Corporate Communication

Fourth Edition

Paul A. Argenti
The Tuck School of Business
Dartmouth College

Boston   Burr Ridge, IL   Dubuque, IA   Madison, WI   New York   San Francisco   St. Louis
Bangkok   Bogotá   Caracas   Kuala Lumpur   Lisbon   London   Madrid   Mexico City
Milan   Montreal   New Delhi   Santiago   Seoul   Singapore   Sydney   Taipei   Toronto

 **McGraw-Hill Irwin**

CORPORATE COMMUNICATION

Published by McGraw-Hill/Irwin, a business unit of The McGraw-Hill Companies, Inc., 1221 Avenue of the Americas, New York, NY, 10020. Copyright © 2007 by The McGraw-Hill Companies, Inc. All rights reserved. No part of this publication may be reproduced or distributed in any form or by any means, or stored in a database or retrieval system, without the prior written consent of The McGraw-Hill Companies, Inc., including, but not limited to, in any network or other electronic storage or transmission, or broadcast for distance learning.

Some ancillaries, including electronic and print components, may not be available to customers outside the United States.

This book is printed on acid-free paper.

1 2 3 4 5 6 7 8 9 0 DOC/DOC 0 9 8 7 6 5

ISBN-13: 978-0-07-299054-6
ISBN-10: 0-07-299054-6

Editorial director: *John E. Biernat*
Publisher: *Andy Winston*
Editorial coordinator: *Amy Luck*
Executive marketing manager: *Rhonda Seelinger*
Project manager: *Dana M. Pauley*
Production supervisor: *Debra R. Sylvester*
Designer: *Cara David*
Photo research coordinator: *Lori Kramer*
Media project manager: *Lynn M. Bluhm*
Cover design: *Chris Bowyer*
Typeface: *10/12 Palatino*
Compositor: *International Typesetting and Composition*
Printer: *R. R. Donnelley*

Library of Congress Cataloging-in-Publication Data

Argenti, Paul A.
    Corporate communication/Paul A. Argenti—4th ed.
      p. cm.
    Includes bibliographical references and index.
    ISBN-13: 978-0-07-299054-6 (alk. paper)
    ISBN-10: 0-07-299054-6 (alk. paper)
    1. Communication in management. 2. Communication in organizations. I. Title.
    HD30.3.A73 2007
    658.4'5—dc22   2005056297

www.mhhe.com

In memory of my father: Nicholas J. Argenti
1918–2003

Preface to the Fourth Edition

This book grows out of more than 25 years of work developing the field of study referred to in this book as *corporate communication*. While the term itself is not new, the notion of it as a functional area of management equal in importance to finance, marketing, and production is more recent. In the last 25 years, senior managers at a growing number of companies have come to realize the importance of an integrated communication function.

In this introduction, I would like to talk a bit more about my expertise, what this book is all about, and why I think everyone involved in organizations today needs to know about this important discipline.

Author's Expertise

For the last 25 years, I have been a professor of management and corporate communication at the Tuck School of Business at Dartmouth College. Prior to that, I taught at the Columbia and Harvard Business Schools.

The tradition of teaching communication has been a long one at Tuck, but as at most schools, the focus was always on skills development, including primarily speaking and writing. The first development in the evolution of corporate communication was an interest among businesspeople in how to deal with the media. Since this mostly involved applying oral presentation skills in another setting, the faculty teaching communication were a logical choice for taking on this new task.

So when I began teaching the first management communication course at Tuck in 1981, I was asked to include a component on dealing with the media. I became interested in this through my study of marketing at Columbia and had already written a case on the subject, which appeared in earlier editions of this book.

Over the years, my interest in the subject grew beyond how companies deal with the media to how they deal with *all* communication problems. As I wrote more case studies on the subject and worked with managers inside companies, I saw the need for a more integrated function. The reason for this is that most companies were conducting communication activities in a highly decentralized way.

For example, the employee communication function at Hewlett-Packard (HP) in the mid-1980s was in the human resources department, where it had always been, when I wrote a case on how HP dealt with voluntary severance and early retirement programs. As I looked at other companies, I found the same basic structure everywhere. Yet the people in those various human resources departments were doing exactly the same thing internally that a communication specialist in the public relations department was doing for the external audience—sending a specific company message to a specific audience.

The same was true of the investor relations functions, which typically resided exclusively in the finance department in most companies until the 1990s. Why? Because the chief financial officer was the one who knew the most about the company's financial performance and historically had been responsible for developing the annual report. Communication was seen as a vehicle for getting that information out rather than as a function in itself.

Again, as I worked with companies on developing new identities and reputations, I found marketing people involved because they had traditionally dealt with image in the context of products and services. Yet those marketing experts didn't always know what was being communicated to the press or to securities analysts by their counterparts in other functional areas.

These experiences led me to believe that corporations and other organizations, from universities to churches to law firms, could do a much better job of communicating if they integrated all communication activities under one umbrella. That was the theory at least, but I could find precious little evidence in practice.

Then, in 1990, I was fortunate enough to be given a consulting assignment that allowed me to put into practice what I had been talking about in theory for many years. I received a call from the chairman and chief executive officer of a major corporation after my picture appeared on the front page of the *New York Times* Sunday business section in an article about how professors were teaching business students about dealing with the media.

Ostensibly, the chairman's call was about how his company could get more credit for the great things it was doing. Specifically, he wanted to know if I had a "silver bullet." My silver bullet, as it turned out, was the development of a new corporate communication function for the company.

This company, like most, had let communications decentralize into a variety of other functional areas over the years, with the predictable result: no integration. The media relations people were saying one thing, the investor relations department was saying another; the marketing team was developing communication strategies for the outside, the human resources department for the inside.

No one except the chairman, who sat at the top of this $30 billion organization, could see the big picture, and none of those intimately involved with the various activities had an inside track on the overall strategy for the firm. Over the next year and a half, the chairman and I came up with the first integrated communication function that had all the different subsets I had tried unsuccessfully to bring together at other companies and even at my own university.

We changed everything—from the company's image with customers to its relationship with securities analysts on Wall Street. Today this company has one totally integrated communication function. This book will explain what all the component parts of that function are all about.

What Is This Book About?

Chapter 1, "The Changing Environment for Business," provides a context for the rest of the book. It describes changes in the environment for business that have taken place over the last half century and their implications for corporate communication. While attitudes about business have never been totally positive, they have reached an all-time low in recent years: Mistrust of and skepticism about corporate entities are high, as are expectations that companies will "give back" to society through philanthropy, community involvement, or environmental protection activities.

In the Arthur Andersen case, an accounting firm faced a large-scale crisis of its own as it found itself implicated in legal proceedings surrounding the widely publicized downfall of one of its auditing clients, Enron. Could an auditor have prevented the collapse of the energy giant or was this a much more complicated situation?

Chapter 2, "Communicating Strategically," explains how companies need to use a strategic approach to communications. In the past, most communication activities were dealt with reactively as organizations responded to events in the world around them. With the framework for strategic communication provided in this chapter, companies can proactively craft communications tailored to their constituencies, and measure their success based on constituency responses.

In the Carson Containers case, which is new to this edition, we find an example of a manager who failed to use a strategic approach to communication in a rapidly changing corporate environment.

In Chapter 3, "An Overview of the Corporate Communication Function," we take a look at the evolution of the corporate communication function and some of the different ways it can be structured within organizations. This chapter also describes each of the subfunctions that should be included in the ideal corporate communication department.

The Dell Computer Corporation case provides an excellent example of how a company built a strong communication function from the ground up.

Chapter 4, "Identity, Image, and Reputation," describes the most fundamental function of a corporate communication department: to reflect the reality of the firm itself through visual images and the right choice of words. The study of identity and image has blossomed in recent years as graphic designers have worked with companies to develop the right look for a particular approach to the marketplace. Additionally, corporate reputation is gaining increased attention as consumers and investors take a more holistic view of companies and their activities, such as corporate social responsibility.

The case for this chapter, new to this edition, allows students to look inside Muzak's new corporate identity program.

Organizations also reflect their identity through advertising. In Chapter 5, "Corporate Advertising," we take a look at how companies use corporate advertising to sell the organization as a whole, as opposed to just the products or services they offer, to the public. Organizations use corporate advertising for a number of reasons: to enhance or alter their image, to present a point of view on a topic of importance to them, or to attract investment.

The exercise at the end of Chapter 5 features print advertisements from some recent campaigns for discussion.

In Chapter 6, "Media Relations," we look at how today's corporate communication function has evolved from the "press release factory" model to a more sophisticated approach of building relationships with journalists before having a specific story to sell them, and targeting the appropriate media for different kinds of stories.

The Adolph Coors Company serves as our case in point for this chapter. In the case, we see how this company dealt with the formidable *60 Minutes* when it approached Coors with a controversial story idea.

One of the most important functions within corporate communication deals with an internal rather than an external constituency: employees. In Chapter 7, "Internal Communication," we look at employee communication's migration away from the human resources area toward a function that is more connected with senior management and overall company strategy.

The Westwood Publishing case explores one company's attempt to deal with voluntary severance and outplacement issues related to layoffs.

In Chapter 8, "Investor Relations," we see how companies use communication strategies to deal with analysts, shareholders, and other important constituencies. In the past, this communication subfunction often was handled by managers with excellent financial skills and mediocre communication skills. Today, as IR professionals interact regularly with the media and need to explain nonfinancial information to investors, strong communication skills are equally critical.

Our case for this chapter, Steelcase, Inc., examines how an IR function was built at that company.

Chapter 9 covers government relations. The business environment historically has fluctuated between periods of relatively less regulation and relatively more, but government relations is always a consideration for companies, whether at the local, state, federal, or international level.

The Disney case provides an example of how a large corporation dealt with challenges from government and local communities in Virginia as it tried to open a historical theme park.

Organizations inevitably will have to deal with some kind of crisis. In Chapter 10, "Crisis Communication," we look at how companies can prepare for the unexpected and provide examples of both good and poor crisis communications, as well as practical steps to creating and implementing crisis communication plans.

Our case at the end of this chapter focuses on Coke in India as it attempts to work its way out of a crisis in this new case involving accusations of environmental contamination in its products.

Why Is CorpComm So Important Today?

Every functional area at one time or another was the newest and most important. But as we enter the 21st century, the importance of communication is obvious to virtually everyone. Why?

First, we live in a more sophisticated era in terms of communication. Information travels with lightning speed from one side of the world to another as a result of technological developments such as the Internet and blogs.

Second, the general public is more sophisticated in its approach to organizations than it has been in the past. People tend to be more educated about issues and more skeptical of corporate intentions. Thus, companies cannot get by on statements like "What's good for General Motors is good for everyone" or "If we build a better mouse trap, customers will beat a path to our door." Maybe not, if they don't know who you are.

Third, information comes to us in more beautiful packages than it did before. We now expect to see glossy annual reports from major corporations. We don't want to walk into grimy-looking stores even for our discount shopping. Gas stations are modern looking and have been "designed" from top to bottom by high-profile New York design firms. The bar is high for a company's message to stand out in this environment.

Fourth, organizations have become inherently more complex. Companies in earlier times (and the same is true even today for very small organizations) were small enough that they could get by with much less sophisticated communications activities. Often, one person could perform many different functions at one time. But in organizations with thousands of employees, it is much more difficult to keep track of all the different pieces that make up a coherent communication strategy.

This book describes not only what is happening in an era of advanced communication but what companies can do to stay one step ahead of the competition. By creating a coordinated corporate communication system, organizations will be able to face the new century with the strategies and tools that few companies in the world have at their fingertips.

I am sure that 20 years from now, when another functional area develops that we cannot even imagine right now, much will have been written about corporate communication, and most complex organizations will have a corporate communication department with many of the subsets described in this book. Until then, however, I hope you enjoy reading about this exciting field as much as I have enjoyed discovering it.

A Note on the Case Method

Throughout this book you will find cases or examples of company situations that typically relate to material covered in each of the chapters.

What Are Cases?

Cases are much like short stories in that they present a slice of life. Unlike their fictional counterparts, however, cases are usually about real people, organizations, and problems (even though the names may sometimes be disguised for proprietary reasons. Thus, a reader has an opportunity to participate in real decisions that managers had to make about a variety of real problems.

The technique of using actual business situations as an educational and analytical instrument began at Harvard in the 1920s, but the use of a "case" as a method of educating students began much earlier. Centuries earlier, students learned law by studying past legal cases and medicine through the use of clinical work.

Unlike textbooks and lectures, the case method of instruction does not present a structured body of knowledge. This often proves frustrating to students who may be used to more traditional teaching methods. For example, cases are frequently ambiguous and imprecise, which can easily confuse a neophyte. This complexity, however, represents what practitioners usually face when making decisions.

In cases, as in life, problems can be solved in a variety of ways. Sometimes one way seems better than others. Even if a perfect solution exists, however, the company may have difficulty implementing it. You also may find that you have a completely different solution to the problem than another student. Try to forget the notion of an "answer" to the problem. The goal in using this method is not to develop a set of correct approaches or right answers, but rather to involve you in the active process of recognizing and solving general management problems.

In class you will represent the decision maker (usually a general manager) in a discussion that is guided by the professor. While the professor may suggest ideas from time to time, or provide structure to ensure that students cover major issues, each student's insight and analytical prowess is displayed in this context. Often a professor will play devil's advocate or pursue an unusual line of reasoning to get students to see the complexities of a particular situation. As a teaching device, the case method relies on participation rather than passive learning.

Although cases come in all shapes and sizes, two categories define the scope of most cases: evaluative and problematic. An evaluative case presents the reader with a description of a company's actions. The purpose of an analysis is thus to evaluate what management has done and then to determine whether the actions were well-founded.

On the other hand, problem cases, which are far more common, describe a specific problem a manager faces, such as whether to launch a new corporate advertising program, to choose one method of handling the media over another, or even to choose one form of communication rather than another. Such problems call for development of alternative strategies leading to a specific recommendation.

Case Preparation

No matter what type of case you're dealing with, a common approach will help you to prepare cases before you have time to develop what will eventually become your own style. In time, you will no doubt find a method that works well and proves more suitable to you. Regardless of the approach, a thorough analysis requires a great deal of effort.

Begin with a quick reading of the case. This gives you a sense of the whole rather than what often can appear as a dazzling array of parts if you start by analyzing each section in detail. You should extract a *sense* of the organization, some impressions of what *could be* the problem, and a working knowledge of the amount and importance of information presented in the case.

A more careful second reading of the case will allow you to begin the critical process of analyzing business problems and solving them. What you should hope to cull from this analysis follows.

Problem Definition

First, you must establish a specific definition of the problem or problems. While this may be clearly stated in the case, usually problem definition is a crucial first step in the analysis. You need to go beyond simple problem definition and look for symptoms as well. For example, as part of the analysis, you might wonder why or how the defined problem has developed in the company. Avoid, however, a repetition of case facts or a historical perspective. Assume that your reader has all the facts you do and choose reasoning that will serve to strengthen, rather than bloat, your problem definition.

Company Objectives

Once you have defined the problem, place it within the context of management's objectives. How does the problem look in this light? Do the objectives make sense given the problems facing management?

In some cases, objectives are defined explicitly, such as "increase stock price by 10 percent this year." If the problem in the case proves to be that the company's investor-relations function is a disaster, this objective is probably overly optimistic.

Goals can be more general as well: "Change from a centralized to a decentralized communication organization in five years." In this instance, a centralized department with independent managers at the divisional level has a good chance of meeting its objectives.

Data Analysis

You next need to analyze information presented in the case as a way of establishing its significance. Often this material appears in exhibits, but you also will find it stated within the case as fact or opinion. Remember to avoid blind acceptance of the data, no matter where they appear. As in the real world, information presented in the case may not be reliable or relevant; but you may find that if you manipulate or combine the data, they ultimately will prove valuable to your analysis. Given the time constraints you will always be under in case analysis and in business, you should avoid a natural tendency to spend more time than you can really afford analyzing data. Try to find a compromise between little or no data analysis and endless number crunching.

Alternative Strategies and Recommendations

After you have defined the problem, identified company objectives, and analyzed relevant data, you are ready to present viable alternative strategies. Be sure the alternatives are realistic for the company under discussion, given management's objectives. In addition, you must consider the implications of each alternative for the company and management.

Once you have developed two or three viable alternative solutions, you are ready to make a recommendation for future action. Naturally, you will want to support the recommendation with relevant information from your analysis. This final step completes your case analysis, but you must then take the next step and explore ways to communicate all the information to your reader or listener.

Cases in the Real World

Here are some further thoughts to help you distinguish a case from a real situation. Despite the hours of research time and reams of information amassed by the case writer, he or she must ultimately *choose* which information to present. Thus, you end up with a package of information in writing. Obviously, information does not come to you in one piece in business. A manager may have garnered the information through discussions, emails, memos, reports, magazines, blogs, and other means. The timing also will be spread out over a longer period than in a case.

Also, given the necessary selectivity of the case writer, you can be sure a specific teaching objective helped focus the selection of information. In reality, the "case" may have implications for several different areas of a business.

Since a case takes place within a particular period of time, it differs in another important way from management problems. These tend to go on and to change as new information comes to light. A manager can solve some of the problems now, search for more information, and decide more carefully later on what is best for a given situation. You, on the other hand, must take one stand now and forever.

Finally, case analyses differ from the realities of management in that students do not have responsibility for implementing decisions. Nor do they suffer the consequences if their decision proves untenable. You should not assume that this removes you from any responsibility. On the contrary, the class (in a discussion) or your professor will be searching for the kind of critical analysis that makes for excellence in management.

Acknowledgments

Without the help and support of the Tuck School at Dartmouth College I could not have completed this book. Over the last 25 years, I have been given funds to write cases and conduct research as well as time to work on the material in this book. I am particularly grateful to Dick West for initially investing in my career here at Tuck and encouraging me to develop a new area of study, and to Paul Danos and Bob Hansen for their continued support more recently.

I also must thank my friends and colleagues at Tuck who first made me sit down and finally produce a text after years of collecting materials and thoughts in files and boxes: John Shank and Mary Munter. The International University of Japan also deserves credit for providing me with the contemplative setting I needed to write the first edition.

Many clients helped me to test the ideas I have developed over more than 25 years, but I am particularly indebted to Joseph Antonini, former chairman and chief executive officer of Kmart, for allowing me to think creatively about the possibilities for a unified corporate communication function. I also would like to thank Jim Donahue and Andy Sigler, formerly chairman and CEO of Champion International, for allowing me to test new ideas with top managers at their company; Nancy Bekavac, president of Scripps College, for allowing me to work on Scripps' identity program and for her helpful comments on Chapter 4; and Valerie Haertel of Alliance Capital Management for her input and help with Chapter 7. David McCourt, former chairman and CEO of RCN, also allowed me to work more recently on developing a corporate communication function in his company. In addition, I thank my many colleagues at Goldman Sachs, where I have been fortunate to work as a consultant for the last eight years, and to Peter Verrengia and all of my colleagues at Fleishman Hillard for their support over the last three years.

I am indebted as well to the students I have taught at Tuck, Erasmus University, Singapore Management University, Hanoi School of Business, the International University of Japan, the Helsinki School of Economics, Columbia Business School, and Harvard Business School. They have tested these ideas in their fertile minds and given me inspiration for coming up with new ways of thinking about corporate communication.

I'd also like to thank Peter Lawrence for his permission to use the Muzak case in Chapter 4, Elizabeth Powell for her permission to use the Disney case in Chapter 9, and Jennifer Kaye for her support overall and help writing the new Coke in India case in Chapter 10.

Many research assistants helped me with this project over the years, but I am particularly grateful to Christine Keen and Patricia Gordon, Mary Tatman, Adi

Herzberg, Thea Haley Stocker, and Abbey Nova for their incredible help with previous editions. This fourth edition would have been impossible to complete without the help of Thea Haley Stocker, Abbey Nova, Kimberley Tait, Suzanne Klotz, and Annette Lyman, my incomparable academic assistant at Tuck. I cannot imagine ever having a better team in place to work on a project like this.

The reviewers who helped with the fourth edition also deserve special thanks for their insightful comments and advice:

Don Bates
Columbia University

Gary Kohut
University of North Carolina–Charlotte

Joel T. Champion
Colorado Christian University

James O'Rourke
University of Notre Dame

Karen Gersten
Evelyn T. Stone University College

Michael Putnam
University of Texas–Arlington

I also wish to thank the reviewers from the previous editions who made this book better through their honesty and input:

Cynthia Buhay-Simon
Bloomsburg University

Margo Northey
University of Western Ontario

Rick Calabrese
Dominican University

J. S. O'Rourke
University of Notre Dame

Carter A. Daniel
Rutgers University

Elizabeth Powell
University of Virginia

Jerry Dibble
Georgia State University

Charlotte Rosen
Cornell University

Jane Gilligan
Clark University

Lynn Russell
Columbia University

Valerie Haertel
Alliance Capital Management

Irv Schenkler
New York University

Suzette Heiman
University of Missouri

Judith Sereno
Medaille College

Chris Kelly
New York University

Robert Stowers
College of William & Mary

Sherron B. Kenton
Emory University

Mary E. Vielhaber
Eastern Michigan University

Joan M. Lally
University of Utah

JoAnne Yates
Massachusetts Institute of Technology

Otto Lerbinger
Boston University

Yunxia Zhu
UNITEC (New Zealand)

My thanks also go to the staff of McGraw-Hill/Irwin, especially my editor, Andy Winston; developmental editor Robin Reed; copyeditor Betsy Blumenthal; editorial coordinator Amy Luck; project manager Dana Pauley and former executive editor at Irwin, Bevan O'Callaghan, who initially signed the book. Their patience allowed me the freedom to develop this material for the four editions over a much longer period of time than I would have guessed it would take at the outset.

Finally, I would like to thank my parents for giving me the raw material in the beginning and the education later on that allowed me to become an academic.

Paul A. Argenti

Hanover, New Hampshire

The author would like any comments or questions as well as corrections to the text. Please write to Professor Paul A. Argenti, The Tuck School of Business, Dartmouth College, Hanover, NH 03755; or e-mail comments to: paul.argenti@dartmouth.edu.

Table of Contents

CHAPTER ONE

The Changing Environment for Business

Most of today's business leaders grew up in a different era from the one they find themselves in now: a typical senior executive grew up during one of the most prosperous and optimistic periods in American history. The difference between the world these people knew in their childhood and the one their grandchildren will face in the 21st century is nothing short of staggering.

The public's current expectations of corporations are also different from what they were 40 or 50 years ago. To attract customers, employees, and investors, companies need to be progressive leaders about a host of global issues and put their vision in a broader social context. Public scrutiny of business is constant and intense, and in the past decade, disillusionment has grown over excesses in executive pay, questionable accounting practices, drug recalls, and moral laxity on the part of corporations.

In this chapter, we will put our discussion of corporate communication in context by looking at some of the events that have influenced the operating environment for business. We begin by looking at a history of public attitudes toward American business and their reflection in popular culture. Next we turn to the effects of globalization (and the antiglobalization backlash) on business. Finally, we look at how improved corporate communication can help companies compete in the constantly changing environment.

Attitudes toward American Business through the Years

Business has never had a completely positive image in the United States. In the 1860s, the creation of the nation's transcontinental rail systems and the concomitant need for steel created hazardous working conditions for steelworkers and railroad builders alike. Soon thereafter, the industrial revolution moved American industry away from a model of small workshops and hand tools to mechanized mass production in factories. This shift had the effect of lowering prices of finished goods, but it also contributed to harsh and dangerous working conditions for laborers. The exploitation of young women and children working in factories only added to negative perceptions of business.

As the patriarchs of big business, the Carnegies, Mellons, and Rockefellers—"robber barons," as they came to be known—were perceived as corrupt businessmen looking out for their own interests rather than the good of all citizens. And yet these negative attitudes toward the first modern corporate businessmen were coupled with envy of their material wealth. Most Americans wanted the lifestyle of these business magnates and came to see the pursuit of wealth and the security it provided as part of the "American Dream."

The 1920s were characterized by a sharply rising stock market and great disparities in wealth distribution. These disparities—between rich and middle-class, between agriculture and industry—made for unstable economic conditions, while speculation in the stock market fueled its growth to unprecedented levels. The stock market "bubble" finally burst in 1929, giving way to the Great Depression, which would last a decade and affect the rest of the industrialized world. It was a dark time for businesses and individuals alike.

By the mid-1940s, however, businesses started rebounding from the Depression as companies geared up for the Second World War. The steel industry, the automotive industry, the military-industrial complex—all of which made the prosperity of the 1950s and 60s a reality—got their start during World War II.

Perhaps the epitome of this era, considered by many a "golden age" were the "Camelot" years of the Kennedy administration. The economy was booming, and in the aftermath of the Cuban missile crisis, the United States felt it had defused the tensions of the Cold War. Even after Kennedy's death, prosperity continued, and public approval of business soared.

Over a period of 30 years, marketing consultancy firm Yankelovich asked the question of American citizens, "Does business strike a balance between profit and the public interest?" In 1968, 70 percent of the population answered yes to that question. By the time Richard Nixon was on his way to the White House, however, the nation was torn apart by civil unrest, with the continuation of the Civil Rights struggle and demonstrations against U.S. involvement in the Vietnam War. Disagreement over the role of the United States in Vietnam marked a serious deterioration in public attitudes toward all institutions, including business. For those who were against the war, the executive branch of government came to stand for all that was wrong with America.

Because it helped make the war possible and profited from the war, American industry was the target of much of the public's hostility. Dow Chemical's manufacture of Napalm and Agent Orange, which would be used to defoliate Vietnamese jungles, led to student protests on American university campuses. Young people in this country came to distrust the institutions involved in the war, whether government agencies or businesses. This represented a dramatic change from the attitudes Americans had during World War II. Those in power failed to see how the Vietnam War was different because Americans were ambivalent about what the country was fighting for.

TABLE 1.1
How Much
Confidence
Do You Have
in These
Institutions?*

	1966	1971	1989
Large companies	55%	27%	14%
U.S. Congress	42%	19%	10%
Executive branch	41%	23%	27%
Supreme Court	51%	23%	26%

Source: *Yankelovich Monitor.*

*Answers reflect those answering most positively.

Toward the end of the 1960s and coinciding with the war in Vietnam, a rise in radicalism in America marked the beginning of a long deterioration of trust in institutions. The events of the early 1970s also contributed to this shift. For example, Watergate only confirmed what most young Americans had believed all along about the Nixon administration. The aftermath of the oil embargo, imposed by Arab nations after the 1973 Middle East war, had even more of an effect on attitudes toward business in America. Cheap, abundant petroleum—the lubricant of the American way of life—suddenly became scarce and expensive as Saudi Arabia and other Arab producers punished the United States for supporting Israel in the war. The cutoff lasted less than three months, but its effects on consumer attitudes are still with us today.

As a result of Watergate, Vietnam, and the oil embargo, by the mid-1970s American attitudes toward business reached an all-time low. In answer to the same question "Does business strike a fair balance between profit and the public interest?" those answering yes in the Yankelovich poll dropped to 15 percent in 1976 when Jimmy Carter took office. This drop of 55 points in just eight years says more about the changing attitudes toward business than a thousand anecdotes.

An opinion research poll that asked the general public to rate their confidence in a number of institutions showed declines in all areas, as shown in Table 1.1. Although figures don't exist for other institutions, we can imagine similar dips in attitudes toward the police, the armed forces, and even organized religion based on how people felt about large institutions in the 1970s.

As you read this, you may be asking yourself whether the 1980s and 1990s, which together constituted the final economic boom of the 20th century, restored America's faith in business to where it had been in the 1960s. They did not and in 2005 a Harris Poll asking the same questions found the responses to be large companies, 17 percent; U.S Congress, 16 percent; White House, 31 percent; and Supreme Court, 29 percent.[1] In answer to the question about whether business strikes a fair balance between profit and the public interest, the percentages climbed back to a high of only 30 percent answering yes in 1984. And the percentages dropped slightly, to 28 percent in 1999 (the last year Yankelovich asked this question). (See Table 1.2.)

The 1990s saw the phenomenal rise of the NASDAQ index to 4,000 points by the end of the decade. Individual investors were actively participating in the equity

[1] Harris Poll, February 8–13, 2005.

TABLE 1.2
Does Business
Balance Profit
and Public
Interest?*

Source: *Yankelovich
Monitor.*

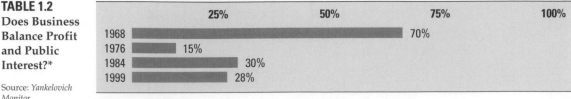

* Percent yes responses.

markets and reaping enormous gains as stock prices seemed to be on an unstoppable upward trajectory. Then, in the spring of 2000, the markets came crashing down. By December, the NASDAQ had sunk to less than half its peak level of 5,000 reached at the beginning of the year. And unfortunately for the 100 million individual investors who had poured money into the market during the Internet-fueled boom of the 1990s, it did not stop there in its downward spiral. By early 2002, these individuals had lost $5 trillion since the "Internet bubble" burst, representing 30 percent of their stock wealth.[2]

In the midst of this market turmoil, the actions of unscrupulous financial analysts (see Chapter 8 for more on analysts) and companies like Enron angered the American public further. By February of 2002, some 81 percent of investors polled "did not have much confidence in those running Big Business."[3] This is not surprising when you consider the many highly publicized stories of top executives who sold millions of dollars' worth of shares in their own failing enterprises, further enhancing their wealth as rank-and-file employees lost much of their retirement savings.

The public also has been embittered by the growing pay gap between senior company executives and ordinary workers that reached enormous proportions over the past decade. Recent figures show that CEOs of large corporations made 411 times as much as the average factory worker.[4] And from 1990 to 2003, employee wages rose 48 percent, as compared with a climb of 315 percent for CEO pay.[5] To add insult to injury, wide disparities exist between executive pension plans and those of the rest of the workforce. General Electric, for example, has a retirement plan for top executives that guaranteed an annual return of at least 10 percent, a rate far better than that which a typical employee could expect on his or her 401(k) plan.[6]

With the bursting of the "dot.com bubble"; the exposure of corporate fraud at large companies such as WorldCom, Adelphia, and Tyco; and the collapse of Enron and its auditor, Andersen, due to fraudulent accounting, Americans perceived

[2] Marcia Vickers, Mike McNamee, et al., "The Betrayed Investor," *BusinessWeek,* February 25, 2002, p. 105.

[3] Ibid., p. 106.

[4] John A. Byrne, "How to Fix Corporate Governance," *BusinessWeek,* May 6, 2002, p. 72.

[5] United for a Fair Economy, "CEO Pay Charts," http://www.faireconomy.org/research/CEO_Pay_charts.html (retrieved July 7, 2005).

[6] David Leonhardt, "For Executives, Nest Egg Is Wrapped in a Security Blanket," *New York Times,* March 5, 2002, p. C1.

business as actively trying to deceive them. This perception was reflected in the media as well, such as in the *NBC Nightly News* segment entitled "The Fleecing of America."

Through the years, the television news media have played a major role in conveying, filtering, and obstructing messages from corporations as well as government and activist groups (see Chapter 6 for more on the media's influence on business). By the late 1990s, the Internet also began to shape attitudes toward business as activist groups gained access to a broadcast forum for its arguments against business. Today, environmental activists, animal rights groups, and shareholder rights proponents now have the ability to get messages out instantaneously to like-minded individuals throughout the United States and the world.

While the media and the Internet are powerful channels for views on business to be expressed and debated, nowhere are the attitudes that prevail in the external environment more clearly defined than in television and film.

Hollywood: A Window on Main Street and Wall Street

Throughout history, literature and the arts have both affected and reflected perceptions about institutions. Greek attitudes about government and religion manifested themselves in theater; Shakespeare shaped notions about English history for generations; and in the United States, cinema and television over the past several decades have reflected some of the public's negative attitudes about business.

For many Americans today, what they see in fictional or "factional" accounts in films and on television helps shape their attitudes more than educational institutions. In fact, Americans spend far more time in front of the television set than they do in the classroom. According to research undertaken by a number of different organizations, the average American household spends approximately 40–50 hours per week in front of the television set. Many have written about what this has done to American society in a broader context over the last 30 years, but in this textbook, we will focus on the relationship between popular culture and business.

The Media Institute, a research organization funded by corporations, has been tracking media coverage of business for over 20 years. Each time it issues a report, the results are the same: businesspeople are portrayed negatively in almost two-thirds of all television programs. Researchers have concluded that half of the time, businesspeople portrayed on television were involved in criminal activities.

In addition, most Americans get their news from television. As a result, the negative portrayals viewers see in fictional programming blend into the negative news they watch on the nightly news. An individual might, for example, watch an episode of *Law and Order: Criminal Intent* in which a woman is framed for murder after raising questions about her company's accounting practices one night, then see an in-depth story about Enron on *Dateline NBC* the following evening. This information all comes from television, all of it is bad, and the net result is the reinforcement of negative perceptions of business.

Films also contribute to a negative business image. One of the most successful films of the late 1970s was called *The China Syndrome*, a movie about a narrowly averted meltdown at a nuclear reactor. A week after the release of the film, a real nuclear accident occurred at Three Mile Island. While everyone would agree that Metropolitan Edison did a poor job of communicating about this accident, few would say that the company was as bad as the one portrayed in the movie. For many Americans, however, the two events were linked, which made their reaction to the events at Three Mile Island that much stronger.

It is eerie how Hollywood has mirrored events in business at exactly the right time. The movie *Wall Street* is another such example. Oliver Stone's movie came out just ahead of the great scandals that rocked the real Wall Street in the late 1980s. Even within the film itself, reality and fiction were intertwined. Gordon Gekko, the evil financial genius meant to represent someone like the notorious arbitrageur Ivan Boesky, makes a speech in the film about greed. "Greed is good, greed purifies, greed cuts through and captures the essence of the evolutionary spirit," Gekko says in a passionate speech at an annual meeting. Months earlier, the real Ivan Boesky had made a similar speech to a group of graduates at the University of California's Berkeley campus.

Released in 2000, the movie *Erin Brockovich* portrayed the real-life story of a single mother who talks her way into a job in a law firm and ends up taking on a major gas and electric company in a lawsuit over toxic waste. The end of 2001 exposed another large energy company, this one for massive accounting fraud. While not literally deadly like the industrial byproducts at the heart of *Erin Brockovich*, Enron's bankruptcy caused financial ruin for many of its employees and investors.

Are these examples instances of "life imitating art"? More likely, it is the other way around. As long as business has a negative public image, movies and television will continue to dramatize real-life tales of corporate wrongdoing. As Hollywood exports a large number of American films to countries around the world, these images become part of a global informational tapestry that we explore in more detail in the next section.

The Global Village

Technology has strengthened communication channels around the globe, disintegrating national borders to produce what Canadian philosopher Marshall McLuhan foresaw decades ago—the creation of a world so interwoven by shared knowledge that it becomes a "Global Village."[7] This trend has had a monumental impact on business, particularly over the last decade.

Out of the top 100 economies, 51 are multinational corporations and the remaining 49 are countries.[8] Thus, it may not be surprising that individuals have begun to turn to large companies to provide the direction that distinct national cultures,

---

[7] Marshall McLuhan and Bruce R. Powers, *The Global Village: Transformations in World Life and Media in the 21st Century* (New York: Oxford University Press, 1989).

[8] Paul A. Argenti and Janis Forman, *The Power of Corporate Communication: Crafting the Voice and Image of Your Business* (New York: McGraw Hill, 2002), p. 83.

communities, and inspirational narratives offered more strongly in the past. Coupled with this is a heightened level of interest in social responsibility on the part of organizations. In Chapter 4, we will discuss the growing importance of corporate social responsibility and its implications for corporate reputation, but generally, the public is looking for companies to demonstrate care for the communities in which they operate from both an environmental and human perspective.

In his book *The Mind of the CEO,* Jeffrey Garten explains, "As the world gets smaller, CEOs will be unable to escape involvement in some of the most difficult political, economic and social problems of our times. There will be no way to avoid operating in countries with fragile economies, weak democratic structures and mega-cities with severely overburdened infrastructures."[9]

Disintegrating national borders, coupled with the liberalization of trade and finance in today's "Global Village," also have fostered an increase in cross-border corporate mergers and the number of multinational corporations. Today, companies tend to specialize in their core competencies and outsource what remains or, alternatively, merge to integrate the suppliers into their own organization. Statistics reveal that $3.4 trillion in mergers took place in 1999, compared with less than $1 billion in 1995.[10] A Goldman Sachs study estimated that 300,000 to 500,000 jobs were lost between 2001 and 2003 to overseas relocations and that as many as 6 million jobs could move overseas by 2013.[11]

Many individuals and communities object to the enormous political clout that large corporations wield today. This sentiment gave rise to the "anti-brand" movement that flourished in the mid-1990s—a decade in which global companies began to replace government bodies as the primary target of many activists worldwide. In 2000, a *BusinessWeek*/Harris Poll indicated that 72 percent of Americans agreed with the statement that business has too much influence. In 2002, 77 percent of respondents thought large corporations hold too much power.[12] In 2000, a *Wall Street Journal*/NBC poll revealed that 48 percent of Americans thought that trade hurt the economy.[13] In 2004, a Chicago Council on Foreign Relations Worldviews survey revealed that 39 percent of Americans thought international trade was bad for the U.S. economy; 64 percent thought it was bad for job security of American workers.[14]

The anti-globalization movement extends beyond traditional union bodies to include young and old consumers, concerned parents and vocal student activists alike. The resulting anticorporate protests were so well attended that in October 1997, Earth First! produced a calendar listing important anticorporate protest dates, announcing the first "End Corporate Dominance Month."[15]

[9] Jeffrey Garten, *The Mind of the CEO* (New York: Basic Books, 2001), p. 24.

[10] Ibid., p. 100.

[11] Sue Kichhoff and Barbara Hagenbaugh, "Economy Races Ahead, Leaving Jobs in the Dust," *USA Today,* October 1, 2003.

[12] Pew Charitable Trusts Survey: Views of Business and Regulation, February 2002.

[13] Garten, *Mind of the CEO,* p. 213.

[14] Chicago Council on Foreign Relations, "Global Views 2004," September 2004, http://www.ccfr.org/globalviews2004/sub/pdf/2004_US_Public_Topline_Report.pdf (retrieved July 7, 2005).

[15] Naomi Klein, *No Logo: Taking Aim at the Brand Bullies* (New York: Picador USA, 1999), p. 327.

Vancouver-based *Adbusters* magazine devotes itself to deriding corporate giants—a practice now officially referred to as *culture jamming*.[16] Plastering the image of Charles Manson's face over a Levi's jeans billboard, hurling pies at Bill Gates, and dumping garbage bags full of shoes outside of Nike Town to protest Pakistani children manufacturing Nike soccer balls for six cents an hour are some of the routine tactics culture-jamming activists are employing to make anticorporate statements to the public. [17]

Anticorporate activism also has benefited from technological advances. The 1999 antiglobalization protests at the World Trade Organization (WTO) annual meeting in Seattle were largely coordinated by extensive online planning.[18] John Delicath, a University of Cincinnati expert on antiglobalization protests, explains that "Starting with the protests against the WTO in Seattle, so-called 'anti-globalization' activists have used the Internet to build relationships and create networks for sharing ideas, information and resources."[19] Ironically, just as technology has helped companies to grow into multinational behemoths, it also has aided their anticorporate adversaries in mounting coordinated campaigns against them.

Continual technological advances also have made it difficult for companies to prevent both positive and negative news about them from reaching individuals in virtually all corners of the world. Media outlets have expanded their reach such that events are no longer confined to local communities; rather, they can create reverberations felt worldwide. By 2010, 3 billion people worldwide are expected to own mobile phones;[20] 236 million U.S. consumers are expected to own a mobile phone, representing 75 percent of the population.[21]

Business leaders today therefore must be prepared not only to handle the international media spotlight but also to proactively counter the advocacy groups looking to use today's media environment to compromise their corporate reputation—and bottom line—globally.

How to Compete in a Changing Environment

Even well respected companies face attacks in this antibusiness environment. Gillette, for example, has been a target of animal rights groups who have successfully used teachers and children to create a stir over the company's research methods. One letter to Gillette's former chairman, Alfred Zeien, said: "Let this be a warning to you. If you hurt another animal, if I find out, one month from [the day] this letter arrives to you, I'll bomb your company. P.S. Watch your back." The letter

---

[16] Ibid., p. 280.

[17] Ibid.

[18] Adam Tanner, "Activists Embrace Web in Anti-globalisation Drive," *Reuters,* July 13, 2001.

[19] Ibid.

[20] Gartner Group 2005, http://blogs.zdnet.com/ITFacts/?p=8227 (retrieved July 1, 2005).

[21] The Diffusion Group, Press release, February 2, 2004, http://www.tdgresearch.com/press028.htm (retrieved July 7, 2005).

came from a sixth grader at a school in Philadelphia. As homework, his teacher had assigned letters to companies about animal testing. [22] While the children's campaign had no effect on market share, the company worried about potential long-term effects: "Long term, this could be a very bad trend for the business," said CEO Zeien.[23]

When Nike faced allegations of unfair labor practices in Asia, including children working in dangerous conditions for low wages, the company initially denied the charges. The media's portrayal of Nike became increasingly negative, and television footage of Asian children working in sweatshoplike conditions furthered the controversy. While protests against Nike for these alleged practices were relatively contained and did not have a considerable impact on sales, the problem of the company's labor and environmental policies continue to reappear in the press.[24] One could question how long this can go on before it does have a measurable effect on the company's profitability.

The entire fast-food industry came under attack with the release of the documentary *Super Size Me* in 2004, which follows the filmmaker as he eats only at a McDonald's for a period of time. The changes to his mental and physical outlook were shocking and the film contributed to putting a spotlight on the marketing of fast food and the problem of obesity in America. So how can managers adapt to the challenges of a business environment that is constantly in flux but seems to be moving in the direction of greater scrutiny and less favorable impressions of corporations? In the next section, we will look at some of the ways companies can stay on course while navigating these choppy waters.

Recognize the Changing Environment

First, managers need to recognize that the business environment *is* constantly evolving. The short-term orientation of today's managers rarely gives them an opportunity to look at the big picture of how this changing environment affects the company's image with a variety of constituencies. Over the long term, this can have damaging results.

McDonald's took note when, in the late 1980s and early 1990s, environmentally conscious consumers raised concerns over the company's use of nonrecyclable plastic "clamshell" packaging for many of its popular sandwiches. Disapproving customers mailed the containers, in addition to thousands of hostile letters, to the company's Oak Brook, Illinois, headquarters. So in August of 1990, McDonald's forged an agreement with the Environmental Defense Fund (EDF), an environmental research and lobbying group, to form a joint taskforce and brainstorm ideas to reduce the company's annual solid-waste production.

The decision tapped into the company's awareness of growing consumer concerns. Edward H. Rensi, then president of McDonald's U.S.A., explained that the

---

[22] Barbara Carton, "Gillette Faces Wrath of Children in Testing of Rats and Rabbits," *The Wall Street Journal,* September 5, 1995, p. A1.

[23] Ibid.

[24] Argenti and Forman, *Power of Corporate Communication,* pp. 10–11.

company had first adamantly insisted that its foam packaging was not detrimental to the environment, only to realize that "our customers just don't feel good about it. So we're changing."[25] More recently, in response to *Super Size Me* and the growing obesity epidemic, McDonald's launched a revamped menu of healthier menu options downplaying its Super Size options. Its public relations effort included giving away pedometers as well as developing a Web site, http://www.supersizeme-thedebate.com, that featured menu plans for eating healthfully at McDonald's.[26]

One of the most important challenges facing senior managers is the profoundly unsettling impact of technological change. Andrew Grove, cofounder and CEO of Intel Corporation, explained, "We make a cult of how wonderful it is that the rate of [technological] change is so fast. But . . . what happens when the rate of change is so fast that before a technological innovation gets deployed, or halfway through the process of being deployed, [an] innovation sweeps in and creates a destructive interference with the first one?"[27] While many agree that technology has helped business, it also has led to greater uncertainty for business leaders and consumers alike.

Unlike many shifts in the market that companies can anticipate by keeping their fingers on the pulse of change, such as evolving consumer tastes, technological innovations can happen swiftly and have profound effects. Companies need to quickly determine what, if anything, they need to do to respond to such changes.

Adapt to the Environment without Compromising Principles

Second, companies must adapt to the changing environment without changing what they stand for or compromising their principles. As an example, in 1995, the Seattle-based coffee company Starbucks adopted guidelines aimed at improving working conditions at its foreign coffee suppliers. Starbucks' guidelines called for overseas suppliers to pay wages and benefits that at least "address the basic needs of workers and their families." For example, the company asked suppliers to allow child labor only when it does not "interfere with mandated education." Global human rights groups applauded the guidelines, saying they substantially widened the possibilities for corporate codes of conduct.

Chemical giant Monsanto faced challenges when its foray into genetically engineered crops met with resistance from protesters who labeled its products "Frankenfoods." Protests were not limited to the company's headquarters in St. Louis, but spread to some of Monsanto's large, visible customers, forcing McDonald's, for one, to announce that they would no longer use the company's genetically modified (GM) potatoes.[28]

---

[25] John Holusha, "Packaging and Public Image: McDonald's Fills a Big Order," *New York Times,* November 2, 1990, p. A1.

[26] Web site of the International Centre for Corporate Social Responsibility, http://www.nottingham.ac.uk/business/ICCSR (retrieved July 8, 2005).

[27] Garten, *Mind of the CEO,* p. 32.

[28] Jonathan Low and Pam Cohen Kalafut, *Invisible Advantage: How Intangibles Are Driving Business Performance* (Cambridge: Perseus Books, 2002), p. 114.

This issue ultimately took its toll on the company's stock price in the late 1990s despite the company's meeting Wall Street expectations. In response, Monsanto adopted a new approach to handling the "GM backlash" through education and outreach. Historically, the company had been perceived as aggressively marketing products that the public did not understand or trust. Now, Monsanto communicated "The New Monsanto Pledge," which outlined five key elements including dialogue, transparency, respect, sharing, and delivering benefits.[29] While the company continued to produce GM foods, its collaborative approach to working with consumer groups and farmers to foster greater understanding of biotechnology's role in food production was viewed positively by many who had previously opposed Monsanto.

Arie de Geus of the MIT Sloan School of Management analyzed the strengths of what he defined as "living companies"—a group of 30 companies ranging in age from 100 to 700 years scattered throughout North America, Europe, and Japan.[30] One of the primary reasons these companies—including DuPont, W.R. Grace, Sumitomo, and Siemens—have managed to endure has been their ability to adapt to the rapidly evolving environment in which they live. De Geus explains: "As wars, depressions, technologies, and politics surged and ebbed, they always seemed to excel at keeping their feelers out, staying attuned to whatever was going on. For information, they sometimes relied on packets carried over vast distances by portage and ship, yet they managed to react in a timely fashion to whatever news they received. They were good at learning and adapting."[31]

Don't Assume Problems Will Magically Disappear

Third, assume things will only get worse and you will be better off in today's complex environment. Hooker Chemical executives in the 1970s had no way of knowing that the Love Canal story would run as long as it did. Had they anticipated the length of the story's appeal, they no doubt would have changed their communication strategy. Most managers assume that the American public has a short memory about problems companies get into. In fact, consumers have longer memories than you might think, as witnessed by boycotts of companies such as Coors, Wal-Mart, Nike, Shell, and Texaco.

Some companies seem to be getting it right, but most are still getting it wrong. Caterpillar Inc., the world's largest manufacturer of construction equipment, allowed itself to get into a battle with one of the strongest unions in the United States, the United Automobile Workers, in the mid 1990s. Despite all that is now known about negotiation and how management should never argue over positions, the company decided to replace 12,600 workers over issues of wages and health benefits.

USX (the former U.S. Steel Corporation), on the other hand, took a different approach. The president of the vast steel operation, Thomas J. Usher, unexpectedly appeared at the offices of the United Steelworkers local to listen to what union

---

[29] Ibid., p. 115.

[30] Arie de Geus, "The Living Company," *Harvard Business Review,* March 1, 1997.

[31] Ibid.

leaders had on their minds about the company's largest mill. The president of the local union said this kind of behavior was unusual: "Other heads of U.S. Steel would never have dreamed of being in the same room with the union people. He is bringing in a breath of fresh air."

No one can say how well either of these companies will fare in the years to come, but this textbook will focus on approaches like USX's. Recognizing that the union's interests are essentially the same as management's is a stretch for managers mired in old-fashioned thinking. The autocratic managers at U.S. Steel that President Kennedy once referred to as "a bunch of S.O.B.'s" would never have been able to step up to the changes in the environment the way Mr. Usher did.

Keep Corporate Communication Connected to Strategy

Fourth, corporate communication must be closely linked to a company's overall vision and strategy. Since few managers recognize the importance of the communication function, they are reluctant to hire the quality staff necessary to succeed in today's environment. As a result, communication people are often kept out of the loop.

Successful companies connect communication with strategy through structure, such as having the head of corporate communication report directly to the CEO. The advantage of this kind of reporting relationship is that the communications professional can get the company's strategy directly from those at the top of the organization. As a result, all of the company's communications will be more strategic and focused (see Chapter 3 for more on structure).

In Chapter 10, we will take a look at how Johnson & Johnson handled the Tylenol cyanide crisis of the early 1980s. Part of what helped the company so successfully deal with this dire situation was the existence of the J&J Credo, a companywide code of ethics that spells out J&J's promises to its many constituencies. This helped guide the company's actions during an episode that could have irreparably damaged the Tylenol brand and possibly J&J itself.

Companies' corporate communications teams play a pivotal role in defining a corporate mission—the cornerstone of a company's overarching strategy—and communicating that mission to internal and external constituents. Given today's rapidly changing environment, a clear-cut corporate mission not only keeps employees aligned with what the company is striving to be, but also can act as a source of stability for consumers weary of the constant change surrounding them.

Conclusion

The business environment is constantly changing. Everyone in business today, whether at a large corporation with a national union to deal with or a small business looking to make its mark in the international arena, needs to communicate strategically. The way organizations adapt and modify their behavior, as manifested through their communications, will determine the success of American business in the 21st century.

Case 1-1

Arthur Andersen

Nothing . . . is duller than accounting—until someone is defrauded. And after every modern financial disaster . . . investors have tended to ask the same question: where were the auditors?[1]

Joseph Berardino, CEO of Arthur Andersen, slept peacefully in a hotel room in Tokyo on November 28, 2001, when he was suddenly awakened by a phone call from one of his colleagues in New York City. "The Justice Department is thinking of indicting Andersen, Joe," said one of his partners. Berardino was instantly awake.

Berardino had remained upbeat about the future of Andersen since he became that company's CEO six months earlier. He had written an essay for the company newsletter a year earlier describing the business world as entering "terrific times. Exciting times for our clients and our people."[2] But an indictment from the SEC could ruin his accounting firm and end the "terrific times" that he'd predicted for Andersen only a few months before.

At the end of 2001, Andersen faced criticism for its botched audits of Enron Corporation, a failed energy-trading firm, and for destroying documents related to the audits. Already Enron's woes had made front-page headlines for weeks. "This is going to be a whole new ballgame," thought Berardino.[3] If the SEC announced that it would subpoena Andersen's files, the story would appear in the nation's

major newspapers the next day. Clearly, Andersen would have to make some sort of announcement about the investigation. He picked up the phone to call David Tabolt, chief spokesman for Andersen, to discuss communication options, especially with the media. "David, it's Joe; how should we respond to questions about this problem?"[4]

FOUNDING OF ARTHUR ANDERSEN

Arthur Andersen and Clarence DeLany cofounded the accounting firm Andersen, DeLany, & Company in 1913. Soon afterwards, in 1918, DeLany left the company and the name changed to Arthur Andersen & Co. After DeLany's departure, Arthur Andersen built his company as its sole leader over the next four decades. Reflecting its leader's strong ethical principles, the firm adopted the motto, "think straight, talk straight."[5]

Andersen grew steadily throughout the Roaring Twenties, Great Depression, and both World Wars. The firm benefited from new government regulations that required more company filings and led to an increasingly complicated tax code for corporations. Andersen continually sought out chances to increase its reach. In 1928, it began the financial investigations that would eventually become its consulting practice. In 1932, it became the bankruptcy trustee for Samuel Insull's failed utility empire. Andersen's branches spread to new locations throughout the United States, and after 1963 it would venture into foreign countries as well.

When Arthur Andersen died in 1947, he left behind a modestly successful, well-established

---

Source: This case was prepared by S. Helen Labun under the direction of Professor Paul A. Argenti in 2002. It was revised in 2005.

[1] Jane Mayer, "The Accountants' War," *New Yorker*, April 22, 2002, p. 64.

[2] John Schwartz and Jonathan Glater, "At Andersen's Helm, a Winner of Battles Who Faces a War," *New York Times*, January 14, 2002.

[3] Ken Brown and John R. Wilke, "Berardino's Hopes of Saving Andersen Were Dashed Following Indictment," *The Wall Street Journal*, March 28, 2002.

[4] This case study is a fictionalized account based on actual events that occurred at Arthur Andersen, LLP.

[5] Bethany McLean and Peter Elkind, *The Smartest Guys in the Room* (New York: The Penguin Group, 2004), p. 143.

firm. He was replaced, after a brief bout of family infighting, by Leonard Spacek. With strong business principles, Spacek quickly ended the arguments over Andersen's successor that had put senior employees at odds with each other, and pulled the managers together to focus on a new era for Andersen, positioning the company to become one of the world's leading accounting firms.[6] By the year 2001, the trademark Andersen would include a worldwide network of operations with annual revenues exceeding $9.3 billion.

EXPANDING SERVICES AT ARTHUR ANDERSEN: 1950–2000

In the 19th century, accounting included primarily bookkeeping responsibilities; over the course of the 20th century, however, the accounting industry moved far beyond this original function. Work at Arthur Andersen eventually included services such as both internal and independent audits, tax process oversight, legal services, and human resource work.

One of the most significant nonauditing functions that Andersen offered its clients was consulting. This piece of the firm's business began early in the company's history and by 1954, Andersen had developed a separate unit for its consulting business. Andersen experienced internal conflicts between accounting and consulting from the time that these two branches split until the year 2000. In Andersen's corporate partnership structure, profits throughout the company were shared. This intensified ill-will between the profitable consulting partners and the lesser-so audit partners. (In 1997, 56 percent of the firm's revenue was brought in by the consulting side, which was also growing at twice the rate of the auditing business.)[7]

Eventually, Andersen established Andersen World, a global corporation that provided an umbrella organization for both consulting and accounting, in the hope that a reorganized company structure could defuse some of the tension. But quarrels only intensified, especially as Andersen Accounting developed its own consulting division to serve those companies not covered under the Andersen Consulting unit.

Power struggles continued between the different departments at Andersen into the 1990s. In the 1990s, the problems of how to combine consulting and auditing work grew in scope as observers outside of Andersen raised questions about potential conflicts of interest at the Big Five accounting firms, all of which derived significant revenues from consulting services. A 2002 report in *The Accounting Review*, for example, calculated that throughout the 1990s, profits from consulting at the Big Five auditors were three times those produced by auditing work.[8] The ratios of an individual executive's annual income often were weighted even more heavily towards consulting. The resulting incentive structure produced rewards for those workers who brought in a high volume of consulting work, not those who performed their duties well as auditors. In the best case, this system advanced the careers of mediocre accountants. In the worst case, Andersen partners approved on poor auditing jobs when executives received high commissions from the consulting business generated by a company's fraudulent financial transactions.

Consulting was not the only relationship between auditors and their clients that came under scrutiny in the 1990s. Individual branches of Andersen each focused on a single large client. Critics accused these offices of losing their neutrality through close associations with the companies they would audit. At Enron, for example, Andersen served not only as an external auditor, but as the company's internal auditor as well.

---

[6] Hoover's Online, "Andersen Overview," 2001; Rick Wartzman, "After WW II, Founder's Death Shook Arthur Andersen Firm," *The Wall Street Journal*, May 1, 2002.

[7] McLean and Elkind, *The Smartest Guys in the Room,* pp. 144–45.

[8] Mayer, "The Accountants' War."

This close connection led to a situation in which Andersen accountants, acting in their capacity as independent auditors, signed off on their own internal accounting work. Andersen accountants also were often checking the work of past, or potential, employers. The "cross-pollination" of employee pools between Andersen's Houston office and Enron headquarters was an established practice. The president, vice president, and chief accounting officer positions were all held by former Andersen employees.[9] Enron was viewed as *the* magical, innovative company at which to work, or the next best thing—to have as a client. As Leigh Anne Dear, a former Andersen accountant, said, "It was like these very bright geeks from Andersen suddenly got invited to this really cool, macho frat party."[10]

Although the SEC would later accuse Andersen partners of actively promoting their own interest over their accounting duties in the new business climate, a large part of the changes seen in the accounting industry were simply responses to changes in business. During a period of incredible economic growth in the 1990s, new forms of assets and liabilities emerged; firms entered into joint-venture agreements and engaged in a variety of business transactions across different markets. The public could now invest in "innovative" companies that had expanded beyond a focus on one or two fields to trade in multiple fields, many of which had little connection to each other. Enron, once a gas pipeline company, was considered a visionary leader in this new environment. The corporation placed a premium on novel ideas, investing in and creating new trading markets for everything from broadband to pulp, and leveraging a large amount of debt to fund these projects. With the high volume of money changing hands in the bull markets, opportunities arose for some executives to divert funds for their personal use.

These new strategies were unprecedented in the accounting world, and so auditors like Andersen had to discover new ways to monitor business effectively. Sometimes they did not succeed.

SETBACKS AT ANDERSEN: 1996–2000

Not all transactions went smoothly as both the business community and auditing firms generated new functions that did not fit easily into the regulatory framework devised by the government in the 1930s. The SEC had begun to adapt, but only slowly, and during the process of changing federal oversight, the Big Five accounting firms entered into more and more political battles. Andersen found itself at odds with government regulators and eventually it came under investigation for several improper auditing jobs.

Two major scandals broke at Andersen during the 1996–2000 period: Waste Management Systems and Sunbeam. Of these, Waste Management proved the most damaging. In 1998, Waste Management, an Andersen client for several decades, restated its earnings to show an overestimate of $1.4 billion over a four-year period. This was the largest restatement in American history (Enron would later reveal a $600 million error—less than half of Waste Management's inflation).

The SEC investigation into this incident turned up several incriminating documents at Andersen offices. As a result, Andersen was levied a $7 million fine by the SEC and paid an additional $75 million to settle the civil lawsuits. Andersen also was handed a cease-and-desist order that prohibited it from engaging in further misconduct. Vowing never to allow this type of situation to arise again, Andersen distributed a memo to the entire partnership stating, "One of the most important lessons from litigation involving our profession is that client selection and retention are among the most important factors in determining our risk

---

[9] Ibid.

[10] McLean and Elkind, *The Smartest Guys in the Room*, p. 146.

exposure . . . [We] have the courage to say no to relationships that bring unacceptable levels of risk to our firm." The company also instituted a document retention policy that encouraged employees to dispose of [nonessential] client documents.[11]

Sunbeam also misstated its earnings for years when that company was an Andersen client, though not to the same degree as Waste Management. Again, Andersen paid exorbitant fines but managed to escape without any official recognition of wrongdoing.[12]

Another blow to Andersen Accounting came in August of 2000, when a lengthy arbitration process ended in the formal separation of its consulting unit to become its own, unaffiliated company. The disputes between the consulting and auditing branches of Andersen reached back almost half a century. Directly following its legal split from Andersen, the consulting firm renamed itself Accenture and launched a massive campaign to reinvent its image, purging itself of any remaining ties with Andersen by emphasizing its historically separate nature (the Accenture Web site credits the company's beginnings to a plan to install a computer in General Electric in 1953 without any mention of accountants). Accenture became a publicly owned company specializing in fast-paced development of innovative technology solutions for its global clients.[13]

Even with its setbacks, at the end of the 1990s, Andersen did not lose its place as a major accounting firm. The company had 1,500 senior partners and retained 85,000 employees in 84 different countries at the start of 2000. At this time, hoping to prepare the company to handle any future crises, management brought in a new CEO: Joseph Berardino.

BERARDINO HEADS ANDERSEN

Joseph Berardino was billed as a crisis manager who could "take Andersen back to its roots," helping the company recover from its recent accounting scandals, along with healing the rift created by the contentious divorce with Andersen Consulting. Berardino had a solid accounting background. He took pride in his skills as an auditor and had been a dedicated employee at Arthur Andersen since he graduated from Fairfield University in 1972. Senior executives greeted him as a "buck stops here" type of CEO who could clean up the dubious bookkeeping that had gotten the company in trouble before.[14]

Unfortunately for Berardino, most of the errors that would lead to Andersen's unraveling were in place long before he took his place as CEO in January of 2001. For example, although he did consolidate top management into a council of 5 (down from 17) to chart a decisive course for the company, the partners who dealt with the 100 top clients had already established a high level of autonomy in their branches. David Duncan, a senior partner in the Houston office who headed the Enron account, had abused this authority when his group approved fraudulent Enron accounts. The inflated earnings in Enron reports that would prompt the SEC investigation had been recorded during the five years prior to Berardino's promotion. The mistakes were well covered, and even if they were completely evident, it was too late for him to undo them; he could only mitigate their repercussions.

Many of the problems Andersen faced were not unique to that company. In truth, for Berardino to truly return accounting to its "roots," to the way it had been before the 1990s, he would have had to change an entire industry, not just one firm. Every auditor had to evaluate a new range of business activities

---

[11] Ibid., pp. 145, 381.

[12] Kurt Eichenwald, "Andersen Misread Depths of the Government's Anger," *New York Times,* March 18, 2002, p. A-1.

[13] Accenture company Web site, http://www.accenture.com (accessed July 30, 2002).

[14] Schwartz and Glater, "At Andersen's Helm."

engaged in by corporations who no longer conformed to traditional financial practices. The other Big Five accounting firms also all combined consulting and auditing work. The Big Five accountants shared so many concerns, in fact, that they had banded together into a single lobbying group to challenge Congress on unwanted regulatory changes and donate large sums to political campaigns sympathetic to their cause.

Berardino himself had earned his reputation while a partner in the accounting world for his dealings with then-chairman of the SEC Arthur Levitt. Berardino challenged Levitt directly when the chairman moved to block Andersen's attempts to rejuvenate its consulting activities following the 2000 Accenture split. Like many in the accounting industry, Berardino argued that consulting work enhanced auditing by giving employees a firsthand knowledge of the industry that they monitored. Berardino understood that auditors were no longer just auditors and he saw no need to challenge what had become standard practice. Berardino played an essential strategic and diplomatic role in hammering out the new SEC auditor-independence rules with Levitt.[15]

By 2001, the accounting industry bore little resemblance to 1913's art of bookkeeping. Auditors faced unprecedented pressure. They monitored businesses that did not fit into established categories. And as technology evolved and information became quickly accessible and transmittable, accountants had greater capacity to add new services to their work, including consulting duties. The potential existed for a reshuffling of auditing practices not only at Andersen, but across every firm in the industry. When sweeping change did occur, it occurred with Arthur Andersen in the media spotlight as a symbol of the accounting industry's failures.

ARTHUR ANDERSEN IN THE PUBLIC EYE

Prior to 2001, most Americans paid little attention to the role of the "Big Five" auditors in the business world. The new business environment of increasingly close auditor–client ties had led to concerns within the industry. Lobbyists for the major accounting firms had established a place for themselves on Capitol Hill, while executives within the firms themselves struggled with questions of proper oversight and possible conflicts of interest. The general public, however, remained mostly disengaged from this debate.

Like all independent auditors, Arthur Andersen always had an indirect responsibility to the public. In its capacity as an independent auditor, Andersen oversaw business transactions and bookkeeping, and verified the profits that each company posted so that potential investors could base their investment decisions on credible information. At the same time, however, it was the large corporate clients that generated profits for Andersen (and subsequently generated the million-dollar annual paychecks for partners like Duncan[16]), and so it was these clients with whom top executives cultivated good relations, to the exclusion of relationships with other key constituencies.

When Enron officials pointed their fingers at the fraudulent bookkeeping behind their company's bankruptcy in 2001, the public began to ask how the $600 million error could have occurred. As the investigation into Enron's business practices progressed, the media and the public both became increasingly critical of Arthur Andersen, which had consistently turned a blind eye to questionable financial transactions. (The company's original "think straight, talk straight" motto had long since been replaced by the "simply the best" slogan.[17]) Andersen had

[15] McLean and Elkind, *The Smartest Guys in the Room*, pp. 374–78, 390.

[16] Ibid., p. 147.
[17] Ibid., p. 145.

faced accounting scandals before, but none of these had Enron's potency. The auditing firm could not escape public censure in the aftermath of the energy giant's demise.

The American public, fueled by images of loyal Enron workers left with no work, no pension, and worthless stock options, immediately condemned Enron executives as criminals. Furthermore, they saw Arthur Andersen as directly implicated in these executives' criminal activities. To many, Andersen would become synonymous with Enron's failure. Whether or not Andersen was unique in its relations with its clients, its Enron association became the symbol of a corporate world in which unscrupulous top executives could use sophisticated financial manipulations for personal profit at the expense of their companies.

In the wake of Enron, the auditing firm that had devoted so much of its time and attention to courting its top corporate clients would have to answer to a new constituency—the American public. Many of Andersen's new critics had no prior knowledge of the accounting business; they had never previously questioned who audited the books of the companies on which they relied for services, employment, or returns on their investments. Instead, average citizens relied on a regulatory structure in place at the SEC to protect them against fraudulent bookkeeping practices. This infrastructure had failed them. Worse, many Americans believed that the auditors charged with enforcing accounting standards had joined forces with the very companies who were abusing these standards. To these critics, Andersen executives had committed a double betrayal, both collecting illegal profits and neglecting their duties as watchdogs. These perceptions were further fueled by accounts of Andersen employees working at Enron, adopting the client's "business casual" approach at work, and socializing at high-level social functions such as the Masters Golf Tournament.[18] Andersen was not alone in questionable auditor–client relations; the accounting industry as a whole had undergone substantial changes through the 1990s. Andersen was alone, however, in its link to the Enron debacle and in bearing the brunt of Americans' outrage over what had happened. The investors to whom Andersen's corporate clients responded would soon demand stricter inspection of accounting procedures. Some would ask for a separation from Andersen. For the first time, a major auditing firm's reputation with the American public would have a direct impact on the future of the company. And Andersen, by November of 2001, was ill-prepared to handle the public constituency.

THE ENRON COLLAPSE

Through the 1990s, Enron enjoyed a very close relationship with the Andersen partners that it hired as accountants. This relationship included the "cross-pollination" of employee pools: both internal and external audits performed by Andersen, and a large volume of consulting work done by Andersen accountants as well. Duncan directly oversaw the auditing of Enron's accounts and exercised significant power in determining the relationship between Andersen and Enron. In 1997, at the young age of 38, Duncan took over running the profitable Enron account.[19] He had personal ties to both Houston, as a graduate and active alumnus of Texas A & M, and Enron, where he regularly joined in company-sponsored events and, like many on Andersen's Enron team, shared office space at Enron headquarters.[20] In addition, Duncan and Rick Causey, chief accounting officer at Enron, had a strong friendship/camaraderie that had developed during the years when Causey worked alongside Duncan at Andersen.[21]

---

18 Ibid., p. 146.

19 Ibid.

20 Thaddeus Herrick, "Were Enron, Andersen Too Close?" *The Wall Street Journal,* January 21, 2002.

21 McLean and Elkind, *The Smartest Guys in the Room,* p. 146.

During the course of the business relationship, Enron proved to be one of Andersen's top four clients, pulling in $52 million in fees for the auditor in 2000 alone. In the later years of the relationship, the Enron account made the Houston office both the biggest and most profitable office in the firm.[22] At one point, during what Andersen now claims was a routine internal team meeting, there was mention that "it would not be unforeseeable that fees could reach a $100 million per year amount," and that Andersen should keep the client, in spite of its nonroutine business practices, including complex partnership companies being formed, and its use of the relatively new mark-to-market accounting principles.[23]

With the distinction of managing one of Andersen's "crown jewel" clients, Duncan was granted personal autonomy in handling the Enron portfolio that extended beyond the Houston office.[24] This gave him the ability to overrule those governance committees that Andersen headquarters had established to ensure proper accounting procedure. Duncan could even remove committee members from ruling on Houston office work. He acted on this power when, in December 1999, Carl Bass, a partner in the Houston office, voiced concerns over bookkeeping and the complex formation of limited partnerships at Enron. Bass was a member of Andersen's Professional Standards Group (PSG), a committee of expert auditors charged with reviewing particularly complicated accounts. Duncan had dismissed PSG objections on four separate occasions prior to 1999. In that December, Bass detected improper records for a sale of options by a special-purpose enterprise owned by an officer at Enron. Although the sale eventually went through as originally recorded, Bass would not drop his complaint over the trans-

action. Over a period of several years, Duncan, on Enron's behalf, petitioned to have Bass removed from the case. Bass was eventually removed from the PSG.[25]

After the complaint about Bass, in February 2001, executives at Andersen once again expressed serious reservations about Enron as a client. And once again the Houston office persuaded top officials not to terminate the contract. By this time, the errors that would lead to Enron's bankruptcy later that year had already accumulated. Congressional investigators would later find that Enron had used outside partnerships owned by Enron executives, like those uncovered in Bass's review, to hide millions of dollars of debt, hedge normally unhedgeable investments,[26] and thereby allow the company to consistently report inflated earnings.

In spite of Duncan's insistence on keeping the Enron account, Andersen headquarters still believed that something had gone wrong in the Houston bookkeeping. Top in-house Andersen counsel had a conference call on October 9, 2001, to discuss the possible need for Enron's accounting restatement. During this call, one Andersen lawyer, Nancy Temple, took down a note stating, "Highly probably some SEC investing[ation] . . . probability of charge of violating C+D in WM [referring to the cease and desist order regarding the Waste Management suit]."[27]

On October 12, 2001, 10 days before the SEC announced its investigation of Enron, Temple sent out an e-mail that reminded employees of the company's document retention policy. This policy had begun after the Waste Management investigation, in which the SEC had uncovered wrongdoing at Andersen using evidence pulled from its Waste Management files.

[25] Mike McNamee, "Out of Control at Andersen," *Newsweek,* April 8, 2002.

[22] Ibid., p. 145.

[23] Ibid., p. 317.

[24] Ibid., p. 145.

[26] Kurt Eichenwald, *Conspiracy of Fools* (New York: Broadway Books, 2005), pp. 222–29.

[27] McLean and Elkind, *The Smartest Guys in the Room,* p. 381.

Upon being reminded to purge documents, Michael Odom, an Andersen Practice director, told Houston employees that "if [the documents are] destroyed in the course of normal policy and litigation is filed the next day, that's great . . . we've followed our policy, and whatever there was that might have been of interest to somebody, uh, is gone."[28] Following Temple's e-mail and Odom's reminders regarding the company policy, employees began to shred all nonessential documents—drafts, notes, internal memos. The team also was encouraged to delete e-mails that were not essential to the audit files.[29] Over the next two weeks, it has been estimated that the Houston office shredded more documents than it normally would have in an entire year. In addition, approximately 30,000 e-mails and electronic files were deleted from computers, and the Portland, Chicago, and London offices commenced shredding their nonessential Enron-related documents.[30] As one Andersen employee later reflected, Duncan and his office were just following company policy and orders.[31]

On October 22, 2001, the SEC publicly announced its probe into Enron's financial transactions. The internal debates at Andersen over these transactions, debates that began in 1999 and continued up to the SEC announcement, indicate that the accounting firm knew that its own role in the energy company's financial trouble might be called into question. If any doubt remained over whether Enron's scandal would reach the auditors, Enron executives settled the matter on October 31 by convening a special committee to investigate Andersen's accounting failures.

Internal communication and documentation revealed that Andersen's higher-ups had recognized Enron as a risky client. Regarding Enron, one partner wrote in early 2001, "Client is a first mover, and expects to push the edges of established convention, and where they can, create new convention . . . often in very grey areas." Internal Andersen documents also noted that Enron's "accounting and financial risk were very significant."[32] Even Duncan had made a note, following a 1998 Andersen audit, stating, "Obviously we are on board with all of these [transactions], but many push limits and have high 'others could have a different point of view' risk profile."[33]

In spite of Andersen headquarters' early realization that their Houston office could come under attack for its treatment of the Enron accounts, almost everyone else at the company remained in the dark about the problem. Branches outside of Houston received little or no preparation for October's crisis. In fact, employees at Arthur Andersen described their preparation as virtually nonexistent. Doug DeRito, the Atlanta partner at Andersen, went so far as to request Berardino's resignation. He was angered by the lack of any internal information flow and declared, "My ability to survive financially [through Enron] is at stake, and I have zero details."[34]

On November 8, 2001, Enron restated its finances back to 1997, revealing a $586 million loss. The company's stock plummeted, and the finger pointing began in earnest. Enron disavowed its books and blamed Andersen's poor accounting standards for allowing millions of dollars' worth of improper transactions to pass without anyone sounding an alarm. Enron had made many unwise business deals, but its officials insisted that the error hadn't been theirs alone, but rather their accountants' as well.

Arthur Andersen had worked hard over the previous century to develop a positive reputation

[28] Eichenwald, *Conspiracy of Fools,* p. 529.

[29] McLean and Elkind, *The Smartest Guys in the Room,* p. 381.

[30] Ibid., pp. 382–83.

[31] Eichenwald, *Conspiracy of Fools,* p. 651.

[32] McLean and Elkind, *The Smartest Guys in the Room,* p. 146.

[33] Ibid., p. 147.

[34] Ken Brown, Ianthe Jeanne Dugan, and Cassell Bryan-Low, "Berardino's Resignation Leaves Andersen's Drama Unresolved," *The Wall Street Journal,* March 27, 2002.

among corporate clients like Enron (see Exhibit 1.1). The firm served these clients not only through external auditing services, but consulting and internal auditing work as well, and oversaw transactions of billions of dollars in the fast-paced financial world of the 1990s. When companies that had hired Andersen as an accountant started to fail, however, the close auditor–client relationships that first attracted clients to Andersen began to appear too close. Federal investigators would soon attempt to separate acceptable company practices from compromising ones in the much-changed accounting world of 2001. And Arthur Andersen would be at the center of this debate.

PROBLEMS FACING ANDERSEN

With the SEC about to announce that it would subpoena Andersen's files regarding the Enron case the next day, Berardino knew that his firm was in danger and needed immediate help. Andersen was already on SEC "probation" for earlier accounting errors with Waste Management and Sunbeam. Partners at the firm had reason to believe that the SEC would investigate its operations even further when it examined Andersen's role as an auditor at Enron. Not only would Andersen be under federal scrutiny, but the heavy media coverage of Enron had placed the accountants under public scrutiny as well. Berardino had never represented Andersen to such a broad audience before, and he had almost no foundation from which to build a new campaign now. It would be difficult to put together a corporate communication strategy given the firm's limited effort in this area, but Berardino knew he had to do something now, or the firm might never recover.

CASE QUESTIONS

1. How does the changing environment for business affect Arthur Andersen's ability to communicate in this situation?

2. Where is the firm most vulnerable, from a communications standpoint?

3. Who needs to be involved in discussions about how to communicate in the face of the SEC investigation of Andersen?

4. What role will Joe Berardino need to play in this situation?

5. What advice would you give Mr. Berardino if you had received his call from Tokyo instead of David Talbot?

EXHIBIT 1.1
Arthur
Andersen &
Co. ad
"What's
Really
Holding
Your
Company
Back?"

What's really holding your company back?

You'll find out when you discover your real business problems—the ones hidden in your underlying business practices.

And that's where our proprietary knowledge base of Global Best Practices can help.

In our trained hands, it lets us compare your operating practices to the best in the business world—within your own industry, and across the board.

So we can gain insight into what's slowing you down. And roll out more creative ways to help you reengineer your operations.

It's designed to be the most thought-provoking resource of its kind. Driven by an advanced application of CD-ROM technology. Updated throughout our global network. And unsurpassed in its depth and scope.

To see a demonstration of our knowledge base or receive a brochure, call 1-800-445-5556, today. And find out how we can help you make lasting progress—on paper and in practice.

*Best Practices.
Putting insight
into practice.*™

ARTHUR
ANDERSEN

ARTHUR ANDERSEN & CO. SC

CHAPTER TWO

Communicating Strategically

In the first chapter, we examined the changing environment for business over the last half century. In this chapter, we explore how these changes have affected corporate communication and why the changing environment requires a different approach to the function from what we have seen in the past.

We begin this chapter with an explanation of the basic theory behind all communication, whether individual or organizational in nature. Much of this theory comes from ideas generated thousands of years ago by Aristotle. More recently, communication experts have adapted these same theories to individuals as they communicate in writing and speech.

Few, however, have looked at how these same basic theories apply in the corporate communication context—that is, in the way organizations communicate with various groups of people. Communication, more than any other subject in business, has implications for everyone within an organization—from the newest administrative assistant to the CEO. Most managers have learned to think strategically about their business overall, but few think strategically about what they spend most of their time doing—communicating.

This chapter discusses how communication theory developed as well as how that theory can be used to establish communication strategies in organizations. The discussion then turns from the application of communication theory to making the critical link between corporate communication and the firm's overall corporate strategy.

Communication Theory

Most theories associated with communication are based on notions that can be traced back thousands of years. In ancient Greece, the subject we now refer to as communication was called *rhetoric*, using language to persuade whoever was listening to do something. Practicing the art of rhetoric was highly regarded by the Greeks.

Aristotle, who studied under Plato and taught in Athens from 367–347 BC, is most often associated with the development of rhetoric as an art. In Aristotle's

FIGURE 2.1
Corporate
Communica-
tion Strategy
Framework.

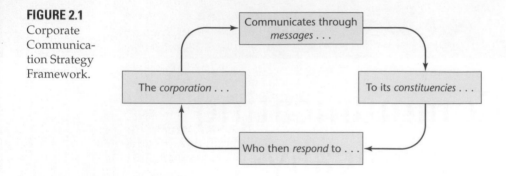

major work, *The Art of Rhetoric*, we can find the roots of modern communication theory.[1] Early in this seminal text, Aristotle defines the composition of every speech:

> [E]very speech is composed of three parts: the speaker, the subject of which he treats, and the person to whom it is addressed, I mean the hearer, to whom the end or object of the speech refers.

Whether an organization is trying to enhance its reputation through corporate advertising, to communicate effectively with employees about the rising cost of health care, to convince shareholders that the company is still worth investing in, or simply to get customers to buy more of its products, using a coherent communication strategy is critical.

This strategy depends on thinking carefully about the same three parts that Aristotle used to describe the components of speech: (1) Instead of a speaker, the first component in a corporate communication strategy is *the organization*. (2) The second component, in place of Aristotle's "person . . . to whom the end or object of the speech refers," is *the constituency*. (3) The final component, which Aristotle describes as "the subject of which he treats," will be referred to as *messages*. The corporate communication strategy framework, seen in Figure 2.1, synthesizes ideas from Aristotle and communications expert Mary Munter[2] to form a useful framework for analyzing corporate communication.

As we look at the interaction among the three variables, we see that each is connected to the others. As communication theorist Annette Shelby states: "The unique interrelationships of these variables determine which messages will be effective and which will not."[3] In addition, the framework is circular rather than linear, which reflects the reality that communication of any kind is an ongoing process rather than one with a beginning and an end.

---

[1] Aristotle, *The Art of Rhetoric* (Cambridge, MA: Harvard University Press, 1975).

[2] Mary Munter, *Guide to Managerial Communication,* 7th ed. (Upper Saddle River, NJ: Prentice Hall, 2005). Please see Chapter 1 for a full discussion of how these same ideas apply to an individual rather than an organization.

[3] Annette N. Shelby, "The Theoretical Bases of Persuasion: A Critical Introduction," *Journal of Business Communication* 23, no. 1 (Winter 1986), pp. 5–29.

Developing Corporate Communication Strategies

Let's further develop each of these variables and apply them to real situations and see how they operate in practice.

Setting an Effective Organization Strategy

The first part of an effective corporate communication strategy relates to the organization itself. The three subsets of an organization strategy include (1) determining the *objectives* for a particular communication, (2) deciding what *resources* are available for achieving those objectives, and (3) diagnosing the organization's *reputation*.

Determining Objectives

An organization, like an individual, has many different reasons for deciding to communicate. For example, a company might want to announce to employees a change in its benefits package for the upcoming year. Let's suppose the organization has decided to eliminate retiree health benefits as a result of increasing health care costs. In this case, its objective is more than just announcing the change; it also must convince employees it has a good reason for taking something away from them. Thus, the objective here is to get employees to accept the change with a minimal amount of protest.

In contrast, let's suppose that a Japanese candy manufacturer has decided to enter the U.S. market. To stimulate interest in its confections, the company decides to produce a brochure that will show and explain what the product is and how it is an extension of Japanese culture. The company's objective, then, is to create a demand among American consumers for something they neither know about nor want.

Notice that in both of these cases, the *response* from the constituency in question is what is most important. That is the basis for defining an objective: *What does the organization want each constituency to do as a result of the communication?* Management communication expert Mary Munter writes in her *Guide to Managerial Communication* that managerial communication is only successful if you get the desired response from your audience.[4] To get that response, you must think strategically about your communication, including setting measurable objectives for it.

Deciding What Resources Are Available

Determining how to communicate about something like an employee benefits plan or introducing a new product into a market depends heavily on what resources are available within the organization, including money, human resources, and time.

Money In our earlier example involving cutbacks in health benefits for employees, the company must decide whether it is better to simply announce the program as clearly as possible to its employees—say, through the company newsletter, via

[4] Munter, *Guide to Managerial Communication.*

e-mail, or on the company's intranet—or to hire a benefits consultant with experience in helping other companies sell scaled-back benefits to employees. The first option looks less expensive than the second in the short term, but if the employees revolt because they feel they are losing something for no good reason, the company might end up spending far more than it would have if it had hired the more experienced consultant in the first place.

Most companies, unfortunately, often err on the side of short-term, inexpensive solutions to communication problems because they are not looking at the problem from the perspective of the constituency in question. This is similar to a problem individuals often have in communicating: they look at their own needs rather than the needs of their audience and end up having difficulty reaching their communication objective.

Human Resources   Human resources are also an important factor in determining the success or failure of a company in achieving its objectives. Typically, too few are assigned to deal with communication tasks, and those involved are often inexperienced or unqualified.

Imagine a company that has just gone public and has decided to create an investor relations function to deal with shareholder relations and communication with securities analysts. It could assign one person to do all of these things, or it could decide that it really needs three. The best approach depends on the size of the company and its shareholder base. Let's look at the case of a well-known, multibillion-dollar company that turned this function over to one person with weak communication skills rather than devote two or three experts to deal with the different constituencies involved. In this company's case, it wasn't a question of whether they could afford to pay more people to do the job correctly; it was the lack of understanding about how important corporate communication really is and the limitations put on the human resources needed to accomplish a specific task.

This Fortune 500 company changed its approach after analysts started to downgrade its stock despite healthy prospects for the company's future. The CEO discovered that the analysts felt that the investor relations person at the company was not interested in giving them sufficient information to rate the company's stock. This led them to believe that something was wrong at the company. The investor relations person, on the other hand, was actually trying to do two or three tasks at the same time and simply could not keep up with the demands of the job. After this incident, the company hired two more professionals to handle the job properly, creating a more effective and efficient investor relations function, and its stock price shot back to where it should have been all along.

Time   Time, like human resources and money, is also a critical factor in determining an organization's corporate communication strategy. Let's look at two approaches for dealing with the same problem involving the allocation of time.

In the case of the Japanese confectioner mentioned earlier, the company decided to produce a brochure (with the help of a communications consulting firm) describing its product more than two years before it was actually necessary.

So much time was involved, however, in getting everyone in the company to buy into both the copy that was developed for the brochure as well as the design that it took almost the full two years to produce an eight-page pamphlet. Cultural differences between Japanese and American business styles contributed to the tremendous amount of time needed to develop the brochure.

For an American firm, it is unheard of to devote so much time to what would be viewed as such a simple project. American firms produce brochures like this from start to finish in a matter of weeks. But is this really a better approach?

The allocation of time, like the allocation of all resources, should be determined by what it will really take to achieve the company's objective rather than to seek a short-term solution. In some cases, this might mean allocating more resources than the organization would like to achieve the desired result; but almost always, the organization is better off allocating the resources up front. Correcting mistakes in corporate communication can be a costly proposition. Too often, qualified communicators are brought in only after a crisis has erupted, or to combat rumors that have materialized to fill a "communications void." This is often the case when a company is in the midst of a merger or acquisition and employees hear details about the company's merger plans through media outlets before they hear it from the company itself. When rampant rumor mills and third-party information inspire fear and uncertainty among employees, productivity and customer service typically suffer—in some cases enough to reduce shareholder value.[5] The company then suddenly has a much larger—and potentially more costly—problem to deal with.

Diagnosing the Organization's Reputation

In addition to setting objectives for a communication and deciding what resources are available to accomplish that objective, organizations also must determine what kind of reputation they have with the constituencies in question. An organization's overall reputation with constituencies is based on several factors. We will get into this in greater detail in Chapter 4 when we talk about image, identity, and reputation, but it is also a critical factor in the development of all communication strategies, whether specifically related to image or not.

Reputation is based on the constituency's perception of the organization rather than the reality of the organization itself. As an example, think about a university that is trying to generate positive publicity in the national press. If the university is not well known outside its region, this might prove very difficult. Its reputation in this situation would be low because national press representatives would have limited experience with the institution compared to an institution that already has a national reputation. Thus, no matter what kind of resources the university puts behind this effort, it will be an uphill battle.

Worse than limited reputation is credibility that is lacking or damaged. Following the highly publicized Bridgestone/Firestone tire recalls of 2000, Firestone sought to rebuild trust among consumers through its "Making It Right"

---

[5] Michael Kempner, "When RUMORS Thrive Your Deal's in Trouble: Damage Control Techniques to Seize the Communications High Ground," *Mergers & Acquisitions*, May 1, 2005, pp. 42–47.

advertising campaign. The ads unveiled the company's action plan for upgrades in manufacturing and quality control in an effort to restore customer confidence in Firestone tires and boost sales. For consumers, however, this was largely a case of "too little, too late." While the first large-scale tire recall took place in August 2000, it was not until April of 2001 that Firestone launched "Making It Right." After months of avoiding responsibility for the tire mishaps and, even worse, engaging in a blame game with Ford over which company was responsible for the fatal accidents—the tires or the Ford Explorer vehicle—Firestone was increasingly perceived by consumers as unconcerned about them and their safety. This loss of credibility proved devastating when the company decided it was finally time to reach out with a message of concern in an effort to rebuild trust with its advertising campaign.

Sometimes, a damaged reputation can result from circumstances beyond an organization's control, not resulting from any specific actions or missteps by the company itself. For example, energy companies faced a collective reputational challenge in the wake of the Enron collapse. Many began having problems with bondholders, regulators, and investors following the scandal as they were presumed guilty of engaging in similar practices as the former energy giant. One possible strategy to combat this "guilt by association" would have been for a company to craft a communication program that would actively seek to distinguish it from Enron in a highly visible way.[6]

We can see that an organization's reputation is an important factor in setting a coherent communication strategy. For simple tasks, this is not a problem; but in other cases, the image credibility an organization has built with a specific constituency can make a huge difference in determining the success or failure the organization has in achieving its objectives. Companies increasingly are recognizing this fact and, accordingly, are dedicating resources to assessing their corporate reputation. One such company is FedEx. Once a year, the company's senior executives gather at its Memphis headquarters to asses the different risks the company faces. In addition to considering the possible financial impact and implications for business continuity of each scenario, they examine what would happen to the company's reputation. "We believe that a strong reputation can act as a life preserver in a crisis and as a tailwind when the company is on the offensive," says Bill Margaritis, FedEx's corporate vice president of worldwide communications and investor relations. In addition to this hypothetical scenario analysis, FedEx conducts a survey quarterly to find out how the company is perceived by external stakeholders, and performs a similar exercise with its employees annually.[7]

The three considerations for creating an effective organization strategy—setting objectives, deciding on the proper allocation of resources, and diagnosing the organization's reputation—are the building blocks upon which all other steps in communication strategy depend. A second set of issues the organization can turn to is an assessment of the constituents involved.

---

[6] Duncan Wood, "Not Cleaning Up Your Act Can Be Costly," *Treasury & Risk Management*, September 2004.

[7] Ibid.

TABLE 2.1
Constituents of
Corporations

Primary	Secondary
• Employees	• Media
• Customers	• Suppliers
• Shareholders	• Government
• Communities	Local
	Regional
	National
	• Creditors

Analyzing Constituencies

Analyzing constituencies is similar to analyzing your audience when you want to plan a speech or write a memo. This analysis determines (1) who your organization's constituencies are, (2) what each thinks about the organization, and (3) what each knows about the communication in question. We will look at each of these in turn.

Who Are Your Organization's Constituencies?

Sometimes the answer to this question is obvious, but most of the time, it will take careful consideration to analyze who the relevant constituencies are for a particular message. Do not be fooled into thinking that it is always obvious who the main constituency is. Usually, constituencies come from a group that is primary to the organization, but a secondary group also can be the focus for a particular communication (see Table 2.1).

Companies have different sets of constituencies depending on the nature, size, and reach (i.e., global or domestic, local versus regional or national) of their businesses. While a company may list its constituencies on a piece of paper, as in Table 2.1, it should resist thinking of them as too fixed or too separate. An organization's primary constituency or constituencies can change over time. In a time of crisis, for example, it may be wise for a company to focus more intently on its relations with the media—which it may normally consider a secondary constituency—to manage its reputation and attempt to minimize negative press. Additionally, constituencies should not be thought about in "silos," as the lines between them can blur. When employees are also shareholders in a company, for instance, they belong simultaneously to two constituency groups. For example, Starbucks officially blends constituencies by offering all employees "bean stock" based on the number of hours they work.[8]

Also recognize that constituencies interact with one another, and an organization must sometimes work through one constituency to reach another. For instance, if a department store is focused on revitalizing a customer service focus to drive more loyalty (and sales) from its customer constituency, it must reinforce this mission with employees before customers will see results. An example of this can be seen in the *employee-customer-profit chain model* created by Sears, which

[8] Kim Fellner, "The Starbucks Paradox," *Color Lines,* Spring 2004, http://www.arc.org/C_Lines.

tracked success from management behavior through employee attitudes to customer satisfaction and, ultimately, financial performance.[9]

Companies should acknowledge the role of their own employees as "brand ambassadors"—given that they interact with a large number of external constituencies, the potential for "word of mouth" goodwill and image building is significant when employees fully understand what the corporation aims to be in the mind of its customers and other constituencies. Nike is a company that is known for its efforts in this area.[10]

Keep in mind also that constituencies can have competing interests and different perceptions of a company. For example, cutting employee benefits may be welcomed by shareholders but in all likelihood will not be popular with employees. Finally, keep in mind that communications intended for one constituency often reach others.

The individual communication experience of one marketing vice president (VP) brings this last point to life. The executive VP to whom he reported had decided to cut the group's administrative support staff due to the increased use of voice mail technology to handle communications while professionals were away from their desks. This vice president detailed his plan for cutting the support staff by almost two-thirds in a memo to the vice president in charge of human resources. The plan involved laying off five assistants in the department over a period of six months. Many of them had been with the firm for several years.

As usual, the marketing VP typed up his thoughts in rough form and e-mailed it to his assistant, asking her to format the letter and print the final draft on his letterhead. Although his assistant was not one of the five affected by the layoffs, she couldn't help but empathize with her colleagues of many years, and within an hour, the marketing VP had a revolt on his hands.

Now obviously, he didn't intend for his assistant to be a part of his constituency, nor did he stop to think about her reaction to the change when he asked her to print the letter to the human resources VP. Nonetheless, she became a conduit to a more important constituency—the employees who would actually be affected by the plan.

This simple example is instructive to organizations seeking to communicate at a more macro level as well. Just as we cannot always control the flow of information to one constituency alone on an individual level, on the corporate level the same set of problems arises.

What Is the Constituency's Attitude toward the Organization?

In addition to analyzing who the constituencies for a particular communication really are, organizations also need to assess what each constituency thinks about the organization itself.

We know from personal experience that it is easier to communicate with people who know and like us than it is with those who do not. The same is true

---

[9] Anthony J. Rucci, Steven P. Kirn, and Richard T. Quinn, "The Employee Customer Profit Chain at Sears," *Harvard Business Review,* January–February 1998, pp. 83–97.

[10] Martin Roll, "10 Steps for Successful Corporate Branding," BizCommunity.com, August 4, 2004, http://www.biz-community.com.

for organizations. If a company has built goodwill with the constituency in question, it will be much easier to reach its objective.

The classic example of good corporate communication is Johnson & Johnson's redemption of the Tylenol brand in 1982, when poisoned capsules killed seven people in Chicago. (See Chapter 10 for more on the Tylenol crisis.) That the company was able to succeed against all odds—when people like advertising executive Jerry Della Femina and several other experts in communication declared Tylenol impossible to save at the time—was a tribute to the hard work the organization had done before the tragedy actually happened. The company was known in the industry, by doctors, by consumers, and by the press as rock solid—willing to stand by its products and do the right thing, no matter what the cost. In this case, the cost ran into the hundreds of millions of dollars, when the company decided to recall over 31 million bottles of Tylenol capsules.

Convincing people to buy a product that had been laced with cyanide was not an easy proposition, but because the company had the trust of many different constituencies, it was able to achieve its objective, which was to revive the brand. If people hadn't trusted the company, or if they had questioned its behavior in any way, this would not have been possible.

When goodwill or trust is lacking, communication can be a struggle. And companies cannot expect to be trusted until they prove themselves trustworthy through concerted actions that demonstrate care, concern, and understanding for their constituencies. Building trust often must start from within the organization—by communicating up and down with employees, hearing them out on the topics that concern them, and making constructive changes based on their input. Companies with high levels of trust with employees are also those that take the time to clearly communicate the company's business goals to employees and help them understand the vital roles they play in achieving those goals.[11]

What Does the Constituency Know about the Topic?

In addition to the constituents' attitudes toward the company, we also must consider their attitudes toward the communication itself. If they are predisposed to do what your organization wants, then they are more likely to help the organization reach its objective. If they are not, however, the organization will have great difficulty in trying to achieve its goals.

Consumers are often wary of new or unknown products. The Japanese confectioner mentioned earlier was a victim of such bias as it tried to convince Americans to buy a product that was well known and liked in Japan but completely foreign to Americans. In Japan, the company is seen as the highest-quality manufacturer of *wagashi*, or candy. The company, Toraya, is one of the oldest companies on earth. It can trace its roots back to the ninth century, and the same family has been in control of the firm for 17 generations. It has been serving the imperial family since its inception.

Given its long history and aristocratic roots, the president of the company assumed that the product would speak for itself in the U.S. market. Since no one

[11] Shari Caudron, "Rebuilding Employee Trust," *Workforce Management,* October 2002, pp. 28–34.

else was around to compete with the firm, middle managers in charge of the U.S. operation assumed that its introduction of *wagashi* would be a huge success.

Unfortunately, they didn't think about how American palates would react to the taste of a candy made out of red beans and seaweed. Most of the people who heard about the product couldn't even pronounce its name, and when they tasted the gelatinous form of the product, known as *yokan*, they didn't like it.

To get consumers in the United States interested in the product, Toraya had to educate people about the role of *wagashi* in Japanese history, and its exclusivity as demonstrated by its aristocratic roots. Those who tasted the product in focus groups early in the process of its introduction to the United States likened the experience to the first time they had tasted caviar or espresso.

Companies that try to sell an idea to the public are always in danger of failing as a result of the lack of information or the negative feelings consumers may have about it. U.S. automaker General Motors (GM) realized, after several failed attempts to penetrate the U.K. market with Cadillacs, that rather than spending money on a U.K. advertising campaign, it was better served to hire an automotive PR specialist to help the company educate people about Cadillac's new approach to the market, including an increased range of right-hand-drive models.[12]

When companies are communicating to their employees about something like a change in benefits—from a defined benefit pension plan to a cash balance plan, for instance—understanding what employees know about the topic, as well as how they feel about it, is critical. Without this insight, time and resources can be wasted on a communications campaign that ends up missing the mark. For example, a company may assume that employees' greatest concern is the competitiveness of their new benefit relative to other companies, when, in fact, they are most concerned about understanding how the new plan differs from the existing one. Absent this knowledge, the company's communication strategy may focus too heavily on the benchmarking issue and fail to address the issue of most concern to this constituency.[13]

Clearly then, after a firm has set objectives for its corporate communication, it must thoroughly analyze all the constituencies involved. This means understanding who each constituency is, finding out what each thinks about the organization, and determining what each already knows and feels about the communication in question. Companies should consider allocating a portion of their marketing budget to this kind of research. Armed with this intelligence, the organization is ready to move to the final phase in setting a communication strategy: determining how to deliver the message.

Delivering Messages Appropriately

Delivering messages appropriately involves a two-step analysis for companies. A company must decide *how* it wants to deliver the message (choose a communication channel) and *what approach* to take in structuring the message itself.

---

[12] Richard Cann, "Cadillac Media Push Aims to Crack the UK," *PRWeek*, July 9, 2004.

[13] "Communicating Cash Balance Plans," *Watson Wyatt Insider*, April 2000, http://www.watsonwyatt.com.

TABLE 2.2
Communica-
tion Channels

Old Channels	New Channels
Speaking	Fax
Writing	E-mail
	Voice mail
	Web conferencing
	Video conferencing
	External Web sites
	Intranets
	Weblogs ("blogs")

Choose a Communication Channel

Determining the proper communication channel is more difficult for organizations than it is for people. An individual's channel choices are usually limited to writing or speaking, with some variation in terms of group or individual interaction. For organizations, however, the channels available for delivering the message are several.

As you can see from Table 2.2, there are now more communication channels then ever before for an organization's internal and external communications. For example, a company looking to reveal a change in top management may decide to announce the change through a press release, which gets the message out to a broad set of constituencies. In addition it also may announce the change in a memo and an e-mail to employees, as well as posting it on the company's intranet.

Even this simple example has multiple channel possibilities. Should the press release go to local media or national media? If the company is global, should it get the message out on an international newswire, such as Reuters? Should it transmit the message through its home page on the Web? Should the message go to employees through visual communications since many companies today have satellite hookups for far-flung operations? Then there is the whole question of *timing*. Should the employees hear about it first? Should the story be given to one reporter before all others, on an exclusive basis?

After GM announced 25,000 planned job cuts by 2008 at the company's annual meeting in 2005, the company had to work fast to calm worker uncertainty about what lay ahead. Sue Melino, staff director of GM's global internal communications department, explained that the company's goal was to ensure that employees were informed about the layoffs as soon as they were released to the public. The company delivered the news to employees through multiple channels: a Webcast of CEO Rick Wagner's speech at the annual meeting, newsletters in company plants, and a segment on GM's daily employee television show. "What we are trying to do," Melino explained, "is provide as much context as we can internally."[14]

When Agilent Technologies, the PC and computer equipment manufacturer spun off from Hewlett-Packard, faced plummeting sales and a grim business outlook in

[14] John N. Frank, "GM Pushes Growth Message in Light of Announced Job Cuts," *PRWeek*, June 9, 2005.

2001, then CEO Ned Barnholt had to communicate some difficult news to investors as well as employees. As he prepared to release a large quarterly loss to Wall Street analysts in August, Barnholt decided that he wanted employees to hear the news from him rather than from CNBC, so he got on the company's public announcement system and delivered the news to Agilent employees himself. Included in the message was straight talk about further job cuts that would have to take place, and also sincere thanks and praise to all the employees who had worked hard to carry out cost-cutting measures and had done whatever they could to help the company.[15] Barnholt won praise from Agilent employees for his candid, direct approach in communicating with them about issues that would affect them, and while the news was not good, they appreciated hearing it from the company's CEO before hearing it from a business network news anchor.

Each time a corporate communication strategy is developed, the question of which channels to use and when to use them should be explored carefully. Before this step, the company needs to think about the best way to structure the message and what to include in the message itself.

Structure Messages Carefully

According to most experts in communication, the two most effective message structures are direct and indirect. Direct structure means revealing your main point first, then explaining why; indirect structure means explaining why first, then revealing your main point.

When should a company choose to be direct and when should it decide to be indirect? Normally, organizations should be as direct as possible with as many constituencies as possible because indirect communication is confusing and harder to understand.

Take the example of Nissan when it introduced the Infiniti series in the United States. Instead of just coming out with photographs of the new cars (as it does now) the company took a more indirect (and typically Japanese) approach by showing impressions of landscapes and creating a mood without actually showing the car. This was a creative success compared to the approach its direct competitor, Toyota's Lexus, took by showing the traditional pictures of cars. Unfortunately, the campaign didn't sell many cars. The company wanted to create a strong identity in the American market through this type of advertising, but this mixture of product and image advertising was completely lost on American consumers.

A third option in terms of message structure is to simply have *no* message. Today, this approach simply doesn't work with a public hungry for the next sound bite and the media looking for an "angle" on the story. Usually, saying that the company cannot talk about the situation until "all the facts are in" is better than just saying "No comment" or nothing at all; but managers (especially in the United States) are often influenced by lawyers who are thinking about the legal ramifications of saying anything. Deciding to be direct often means taking the court of

---

[15] Daniel Roth, "How to Cut Pay, Lay Off 8,000 People, and Still Have Workers Who Love You," *Fortune,* February 4, 2002, pp. 62–68.

public opinion into consideration as well, which, to some companies, is often far more important than a court of law.

Constituency Responses

After communicating with a constituency, you must assess the results of your communication and determine whether the communication had the desired result. In some instances, this feedback can be gathered nearly immediately after the delivery of an important message or set of messages. For example, employees can be given a short questionnaire to confirm an understanding of the main points of the communication and uncover areas where they would have wanted more information or clarification. In other cases, it may take some time to measure the success of the communication, such as determining whether sales rose in response to an advertising campaign. After the results are in, you must determine how you will react. Has your reputation changed? Do you need to change your communication channel? Hence the circular nature of the corporate communication framework.

Creating a coherent corporate communication strategy, then, involves the three variables we have discussed in detail above: defining the *organization's* overall strategy for the communication, analyzing the relevant *constituencies*, and delivering *messages* appropriately. In addition, the organization needs to analyze constituency *responses* to determine whether the communication was successful. Figure 2.2 summarizes this more complete version of the corporate communication strategy model introduced earlier.

FIGURE 2.2
Expanded Corporate Communication Strategy Framework.

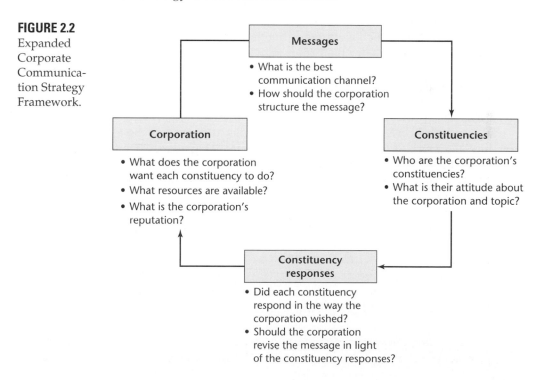

Messages
- What is the best communication channel?
- How should the corporation structure the message?

Corporation
- What does the corporation want each constituency to do?
- What resources are available?
- What is the corporation's reputation?

Constituencies
- Who are the corporation's constituencies?
- What is their attitude about the corporation and topic?

Constituency responses
- Did each constituency respond in the way the corporation wished?
- Should the corporation revise the message in light of the constituency responses?

Conclusion By creating a coherent communication strategy based on the time-tested theories presented in this chapter, an organization is well on its way to reinventing how it handles communications. Just as important for the firm, however, is its ability to link its overall strategy to its communication efforts.

In the last 20 years of the 20th century, the field of strategy blossomed with intriguing ideas from academics like Michael Porter,[16] Gary Hamel and C. K. Prahalad,[17] James C. Collins and Jerry E. Porras,[18] Adrian Slywotzky,[19] and Richard A. D'Aveni.[20] Their ideas drove strategy at large corporations and small businesses alike. None of them, however, focused on how to implement their ideas through the use of an effective corporate communication strategy.

For example, Prahalad and Hamel's "Strategic Intent"[21] is based on the idea of generating an intense single focus for an organization like President Kennedy's desire to send a man to the moon in the 1960s or British Airways' quest to become the "World's Favourite Airline." To be effective once it has been developed, however, this sort of strategy must be communicated to everyone in the organization. Managers should develop a method for communicating this kind of plan using the corporate communication strategy framework presented in this chapter.

In addition, as discussed in Chapter 1, firms face increased scrutiny from external forces (take Greenpeace on the environmental front) and key constituencies (such as shareholder groups like the one that fought former CEO Carly Fiorina at Hewlett-Packard over the merger with Compaq). By linking corporate strategy to corporate communication, managers can mitigate the potential loss in reputation (see Chapter 4) that can result from a weak or negative response from the organization to these external groups.

The extent to which an organization is affected by external forces also is determined by what industry the firm is in, where it does business, and how public its operations are. In addition to staying competitive, then, the question of how the firm is perceived externally must be considered. Just as the company's awareness about competitive forces protects it from competitors, its awareness of external forces also protects it from attacks.

That Johnson & Johnson consistently ranks at or toward the top of a number of highly publicized reputation surveys is not surprising when you consider the care the

[16] Michael Porter, "How Competitive Forces Shape Strategy," *Harvard Business Review* 57, no. 2 (March–April 1979), pp. 137–45.

[17] Gary Hamel and C. K. Prahalad, "Competing for the Future," *Harvard Business Review* 72, no. 4 (July–August 1994), pp. 122–28.

[18] James C. Collins and Jerry E. Porras, *Built to Last: Successful Habits of Visionary Companies* (New York: Harper Business, 1994).

[19] Adrian Slywotzky, *Value Migration: How to Think Several Moves Ahead of the Competition* (Boston: Harvard Business School Press, 1996).

[20] Richard A. D'Aveni, *Hypercompetition: Managing the Dynamics of Strategic Maneuvering* (New York: Free Press, 1994).

[21] C. K. Prahalad and Gary Hamel, "Strategic Intent," *Harvard Business Review* 67, no. 3 (May–June 1989), pp. 63–76.

company takes to ensure a strong connection between vision and communication. This was evidenced during the Tylenol crisis, when the company lived up to the values codified in the J&J Credo (see Chapter 10) in the caring manner in which it attended to the needs of its constituencies.

When developing an overall strategy, firms need to consider their corporate communication effort as manifested in the company's vision and mission statement. By doing so at the inception of an overall strategy, the firm avoids repercussions later. Since all organizations operate at the behest of the public will, this egalitarian approach to communications will be appreciated by a society that has come to depend on its organizations more than ever before.

Carson Container Company

Carson Container Company was a large regional plastic, injection-molding, container manufacturer supplying single-serving containers to small food and beverage producers. Carson had 30 plants, located primarily in the eastern part of the United States. Their procurement procedures were not coordinated. Carson's corporate headquarters had even encouraged plant managers to act as separate entities. In addition, each plant bought many items from local suppliers. Carson's decentralized approach to procurement was indicative of its overall strategy toward dealing with its constituencies including employees, customers, shareholders, and communities.

The noncarbonated beverage market (specialty juices and waters) took off in the late 1990s/early 2000s, and thus demand for Carson's bottles heated up. As it became clear that this trend would continue through the coming years, Carson faced increasing competitive pressures to drive prices down, and company management recognized that dealing with such a fragmented supplier base was hindering "efficiency" at the company. Michael Bundy, the company's president, hired an experienced materials manager, Rick Haskell, as Vice President of Corporate Procurement, a new position in the company. Bundy gave Haskell lots of flexibility in organizing his work and placed Patricia Friberg as Haskell's executive assistant. Gunn had worked for 15 years at Carson in several different positions and thus knew many plant employees. Haskell's appointment was announced in the employee newsletter published at headquarters and in a memo to plant managers.

Source: This is a fictional case based on real events as well as ideas presented in both the "Dashman Company" case (9-462-001) published by HBS Case Services, Harvard Business School, Boston, 1947, and the "Marathon Plastics" case published in W. H. Newmann, E. K. Warren, and J. E. Schnee's *The Process of Management*, 5th ed. (Englewood Cliffs, NJ: Prentice Hall, 1982).

Haskell wanted to centralize the company's procurement procedures and reduce the number of suppliers overall. To begin the process, he asked each of the executives who handled materials management in the various plants to clear with headquarters all contracts over $100,000. Haskell thought that if headquarters was going to coordinate in a way that would help each plant and Carson overall, he had to know about contracts being negotiated at least a week before they were going to be signed. He discussed the idea with Michael Bundy, who discussed it with the board of directors, who approved the idea.

Carson's plants made purchases and negotiated deals with suppliers continuously, but the beginning of its busiest buying season was only two weeks away when the new plan was put into place. Haskell drafted a memo to send to the 30 plant materials managers:

Dear Materials Manager:

Carson's board of directors has approved a new procurement process. Henceforth, all materials managers in each plant will alert the Vice President of Corporate Procurement about contracts above $100,000 that they plan to negotiate at least a week before the day they will be signed.

I know you must understand that this change is critical to coordinate the procurement requirements at Carson and consolidate relationships with national suppliers when we are finding it more difficult to secure good deals at the local level. This step will provide us in the head office the information we need to see that each plant procures the optimal supply of materials at the best prices. As a result, the goals of each plant and for Carson as a whole will more likely be achieved.

Sincerely,
Richard Todd Haskell II
Vice President, Procurement

Haskell gave Patricia the memo and asked for her input. She told him she thought the memo was great. She said, however, that, since he had met only three of the materials managers, he might like to meet all of them and discuss procurement with each of them individually. Haskell declined because he had so many things to do at home and in his office that he was unable to travel. He also felt it would cost too much to visit all the plants, and he was keenly aware of the need to limit spending.

Over the next few days, responses came in from all but a few plants. Some managers wrote longer responses, but the following e-mail message was typical:

Dear Dick:

Welcome to Carson! We wish you every success as the new procurement coordinator. We got your recent communication about notifying headquarters a week in advance of our intention to sign contracts with suppliers. This suggestion seems very practical. We would like to let you know that you can be sure of this plant's cooperation in your new job.

Best regards,

Over the next several weeks, headquarters heard nothing from the plants about contracts being negotiated with suppliers. Carson executives in other departments who visited the plants frequently reported that they were quite busy, and the usual procedures for that time of year continued.

CASE QUESTIONS

1. What problems does Carson Container Company have that will affect its communications?
2. What specific problems does Mr. Haskell have as a result of his communications to materials managers?
3. How would you analyze this case in terms of the expanded corporate communication strategy framework (Figure 2.2)?
4. What advice would you give Haskell to help solve his and Carson's problems?

CHAPTER THREE

An Overview of the Corporate Communication Function

The past two chapters painted a broad picture of the business environment and provided a framework for communicating strategically. Against this backdrop, we turn now to a discussion of the corporate communication function itself. A growing number of companies recognize the value of corporate communication and are adapting their budgets and internal structures accordingly. The *PRWeek*/Weber Shandwick 2005 Corporate Survey estimated average future corporate communication budget increases of 24 percent within a year's time.[1]

This chapter traces the evolution of corporate communication and the developments in recent years that led to a heightened recognition of the field. After examining the roots of corporate communication, we then discuss the most appropriate structure for the function within an organization, including reporting relationships. We also showcase each corporate communication subfunction that is explored in greater detail later in this book.

From "PR" to "CorpComm"

Public relations (PR), the predecessor to the corporate communication (Corp-Comm) function, grew out of necessity. Although corporations had no specific strategy for communications, they often had to respond to external constituencies whether they wanted to or not. As new laws forced companies to communicate in many situations they hadn't previously confronted, the constant need for a response meant that dedicated resources were required to manage the flow of communications.

---

[1] Weber Shandwick, "Corporate Survey 2005," *PRWeek*, June 27, 2005.

This function, which was tactical in most companies, was almost always called either "public relations" (PR) or "public affairs." Typically, the effort was meant to prevent the press from getting too close to management. Like a Patriot missile, designed to stop incoming missiles during war, the old PR professional was asked to protect the company from bad publicity, often by "spinning" damaging news in a positive light. Thus, the term "flack" came to be used to describe what PR people were actually doing: shielding top managers from "missiles" fired at them from the outside.

The "flack" era of public relations lasted for a number of decades, and when companies needed other communications activities, public relations personnel were the obvious choice to take them on. In the 1960s, for instance, it was not unusual to find public relations officials handling speechwriting, annual reports, and the company newsletter. Given that the majority of work in this area involved dealing with the print media (television wasn't truly a factor until the early 1970s), many companies hired former journalists to handle this job. The former-journalist-turned-flack brought the organization the first dedicated expert in the area of communication.

Until recently, the top managers in large companies came from backgrounds such as engineering; accounting; finance; production; or, at best (in terms of under-standing the company's communication needs), sales or marketing. Their understanding of how to communicate depended on abilities they might have gained by chance or through undergraduate or secondary school training rather than years of experience. Given their more quantitative rather than verbal orientation, these old-style managers were delighted to have an expert communicator on board who could take the heat for them and offer guidance in times of trouble.

PR professionals often were seen as capable of turning bad situations into good ones, creating excellent relations with their former colleagues in journalism, and helping the chief executive officer become a superb communicator. In some cases, this was true, but for the most part, the journalists were not the answer to all of the company's communications problems. When situations turned from bad to worse, they were the obvious ones to blame—easy scapegoats for irresponsible managers.

The First Spin Doctors

In addition to the internal PR staff, outside agencies often helped companies that either couldn't afford a full-time person or needed an extra pair of hands in a crisis. The legends of the public relations field—such as Ivy Lee; Edward Bernays; David Finn; Harold Burson; and, more recently, Howard Rubenstein and John Graham—helped the public relations function develop from its journalistic roots into a more refined and respected profession.

For many years, PR agencies dominated the communications field, billing companies hefty fees for services they could not handle in-house. Few large companies were willing to operate without such a firm for fear that they might be missing an opportunity to solve their communications problems painlessly by using these outside "spin doctors."

Some of the top public relations firms today—such as Fleishman Hillard, Hill & Knowlton, and Burson-Marsteller in the United States; Shandwick in the United

Kingdom and the United States; and Cosmo PR in Japan—still provide some of the best advice available on a number of communications-related issues. But outside agencies cannot handle all the day-to-day activities required for the smooth flow of communications from organization to constituents. Therefore, they often work alongside in-house communication professionals on strategic or project-based communications activities.

A New Function Emerges

By the 1970s, the business environment required more than the simple internal PR function supplemented by the outside consultant. The rise in importance and power of special-interest groups, such as Ralph Nader's Public Interest Research Group (PIRG) and environmentally oriented organizations such as Greenpeace, forced companies to increase their communications activities. During the Arab oil boycott and embargo in the 1970s, the entire oil industry came under fire as consumers had to wait hours for a tank of gasoline while big oil companies reported what many consumer groups felt were "obscene" profits running into the hundreds of millions of dollars.

This led Mobil Oil to develop one of the most sophisticated public relations departments of its time. Mobil's Herb Schmertz revolutionized the field by solving communications problems with strategies that no one had thought of before. His series of advertisements, called "issue ads" (see Chapter 5 for more on this subject), which ran on the *New York Times* and the *Wall Street Journal* op-ed pages once or twice a week, directly attacked the allegations of both "obscene" profits and hoarding of oil to inflate prices. Instead of merely reacting to these allegations, the Mobil issue ads put the blame on the government, explained why the oil companies needed hefty profits for exploration, and refocused discussion on other issues the company's CEO thought were important to shareholders.

With a budget in the tens of millions of dollars, Schmertz created a new communications function that changed the nature of Mobil's communications effort from old-style public relations to the first significant corporate communication department. A senior vice president of the corporation, Schmertz was also one of the very few communications executives with a seat on the board of directors—further proof of Mobil's commitment to enhanced communications.

Thus, as individual corporations and entire industries were increasingly scrutinized and had to answer to a much more sophisticated set of journalists, the old-style public relations function was no longer capable of handling the flack. As a result, what at first had been deemed a waste of resources at Mobil in the early 1970s became the norm in corporate America. The focus now shifted to structuring these new departments effectively to fit the function into the existing corporate infrastructure.

In more recent years, the corporate communication function has continued to evolve to meet the demands of the ever-changing business and regulatory environments. At the outset of the millennium, a string of financial scandals at corporations including WorldCom and Enron resulted in the Sarbanes-Oxley Act of 2002, which made full disclosure, transparency, and corporate responsibility the expected norm for companies large and small. The need to maintain this level of transparency has elevated the corporate communication function within companies to a new strategic level. Messages, activities, and products—from investor conferences and annual reports to philanthropic activities and corporate advertising—are now analyzed by regulators, investors, and the public at large with unprecedented scrutiny. And the proliferation of online communication vehicles, including Web portals, instant messaging, and Weblogs, or "blogs," has accelerated the flow of information and the public's access to it to record speeds.

Under this higher-resolution microscope, the clarity, alignment, and integration of communications to all constituents have the ability to make or break a corporate reputation. As a result, 77 percent of in-house communicators cite spending a "moderate amount" or "great deal" of time developing integrated communications.[2]

To Centralize or Decentralize Communications?

One of the first problems organizations confronted in structuring their communication efforts was whether to keep all communications focused by *centralizing* the activity under one senior officer at headquarters or *decentralizing* the activities and allowing individual business units to handle communications. The more centralized model provided an easier way for companies to achieve consistency in and control over all communication activities. The decentralized model, however, gave individual business units more flexibility in adapting the function to their own needs.

The same structural challenges persist today, and the answer to the centralization/decentralization debate often depends on a company's size, the geographic dispersion of its offices, and the diversity of its products and services. For organizations as large and diversified as General Electric, for example, the question is moot: There is no way such a sprawling organization involved in activities as diverse as aerospace and network television could remain completely centralized in all of its communication activities.

The same is true for Johnson & Johnson (J&J): With more than 110,000 employees in more than 200 operating companies in 57 different countries, complete centralization of communications would be difficult, if not impossible. Instead, Bill Nielsen, former corporate vice president of corporate communication at J&J, described the function as "a partnership of professionals in communication."[3] J&J even avoids centralizing its external communication counsel with a single public relations firm. Instead, the company uses both small firms on a project basis and large, global agencies with resources around the world, amounting to a total of over 20 different agencies worldwide to support various elements of its business.

Global events and economic trends also affect decisions about the structure of an organization's communication function. Not only did the shock of the September 11,

[2] Ibid.
[3] Interview with Bill Nielsen, February 2002.

2001, attacks teach companies the importance of expecting the unexpected in terms of crises, but it also gave decentralized communication structures a new appeal for many companies. As Jim Wiggins, first vice president of corporate communication for Merrill Lynch at the time, explained, "Companies will have to look at less centralization of key activities if we now live in a world where terrorism is a key possibility."[4]

Increased security threats are not the only catalyst for the decentralization of communications; economic downturns can have a similar effect. Consider a major international airline that imposed significant staff reductions on its corporate communication department due to across-the-board cost cuts. As a result, the director of communications explained that the department became more selective about what they committed to, saying: "We don't do everything for everybody anymore." Instead, other departments throughout the company established communication positions, doing some of the activities formerly handled by the centralized corporate communication department.[5]

In instances of scaled-back budgets, delegating tasks is doubly important because economic uncertainty also can force the communications department to handle activities they would generally outsource to a full-time PR agency. *PRWeek*'s 2005 Corporate Survey revealed that fewer than 60 percent of responding corporations retained an external PR agency, a decline from prior years' survey results.[6]

While decentralization allows for more flexibility in tough economic times, these advantages are not without accompanying risks. Dispersing corporate communications across individual operating units without some central oversight significantly raises the potential for inconsistent messages. In decentralized structures, a company's communication professionals must be diligent about assuring quality, consistency, and coordination of messages across the board.[7] Companies often require formal mechanisms to ensure that this coordination takes place.

Perhaps, then, finding a middle ground between a completely centralized and a wholly decentralized structure is preferable for large companies. For example, a strong, centralized, functional area can be supplemented by a network of decentralized "operatives" who adapt the function to the special needs of the independent business units. As we will see in the case at the end of this chapter, Dell organizes its corporate communication staff using an approach that follows how its businesses are organized: a "matrix" based on customers, products, and geography. While the more than 80 team members are physically located within the businesses they support, Lynn Tyson, who heads up the team, sits at headquarters among Dell's corporate staff, interacting constantly with senior management. This combination of centralized communication management with "operatives" dispersed throughout the various business units has proved successful for Dell, a company with over 50,000 employees who live and work in more than 30 countries.

[4] Shane McLaughlin, "Sept. 11: Four Views of Crisis Management," *Public Relations Strategist,* January 1, 2002, pp. 22–28.

[5] Jack LeMenager, "When Corporate Communication Budgets Are Cut," *Communication World* 3 (February 3, 1999), p. 32.

[6] Weber Shandwick, "Corporate Survey 2005.".

[7] LeMenager, "When Corporate Communication Budgets Are Cut."

Where Should the Function Report?

Surveys conducted over the last decade have consistently shown that a high percentage of the average CEO's time is spent communicating. Research conducted at the Tuck School of Business suggests that, on average, Fortune 500 company CEOs spend between 50 and 80 percent of their time on communication activities. To choose an example from the 1980s, Johnson & Johnson CEO James Burke estimated that he spent over 40 percent of his time as CEO communicating the J&J Credo alone (see Chapter 10 for more on the Credo).[8]

CEOs generally devote their time to communicating their company's strategic plan, mission, operating initiatives, and community involvement both internally and externally. Michael Useem, management professor at the Wharton School of the University of Pennsylvania, estimates that due to investors' increasing demands for companies to deliver short-term results, about one-third of a CEO's time is devoted to capital markets and to communications with up to four dozen analysts and investors.[9]

Consider the prominent position Citigroup CEO Charles ("Chuck") Prince took in 2005 when announcing and leading the company's commitment to engraining ethics in its cultural fabric in the wake of a number of regulatory and legal scandals, one of which resulted in the closing of the Citigroup Private Bank in Japan. As Prince explained: "This is job one. If I don't own this, I don't think it will succeed. If you delegate this, people will know instantly you are not sincere."[10] The campaign—internally named "The Company We Want to Be"—includes an annual ethics training session for all employees and a global road-show each year at which Prince can hear firsthand the concerns and ideas of Citigroup employees from across the 100 countries in which it operates. At the outset of its launch in March 2005, Prince estimated that he was devoting at least half of his time to the campaign.[11]

In many respects, CEOs themselves are an embodiment of the corporate brand. As such, their behavior and commentary can easily and markedly affect a company's financial performance. Recall Martha Stewart, founder and CEO of Martha Stewart Living Omnimedia, sentenced to five months in prison in 2004 after being found guilty on four counts of obstructing justice and lying to investigators regarding a stock sale. Expectations of a nonguilty verdict caused the company's stock price to rally prior to the announcement, only to nose-dive 22 percent on the NYSE following the guilty verdict.[12]

All of this implies that the CEO should be the person most involved with both developing the overall strategy for communications and delivering consistent messages to constituencies. Ideally, the corporate communication

---

[8] James C. Collins and Jerry I. Porras, *Built to Last* (New York: Harper Business, 1994, 1997), p. 80.

[9] Nanette Byrnes, "The 21st Century Corporation: The New Leadership: Chief Executive Officer: The Boss in the Web Age," *BusinessWeek* 3696, (August 28, 2000), p. 102.

[10] Alan Murray, "Citigroup's Prince Begins to Usher in New Culture of Ethics," *The Wall Street Journal*, March 2, 2005, p. A2.

[11] Ibid.

[12] Jim Robinson, "Leader of the Brand—Keeping the Best CEOs in Step," *Management,* June 1, 2005, p. 26.

FIGURE 3.1 Ideal Structure for CorpComm Function

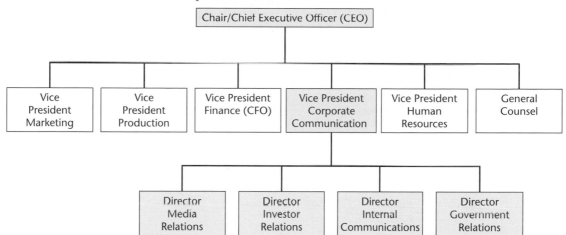

function will have a direct line to the CEO. (See Figure 3.1 for a sample corporate communication reporting structure.) Nearly half (46 percent) of respondents to *PRWeek*'s 2005 Corporate Survey said their company's head of communications reported directly to the CEO, president, or chairman.[13] (See Tables 3.1 and 3.2 for details of the study.) Even if reporting lines do not, on paper, go directly to the CEO, the head of corporate communication must have access to the highest levels of senior management and those executives must believe in the value and necessity of corporate communication as a way to achieve corporate goals. Without this connection, the communications function will be less effective and far less powerful.

To keep the number of direct reports to the CEO down to a handful of senior executives (often the biggest stumbling block to getting the corporate communication function "plugged in" at the top), some companies have corporate communication report to a strategic planning function. Given the importance of tying

[13] Weber Shandwick, "Corporate Survey 2005."

TABLE 3.1
Where Corporate Communication Reports

Source: Weber Shandwick, "Corporate Survey 2005," *PRWeek*, June 27, 2005.

Communications Head Reports to:	Total (Percent of Companies)
Chairman/CEO/president	45.6
Head of marketing	31.6
Other	14.0
Chief operating officer	4.8
Head of human resources	1.8
Chief financial officer	1.3
General counsel	.9

TABLE 3.2
Title of Senior
Communica-
tion Executive

Source: Weber
Shandwick,
"Corporate Survey
2005," *PRWeek*,
June 27, 2005.

Title	Total (Percent of Companies)
Senior vice president	17.1
Vice president	31.1
Director	26.3
Manager	17.1
Other	8.3

communications to the overall strategy of the firm, this may benefit the growing corporate communication function.

When Union Carbide Corporation was dealing with the aftermath of its Bhopal plant accident in India in 1984, the company transferred its communication responsibilities to the vice president of strategic planning. In a letter to executives, the chairman and CEO of the company at the time, Robert Kennedy, said:

> The Corporation's strategic direction is a key element of our communication to shareholders, employees and the public at large. . . It is therefore more important than ever to be open and consistent in our communications to all of these groups, to keep them informed of our progress as we implement strategy, and to make sure that we address the special concerns and interests of all the groups and constituencies with a stake in Union Carbide's future. . . To ensure the closest possible alignment of our communications with management directed at strategic planning developments, the management of those functions is being consolidated under . . . [the] Vice President of Strategic Planning and Public Affairs.[14]

In some cases, however, the function still reports to the catch-all executive vice president (EVP) in charge of administration. This person also has responsibility for areas such as personnel, security, and buildings and grounds. This structure can present tremendous problems for the communication function—especially if the EVP has little knowledge of or lacks an interest in communications.

Gerald Swerling, head of the graduate public relations program at the University of Southern California's Annenberg School of Communication, observed that the increased recognition of communications and public relations by senior management over the last decade has caused an increasing number of CEOs to "demand that there be PR professionals at the strategic planning table for new products and initiatives."[15] And while a 2005 Burson-Marsteller study revealed that only 15 percent of the largest revenue-producing Global 500 companies have corporate communication expertise in boardrooms, 81 percent of the same companies have corporate communication executives on their senior management teams.[16]

When senior management places value on the function, employees will begin to perceive communications rightfully as a critical management tool.[17] Now let's take a look at what that function should include.

---

[14] Letter from Union Carbide's CEO, Robert B. Kennedy, to Executive List, dated March 5, 1992.

[15] Richard Nemec, "PR or Advertising-Who's on Top?" *Communication World* 4 (February 3, 1999), p. 25.

[16] Craig McGuire, "Market Focus: Corporate Boards—Board Games," *PRWeek*, June 27, 2005, p. 25.

[17] LeMenager, "When Corporate Communication Budgets Are Cut."

TABLE 3.3
Functions
Included in
Corporate
Communica-
tion
Department

Source: Weber
Shandwick,
"Corporate Survey
2005," *PRWeek,*
June 27, 2005.

Function	Total (Percent of Companies)
Media relations	87.3
Online communications	68.4
Marketing	65.4
Special events	64.9
Product/brand communications	63.6
Crisis management	60.1
Employee/internal communications	58.8
Community relations	55.3
Product/brand advertising	51.3
Reputation management	46.9
Issues advertising	34.2
Public affairs/government relations	32.5
Cause-related marketing	27.6
Financial/Investor relations	26.3
Annual/quarterly report	25.9

The Functions within the Function

According to recent surveys, over half of the heads of corporate communication departments oversee communications functions that include media relations, online communications, marketing, special events, product/brand communications, crisis management, employee/internal communications, community relations, and product/brand advertising.[18] Forty-seven percent include reputation management within the corporate communication function; just over 32 percent include a public affairs/government relations function; 26 percent reported overseeing investor relations, and 26 percent listed the company annual or quarterly report as being within communications' sphere of responsibility.[19] (See Table 3.3.) While not every company can include all the subfunctions listed here under one umbrella, to operate most effectively, a majority of these functions must be included in the overall communication function.

The best approach to building a corporate communication function is to begin with the most global and strategic issues and then move into the narrower aspects of the function. We begin this section with a discussion of identity and image, and then move on to the various subfunctions of corporate communication.

Reputation Management

Difficult to classify as a separate subfunction, an organization's reputation management strategy is the most critical part of any corporate communication function. (In the next chapter, we explore these constructs in greater detail.) What is the

---

[18] Weber Shandwick, "Corporate Survey 2005."

[19] Ibid.

difference between image and identity, the subsets of reputation and how do they shape the operations of a corporate communication department?

Image is the corporation as seen through the eyes of its constituencies. An organization can have different images with different constituencies. For example, cigarette companies might be reprehensible to many American consumers looking for a healthier lifestyle but a delight to Philip Morris shareholders reaping the profits from international sales of the same product. On the other hand, customers might have been perfectly happy with what Macy's had to offer in its many stores throughout the United States, but securities analysts were reluctant to recommend the parent company's stock knowing that inevitably it would enter bankruptcy.

Determining what the organization's image is with different constituencies is usually less obvious than in the examples above—particularly given the increasingly blurred lines separating one constituency from another, as discussed in Chapter 2. For example, many employees today are encouraged to own stock in their own company and can be the most visible ambassadors of their company's brand by also being a consumer of its products or services. The corporate communication department should conduct marketing research to understand and monitor each constituency's evolving needs and attitudes. Obviously, the organization cannot please everyone, but by monitoring what constituencies are thinking about, it can make a conscious effort to avoid creating hostility with a particular group. A similar monitoring system also can be used regularly to gauge the impact and success of the company's communication activities.[20]

Unlike its image, however, the organization's *identity* should not vary from one constituency to another. Identity consists of a company's defining attributes, such as its people, products, and services. An organization has some kind of identity whether it wants one or not, based in part on the visual components it presents to the world. People all over the world know Coca-Cola's red can and white script lettering and McDonald's golden arches in front of a store, whether it's in Shanghai, China, or Providence, Rhode Island.

Since identity building and maintenance require a variety of skills, including the ability to conduct marketing research, to design attractive brochures, and to enforce identity standards and cohesion, it may be spread around several different functions in the absence of a single, centralized corporate communication function. For example, the marketing research needed to determine a firm's image with various constituencies might be a minor byproduct of the overall marketing research effort currently under way at a company, to determine customer attitudes toward particular products and services rather than the firm as a whole.

Determining how a firm wants to be perceived with different constituencies and how it chooses to identify itself is the cornerstone function of corporate communication. If the firm is making serious changes in its identity, this subfunction can easily be a full-time job for a team of corporate communicators for a period of time.

---

[20] Heyman Consulting, "State of U.S. Corporate Communications," prepared for Prof. Janis Forman, The Anderson School at UCLA, May 31, 2001, p. 32.

At nearly all companies, outside agencies specializing in identity and image, such as Lippincott & Margulies, Siegel and Gale, or Landor, would definitely be involved in the makeover as well, if the company alters significant components of its identity. These changes can range from the merely cosmetic—to keep the "look" of the company up-to-date—to the more momentous—such as a name change or a new logo.

Corporate Advertising and Advocacy

A company's image also can be enhanced or altered through *corporate advertising*. This subfunction of corporate communication is different from its product advertising or marketing communications function in two ways. (See Chapter 5 for more on corporate advertising.)

First, unlike product advertising, corporate advertising does not necessarily try to sell a company's particular product or service. Instead, it tries to sell the company itself—often to a completely different constituency from customers. For example, General Electric announced a commitment of a substantial portion of its $90 million corporate advertising budget in 2005 to "Ecomagination"—a marketing campaign not only promoting its environmentally friendly products but also positing GE as an eco-friendly company and leader in corporate responsibility.[21] Underpinning the campaign was GE's promise to improve its energy efficiency 30 percent while also cutting greenhouse-gas emissions by 1 percent by 2012.[22]

Adding a new layer to traditional television and print campaigns, corporations also are turning to the ever-growing Internet "blogosphere" to create viral marketing campaigns that can influence consumers' opinions. In 2005, Microsoft employees were writing approximately 1,500 blogs, some devoted to corporate recruiting by focusing on the employee experience at Microsoft, as well as available positions and hiring trends.[23] Whether online or off, employees are important word-of-mouth advertising vehicles for a company's advocacy efforts. GE kept this in mind in its "Ecomagination" launch, conducting a simultaneous internal communication program that featured a children's magazine conveying Ecomagination's core messages to employees' children and local communities.[24]

When upscale discount retailer Target ran an extensive corporate advertising campaign in the late 1990s featuring products ranging from satin lingerie to earplugs, accompanied only by the product name and Target's bull's-eye logo, the goal was not just to sell more of these products, but also to showcase the company's diverse merchandise and potential to be the discount retailer that "looks like Barneys, priced like Kmart."[25] In much the same way, the aerospace and defense firms that advertised extensively in publications such as *The New Republic* in the 1980s were not trying to sell F-15s to liberals, but rather to influence public opinion and facilitate approval for increases or allocations in the defense budget.

[21] Matthew Creamer, "GE Sets Aside Big Bucks to Show off Some Green," *Advertising Age* 76, no. 19 (May 9, 2005), p. 7.

[22] Daren Fonda and Perry Bacon Jr., "GE's Green Awakening," *Time,* July 11, 2005, p. A10.

[23] Sarah E. Needleman, "Blogging Becomes a Corporate Job; Digital 'Handshake'?" *The Wall Street Journal,* May 31, 2005, p. B1.

[24] Creamer, "GE Sets Aside Big Bucks."

[25] Shelly Branch, "How Target Got Hot," *Fortune,* May 24, 1999, p. 169.

Even though product advertising is the purview of the marketing department in most large companies, corporate advertising is often run from the CEO's office or through corporate communication departments instead. During the 1980s and 1990s, this was the fastest-growing segment of the advertising industry, as senior officers tried to present a coherent company image for opinion leaders in the financial community.

An important subset of corporate advertising is *issue advertising*. Business and policy groups in the United States spent more than $404 million on issue ads in 2003 and 2004, with some companies using the approach as a key supplement to or in lieu of government lobbying.[26] This type of advertising attempts to do even more than influence opinions about the company; it also tries to influence the attitudes of a company's constituencies about specific issues that affect the company. Recall Mobil's extensive issue advertising campaign during the oil crisis, described earlier in this chapter. Over the years, Philip Morris has spent millions on issue ads covering topics ranging from domestic violence to youth smoking prevention in an effort to put a more caring face on a company many hold in contempt for its role in producing addictive, carcinogenic tobacco products. Another example is when U.S. home mortgage lender Fannie Mae spent $87 million on an advertising campaign in 2003 to help curtail Congress's efforts to create a more stringent regulator to oversee its operations and have the authority to alter its capital standards.[27]

As we will see in Chapter 5, however, issue advertising is risky. By taking a stand on a particular issue, the company is automatically creating a negative image with one or several constituencies. Many companies take this risk nonetheless, facing the consequences of adding their opinions to debates that they consider important.

Media Relations

While the old-style public relations function focused almost exclusively on dealing with *media relations* may be a thing of the past, the subfunction we now refer to as media relations is still central to the corporate communication effort. Most of the average company's corporate communication staff typically reside within this subfunction, and the person in charge of the communications department as a whole must be capable of dealing with the media as a spokesperson for the firm. Although the media relations subfunction started off as a "flacking" service for managers in response to requests from news organizations, today the best corporate communication departments actively set the discussion agenda of the firm in the media. (See Chapter 6.) There is little debate about whether media relations, unlike other subfunctions, should come under the purview of corporate communication versus other corporate functions.

Technology has helped companies communicate through the hundreds of media services available from virtually anywhere in the world. Satellite uplinks

---

[26] Ben Goddard, "Issue Ads Turn up the Heat," *The Hill,* March 17, 2005, p. 19.

[27] Bloomberg News, "Fannie Spent $87 Million on Ad Campaign," Los Angeles *Times,* April 13, 2005, p. C-3.

are available at most corporate headquarters, and companies can put their press releases out to wire services electronically or through the Internet without making a single phone call. Despite these advances, the relationship between business and media remains largely adversarial, although positive relationships between sources and reporters are much more common today than in the past. Since the media and business rely on one another to a certain extent, most companies try to make the best of these relationships.

Marketing Communications

The marketing communications department coordinates and manages publicity relating to new or existing products and also deals with activities relating to customers. It also may manage corporate advertising.

Product publicity almost always includes sponsorship of events for major corporations, such as golf tournaments, car races, and even marathons. In addition, celebrities often are involved in these activities, which requires coordination within the company. Given how important such events and sponsorship agreements can be in shaping a company's reputation, corporate communication experts are often involved in setting the events' agenda.

Customer relations activities have increasingly become a part of corporate communication as a result of pressure groups among consumers that try to exert their influence on an organization. Rather than simply making sure the customer is happy with the product or service, as in the past, companies today must get involved in quasi-political activities with constituencies claiming to represent a firm's customers.

For example, the conservative Reverend Donald Wildmon has pursued a family-oriented agenda against a number of companies that sell products he deems unfit for families. Waldenbooks was vilified in the mid-1990s for selling sexually explicit literature in its stores. By organizing conservative church groups, Wildmon was able to apply pressure on Waldenbooks to stop selling literature ranging from what most people would consider simply erotic to literature with bad language in it. Disney was the focus of a boycott by Southern Baptists in 1997 for its liberal policies toward homosexuals. A year later, the Concerned Women for America (CWA) joined the protests for a Christian boycott of the company, asserting that Disney consciously laced their movies with messages of witchcraft, exemplified by such classics as *Fantasia*, *Peter Pan*, and *Escape from Witch Mountain*.[28] In 2005, the American Family Association, Focus on the Family, and the American Decency Association successfully lobbied for companies including Kellogg, Lowe's, Tyson Foods, and S.C. Johnson to stop buying additional advertising space on U.S. television shows with gratuitous violence and adult content such as ABC's *Desperate Housewives*.[29]

More informed consumers—able to examine the messages and advertising thrown at them with a discerning eye—mean that marketing communications teams must ensure that product and brand promotions are sending the right messages.

[28] Sylvia Weedman, "Bothered and Bewildered," *American Prospect*, May 1, 1998, p. 10.
[29] Jay Greene, and Mike France, with David Kiley, "Culture Wars Hit Corporate America," *BusinessWeek*, May 23, 2005, p. 90.

Internal Communications

As companies focus on retaining a contented workforce given changing values and demographics, they have to think strategically about how they communicate with employees through *internal communications*. (See Chapter 7 for more on this subfunction, also referred to as *employee communication*.) While strong internal communications have always generated a more engaged, productive, and loyal workforce, the bursting of the dot-com bubble, the collapse of several of America's most respected firms, and the proliferation of outsourcing jobs to foreign countries in recent years have further necessitated strong communication channels between management and employees to win employee trust and loyalty.

Often, internal communications is a collaborative effort between the corporate communication and human resources departments, as it covers topics from employee benefit packages to the company's strategic objectives. More and more, companies are making sure their employees understand the new marketing initiatives they are communicating externally, and are uniting the workforce behind common goals and corporate strategies. This type of communication requires the expertise of strong corporate communicators who are also well-connected to senior management and the corporate strategy process.

Additionally, difficult economic times, layoffs, and uncertainty require open, honest communication from senior management to all employees. The sensitive nature of some of these messages further speaks for the involvement of seasoned communications professionals alongside their human resources counterparts and, most importantly, of the CEO or of senior executives who are the individuals communicating messages to internal and external audiences most frequently.

Finally, as mentioned earlier under "Identity and Image," due to the blurring of constituency lines, companies must recognize that employees now also may represent investors and members of community advocacy groups—making thoughtful communications even more critical.

Investor Relations

Investor relations (IR) has emerged as the fastest-growing subset of the corporate communication function and an area of intense interest at all companies. (See Chapter 8 for more on investor relations.) Traditionally, investor relations was handled by the finance or treasury department, often reporting to the company's chief financial officer, but the focus in recent years has moved away from "just the numbers" to the way the numbers are actually communicated to various constituencies.

IR professionals deal primarily with securities analysts, who are often a direct source for the financial press, which this subfunction cultivates in conjunction with experts from the media relations area. IR professionals also interact heavily with both individual and institutional investors. They also are highly involved with the financial statements and annual reports that every public firm must produce.

Given the quantitative messages that are the cornerstone of the IR subfunction, as well as the need for IR professionals to choose their words carefully to avoid any semblance of transferring inside information, this subfunction must be a coordinated effort between communications professionals and the chief financial officer, comptroller, or vice president for finance. The need for this coordination has only increased in recent years with more stringent regulatory demands in the age of Sarbanes-Oxley and Reg FD.[30]

Corporate Social Responsibility

Many companies have a separate subfunction in the human resources area to deal with community relations and a foundation close to the chairman that deals with philanthropy, but the two should be tied closely together as companies take on more responsibilities in communities in which they operate.

The 2004 Cone Corporate Citizenship Study revealed that 77 percent of Americans believe companies have a responsibility to support causes, a belief they will back by rewarding them with increased customer loyalty and purchases.[31] The study also found that 91 percent of Americans "have a more positive image of a product or company when it supports a cause."[32]

There are also serious internal implications to a strong corporate citizenship record: Employees are 40 percent more likely to report pride in their company's values when their company supports social issues and are nearly 25 percent more likely to be loyal to employers versus employees with companies lacking corporate citizenship programs.[33] Thus, given the importance of the constituencies involved and the importance this has in shaping the image of the firm, this subfunction also needs to be housed within the corporate communication function—or work very closely with it.

Corporate philanthropy also has become increasingly important as companies are expected to do more than just give back to the community. Firms now feel a greater obligation to donate funds to organizations that could benefit the firm's employees, customers, or shareholders. Examples of this include donations to universities that might be conducting research in the industry and organizations representing minority interests.

And with increased globalization and international corporate expansion, constituents' expectations for corporate citizenship also have grown more global in scope. Twenty-two percent of Americans want companies' community efforts to focus globally, up from 9 percent in 1997.[34] In December 2004, the devastating tsunami that struck 11 countries in Southeast Asia, killing 180,000 people, demonstrated this broadened focus; the U.S. Chamber of Commerce's Center for Corporate Citizenship reported that more than 400 U.S. companies donated $528 million to the tsunami relief efforts, many of these representing a company's first-time disaster relief donation.[35]

[30] Weber Shandwick, "Corporate Survey 2005."

[31] "Corporate Citizenship: Doing Well by Doing Good," *PR News* 61, no. 23 (June 8, 2005).

[32] Angela Maas, "Employers' Tsunami Relief Effort Matching Contributions Reflect Employees' Priorities," *Employee Benefit News,* March 1, 2005.

[33] "Cause-Related Marketing Initiatives Distinguish Company Brand," *Retail Merchandiser,* May 11, 2005.

[34] Maas, "Employers' Tsunami Relief Effort."

[35] Michael Casey, "Tsunami Prompts Companies to Play Greater Role in Humanitarian Relief Efforts," Associated Press, June 28, 2005.

In turn, many companies are publishing environmental and social performance information in the same manner as they would traditionally report financials. Thirty-nine companies in the S&P 100 index issue "corporate sustainability" reports, outlining standards and the efforts they are making to uphold them.[36] Similarly, the number of CEOs reporting on corporate philanthropic, community, and volunteer activities in annual report letters increased 125 percent between 1999 and 2004.[37]

Government Relations

The *government relations* function, also referred to as *public affairs*, is more important in some industries than others, but virtually every company can benefit by having ties to legislators on both a local and a national level. (See Chapter 9 for more on government relations.) Many companies have established offices in Washington to keep a finger on the pulse of regulations and bills that might affect the company. Because of their critical importance in heavily regulated industries such as public utilities, government relations efforts in such companies are often both staffed internally and supplemented by outside government relations specialists in Washington.

Either firms can "go it alone" in their lobbying and government affairs efforts, or they can join industry associations to deal with important issues as a group. For example, the Edison Institute acts as a lobbying group for electric companies. Either way, staying connected to what is happening in Washington through a well-staffed and savvy government relations team is important to virtually all businesses given the far reach of government regulations within industries from pharmaceuticals to computer software. As companies expand internationally, building or outsourcing government relations efforts in key major foreign hubs—for example in Brussels to concentrate on European Union legislation—will become equally important.

Crisis Management

While not really a separate function requiring a dedicated department, crisis communications should be coordinated by the corporate communication function, and communications professionals should be involved in crisis planning and crisis management. Ideally, a wider group of managers from throughout the organization—including the senior management spokesperson who will be facing the public—are included in all planning for such eventualities. (See Chapter 10 for more on crises.)

While company lawyers typically need to be involved in crises, this presents problems for both the organization and the corporate communication function, since lawyers often operate with a different agenda from their communications counterparts, not always considering how actions can be perceived by specific constituencies or the public at large. A recent study on the subject of communication

---

[36] Fonda and Bacon, "GE's Green Awakening."

[37] andBEYOND Communications, "Scrooge Takes a Holiday: 50 Percent More CEOs Report on Corporate Social Responsibilities," December 27, 2004, http://www.andbeyondcom.com.

versus legal strategies stated: "legal dominance is shortsighted and potentially costly . . . organizations [must] reconcile the often contradictory counsel of public relations (PCC) and legal professionals and take a more collaborative approach to crisis communication."[38]

Working collaboratively with in-house counsel and, importantly, senior management, corporate communications professionals can make the difference between good and poor crisis management. We will see examples of both in Chapter 10.

Conclusion

The success of a company's communication strategy is largely contingent on how closely the communication strategy is linked to the strategy of the business as a whole.[39] In addition to thoughtful design and careful planning of firm strategy, a company must have a strong corporate communication function to support its mission and vision.

While the investor relations function could be in the treasury department of a company, the internal communications function within the human resources department, and the customer relations function within the marketing department, all of these activities require communication strategies that are connected to the central mission of the firm.

Corporate communications professionals must be willing to perform a wide variety of subfunctions within the function, and their roles will continue to broaden and diversify as globalization and information flows from a variety of sources demand that communications be strategic and purposeful. The greater number of multinational firms and the increasing demand for senior management to travel and speak in international venues place additional pressure on the communication function to communicate successfully with even more diverse, foreign audiences.[40]

While many corporations have made strides in building strong corporate communication functions that are closely aligned with overall strategy, there is still much work to be done. A poll released by Gallup in June 2005 revealed that public confidence in "big business" was the second-lowest rated of all institutions in the United States, tied with the U.S. Congress with a 22 percent vote of confidence.[41] In light of this, managing reputation and building trust are more important than ever, and a strong corporate communication function is a means to achieve those goals.

---

[38] Kathy R. Fitzpatrick, and Mareen Shubaw Rubin, "Public Relations vs. Legal Studies in Organizational Crises Decisions," *Public Relations Review* 21 (1995), p. 21.

[39] David Clutterbuck, "Linking Communication to Business Success: A Challenge for Communicators," *Communication World*, April 1, 2001, p. 30.

[40] Norm Leaper, "How Communicators Lead at the Best Global Companies," *Communication World* 4 (April 5, 1999), p. 33.

[41] Ibid.

Dell Computer Corporation

Elizabeth Allen sat in her cubicle at Round Rock One, Dell Computer Corporation's headquarters building outside of Austin, Texas, in early April 2002, scrolling through the 35 e-mails that had arrived in her inbox since she left the office the previous evening. Allen, vice president for corporate communication at Dell, was preparing for the weekly staff meeting she chaired, scanning her messages for any last-minute agenda items from her team of senior communications directors around the globe.

A message from Noriko Iijima, Dell's director of Japan communications, caught Allen's eye. The brief e-mail called Allen's attention to an article published in a leading Japanese business weekly that criticized Dell's lack of spending on research and development. Disturbingly, the comments came from the president and chief operating officer (COO) of Sony, with whom Dell historically had a strategic relationship. Iijima had contacted the PR team at Sony, but did Allen have any thoughts on what else Dell should do to remedy the situation? Allen needed to give this some thought before the meeting began. She also forwarded the e-mail to chairman and CEO Michael Dell.

DELL COMPANY BACKGROUND

Dell Computer Corporation (Dell) was founded in 1984 by Michael Dell, who began selling random-access memory (RAM) chips and disk drives for IBM personal computers (PCs) from his college dorm room at the University of Texas in the early 1980s. Soon thereafter, he began making IBM clones and selling them direct to consumers, saving his customers as much as 40 percent by eliminating the standard retail markup. In 1988 Dell started selling PCs to larger customers, including government agencies. The company went public that same year.[1]

Nearly two decades later, Dell had nearly 35,000 employees and its products included desktop and laptop computers, storage products, servers and server appliances, and workstations. The company also provided warranty services, product integration and installation, Internet access, and technology consulting. Dell offered these products and services to a customer base comprised of several segments: Large and Global Businesses, Education and Health Care, Government, Small Businesses, and Consumers.[2]

The cornerstone of the company's strategy remained the direct business model Michael Dell pioneered from his dorm room. "Cutting out the middleman" had enabled Dell to undercut competitors' prices by a wide margin and gain 30 percent of the U.S. market for PCs and 14.3 percent of the global PC market by 2002.[3] The direct model also put Dell closer to its customers, helping the company anticipate trends that could shape future product offerings. It also allowed Dell to deal directly with any customer concerns or post-sale service issues, again giving the company direct access to valuable information that would help it build even better products. Dell's commitment to direct accountability led the company to develop

Source: This case was prepared by Thea Haley under the supervision of Professor Paul A. Argenti at the Tuck School of Business at Dartmouth. All information in this case came from public and company sources, including an interview with Elizabeth Allen in June 2002.

[1] Hoover's Company Profile Database—American Public Companies, 2002.

[2] Dell company Web site, http://www.dell.com/us/en/gen/corporate/investor/investor_030_rep02.htm (retrieved July 1, 2002).

[3] Amy Tsao, "Can Dell Keep Beating Odds?" *BusinessWeek Online,* June 18, 2002.

"The Soul of Dell," the corporate philosophy that "defines the kind of company [it is] and aspires to become, serves as a guide for actions around the world, and ultimately forms the basis of its 'winning culture.'" The philosophy focused on five major areas including customers, the Dell Team, direct relationships, global citizenship, and winning.[4]

To maintain its position as the low-cost provider, Dell focused heavily on controlling expenses. The company's operating costs, including research and development (R&D), totaled about 10 percent of revenue in 2001, versus 20 percent at Compaq, 21 percent at Gateway, and 45 percent at Cisco.[5] In addition, Dell operated under a just-in-time manufacturing model—one in which its parts inventory remained on its books often for less than 72 hours. While other computer manufacturers including HP and IBM turned their inventories 8.5 and 17.5 times per year respectively, Dell turned its more than 100 times per year.[6]

Throughout the 1990s, Dell enjoyed average annual sales growth of nearly 60 percent.[7] The company gained market share across a number of its businesses and forced rivals with more bloated cost structures to compete on price, ultimately cutting into their margins. The PC market was growing by more than 15 percent a year, and the decade culminated in an upswing on technology spending as companies prepared for the unknown of "Y2K."[8] Dell's stock price hit an all-time high of $58 a share in March of 2000, but that same year would mark the beginning of a dramatic sell-off in the NASDAQ and spell trouble for the entire technology sector.

By 2001, the outlook for PCs had turned somber amid a soft economy and a slump in corporate spending on technology. As Dell continued to lower prices to attract demand in a stagnant market, its gross profit margins thinned from 21.3 percent in 2000 to 17.6 percent in 2001.[9] While the company predicted that computer demand would rebound in 2002 as PCs purchased to prepare for Y2K reached their "usual retirement age" of three years, in fact, many companies were extending the lives of their systems and forgoing new purchases.

Given its aggressive pricing to maintain sales in this environment, Dell engaged in equally aggressive cost-cutting in 2001, slashing $1 billion in operating and manufacturing costs that year and setting the same ambitious goal for 2002.[10] To achieve these savings, Dell was forced to cut jobs in 2001 for the first time in the company's history, eliminating 1,700 positions (nearly 8 percent of its 22,000 jobs at its Round Rock, Texas, headquarters and 4 percent of its total workforce). Shortly thereafter, it announced that another 3,000 to 4,000 would be cut as the company remained committed to ratcheting down expenses.

A NEW DIRECTION FOR DELL?

Continuing to focus on costs would not be the only solution to keeping Dell competitive, however: the company recognized that it needed to continue to diversify beyond the PC and also penetrate new geographic markets for all of its products. Additionally, Dell sought to bolster its services business, providing ongoing support and consulting services to large business clients.

Accordingly, the company began to focus heavily on higher-margin "enterprise computing" products such as servers, storage devices, switches, and even mainframelike computers.[11]

[4] Dell company Web site.

[5] Daniel Fisher, "Pulled in a New Direction," *Forbes,* June 10, 2002, pp. 102–12.

[6] Bill Breen and Michael Aneiro, "Living in Dell Time," *Fast Company,* no. 88 (November 2004).

[7] Hoover's Company Profile Database.

[8] Andy Serwer, "Dell Does Domination," *Fortune,* January 21, 2002, pp. 71–75.

[9] Ibid.

[10] Fisher, "Pulled in a New Direction," p. 104.

[11] Ibid.

While 27 percent of Dell's sales came from enterprise products in 2002 versus 73 percent from desktops and notebooks, Dell was gaining a foothold in servers. In 2001, Dell's server unit's sales grew 27 percent and revenues stayed flat while industrywide, shipments fell 2.3 percent and revenues dropped nearly 20 percent.[12] Estimates showed that by 2002 Dell was the world's No. 2 server manufacturer and No. 1 in the United States.[13]

For storage products, Dell acquired storage area network equipment maker ConvergeNet in 1999, and in 2001, entered into an alliance with EMC to resell EMC's mid-priced Clarion storage systems.[14] The alliance also included a co-branded line of enterprise storage systems.

As Dell made inroads into these new product areas, however, skeptics raised questions as to the company's ability to compete in the arena of higher-end, more complex products and services. For one, enterprise computing businesses were research-intensive. In keeping with its lean cost structure, historically Dell had spent a fraction of what rivals did on R&D, instead forming cooperative R&D programs with other companies or licensing technology needed to develop or enhance its own products. Whether this model could persist in the realm of enterprise computing remained to be seen. Additionally, Dell had proven itself as a successful low-cost producer of commoditized products—PCs—and while enterprise products were arguably headed in that direction, they remained comparatively less standardized, and the barriers to entry were high.

Analysts and industry observers who had witnessed Dell's rise to dominate the PC business based on an innovative business model, however, were optimistic that these endeavors would provide the company with new sources of growth. While most acknowledged that the heady days of double-digit revenue growth were probably over for Dell, the fact that its price–earnings multiple in mid-2002 was 36 times expected earnings versus the overall market's multiple of 22 was a testament to this optimism.[15] Clearly, growth was expected to come from somewhere.

CORPORATE COMMUNICATION AT DELL

Elizabeth Allen, 48, joined Dell in January 2000 from global office supply retailer Staples, Inc., where she had been vice president of corporate communication. Allen's career in corporate communication also had included senior roles at technology conglomerate Raytheon and defense contractor Loral Corp. Compared to these organizations, Dell was different for Allen in many ways.

Most surprising to her was that Dell's corporate communication staff included 120 professionals. The largest team she had managed prior to joining Dell had totaled about 12 at Raytheon; at Loral and Staples, it had been three or four. And while Allen's prior communication roles had reported either directly to the CEO or the CFO, at Dell she reported to Tom Green, who headed up four corporate functions at Dell: human resources, legal, administration, and corporate communication. Green reported to chairman and CEO Michael Dell and president and COO Kevin Rollins. Allen initially was surprised to learn that investor relations (IR) did not come under Green's umbrella, nor that of the CFO, but instead reported directly to Rollins.

But Allen would soon learn that the lines on the company's organizational charts did not dictate how things worked in practice; the organization was more complex and more fluid than what could be depicted on a flat sheet of paper. For instance, she was pleased to find that her reporting relationship to Green

---

[12] Andrew Park and Spencer E. Ante, "Who Will Master the Server Biz?" *BusinessWeek,* June 24, 2002, p. 92.

[13] Tsao, "Can Dell Keep Beating Odds?"

[14] Hoover's Company Profile Database.

[15] Fisher, "Pulled in a New Direction," p. 103.

did not hamper her ability to gain direct access to Dell and Rollins. She noted that "A lot of CEOs talk about communication, but Michael believes it and lives it."[16] The "direct" premise on which Dell built his company also was reflected in Rollins' approach to communications: "The message doesn't get filtered. . . I'm always communicating . . . and it's not one-way communicating. There is no middleman to intrude [because] if I'm cut off from the direct line, I'm useless."[17]

Allen also found that in spite of the organizational structure, she was able to work closely with her IR counterpart. In fact, Lynn Tyson, Dell's IR head, sat in the cubicle adjacent to Allen and had become one of her closest colleagues over her first two and a half years at the company. As Dell himself once reflected, "We don't let structure get in the way of communicating [here]."[18]

The structure of Dell's corporate communication function was more complex than anything Allen had seen before. "If you didn't understand the Dell organization," she explained, "you couldn't figure out how corporate communication was structured." While a small part of the staff sat within corporate management at Round Rock One with Allen, the vast majority of Dell's corporate communication staff were dispersed through each of the company's business units. Dell's large corporate communication team was organized through a loose "matrix" based on customers, products, and geography. Additionally, Allen described the structure of the function as "not consistent regionally. It was opportunistic." Depending on the client base and products sold in different regions, different specializations were needed among the staff, and thus the corporate communication function was tailored to best support the shape of the business within

each region. For instance, CorpComm was more heavily staffed in the Americas region than in some of Dell's overseas offices. But the organic and fluid structure, coupled with senior management's commitment to communications, set the tone for the entire function. It enabled the company to deliver what Rollins proudly termed a "boringly consistent message" (with no rogue messages filtering through to constituencies) that served to maximize the company's reputation and credibility.[19]

Five regional directors reported to Elizabeth, as well as directors for subfunctions including employee communication, corporate public relations, chairman's communication, and a specialized group for Dell's Enterprise Service Group. Regional corporate communication directors outside the United States had a solid reporting line to Allen and a dotted line to their respective regional business heads.

DELL'S AGENCY RELATIONSHIPS

Like most large, complex organizations, Dell had relationships with a number of public relations firms. These included: GCI Group, responsible for manufacturing and sales for various product and customer groups in the United States, Canada, and Latin America and also for local country PR in 12 countries; Walt & Company, a small Silicon Valley firm specializing in server and storage PR; Dittus Communications, a Washington-based public affairs agency specializing in the tech industry; SS&K, a New York–based firm that specialized in strategic and creative communications (the firm was 40 percent owned by Michael Ovitz's Creative Artists firm); Cone Communications, which did strategic philanthropy work for Dell; Matlock & Co., which handled diversity issues; Ogilvy PR, which dealt with regional communications in Europe; and a variety of smaller shops outside the United States that worked at the local level.

---

[16] Elizabeth Allen, interview transcript (during interview with Michael Dell), June 2002.

[17] Kevin Rollins, interview transcript, June 2002.

[18] Michael Dell, interview transcript, June 2002.

[19] Kevin Rollins, transcript of NIRI Conference.

Unlike the crisis orientation and retainer-based relationships that characterize many firms' links to agencies, Dell hired PR firms for specific projects within specific individual Dell businesses. Dell's relationship with GCI was unique, however, as it became the primary agency working with Dell in the Americas region. When GCI won the Dell account, both Dell and GCI interviewed everyone they hired to work on the account. Many of GCI's staff assigned to the Dell account sat in Round Rock and worked closely on a day-to-day basis with their client, allowing for a unique working relationship that transcended the "us and them" mentality that sometimes characterizes agency relationships.

In addition, Dell and GCI continually evaluated the relationship, reviewing budget targets and results achieved on at least a quarterly basis. Because GCI management looked at all billings across all businesses each quarter, both Dell and GCI management could see whether time and resources were being deployed in accordance with the company's strategic objectives, and, if they were not, shift them around as appropriate. Given the strong focus on costs at Dell, this discipline enabled Allen, along with Barry French and Dwayne Cox, co-heads of Americas corporate communication, to keep Dell and Rollins apprised of what concrete results were generated from GCI's work and reassure them that their agency budget was being allocated in line with business needs.

TEAM COMMUNICATIONS

In 2001, Dell's corporate communication team was pared down to approximately 80 full-time professionals through a careful process of reviewing each individual and each position as part of a larger cost-cutting program. Of the remaining staff, approximately 50 were based in the United States and the remainder in Dell's regional offices abroad. It was the first time Allen had direct reports outside the country, and when she joined Dell, Allen herself had won-

dered how best to communicate with such a large, globally dispersed team. She soon discovered that one of the features of the Dell culture would be a great help in this regard: e-mail. "There's a joke that the phone never rings at Dell," Allen said, adding that Dell's e-mail-based culture was part of the work environment that Michael Dell himself fostered at the company. Coupled with a flat corporate hierarchy, this environment made it relatively easy to communicate and to get the "ear" of senior management. "When I need to talk to Michael [Dell] or Kevin [Rollins] about something," Allen said, "I don't need to get a meeting with them. I e-mail them, and they e-mail me back."

In terms of communicating with her staff, e-mail was an efficient means given the dispersion of the team across time zones. When Allen came to Dell, she followed in the footsteps of an individual who had managed Dell's corporate communication function for 10 years. As those 10 years passed and the staff grew in numbers, Allen's predecessor, Michele Moore, began to employ a more formal and structured approach to communications among the team, including standing meetings and conference calls.

Allen had the unusual experience of overlapping with Moore for a full year before Moore retired and was grateful that her predecessor let her step in and try her own approach to managing the team during that time. "If Michele [Moore] had been a different person, that could have been a really tough year," Allen commented. As her own management style took shape at Dell even as Moore remained in the picture, Allen acknowledged that it was a bit different from her predecessor's. "I'm more of a management-by-walking-around type of person," Allen explained, "and I find that between our weekly two-hour meeting and my checking in with people informally as issues arise, there is enough cohesion for the group to really work well."

When PR agency representatives who sat inside Dell were added to Allen's staff total, that number approached 100. And still dozens more worked within the various agencies mentioned previously, adding to the complexity of communications at the company. Just as it turned to e-mail technology to communicate within the firm, Dell looked to the Internet as a means of staying connected to these agencies, using its own extranet for file sharing and online dialogue about specific issues. It seemed that Dell's "direct" model applied not only to its product distribution strategy, but its communications as well.

CORPORATE COMMUNICATION AND CORPORATE STRATEGY

At Dell, company strategy typically came from senior management rather than from a formal strategy process. The reputation of the firm, in fact, was still very much connected to its founder, Michael Dell, the scrappy new kid who found a better way. For many years, as Dell powered past many of its closest competitors in PC sales, it was the power of the Dell story that "sold the company."

As Dell moved up the chain into higher-end systems and services, however, it was doubtful this story would be as powerful. As Barry French, director of public affairs, explained, "We want big companies to feel as comfortable using our products as consumers now do. But they do not yet see us as network designers, which is part of our challenge. We are moving from a manufacturing company to a fancy network designer. This is an especially tough job in such a lean, mean environment."

In 2001, Elizabeth Allen was appointed to Dell's Global Executive Committee, giving her even more direct access to information about Dell's strategic direction. Allen did not, however, describe herself as "formulating strategy," but rather as raising concerns and questions along the way that constituencies both within and outside the organization were likely to have about a given strategic decision and ensuring that management understood how it should be communicated. Michael Dell noted that this role

of communications in relation to the company strategy was very important, because "Communication is not an afterthought, but rather an integral part of the process."[20] To this end, Allen also was extensively involved with the many communication issues around implementation, explaining, "While strategy is always viewed as the 'cool' part of the process to be involved with, execution is where you can really make a difference."

Dell would find in late 2002 that its commitment to communications played a direct role in allowing the company to implement strategy, even during a crisis situation. In late September/early October 2002, over 10,000 union dockworkers staged a 10-day labor lockout, closing 29 U.S. West Coast ports. The shutdown threw a major wrench in the global economy and supply chain by essentially holding both raw and finished goods hostage on cargo ships outside the closed ports. However, while entire industries were crippled by the lockout, Dell averted a major meltdown. Because Dell had already set a precedent of being in constant communication with its counterparts and suppliers in Malaysia, Taiwan, and China, along with its U.S.-based transport partners, the company was alerted of the strike possibility almost six months prior to the incident. Armed with the information, Dell was able to successfully develop and implement a contingency plan that enabled the company to uphold "The Soul of Dell," maintain and reinforce its overall strategy and business objectives, and emerge from the crisis virtually unscathed (from both the customer perspective and the financial perspective). As one reporter reflected after the global crisis came to a close, "In the end, Dell did the impossible: It survived a 10-day supply-chain blackout, with roughly 72 hours of inventory, and it never delayed a customer order."[21]

[20] Dell, interview transcript.

[21] Breen and Aneiro, "Living in Dell Time."

CONCLUSION

Nearly two hours after it began, Allen's weekly corporate communication staff meeting had wrapped up and she made her way back to her desk, thinking about the most pressing follow-up items she would want to get to that day. She had another meeting about Dell's proxy statement in 15 minutes but figured she had time to check e-mail before that began. Scanning the senders and subject lines of the 25 new messages that had arrived since she left for her meeting, Allen quickly found a message from Michael Dell in response to the e-mail she'd forwarded from Noriko Iijima earlier that morning and opened it up.

CASE QUESTIONS

1. Given how the case describes Dell's overall business structure, what are the strengths and weaknesses, structurally, of its corporate communication function as described in this case?

2. What challenges do you foresee for Elizabeth Allen and her team going forward and what advice would you give her?

3. What role could corporate communication play at Dell to help the company advance its strategic goals?

CHAPTER FOUR

Identity, Image, and Reputation

Chapter 3 covered the various components of the corporate communication function. This chapter will examine the first and most critical part of that function: a corporation's identity and image. The chapter also will address how a close alignment between a company's identity and image generates a strong reputation.

Looking at an example of this at the personal level might be a good place to start. People choose certain kinds of clothing, drive particular cars, or style their hair a certain way to express their individuality. The cities and towns in which we live, the music we prefer, and the restaurants we frequent all add up to an impression, or identity, that others can easily distinguish.

Consider the following scenario: A gray-haired man pulls up to a toll booth in an Audi A8, dressed in a gray Broni suit, wearing a gold Patek Philippe watch. After he pays his toll with an EZ Pass and drives on, a middle-aged man in a Toyota Camry pulls up. He is dressed in blue jeans and a plaid button-down shirt and wears a Seiko digital watch. He pays for his toll in cash. Even for people with little understanding of American culture, these quick glimpses of the two men speak volumes about them to observers. (Whether those impressions are right or wrong is another issue.)

The same is true for corporations. Walk into a firm's office and it takes just a few moments to capture those all-important first impressions and learn a great deal about the company. The effort is relatively easy to understand at the personal level, but significantly more difficult at the organizational level. One reason for this complexity is that many potential identity options exist. Take, for instance, the following example from the hotel industry:

An executive and her husband decide to treat themselves to one of life's great pleasures: a weekend in a suite at the Oriental Hotel in Bangkok. During their stay, their daily copies of the Asian *Wall Street Journal* and *Herald Tribune* are ironed for them to eliminate creases; the hotel staff, omnipresent, run down the hallway to open their door lest they should actually have to use their room keys; laundry arrives beautifully gift-wrapped with an orchid attached to each package; every night, the pillows are adorned with a poem on the theme of sleep; and, outside the lobby, Mercedes limos are lined up, ready to take the couple anywhere at any time of the day or night.

A few weeks later, they return to the United States and she is giving a presentation to a group of fellow executives at a midwestern resort. A *USA Today* appears on the outside doorknob squeezed into a plastic bag; the staff, invisible if not for their cleaning carts left unattended in the hallway, are unable to bring room service in under 45 minutes; her pillow is "adorned" with a room-service menu for the following morning and a piece of hard candy; the vehicle waiting to whisk guests to various destinations is a Chrysler minivan; and for flowers, the resort provides silk varietals in a glass-enclosed case that plays the song "Feelings" when the top is lifted.

Both hotels have strong identities, and the choices each has made about its business is at the heart of what identity and image are all about. These choices contribute to and shape the reputation of these hotels and, more generally, convey the identity and image of any institution.

Just what are identity, image, and reputation? How do organizations distinguish themselves in the minds of customers, shareholders, employees, communities, and other relevant constituencies? Above all, how does an organization manage something so seemingly ephemeral as an identity?

What Are Identity and Image?

A company's *identity* is the visual manifestation of the company's reality as conveyed through the organization's name, logo, motto, products, services, buildings, stationery, uniforms, and all other tangible pieces of evidence *created by the organization* and communicated to a variety of constituencies. Constituencies then form perceptions based on the messages that companies send in tangible form. If these images accurately reflect an organization's reality, the identity program is a success. If the perceptions differ dramatically from the reality (and this often happens when companies do not take the time to analyze whether a match actually exists), then either the strategy is ineffective or the corporation's self-understanding needs modification.

As we discussed in Chapter 3, *image* is a reflection of an organization's identity. Put another way, it is the organization as seen *from the viewpoint of its constituencies.* Depending on which constituency is involved, an organization can have many different images. Thus, to understand identity and image is to know what the organization is really about and where it is headed. This is often hard for anyone but the CEO or president to grasp. What, for example, is the reality of an organization as large as ExxonMobil, as diversified as General Electric, or as monolithic as Mitsubishi?

Certainly the products and services, the people, the buildings, and the names and symbols are a part of this reality. While there are inevitably differences in how the elements are perceived by different constituencies, it is this cluster of facts, this collection of tangible and intangible things, that provides the organization with a starting point for creating an identity.

Organizations can get a better sense of their image (as conveyed through visual identity) by conducting research with constituents. This research should be both

FIGURE 4.1

qualitative and quantitative in nature and should try to determine how consistent the identity is across constituencies. As an example, Arthur D. Little (ADL), the global consulting firm, found through research that its image was not clear to a variety of constituencies. Was the organization a consulting firm? A think tank? Was it involved in engineering? Defense? By asking people what they thought about the organization, ADL was able to find out perceptions of its image and discovered that it was unclear.

While image can vary among constituencies, identity needs to be consistent. One constituency, for example, might see ADL as a consulting firm that is too involved in the defense sector and therefore might have a negative image of the company; another constituency might be delighted with the extensive work the consulting firm has done to help the defense industry become stronger over the last 20 years and might then have a positive image of the firm. But at least they both have the firm's identity right. It is involved in defense work and is a consulting firm. That could be either positive or negative, depending on whom you ask, but at least it's accurate.

The logo that Dartmouth's Tuck School adopted twenty years ago (see Figure 4.1) was a carefully crafted visual designed to reflect what faculty and officers felt was the reality of the school: It is the oldest graduate school of business (founded in 1900), it is prestigious (a member of the Ivy League group of schools, Tuck is part of a great university—Dartmouth), and it is elite (usually ranked in the top 5). The symbol conveys all of these meanings, but they can add up to very different images, depending on whom you ask.

For example, some potential students might think that "old" and "Ivy League" mean stodgy or conservative; others might think that prestige is great and this is the best place to go for graduate business training. Whatever their decision about the school, the logo should reflect accurately what the place is all about. Then constituents can decide whether that is an image they like or not.

Differentiating Organizations through Identity and Image

Given how every industry today faces global competition and companies are trying to manage with limited resources, an organization's identity and image might be the only difference that people can use to distinguish one company from the next. Is there really any difference between buying a tank of ExxonMobil gasoline and a tank of Shell gasoline? Given that the same distributor often sells the same gasoline to dealers in the United States, the answer would seem to be no. Yet consumers make distinctions about such homogeneous products all the time based on what the *company's* image is all about rather than the product itself.

If an ExxonMobil and a Shell station sit two blocks apart and your gas needle is approaching E, where will you go? You might have strong negative feelings about ExxonMobil, for example, because of the oil spill at Valdez. Or, conversely, you may be delighted by the consistent returns to shareholders that this behemoth provides.

You see the Shell logo and you might recall some of the advertising the company sponsored as part of its "Energy for People Now and in the Future" cleaner energy/liquefied natural gas (LNG) campaign, "People Like Natural Gas." One of the recent print ads addressed the benefits of LNG by relaying the story of a small Japanese noodle manufacturer's business flourishing when using the energy alternative. On the other hand, you may see Shell and think back to the company's attempt in the early 1990s to dump the Brent Spar oil platform into the Atlantic Ocean. You also saw the award winning environmental responsibility efforts the company undertook, the "Profits and Principles" campaign, but the stigma of Brent Spar still lingers in your mind.

Now, when you decide to buy gasoline, aside from the location of the gas station, these factors are really the only differences between the two companies (given similar prices). Both tanks of gas will keep the car going, both tanks of gas have approximately the same octane rating, and both service stations will offer varying service quality. If, however, you are focused on shareholder value, this might convince you to buy ExxonMobil gasoline. Maybe you instead appreciate Shell's efforts to educate you about cleaner energy sources and feel an affinity for a company that is making a concerted effort to promote environmentally friendly energy. Alternatively, you may feel morally bound to boycott ExxonMobil as a result of the Valdez oil spill or Shell because of Brent Spar.

As products become much the same all over the world, consumers are increasingly making distinctions based on notions other than the product itself, thereby making image and identity even more powerful differentiators. We will now turn to a more in-depth discussion of first identity and then image. We then conclude with a discussion of how these come together to create an organization's reputation.

Shaping Identity

Because identity-building is the only part of reputation management an organization can control completely, we will first discuss some of the things that contribute positively to corporate identity: an inspirational corporate vision, careful corporate branding (with a focus on names and logos); and, importantly, *consistent* self-presentation.

A Vision That Inspires

Most central to corporate identity is the vision that encompasses the company's core values, philosophies, standards, and goals. Corporate vision is a common thread that all employees, and ideally all other constituencies as well, can relate to.

Thinking about this vision in terms of a narrative or story of sorts can help ensure the overall coherence and continuity of a company's vision and the collective messages it sends constituencies.[1]

Cees B. M. van Riel, a professor at Erasmus University in the Netherlands, links the importance of narratives to successful corporate reputations. He explains that "communication will be more effective if organizations rely on a . . . sustainable corporate story as a source of inspiration for all internal and external communication programs. Stories are hard to imitate, and they promote consistency in all corporate messages."[2] External constituencies rely on articles in publications, television ads, discussions about the company with other people (e.g., family, friends, and colleagues), and direct interaction with company employees for information about a company and the story it is telling.

The most appealing of stories, literary and corporate, often involve an underdog—an unsung hero that audiences can admire and rally behind. Going against the grain can instill a sense of noble purpose in the actions of a hero—or an entrepreneur—who hopes to do things differently. Consider Steve Jobs, the founder of Apple Computer. His unwillingness to succumb to IBM and Microsoft had "hero appeal" that did wonders for Apple's brand.

Names and Logos

Just as our society demands top-10 lists and rejects the full story in favor of sound bites, it also prizes *brands* as identification tags that can allow us to gauge everything around us quickly and effortlessly. Given this phenomenon, a company's value can be significantly influenced by the success of its corporate branding strategy. Coca-Cola, for example, has a value that far exceeds its total tangible assets because of its strong brand name.

Branding and strategic brand management are critical components of identity management programs. While it is beyond the scope of this book to fully explore corporate branding, this chapter will focus on a subset of corporate branding—names and logos—to help illustrate the conscious actions organizations can take to shape their identity and differentiate themselves in the marketplace.

Companies often institute name changes either to signal identity changes or to make their identities better reflect their realities. Andersen Consulting's name change to Accenture is an example of the former. In late 2000, Andersen Consulting, the global technology and consulting company that had separated from its founding parent Arthur Andersen earlier that year, announced a name change that would take effect January 1, 2001. The new company would be called *Accenture*, a play on the words "accent" and "future" that, according to James E. Murphy, the company's global managing director for marketing and communications, was meant to be "a youthful and dynamic expression of the firm's new positioning as a

---

[1] Cees B. M. van Riel, "Corporate Communication Orchestrated by a Sustainable Corporate Story," in *The Expressive Organization,* ed. Majken Schultz, Mary Jo Hatch, and Mogens Holten Larsen (Oxford: Oxford University Press, 2000), p. 163.

[2] Ibid.

bridge builder between the traditional and new economies."[3] The name also clearly distinguished the company's identity from that of its former parent, Arthur Andersen, which had its own, competing consulting division at the time.

Philip Morris provides an example of the second name-change scenario. Recognizing that it was known as a tobacco company despite its reality of being a diversified company with a number of lines of business (indeed, the company is also America's largest food company through its Kraft division), Philip Morris proposed a name change for itself in late 2001. The company chose the name *Altria*, derived from the Latin word *altus*, meaning "high."[4]

Reactions to the name-change proposal were not positive. Some saw the move as an attempt by the company to distance itself from tobacco litigation. This possible motive aside, while it was understandable that the company wanted its identity to reflect more accurately its reality as a diversified company, the proposed name change would not achieve that goal—for a name change alone will never single-handedly fix a perception problem. Such a change must be part of a broader identity program that is clearly explained to the company's constituencies. To many people who only read of the name change in the press, it was not clear why a Latin word meaning "high" would better reflect what Philip Morris was all about.

Another example that illustrates the importance of properly communicating about name changes (and the risks inherent in not doing so) is Nissan in Japan. To consolidate the company's brands worldwide, an edict from Nissan's company headquarters in the early 1980s eliminated the well-known Datsun brand name from the U.S. market in favor of the company name Nissan. This name change took over five years to complete because dealers refused to pay for new signs and resisted the change in general. In addition, the name change confused customers. Virtually everyone in the late 1960s and early 1970s knew about the Datsun 240Z and the company's line of small cars that helped Americans get through the first oil crisis.

After the name change, however, some customers thought that Nissan was a subsidiary of Toyota, its archrival. Even after almost a decade, the new name Nissan was still less known in America than the old Datsun name. As this example illustrates, while organizations can differentiate themselves based on identity through names and logos, they also can risk losing whatever identity they have built up very quickly through changes in the use of names and logos that are not communicated properly.

Logos are another important component of corporate identity—perhaps even more important than names because of their visual nature (which can allow them to communicate even more about a company than its name) and their increasing prevalence across many types of media. When upscale discount retailer Target placed an ad in the *New York Times* in 1999 depicting only its bull's-eye logo and inviting readers to call a toll-free number if they knew what the symbol meant,

---

[3] Howard Wolinsky, "Consulting Firm to Change Name; Andersen Consulting to Be Accenture," *Chicago Sun-Times*, October 27, 2000, p. 64.

[4] David Lazarus, "Name Change Is an Exercise in Futility; So What's in a Name? Lots of Spin," *San Francisco Chronicle*, December 5, 2001, p. B1.

A young woman in Hanoi, Vietnam, sports a counterfeit version of the Nike swoosh on her hat.

its phone lines were tied up immediately. The company was soon forced to shut down the toll-free number due to the staggering response.[5]

One of the most recognizable logos in the world today (perhaps second only to Coca-Cola's) is Nike's "swoosh," which was designed for Nike founder Phil Knight by Portland State graduate Carolyn Davidson in 1972 for $35. Some experts believe the swoosh is better known today than McDonald's golden arches. Golfing sensation Tiger Woods wears the swoosh on his hat and clothes. Lance Armstrong cycled through seven consecutive Tour de France triumphs with the swoosh on his yellow jersey. Teams in hockey's Canada Cup and national soccer teams also have worn the swoosh in competition. With Nike as their sponsor, 700 winter athletes at the 2002 Winter Olympics in Salt Lake City sported the swoosh outside competition.[6]

Logos can be simply symbols, like the Nike swoosh, or they can be symbols that *represent* names, like the Target "bull's eye" or Arm & Hammer's arm and hammer. Logos can be stylized depictions of names or parts of names (like the "golden arches" that form the "M" in "McDonalds"), or stylized names with added mottos or symbols. Accenture's logo, for example, is the company name with a "greater than" symbol above the "t" that is meant to connote the firm's goal of pointing the way forward and exceeding clients' expectations.[7]

Firms that specialize in identity management and design should be involved with the process of logo creation for a company. Later in this chapter, we will take a closer look at the processes behind creating new names and logos as part of an overall identity program.

Putting It All Together: Consistency Is Key

An organization's vision should manifest itself consistently across all its identity elements, from logos and mottos to employee behavior. Overnight package-delivery pioneer FedEx is a good example of this. In the 1990s, the company had noticed that customers routinely referred to it as "FedEx," rather than using its official name, the multisyllable "Federal Express." Additionally, office workers were beginning to use "FedEx" as a verb; few people said they would "UPS a package" or "Airborne Express a letter." Instead, it was "Let's FedEx this." The company thus decided to use the abbreviation already used by thousands of customers (and competitors' customers) as its official name. On June 23, 1994, Federal Express changed its name to *FedEx* and paired it with a distinctive new motto: "The World on Time." As a launch advertisement read in 1994: "We're changing our look to FedEx. Isn't that what you call us anyway?" (See Figure 4.2 on page 76.)

[5] Shelly Branch, "How Target Got Hot," *Fortune*, May 24, 1999, pp. 169–74.

[6] John Roberts and Bill Whitaker, "Olympics Too Commercial?" *CBS Evening News with John Roberts*, February 10, 2002.

[7] Sandra Guy, "Consultant to Launch Big Effort to Advertise Its New Identity," *Chicago Sun-Times*, November 16, 2000, p. 66.

By officially making the company name synonymous with punctual overnight delivery ("The World on Time"), FedEx demonstrated that it was in touch with what its customers wanted from the company and made an open commitment to reinforce the same message throughout its organization. With the new motto and logo, FedEx's clean and pressed uniforms, immaculate transport vehicles and service centers, and an employee mantra of "service without excuse" all echoed a consistent commitment.[8]

Michael Glenn—executive vice president, market development and corporate communications for FedEx—explained that by embracing its one-word association, "FedEx and its name have changed their environment from morally neutral to morally charged."[9] By putting its promise to deliver "The World on Time" on every package, truck, and plane, FedEx ensured that every pick-up, delivery, and customer interaction would reinforce that promise. The new name and logo showed that the company was in touch with its customers, and FedEx's advertising of this new identity reinforced the message that its customers mattered.

Identity Management in Action

The dual nature of identity and image—embodied in physical objects yet inextricably tied to perceptions—creates a special dilemma for decision makers. In a world where attention is focused on quantifiable results, the emphasis here is on qualitative issues. Devising a program that addresses these elusive but significant concerns requires balancing thoughtful analysis with action. Here is a method that has been successfully used by many organizations to manage the identity process.

Step 1: Conduct an Identity Audit

To begin, an organization needs to assess the current reality. How does the general public currently view the organization? What do its various symbols represent to different constituencies? Does its identity accurately reflect what is happening, or is it simply a leftover from the past?

To avoid superficial input and objectively respond to these questions, consultants from the hundreds of "identity firms" conduct in-depth interviews with top managers and those working in areas most affected by any planned changes. They review company literature, advertising, stationery, products and services, and facilities. They also research perceptions among the most important constituencies, including employees, analysts, and customers. The idea is to be thorough, to uncover relationships and inconsistencies, and then to use the audit as a basis for potential identity changes.

In this process, executives should look for red flags. We saw that FedEx took action after learning that its customer constituency was no longer using its official name. Typical problems include symbols or names that conjure up images of earlier

---

[8] "Chapter 11: The Image Is the Reality (If You Work at It)," *The World on Time*, July 1, 1996, p. 115.

[9] Ibid.

days at the company or just generally incorrect impressions. Once decision makers have the facts, they can move to create a new identity or institute a communication program to share the correct and most up-to-date profile of the company.

While the identity audit may seem a fairly straightforward and simple process, it usually is not. Often the symbols that exist and the impressions that result are not how the organization sees itself in the present at all. Companies trying to change their image are particularly difficult to audit because the vision that top executives have of what the company *will be* is so different from what the reality currently *is*. Often executives disregard research that tells them how constituents' perceptions about the organization differ from their own. Such cognitive dissonance is the first challenge in managing identity for executives. The reality of the organization must be far enough along in the change process so that the new image the company is trying to adopt will actually make sense, some day at least, to those who will encounter this company in the years ahead.

Step 2: Set Identity Objectives

Having clear goals is essential to the identity process. These goals should be set by senior management and must explain how each constituency should react to specific identity proposals. For instance: "As a result of this name change, analysts will recognize our organization as more than just a one-product company"; or "Putting a new logo on the outside of our stores will make customers more aware of dramatic transformations that are going on inside." It is extremely important, however, that emphasis be placed on *constituency response* rather than company action.

That's where problems often start. Most managers—particularly senior managers—are internally focused and thus have great difficulty in getting the kind of perspective necessary to see things from the viewpoint of constituents. Consultants can certainly help, but the organization as a whole must be motivated to change and willing to accept the truth about itself, even if it hurts.

In addition, change for the sake of change, or change to meet some kind of standardization worldwide (which was true in the case of Nissan), is not the kind of objective that is likely to meet with success. Usually, such arbitrary changes are the result of a CEO's wanting to leave his or her mark on the organization rather than a necessary step in the evolution of the company's image.

A positive example of clear objectives leading to necessary change is Kentucky Fried Chicken's desire to change its image and menu in the mid-1990s as a result of changes in American dietary habits. The strong corporate identity of this company worldwide (it has one of its biggest restaurants on Tiananmen Square in Beijing and can be found in remote corners of Japan) conjures up images of Colonel Sanders's white beard, buckets of fried chicken, salty biscuits, and gravy.

To an earlier generation, these were all positive images closely connected with home and hearth. Today, however, health-conscious consumers are more likely to think of the intense cholesterol, the explosion of sodium, and gobs of fat in every bucket of the Colonel's chicken. Thus, the company tried to reposition itself with health-minded consumers by offering broiled chicken and chicken salad sandwiches. The company's goal was to change the old image and adopt a more health-conscious positioning.

To do so, executives decided to change the name of the 5,000 restaurants grad-ually to just "KFC." The obvious point was to eliminate the word "fried." While most identity experts would agree that it is very difficult to create an identity for a restaurant out of initials alone, this one has the well-known Colonel to go along with the change. The communication objective for this particular change made a great deal of sense, and put KFC in a better position to sell to a more nutrition-minded set of customers.

Step 3: Develop Designs and Names

Once the identity audit is complete and clear objectives have been established, the next phase in the identity process is the actual design. If a name change is neces-sary, consultants must search for alternatives. This is a step that simply cannot happen without the help of consultants because so many names are already in use that companies need to avoid any possibility of trademark and name infringe-ment. Even so, options for change can still number in the hundreds. Usually, cer-tain ones stand out as more appropriate. The criteria for selection depend on several variables.

For example, if the company is undergoing a global expansion, the addition of the word "international" might be the best alternative. If a firm has a lot of equity built into one product, changing the name of the corporation to that of the product might be the answer, as happened when Consolidated Foods changed its name to "Sara Lee." We have already seen that Federal Express changed its name to reflect what its constituencies were already calling it and that Andersen Consulting chose a new name, Accenture, that would give it a distinct identity from its former parent by shedding any vestiges of the Andersen name.

Companies also should ensure that logos continue to reflect accurately the com-pany's reality, and should consider modifications if they do not. Dunkin' Donuts is a good example of this. The popular baked-goods chain is known in the Northeast (where more than two-thirds of its U.S. stores are located) as much for the 2 million cups of coffee it sells daily as for its delicious doughnuts.[10] As the company expanded into new markets where its brand was unfamiliar, it recog-nized the importance of emphasizing the "coffee connection," particularly given the proliferation of bagel chains and upscale coffee chains in many of the markets it was entering. Accordingly, it added the image of a steaming cup of coffee to its existing logo, which is simply the Dunkin' Donuts name in balloonlike pink and orange letters.

The process of designing a new look or logo is an artistic one, but despite con-tracting professionals to develop designs, many company executives get very involved in the process, often relying on their own instincts rather than the work of someone who spent his or her entire career thinking about design solutions. One CEO of a multibillion-dollar company designed what he thought would be the per-fect logo for his company on a napkin. After several weeks of design exploration by

---

[10] Chris Reidy, "Expanding Dunkin' Donuts Brews Up New Logo That Includes Cup of Coffee," *Boston Globe*, January 15, 2002, p. D5.

a reputable design firm, he kept coming back to that same napkin design. Until the designer finally presented an exploration that resembled the napkin design, each of the suggestions was rejected. When the CEO saw his own idea come back at him, he was happy. Everyone else agreed that it was not the best design, but it was adopted and is in use today.

Obviously, there has to be a balance between the professional opinion of a designer and a manager's own instincts. Both need to be a part of the final decision whether a name change or just a new logo is involved. In some cases, designers and identity consultants are perfectionistic or idealistic, presenting ideas that are unrealistic or too avant-garde for typically conservative large corporations. In the end, strong leadership must be exerted to effect the change, no matter what it is, for it to succeed.

Step 4: Develop Prototypes

Once the final design is selected and approved by everyone involved, consultants develop models using the new symbols or name. For products, prototype packaging shows how the brand image may be used in advertising. If a retail operation is involved, a model of the store might be built. In other situations, the identity is applied to everything, including ties, T-shirts, business cards, and stationery, to see how it works in practice.

During this process, it is common for managers to get cold feet. As the reality of the change sinks in, criticism mounts from those employees who have not been involved in the process and from others because they do not have a good sense of the evolution and meaning of the design. At times, negative reactions from constituents can be so strong that proposals have to be abandoned and work started all over again.

To prevent this failure, a diversity of people and viewpoints should be involved in the entire identity process. The one caveat is to avoid accommodating different ideas by diluting concepts. A company should not accept an identity that is simply the lowest common denominator. Two ways to deal with the task are to let a strong leader champion the new design or to set up a strong committee to work on the program. In either approach, everyone has to be informed about the project and involved in it from the beginning: the more people involved in the process from its inception, the less work necessary to sell the idea after much hard work has already taken place.

Step 5: Launch and Communicate

Given the time involved and the number of people included in the process, news about future changes can easily be leaked to the public. Sometimes such publicity is a positive event, as it can create excitement and a sense of anticipation. Still, such chance occurrences are no substitute for a formal introduction of the company's new identity. To build drama into the announcement, public relations staff should be creative in inviting reporters without giving away the purpose. One company sent six-foot pencils and a huge calendar with the date of the press conference marked on it to announce their change.

FIGURE 4.2

At the press conference itself, the design should be clearly displayed in a variety of contexts, and senior executives must carefully explain the strategy behind the program. As additional communication tools, corporations might want to use advertising (see Figure 4.2), Webcasts, or video news releases and satellite links (see Chapter 6). Whatever the choice, remember that presenting an identity, particularly for the first time, is a complex process, as it is easy for constituencies to interpret the change as merely cosmetic rather than strategic.

Step 6: Implement the Program

The final stage is implementation. This can take years in large companies and a minimum of several months for small firms. Resistance is inevitable, but what is frequently shocking is the extent of ownership constituents have in the old identity.

Usually, the best approach to ensure consistency across all uses for a new identity program is to develop identity standards. A standards manual shows staff and managers how to use the new identity consistently and correctly. Beyond this, someone in the organization needs to monitor the program and make judgments about when flexibility is allowed and when it is not. Over time, changes will need to be made in some standards—for instance, when a modern typeface chosen by a designer is not available for use everywhere.

Implementing an identity program is a communication process involving lots of interpersonal savvy and a coordinated approach to dealing with many constituencies. In addition to communicating its new identity program *within* the organization, Accenture, for example, had to train more than 100 other firms, including ad agencies, printers, and Web designers, on how to use its new logo.[11]

Image: In the Eye of the Beholder

We just explored some of the means by which a company can manage its identity. An organization's *image* is a function of how constituencies perceive the organization based upon all the messages it sends out through names and logos, and through self-presentations, including expressions of its corporate vision.

Constituencies often have certain perceptions about an organization *before they even begin to interact with it*. The perceptions are based on the industry, what they have read about the organization previously, what interactions others have had that they have been told about, and what visual symbols they recognize. Even if you have never eaten a hamburger at McDonald's, you have certain perceptions about the company and its products.

After interacting with an organization, the constituencies may have a different image of it than they did before. If this happens, the goal is to have that image be better, not worse. One bad experience with a Verizon operator can destroy a relationship for a lifetime with a customer. One aloof salesperson at Bergdorf Goodman in New York could turn a shopper off to the store forever. That's why organizations today are so concerned with the quality of each and every interaction. The credibility

[11] Guy, "Consultant to Launch Big Effort to Advertise Its New Identity," p. 66.

that a company acquires through the repeated application of consistently excellent behavior will determine its image in the minds of constituents in a much more profound way than a one-shot corporate advertising campaign.

Organizations should seek to understand their image not only with customers, but also with other key constituencies such as investors, employees, and the community (keeping in mind, as discussed in Chapter 2, that some of these may overlap). Often, a company's image with a given constituency is driven not only by its own unique corporate identity, but also by the image of the industry or group it belongs to. Internet companies rode this phenomenon in both directions from the late 1990s into the new millennium. Before the bursting of the dot-com bubble in 2000, virtually all e-based companies (or Internet companies) rose together on a tide of investor optimism with a collectively vibrant, cutting-edge image. Similarly, when that tide turned and investors wanted tangible products, real business plans, and seasoned management again, these companies all suffered, and so did their collective image.

Turning to the employee constituency, a company's image with its employees is particularly important because of the vital role employees play with the company's other constituencies. Starbucks Coffee has built one of the strongest brands and reputations in America by creating an equally powerful story and unified culture that begins inside and works its way out. Chairman Howard Schultz explains the philosophy: "We built the Starbucks brand first with our people, not with consumers, the opposite approach from that of the crackers-and-cereal companies. . . . [b]ecause we believed this was the best way to meet and extend the expectations of employees who were zealous about good coffee."[12] The enthusiasm of Starbucks' *baristas* is meant to be contagious, personally connecting them with their customers. Every barista is meant to play such a key role in generating customer loyalty that Starbucks refers to each one as a "partner," the official name for a Starbucks employee.[13]

As former CEO of Procter & Gamble Ed Artz once observed, "Consumers now want to know about the company, not just the products."[14] The day-to-day behavior of employees, from Starbucks' baristas to its executives, can rank just as high as product or service quality as the source of a strong corporate image that is aligned with the company's identity.

Building a Solid Reputation

The foundation of a solid reputation exists when an organization's identity and its image are aligned. Charles Fombrun, New York University professor emeritus and author of the book *Reputation*, says that "in companies where reputation is valued, managers take great pains to build, sustain, and defend that reputation by following practices that (1) shape a unique identity and (2) project a coherent and consistent set

---

[12] "No Ordinary Joe," *Reputation Management* 4, no. 3 (May–June 1998), p. 54.

[13] Ibid.

[14] Kevin L. Keller, "Building and Managing Corporate Brand Equity," in *The Expressive Organization*, ed. Majken Schultz, Mary Jo Hatch, and Mogens Holten Larsen (Oxford: Oxford University Press, 2000), p. 118.

FIGURE 4.3   Reputation Framework.

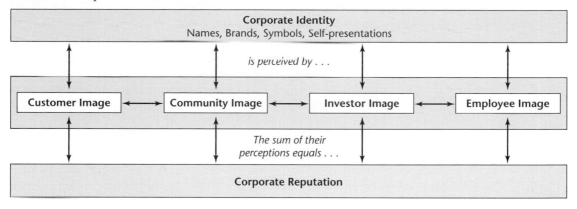

of images to the public."[15] (Figure 4.3 presents a visual representation of the relationship between identity, image, and reputation.)

Reputation differs from *image* because it is built up over time and is not simply a perception at a given point in time. It differs from *identity* because it is a product of both internal and external constituencies, whereas identity is constructed by internal constituencies (the company itself).[16] Additionally, as depicted in Figure 4.3, reputation is based on the perceptions of *all* constituencies.

Why Reputation Matters

The importance of reputation is evidenced by several prominent surveys and rankings that seek to identify the best and the worst among them: *Fortune*'s "Most Admired" list; *BusinessWeek* and Interbrand's "Best Global Brands" ranking; and Harris Interactive and the Reputation Institute's Reputation Quotient (RQ) Gold Study, featured in *The Wall Street Journal*, are just a few. Such highly publicized rankings have gained so much attention that some corporate PR executives' bonuses have actually been based on *Fortune*'s list of America's Most Admired Companies.[17] Between 1999 and 2000, the number of CEOs responding to the *Chief Executive* magazine–Hill and Knowlton Corporate Reputation Watch survey who said they were formally measuring corporate reputation doubled, from 19 percent to 37 percent.[18] In response to this demand, many public relations firms and consultancies now offer reputation measurement and management services to their corporate clients.

What motivated this level of interest? A strong reputation has important strategic implications for a firm, because, as Fombrun notes, "it calls attention to

[15] Charles J. Fombrun, *Reputation: Realizing Value from the Corporate Image* (Boston: Harvard Business School Press, 1996), pp. 5–6.

[16] Pamela Klein, "Measure What Matters," *Communication World* 16, no. 9 (October–November 1999), pp. 32–33.

[17] Matthew Boyle, "The Right Stuff," *Fortune*, March 4, 2002, pp. 85–86.

[18] Peter Haapaniemi, "What's in a Reputation?" *Chief Executive*, March 2000, pp. 48–51.

a company's attractive features and widens the options available to its managers, for instance, whether to charge higher or lower prices for products and services or to implement innovative programs."[19] As a result, the intangible entity of reputation is undoubtedly a source of competitive advantage. Companies with strong, positive reputations can attract and retain the best talent, as well as loyal customers and business partners, all of which contribute positively to growth and commercial success. In four out of the five years between 1994 and 1999, an investor who owned stock in *Fortune*'s most admired companies would have earned returns that beat the S&P 500.[20]

Reputation also can help companies to weather crises more effectively. For example, strong reputations helped Johnson & Johnson (J&J) survive the Tylenol cyanide tampering crisis in the early 1980s (see Chapter 10 for more on J&J's handling of the Tylenol crisis) and allowed Coca-Cola's contamination cases in India in 2004 to come and go without measurable long-term damage to the firm; in the Harris Interactive–Reputation Institute RQ Gold Study for 2004, the companies ranked number one and number three, respectively.[21]

The changing environment for business, as discussed in Chapter 1, has implications for reputation. The proliferation of media and information, the demand for increased transparency, and the increasing attention paid to social responsibility all speak for a greater focus on the part of organizations on building and maintaining strong reputations. Public confidence in business is low, and public scrutiny of business is high. The collapse of energy giant Enron in 2001 dragged its auditor, Andersen, down with it in an accounting scandal that not only irreparably damaged both firms' reputations (and indeed their chances for survival), but also heightened public mistrust of large corporations in general—particularly those with complex accounting—and of the entire accounting profession.

Against this backdrop, organizations are increasingly appreciating the importance of a strong reputation. How does an organization know where it stands? Since reputation is formed by the perceptions of constituencies, organizations must first uncover what those perceptions are and then examine whether they coincide with the company's identity and values. Only when image and identity are in alignment will a strong reputation result.

Measuring and Managing Reputation

In assessing its reputation, an organization must examine the perceptions of *all* its constituencies. As mentioned earlier, many PR firms have developed diagnostics for helping companies conduct this research. While one size does not fit all when it comes to measurement programs, all of them require constituency research.

Employees can be a good starting point, as they need to understand the company's vision and values and conduct themselves in every customer interaction with those in mind. An organization runs into trouble when it does not practice the

---

[19] David A. Aaker, *Building Strong Brands* (New York: Free Press, 1996), p. 51.

[20] Klein, "Measure What Matters."

[21] Annual RQ 2004, http://www.harrisinteractive.com.

values it promotes. As an example, IBM long espoused the value of lifetime employment. In the early 1990s, however, the company went through severe downsizing, and a joke that circulated throughout the company was "IBM means 'I've Been Misled.'" Clearly, employees did not feel that IBM was true to its own values, and this disillusionment caused IBM's reputation to suffer.[22]

Customer perceptions of an organization also must align with the organization's identity, vision, and values. In the late 1990s, Burberry learned what can happen to corporate reputation when this is *not* happening, and how the reputation can be saved by taking aggressive steps to restore these connections.

When Rose Marie Bravo became CEO of Burberry in 1997, the company was facing a number of challenges. Profits were plummeting, and while some of this could be explained by the Asian economic crisis of the mid-1990s (by 1996, Asian consumers—at home and abroad—generated two-thirds of the company's revenues, causing the downturn to dramatically affect Burberry's sales),[23] internal factors were also at work. For one, prior to Bravo's arrival, instead of maintaining a cohesive Burberry brand across the globe, the company allowed each country's management team to develop the brand as it desired in the local market. As a result, when customers thought of Burberry, what came to mind depended on their geographic location. In the United States, it meant $900 raincoats and $200 scarves; in Korea it meant whiskey; and in Switzerland it meant watches. Bravo explained that, before her arrival, "[Burberry] had a disparate network of licensees marketing Burberry around the globe. It wasn't a coherent business. Each country was representing its own version of Burberry. Demand slowed. The business needed a clean up. The brand was over-exposed and over-distributed."[24]

Not only was the company having trouble deciding what it was selling, but also it was struggling with how it was positioning its products. Burberry's inability to decide whether it was targeting upper- or lower-end consumers in Asia, for example, led to its products being sold in bulk to discount retailers. This undermined the image the exclusive, high-end Burberry boutiques were trying to generate in that same market. Bravo realized that Burberry had to sharpen its focus and concentrate on high-end retailing alone to send a consistent message to consumers. Additionally, she recognized that by speaking primarily to older males as a high-end men's raincoat retailer, the company was not catering to a key consumer constituency—women—as effectively as it could.

Recognizing that the Burberry store portfolio needed to reflect the high-end focus of the brand, Bravo upgraded the flagship store in London and doubled the size of the New York store. Even more importantly, Burberry began to rein in its detached network of franchises to allow the company greater control over consistency of product and identity. The most visible turning point was a print advertising campaign featuring supermodel Kate Moss in a Burberry plaid bikini. These

---

[22] Mary Jo Hatch and Majken Schultz, "Are the Strategic Stars Aligned for Your Corporate Brand?" *Harvard Business Review*, February 2001, pp. 129–34.

[23] Lauren Goldstein, "Dressing Up an Old Brand," *Fortune*, November 9, 1998, pp. 154–56.

[24] Quoted in Nigel Cope, "Stars and Stripes," *Independent*, June 6, 2001, Online Lexis-Nexis Academic, August 2001.

ads pushed Burberry's sales up dramatically and the average age of its customer down considerably by putting a fresh, playful face on a venerable fashion brand that, though esteemed for its nearly 150-year heritage, was looked upon by younger constituencies as stodgy and by many women as "not for me."

These initiatives, from store renovations to a more unified product focus across all franchises to the elimination of discount retailing, created a cohesive image and firmly established Burberry as a luxury brand, greatly enhancing its reputation around the world.

Corporate Philanthropy and Social Responsibility

Every organization today needs to consider corporate philanthropy and social responsibility when thinking about its own reputation. A 2001 survey conducted by public relations firm Hill & Knowlton revealed that three-quarters of Americans consider social responsibility issues when making their investment decisions.[25] Many others factor it in when deciding where to purchase goods and services. The Shell and ExxonMobil example earlier in this chapter provides an example of this.

Despite these findings, corporate philanthropy is not without its perils. As we saw in Chapter 1, trust in business is low, and efforts to publicly "do good" can be perceived as self-serving, particularly in the case of "strategic giving," in which the charitable activity relates directly to the business the company is in. Alternatively, when companies are too silent about what they are doing for the community or the environment, they face criticism for being apathetic or greedy.

Philip Morris provides a good example of the former. The company's advertising campaign touting its charitable activities met with skepticism from the public, many of whom viewed these ads as an attempt by Philip Morris to "undo" its negative image as a big tobacco company rather than as a manifestation of true concern for the community. Despite continued spending on promoting its philanthropic activities, the company still ranked 48 out of 60 in the Harris Interactive–Reputation Institute 2004 RQ Gold Study.[26]

Catastrophic events on September 11, 2001, provided another proving ground for companies' social responsibility communications programs. Procter & Gamble provided more than $2.5 million in cash and products to relief efforts, but because it did not publicize these activities, the company was accused in the Harris–Reputation Institute Study of doing "absolutely nothing to help."[27] P&G had consciously taken a low-profile approach to avoid being seen as "capitalizing on disaster," and that approach backfired.

How can companies reconcile the public's desire for them to do good things for the community and the environment with their equally strong skepticism about corporate motives? Why do some companies' efforts to make their good deeds known meet with approval and others' with disdain? First, corporate philanthropy

---

[25] Editorial staff, "Companies Fail Social Investors: Most Investors Value Corporate Responsibility, Few Are Satisfied," *Investor Relations Business*, August 6, 2001, p. 13.

[26] Annual RQ 2004, http://www.harrisinteractive.com.

[27] Ibid.

and social responsibility programs should be consistent with a company's vision to be perceived as credible, rather than as simply "check-the-box" activities or attempts to burnish a tarnished image.

Second, the means by which a company demonstrates its caring for the community should be carefully considered, using the communication framework provided in Chapter 2. If the company understands each of its constituencies—what the constituency members are concerned about, what is important to them, and what they already think about the company—it will be well positioned to structure the right kinds of programs and choose the right *channels* through which to communicate them. For instance, it may decide to describe its community outreach or environmental activities in its annual report or on its Web site rather than through advertising. It may decide that sponsoring a program that allows and encourages employees to volunteer their time in the community will be more effective than giving money to a local charity.

In the changing environment for business, corporate philanthropy and social responsibility are gaining visibility and importance in the eyes of many constituencies. A company that has a good understanding of its own constituencies and what is important to them, and that gives thought to how to tie such programs into its corporate vision, will be well positioned to create programs that will enhance its reputation.

Conclusion

Most managers who have not thought about corporate reputation tend to underestimate its value. This is partly due to a lack of understanding about what corporate image, identity, and reputation are all about and what they do for an organization; but skeptics should understand that an inappropriate or outdated identity can be as damaging to a firm as weak financial performance. Individuals seek consistency, and if perceptions about a corporation fail to mesh with reality, constituents take their business elsewhere.

Executives, then, need to be fully aware of the tremendous impact of identity, image, and reputation and must learn how to manage these critical resources. An organization with a clear corporate identity that represents its underlying reality and is aligned with the images held by all of its constituencies will be rewarded with a strong reputation. Reputational success, in turn, matures into pride and commitment—among employees, consumers, and the general public—and these qualities are irreplaceable assets in an intensely competitive global business environment.

Muzak

Say the name "Muzak" and chances are the term "elevator music" comes to mind. That image is a holdover from the 1920s when General George Squier used military-messaging technology (i.e., power lines) to pipe soothing music into a new contraption called the elevator to calm nervous riders. The resounding success of that early venture became hard to live down. Even though Muzak had long since gone on to develop the world's largest digital music library with songs by original artists, the public perception of elevator music stuck.

It was a liability that Muzak's sales force and franchisees worked hard to overcome. As often as not, they distanced themselves from the brand. At a sales meeting several years ago, Kenny Kahn, Muzak's vice president of marketing, asked Muzak's salespeople to lay their business cards on the table. No two were alike. "We had 200 offices and 3,000 employees and 450 versions of our business card," Kahn recalls. "If we had 1,000 Muzak trucks, they all looked different. We were so insecure about our own identity that our business cards and trucks often looked more like our vendors' identities than our own. The names Bose and DishNetwork appeared more prominently than Muzak."

By 1997, benign neglect of the Muzak brand had begun to take its toll. Kahn admits, "The parent company was losing serious cash. It had insufficient cash flow, increased debt, negative growth and an unbelievably horrible corporate culture. Then there was the franchise organization, which was wealthy. It was desperately afraid of change and had lost all faith in the parent company and felt they couldn't count on us to deliver a brand or pretty much any-

thing else." On the plus side, Kahn added, "Muzak had a new senior management team that was hell bent on change."

Its mandate to Kahn was to revitalize the brand, and he made the rounds of top ad agencies. Greeted warmly at first, Kahn noted that their enthusiasm cooled when he told them his modest budget. One person who didn't flinch was designer Kit Hinrichs, a partner of Pentagram. "When he said he'd love to help us rebuild our identity, I had to ask him why," Kahn recalls. "I'll never forget his answer. He kind of smiled and said, 'Well, if I fail, no one will ever know. But if I succeed, Muzak will tell the world.'"

Hinrichs' recollection was that he saw a company receptive to change. "We came in at the crossroads," he says. "Muzak's new management had done a lot of ground work before they engaged us. While Muzak was still making money, they saw a ceiling they couldn't rise above because of the way they were perceived. They knew they needed to turn that around to attract more premium accounts."

Pentagram's visual audit of Muzak materials and nationwide interviews confirmed everything Kahn had said. Pentagram associate Brian Jacobs, the lead designer on the project, says, "Muzak was so fragmented in the way it communicated that its brand looked different in every city and region and even between franchisees and company sales offices."

A first step was to develop a unifying symbol for Muzak that could go on everything from business cards to trade show booths, videos, and sales materials. Pentagram explored dozens of directions, including wordmarks, symbols, and a complete name change (which Muzak ruled out). In the end, a silver-and-black M in a circle prevailed. "Shifting from featuring the name Muzak to a strong symbol took the emphasis off the wordmark and said, 'Here's a different company

Source: © 1995–2002. Corporate Design Foundation, *@ Issue: The Journal of Business and Design,* vol. 7, no. 1. This case was written under the direction of Peter Lawrence, Chairman, Corporate Design Foundation. Reprinted by permission.

that happens to be Muzak,'" Jacobs explains, "The simplicity of the logo worked well on all kinds of diverse applications and wouldn't conflict with current graphic trends that might be used on marketing materials. Also, choosing silver and black as Muzak's signature colors gave the logo an elegant simplicity. The colors were bold yet neutral so you weren't forced to plan your design around them."

Another significant change was to depict Muzak's business as an art instead of a science. For years, Muzak's brand message focused on showing a correlation between physiological/psychological responses and music—first in elevators and then in the workplace. In the 1960s, Muzak coined the term "stimulus progression" to show how piping the right music into an office setting helped to enhance employee productivity. Even though the company had begun offering foreground music (FM-1) programmed with current original artist hits in 1984, its promotional materials continued to talk in a scientific tone, supported by serious-looking charts and graphs. What the materials failed to convey was the emotional and creative power of music and how Muzak's "audio architects" could skillfully capture the mood and energy of a brand, whether a company, spa, restaurant, or retail outlet, much like graphic designers are able to capture a company's visual identity through imagery. In fact, Muzak described its expertise as "audio imaging."

Pentagram sought to portray Muzak as an organization of young, hip, and knowledgeable audio architects who use music to reinforce their clients' own identities. To ensure that would-be clients took notice, Pentagram created an oversized corporate capabilities brochure featuring bold colors, graphic typography, and brief evocative text that emphatically began "Muzak is emotion."

The brochure set off a firestorm within the company. "Everyone was looking for the bullet points," says Kahn. Since marketing materials are billed back to the franchise organizations and sales force, modest print pieces and

PowerPoint presentations were more often the norm. The new capabilities book was panned as lavish, unwanted, and unnecessary. Backed by senior management, Kahn recalls, "We said, look, we're about art and what we're designing for clients is about art. This piece was not created for you; it was created for your clients. The day the client has a problem with this, then we will have an issue."

Though unconvinced, franchisees and salespeople began to take the brochure out. Kahn says, "We quickly started getting calls. Someone reported he had been stood up for an appointment but left the brochure behind. By the time he got back to the office, there was a message from the person saying, 'I want to see you.' Somebody had signed an 18-store furniture chain from leaving the brochure behind and giving a presentation with our new story. The next day somebody else signed a national firm with 37 locations. Such accounts are big business for us. We were hoping for the mom-and-pop stores when, in reality, regional and national companies were signing on. When something like that happens in a sales organization, word spreads fast."

Not only are sales personnel finding it easier to book appointments, they are finding it easier to make the presentations and follow-through. In addition to the capabilities brochure, Pentagram developed a multimedia software sales presentation, segment-specific brochures, and teaser postcards. The contemporary look of the pieces garnered new respect from clients. It also had the same effect on current and new employees. "We found ourselves attracting very bright, talented young people who in the past wouldn't come to work for Muzak. Now they are lining up to work here," Kahn says.

"Today you could not find a more revitalized company than Muzak," he adds. "Financially, three years ago we were losing cash, no cash flow, stunted growth. Today we have grown by 16 percent three years in a row. Cash flow is terrific. The company is valued at $750 million, up from $100 million in 1997."

Restored confidence in its future encouraged Muzak to move its corporate headquarters from

Seattle to Fort Mill, South Carolina, in 2000. Pentagram's architectural partner James Biber in New York was brought on to design a new headquarters building for the company Muzak had become. Muzak was drawn to a new 100,000-square-foot industrial warehouse space outside of Charlotte, which seemed less traditional than a high-rise office and more in line with its new artistic identity. "Jim helped us figure out what sort of culture we wanted to create and was able to bring concepts from around the world into the design," says Kahn. Biber sensed the space's potential for exuding an urban energy. "In every presentation, we tried to show aerial views of Italian cities for the notion that the space defined within these cities creates a forum for social interaction," explains Biber. "A work space is as much a social place as a functional place. People don't just go there to earn money; they go to an office for social interaction and for a sense of community. Italian cities work beautifully because there are all these specific defined public spaces and also a network of more private ways."

Reflecting on how an Italian piazza (town square) serves as a crossroad, gathering place and intimate heart of a city, Biber configured the interior with a piazza at its center and bridges joining open areas. There are 22 conference rooms, desks on wheels, and no private offices—not even for CEO Bill Boyd.

Throughout the building, the visual language of the brand is presented in subtle and impactful ways. The circle, which is a key part of Muzak's new identity, is integrated into the architecture. "The building is incredibly unique," exclaims Kahn. "Our clients arrive here and realize that we're figuring out something here and it is really special."

The dynamic energy and innovative design of the place have made a visit to Muzak headquarters a destination in itself for clients. "Companies in trend-setting industries come away with the feeling that Muzak is cooler than they are," comments Hinrichs. "This gives them the confidence to entrust their audio identity to Muzak.

"Even so, public perception won't change overnight," cautions Hinrichs. "That will take

place as Muzak becomes known for giving voice to major brands. But Muzak understands that a brand is not just a logo; it is everything you do. You have to manage it and its evolution or the brand becomes stale or fragmented. Kenny saw from the beginning that his job as marketing VP was creating the tools of the brand and then managing the way they are used."

While Kahn understood that changing public perception would take time, he noticed major differences immediately. "Although the world still thinks of us as the elevator music company," he says, "we're able to get the right appointments, with the right retailers, the right restaurant chains, and the people in our business who we want to do business with."

What changed, he says, was that "we have a new way of talking about the company. The product has a face. It has meant everything in the world internally to our culture. Pentagram gave us a visual foundation that lets us actively and creatively show people what music can do for them. Design has not only been great for Muzak's business; design has given Muzak its soul."

CASE QUESTIONS

Imagine yourself in the position of Kenny Kahn. You are working with Pentagram to redesign Muzak's identity/image. Upper management is keen for change but the company's franchise structure, along with its longstanding identity, provides resistance.

1. How much change did Muzak need to communicate through its identity system to change perceptions of the company?

2. What other corporate communication "levers" did Muzak have at its disposal to signal change?

3. How did changing its identity help/hurt Muzak's overall strategy? Short-term? Long-term?

4. How important is it, and should the parent company educate franchisees about the new identity?

CHAPTER FIVE

Corporate Advertising

In the preceding chapter, we discussed the importance of creating a coherent identity, image, and reputation. Of the many options available for organizations to communicate their identity, paid corporate advertising is the easiest and fastest. As a result, most large corporations use some form of corporate advertising, which acts as an umbrella covering any product associated with that company. Because of this strong association, any corporate advertising campaign should be

- *Strategic:* Looking toward the future of the company so that it will have longevity and won't become stagnant or "old news."
- *Consistent:* In keeping with images of products or businesses of the company. Image advertising cannot be viewed as a separate corporate message; rather, it must fit with company vision.

In this chapter, we will study the role of corporate advertising and how it can shape an organization's image. The chapter addresses this topic by first defining corporate advertising, then looking back at its history, and finally, discussing who uses this form of advertising and why.

What Is Corporate Advertising?

Corporate advertising can be defined as paid use of media that seeks to benefit the image of the corporation as a whole rather than its products or services alone. Because all of a company's advertising contributes to its image, both product and corporate advertising should reflect a unified strategy. Corporate image advertising should "brand" a company the way product advertising brands a product.

A major difference between corporate and product advertising is who pays for each of the two types of advertising. A company's marketing department typically is responsible for all product-related advertising and pays for such ads out of its own budget. Corporate advertising, on the other hand, falls within the corporate communication area and either comes out of that budget or, in some cases, is paid for by the CEO's office.

Corporate advertising should present a clear identity for the organization based on a careful assessment of its overall communication strategy (see Chapter 2), and it generally falls into three broad categories: image advertising, financial advertising, and issue advocacy. Let's take a closer look at each of the three categories to understand what corporate advertising is all about.

Advertising to Reinforce Identity or Enhance Reputation

Many companies use corporate advertising to strengthen their identities following structural changes. As companies merge and enter new businesses, they need to explain their new vision, organization, and strategy to constituents who may have known them well in an earlier incarnation but are struggling to understand the new organization. These typically larger organizations often need to simplify their image to unify a group of disparate activities.

Tyco used corporate advertising to rehabilitate its image in the wake of corporate fraud by former CEO Dennis Kozlowski and former CFO Mark Swartz. Under Kozlowski, Tyco had become a confusing conglomerate of business units built by aggressive acquisitions. Even the company's own employees were unsure what businesses Tyco was in. Following operational improvements, new CEO Ed Breen hired Jim Harman from General Electric as Vice President of Corporate Advertising and Branding. Harman, who had overseen GE's "We bring good things to life" campaign, was tasked with demonstrating the breadth of Tyco's businesses, products, and services. Tyco used the tagline "a vital part of your world" in several print ads that portray the company's products and services as integral to daily life. The ads feature a background of more than 6,500 words listing Tyco products and services. The words form a picture, such as a baby or a firefighter, demonstrating the importance and vitality of Tyco's offering. And indeed, in 2005, Tyco won an award for best corporate advertising from *IR Magazine*.[1]

We discussed in the previous chapter the need for organizations to manage their identity, image, and reputation with a variety of constituencies. When companies analyze their image with constituencies, they can then apply these findings to their corporate advertising strategy. If an organization's identity is very different from how it is perceived externally, for instance, it can use corporate advertising to close that gap.

In the last chapter we saw how Burberry used a fresh print advertising campaign featuring a model in a Burberry plaid bikini to change perceptions among consumers that the brand was (a) not for women and (b) stiff and stodgy. Corporate advertising can be an efficient mechanism for changing impressions about organizations if changes have really taken place. At Burberry, CEO Rose Marie Bravo was indeed expanding Burberry's women's clothing and accessory lines and working to raise Burberry's profile as a high-end retailer when the new ads appeared in print.

Effective image advertising also allows companies to differentiate themselves from rivals. For example, Target Corp., which won *Advertising Age* magazine's Marketer of the Year award in 2000, established itself as an upscale discounter with an edgy, high-energy image. Recognizing that competing on price would put the company head-to-head with low-price leader Wal-Mart, the company chose a different path. Target's "pop art" campaign, which broke in the spring of 2000, incorporated products into print and television ads in memorable ways. The "Color My World" spot, for example, featured Coca-Cola as part of a "red"

[1] Suzanne Vranica, "Tyco Aims to Put Its Woes Behind It," *The Wall Street Journal*, June 15, 2004.

Dow lets you do great things.

That special kind of person who cares enough to want to make an impact on world hunger.

1. SING: YOU'RE ON YOUR WAY, THE WORLD IS OPENING ITS DOORS.

2. HER (VO): I never understood when Mom made me clean my plate 'cause...

3. "there were places where kids were starving."

4. Now, I'm about to walk into a Dow laboratory, to work on new ways...

5. to help grow more and better grain for those kids who so desperately need it.

6. SING: YES, YOU CAN MAKE A DIFFERENCE IN WHAT TOMORROW BRINGS.

7. HER (VO): I can't wait.

8. SING: 'CAUSE DOW LETS YOU DO GREAT THINGS.

"Feed The Children" :30

*Trademark of The Dow Chemical Company

Dow was best known to baby boomers for its connection to Vietnam and defense through its products, Napalm and Agent Orange. This corporate advertising campaign from the late 1980s sought to change that image with a new generation. Its tag line, "Dow lets you do great things," ran into the mid-1990s. Courtesy The Dow Chemical Company.

theme that launched the red line of clothing from sportswear company Mossimo.[2]

Advertising and public relations (PR) professionals credited Target with creating product spots such as these that were also effective brand builders for the company overall. In addition to conveying the company's desired image, the ads also prominently featured Target's bull's-eye logo on everything from the wallpaper in the background to the actors' clothing, solidifying the link between the company's identity and fun, "hip" merchandise. Target also has lived up to the promises of its advertising (delivering low-priced, well-designed products), which is critical to the success of any corporate advertising campaign.

Advertising to Attract Investment

In Chapter 8 we will look at the importance of a strong investor relations function. One of the tools that companies use to enhance their images in the financial

[2] Alice Z. Cuneo, "On Target; Retailing Stardom: Spritely Marketing Makes It Chic to Buy Cheap," *Advertising Age*, December 11, 2000, p. 1.

community is financial-relations corporate advertising. This kind of corporate advertising can stimulate interest in a company's stock among potential investors as well as buy-side and sell-side analysts (see Chapter 8 for more on analysts). Given the hundreds of companies analysts cover, a good corporate advertising campaign can stimulate their interest to take a closer look at a particular one.

While analysts do focus heavily on company financials, in a survey of 200 research analysts—each of whom covered approximately 80 companies—"strength of management" was the number-one factor influencing the decision to invest in a company.[3] Analysts place a high value on CEOs who express a coherent vision for their organizations, and as James Gregory of Corporate Branding LLC explains, "the CEO's ability to paint a picture of the company's future is the linchpin of a successful corporate advertising campaign."[4] For these reasons, companies' CEOs are often featured in corporate advertisements targeted at the financial community.

Some corporate advertisers assert that a strong financially oriented corporate advertising campaign can actually increase the price of a company's stock. A W.R. Grace campaign that ran in the early 1980s is often cited as evidence of this. The television campaign, which ran as the company's "Look into Grace" series, highlighted the company's financial and business attributes and then asked, "Shouldn't you look into Grace?" Attitude and awareness studies of the ad campaign in test markets showed that its awareness and approval ratings were much higher after this campaign ran. In addition, the company's stock price increased significantly during the test campaign, although it did not go any higher with later campaigns. Corporate advertising expert Thomas Garbett, writing in the *Harvard Business Review*, stated that

> I interpret the relationship between corporate campaigns and stock pricing this way: advertising cannot drive up the price of a reasonably priced stock and, indeed, doing so might not be entirely legal; it can, however, work to ensure that a company's shares are not overlooked or undervalued.[5]

Professors at Northwestern University's Kellogg School of Business studied this trend using econometric analysis of the link between corporate advertising and stock price. They determined that, indeed, corporate advertising does have a statistically significant positive effect on stock prices. They further determined that the positive influence from such campaigns averaged 2 percent and was particularly strong during bull-market periods, such as in the mid- to late 1990s.

The implications of this study, if true, are exciting for companies. Even a one-point increase in the stock price can translate to the tens or hundreds of millions of dollars for large companies with many shares of stock outstanding. In addition, an improvement in stock price that improves the company's price-earnings ratio can present opportunities for stock options and dividends for employees.

Some companies view building their brand with investors as more important than doing so with customers. As Gary Patrick, founder of Patrick Marketing

---

[3] James R. Gregory, "The Impact of Advertising to the Financial Community," *BusinessWeek* special publication, 1999, p. 4.

[4] Ibid.

[5] Thomas F. Garbett, "When to Advertise Your Company," *Harvard Business Review*, March–April 1982, p. 104.

Group, explained, "There are business-to-business companies advertising during *Friends* or prime time baseball—clearly all they're doing is advertising to potential investors and Wall Street."[6]

Advertising to Influence Opinions

This kind of advertising often is called *issue* or *advocacy advertising* and is used by companies to respond to external threats from either government or special interest groups. Issue advertising typically deals with controversial subjects; it is a way for companies to respond to those who challenge the status quo.

Many companies started using issue advertising in the late 1970s and early 1980s to meet the challenges of what was perceived as an antibusiness media. By taking issues directly to the consumer, companies can compete with journalists for a share of the reader's mind. As a result, issue advertisements often are purposely placed on op-ed pages in prominent newspapers such as *The New York Times*, *The Wall Street Journal*, and *The Washington Post*. Perhaps the most famous example of this kind of advertising is Mobil Oil's series of issue advertisements, which ran for over 20 years. What began as a dialogue about the oil embargo in the early 1970s expanded to become a sort of bully pulpit for this powerful organization as it advocated positions on a wide variety of topics.

Many other organizations also have adopted the op-ed style for their advocacy ads. This includes Amway, whose approach typifies the more positive approach used by companies dealing with environmental issues. Amway ran a series of ads that positioned the company as environmentally aware. One had a photograph of five Amway distributors and the headline "Find the Environmental Activist." The copy goes on to explain that everyone in the ad is an environmental activist and that all Amway distributors are committed to the cause of environmental awareness. The tag line reads "And you thought you knew us."

This advertisement also reveals the problem, however, with much issue advertising. As David Kelley pointed out in an essay on the subject of issue advertising in the *Harvard Business Review*, most companies "pay too much attention to the form and too little to the content of the message."[7] Does the tag line in the Amway ad, for example, imply "You thought we were a bunch of polluters because we specialize in detergents that come in huge containers"? Or does it mean "You thought we were just selling detergents when what we are really doing is protecting the environment"? Either way, the advertisement seems to be playing into the hands of critics rather than setting the agenda for the argument. Since the advertisement is so short, it never gets across the point that this company is trying to make. That is, they would like to argue directly with critics who charge Amway with environmental neglect.

Since companies typically are more conservative than their adversaries, their arguments often fall short of the mark. It is extremely difficult for a large corporation to take on a tough issue in the marketplace without offending someone. When

---

[6] "Marketers Use TV Advertising to Attract Investment," *Investor Relations Business*, November 12, 2001, p. 17.

[7] David Kelley, "Critical Issues for Issue Ads," *Harvard Business Review*, July–August 1982, p. 81.

In this advertisement, Microsoft combines advocacy of the benefits to schools of computers and Internet access with awareness of its own, related corporate social responsibility programs. Courtesy of Microsoft

THE FOURTH R: REVOLUTION

Rarely in America's history has there been such a strong consensus, and opportunity, to dramatically improve our educational system. The national discussion now underway—from the White House to the halls of Congress to local school board meetings—offers a chance to enrich the learning experience for all students, enhance teaching excellence, promote parental involvement, and help schools develop relevant curriculum and deliver services efficiently. Ensuring that tomorrow's citizens are better educated and informed is a sure way to strengthen our democratic and economic future.

While technology is not an end in itself, a combination of powerful software, the personal computer, a new generation of digital devices and the Internet holds the potential to significantly enhance the educational environment. Through the appropriate use of technology in schools we have the capacity to:

- Create a more stimulating learning environment for students, including increased access to individualized educational programs
- Enhance teacher quality by providing professional development and new tools that teachers need to teach to high standards
- Empower schools to be responsive and operate efficiently through the use of information systems that support accountability and continuous improvement
- Increase parental awareness and involvement in their children's learning and school activities, and
- Close the digital divide and create new educational and workplace opportunities—especially in math, science and high-tech fields—for minorities and women.

According to the U.S. Department of Education, today only one in five teachers feels prepared to use computers and the Internet for instruction. To address this issue, Microsoft is involved in a number of efforts, including an online resource network for teachers, and programs that support the training of more than 1.5 million teachers annually in the use of technology as a teaching and learning tool. All the technology in the world won't make a difference in student achievement without well-trained teachers who know how to use it effectively.

Today, there are many tools that help teachers provide a rich environment for learning: encyclopedias and reference materials, productivity tools, and, of course, the Internet. But managing information in the classroom has long been a difficult and time-consuming process. With the launch next month of a new Web-based curriculum-management platform, Encarta Class Server, teachers will be able to manage curriculum standards, lesson plans, content, assignments and assessment more effectively. This will enable them to spend more time developing rich learning materials. Students will have greater opportunities to access related information over the Internet, and parents will be able to participate in their children's education by tracking their progress and communicating with teachers over the Web.

Education leaders also face a challenge running efficient and accountable schools. For example, administrators often collect a great deal of student data, but frequently lack the tools to correlate and analyze that data for better decision making and improvement of their schools. In response to this challenge, Microsoft and more than 100 education software developers are creating the Schools Interoperability Framework—an innovative technical standard that will enable the sharing of data among school software applications that manage student information, library, transportation and food service systems.

For many young people, computers and the Internet are opening up a rich new world of information and learning. As Dr. Rudy Crew, former Chancellor of New York City Public Schools and now executive director of the Institute for K-12 Leadership at the University of Washington, said recently: "Technology offers a window through which many children now have access to a set of strategies or skills they didn't before." And research has shown that students write better and collaborate more on projects when they have access to a computer.

The danger is leaving some of those students behind. In particular, it is crucial that young women and minorities are encouraged to enter fields such as computer science, math and engineering. The challenge for educators, government leaders and industry is to work together to ensure that every student has access to the learning tools that will prepare them for success in our increasingly knowledge-based economy.

This is one in a series of essays on technology and its impact on society. More information is available at microsoft.com/issues.

Microsoft

© 2001 Microsoft Corporation

companies try to please everyone, they ultimately dilute the power of their own messages.

If a company decides to pursue an advocacy campaign, senior management must have the courage to argue forcefully for its ideas and must not be afraid to alienate certain constituencies in the process. For example, when the major book-sellers took on the conservative groups that called for a purging of all "dirty" books, they won the argument with advocates of first amendment rights but lost with family-oriented religious groups. Organizations should thus proceed into the world of issue advertising with extreme caution and with a full understanding of its inherent risks.

The History of Corporate Advertising in America

Interestingly enough, one of the earliest documented corporate advertisements was issue-oriented. According to expert Thomas Garbett, the earliest corporate ad, paid for by the American Telephone and Telegraph Company (AT&T), started its run in June of 1908. The ad had, as its headline, "Telephone service, a public trust," and went on to defend the company's point of view as follows:

> The widespread ownership of the Bell Telephone System places an obligation on its management to guard the savings of its hundreds of thousands of stockholders. Its responsibility for so large a part of the country's telephone service imposes an obligation that the service shall always be adequate, dependable and satisfactory to the user. . . There is then in the Bell System no incentive to earn speculative or large profits. Earnings must be sufficient to assure the best possible service and the financial integrity of the business. Anything in excess of these requirements goes toward extending the service or keeping down rates.[8]

Obviously, in the early part of the 20th century, AT&T had to defend its (then) monopoly status and combat the assumption that it couldn't possibly be acting in the public's interest given the lack of competition. AT&T hoped that the public, as a result of reading the advertisement, would have more faith in the company and its honest intentions.

A decade later, many companies were running corporate advertisements. Herbert F. deBower's 1917 textbook, *Modern Business*, defines issue advertising in a way that is still relevant today:

> Copy that is intended to make people "think something" is termed "molding public opinion" copy. It is used for pure publicity—to direct public sentiment for political or legislative purposes, and frequently to advertise an industry. An advertisement which aims to induce a general impression favorable to some policy, act, or product, obviously employs copy designed to influence public opinion.[9]

By midcentury, "institutional advertising," as it was called, was widely used throughout the United States. Garbett describes one of the most interesting reasons for the increased use of this form of advertising during World War II:

> [Corporate] advertising was broadly used during the [second world] war. Although few peacetime products were available for sale to the public, some advertisers realized that if they stopped advertising for several years, it would be difficult to regain their prestige after the war. A younger generation of consumers would come into the market unfamiliar with their products. The advertising of the period frequently took the form of telling what the company was manufacturing for the Armed Forces. . . In many cases the advertisers expressed regret that their products were not available to the public and promised improved products after the war.[10]

One advertisement that captured the essence of what companies were doing was a hybrid product and image ad. Lucky Strike cigarettes at the time had a green package that was made from some derivative of copper. The cigarette company was forced to give its copper over to the government for the war effort. In changing its packaging to white from green, the company adopted an innovative ad campaign with the headline: "Lucky Strike Goes to War!"

---

[8] Thomas F. Garbett, *Corporate Advertising* (New York: McGraw-Hill, 1981), p. 120.

[9] Ibid., p. 9.

[10] Ibid.

After World War II, corporate advertising faded from view until its revival in the 1970s, when oil companies found themselves battling allegations of exorbitant profits during the oil crisis. As special interest groups gained power throughout the 1970s and 1980s, and as media interest in corporations also increased, companies again turned to corporate advertising to defend themselves.

Today, corporate advertising is highly visible and intensely scrutinized by constituencies. Magazines from *Advertising Age* to *BusinessWeek* to *IR Magazine* feature annual "best of" lists praising corporate campaigns deemed to be best overall or most memorable. Advertising also has gained recognition by investors and Wall Street analysts whether or not ads are explicitly targeted at the financial community. In fact, a study in the *Journal of Advertising* indicated that when a company announces a relationship with a new advertising agency, investors perceive this as indicative of strategic changes within the company.[11] Additionally, equity analysts often discuss companies' advertising campaigns in their research reports and share opinions on new campaigns with the press.

These trends only reinforce the notion that corporate advertising should be aligned with company vision and consistent across advertising media (print, television, Web, etc.). When you consider that, on any given day, the typical U.S. consumer is exposed to between 3,000 and 5,000 advertisements,[12] you begin to appreciate the importance of consistent, memorable corporate advertising.

Who Uses Corporate Advertising and Why?

According to recent studies, over half of the largest industrial and nonindustrial companies in the United States have corporate advertising programs of one sort or another. Usually, a direct correlation exists between size and the use of corporate advertising: The bigger the company, the more likely it is to have a corporate advertising program. Since large corporations tend to have more discretionary income, this makes sense. In addition, larger companies tend to be more diversified and thus have a greater need to establish a coherent reputation out of a variety of activities, products, and services.

Corporate advertising also is used heavily by companies within more "controversial" industries: Cigarette companies, oil companies, pharmaceuticals, and other large industrial companies all have image problems to deal with, from concerns about health, to drug recalls, to pollution. Overall, heavy industry spends more on corporate advertising than consumer-packaged-goods firms, which lead all other industries in product advertising. This may be related to the presence in consumer products companies of a strong marketing focus that concentrates more on the four P's of product, price, promotion, and place (distribution) than developing a strong reputation.

A good corporate advertising program can clarify and enhance a company's reputation, and the absence of one can hurt packaged goods companies and retailers as

---

[11] Robin A. Coulter, Gerald Zaltman, and Keith S. Coulter, "Interpreting Consumer Perceptions of Advertising: An Application of the Zaltman Metaphor Elicitation Technique," *Journal of Advertising*, January 1, 2001, p. 1.

[12] Ibid.

well. In contrast to the Target example mentioned earlier, Kmart Corp. has struggled with its corporate image in recent years and, critics argue, has failed to differentiate itself from rivals such as Target and Wal-Mart. The company seems to have vacillated between trying to compete on price (it revived its "Blue Light specials" with much fanfare in 2001) and marketing brand names such as Martha Stewart. This lack of clarity left customers with no clear, differentiated perception of the company. Let's now take a closer look at some of the reasons companies invest in corporate advertising campaigns.

Increase Sales

The relationship between corporate advertising and sales is less clear than that between product advertising and sales, because corporate advertising is meant to do things that *eventually* boost sales but likely won't directly or immediately do so. This creates a problem for managers trying to introduce corporate advertising into companies that have a heavy financial orientation. The numbers-oriented manager often will cite the lack of a direct connection between corporate advertising and sales as the best reason not to use corporate advertising.

Even so, there are growing efforts to identify a closer relationship between corporate advertising and sales. As a senior vice president of the Association of National Advertisers (ANA) remarked, "As has been seen in other marketing communications areas, corporate advertising managers are becoming more concerned with determining the Return-on-Investment (ROI) of their efforts."[13]

While measuring the return on investment for individual marketing disciplines began 75 years ago with the monitoring of results from direct-mail campaigns, attempts to determine the ROI from integrated marketing campaigns are more recent. Several agencies, including Grey Global Group, McCann-Erickson WorldGroup, and J. Walter Thompson, are using new tools to better quantify results for clients, including measures such as cost per sale or cost per lead.[14] This sort of analysis can help companies make a stronger case for advertising budgets in difficult economic times and also may aid with their financial projections The rise of the Internet has made it increasingly easy to measure newer forms of advertising, such as advertising banners placed on Web sites and in e-mail advertisements.

In 2000, AT&T Business Services took the unusual step of asking agencies competing for a $100 million business-to-business advertising assignment to project the return on investment of their proposed campaigns, and also to recommend which of the company's services should be most heavily advertised. In the future, "Advertising won't be treated as an expense, but as a strategic investment," said marketing vice president Bill O'Brien.[15] Through corporate advertising, companies can draw out features about themselves that they think will appeal to the public and, as a result, make consumers want to buy products from them. For

[13] Association of National Advertisers' Web site, http://www.ana.net/news/1998/ 04_01_98.cfm (retrieved April 29, 2002).

[14] Laura Q. Hughes, "Measuring Up," *Advertising Age*, February 5, 2001, p. 1.

[15] Kathleen Sampey, "AT&T: Ads Are Investment; Shops Must Project ROI," *Adweek*, July 31, 2000, p. 6.

Tiffany & Co.
and The Susan G. Komen Breast Cancer Foundation
Celebrate A Decade of Promise for the Twenty-First Century
with a commemorative gift set inspired by the courageous colors
of those racing for the cure. A limited-edition thirty-six-inch silk jacquard
scarf and TIFFANY™ 100 ml Eau de Parfum. The set, $100.
Available at Tiffany & Co. and select department stores.
To inquire: 800-526-0649.

10% of the proceeds to benefit The Susan G. Komen Breast Cancer Foundation.

©T&CO. 1994

TIFFANY & CO.

NEW YORK ATLANTA BAL HARBOUR BEVERLY HILLS BOSTON CHICAGO DALLAS HOUSTON HONOLULU PALM BEACH
PHILADELPHIA SAN DIEGO SAN FRANCISCO SOUTH COAST PLAZA TORONTO TROY WASHINGTON DC

instance, S. C. Johnson & Son, the maker of such brands as Glade, Pledge, Windex, and Ziploc, learned that 80 percent of consumers believed family-owned companies made products they could trust, versus only 43 percent who said the same of publicly owned companies. In response, the company rolled out a $450 million campaign highlighting the family heritage of S. C. Johnson, with the tag line, "S. C. Johnson—a Family Company."[16]

Returning to our Kmart example, after entering Chapter 11 bankruptcy proceedings in 2002, the company looked to corporate advertising as a mechanism to bring customers back and revitalize sales, pouring $40 million into its "The Stuff of Life" corporate advertising campaign. With television spots directed by filmmaker Spike Lee, the campaign attempted to make what the company's marketing chief called "an emotional bond" with customers.[17] By positioning Kmart as a part of the lives of everyday families, Kmart hoped to attract sales by projecting a staying power that would overcome the public's perception that it was going out of business. In late 2004, Kmart announced the acquisition of Sears, a rival retailer.

Create a Stronger Reputation

We talked about the importance of reputation in the last chapter. The best corporate advertising creates goodwill and enhances reputation by letting constituents in on what the organization is all about, particularly if it does beneficial things that people might not be aware of.

Amoco Chemical Company, acquired by BP in 1998, created a campaign that won an award from *BusinessWeek* in the late 1990s and is a good example of this sort of advertising. One of the print ads for this campaign showed an airplane landing at night with the headline "Amoco Helps Make Coming Home a Little Safer." The ad went on to explain that the lighting masts use durable resin compounds based on material from Amoco Chemical. While the advertisement was visually appealing, another reason that this campaign made it into *BusinessWeek*'s "most memorable" list that year was the concept that chemicals are used for things most people don't even think about that make our lives better. The tag line, also memorable, read, "The Chemistry Is Right at Amoco." Learning more about the good things that come out of Amoco shifted some people's perceptions away from thinking of Amoco as another "big oil" company and a producer of environmental pollutants.

Companies also look to build credibility and enhance reputation by using endorsements from a third-party organization (TPO).[18] Just as individuals rely on the *Zagat Survey* to confirm their choice in restaurants, many find this type of "seal of approval" advertising helpful in assessing companies, particularly lesser-known ones. An endorsement by a trusted and recognized TPO can

---

[16] Jack Neff, "S.C. Johnson Ads to Stress 'Family Owned,'" *Advertising Age*, November 13, 2001, p. 3.

[17] Bruce Horovitz, "Kmart Hopes Spike Lee Ads Do the Right Thing," *USA Today*, February 22, 2002, p. 3B.

[18] Dwane Hal Dean and Abhijit Biswas, "Third-Party Organization Endorsement of Products: An Advertising Cue Affecting Consumer Prepurchase Evaluation of Goods," *Journal of Advertising*, January 1, 2002, pp. 41–58.

inspire confidence in the consumer. Third parties can provide ratings or rankings of a company or its services, or they can be used as the subject of a story that illustrates how the company provided a service to them.

An example of the former is an advertisement for a Van Kampen mutual fund that mentions the fund's five-star rating by the Morningstar investment guide. Xerox Corp. launched a series of print ads using the other approach. One of these shows the Xerox name in large print with a car key sitting on top of it. The copy reads, "Enterprise Rent-A-Car wanted to reduce operational costs. Xerox found the key to success by moving 1.7 million documents onto their intranet every month." Another ad talks about how the company helped Honeywell lower its operational costs by millions of dollars. While Xerox already had the name recognition that many smaller companies using TPO advertising do not, it was largely for photocopying equipment. This series of ads, with the tag line "There's a New Way to Look at It," revealed a much broader set of capabilities. Being able to talk about projects it had undertaken for large, well-known companies provided Xerox with more credibility as it attempted to boost its image as a more comprehensive service provider.

Corporate advertising also is widely used by companies to publicize their philanthropic activities, which, as discussed in the previous chapter, also can lead to an enhanced reputation. These advertisements can create bizarre associations between otherwise diametrically opposed sectors of society such as cigarette manufacturers and the arts (Philip Morris), opera and oil (Texaco), and supertanker manufacturers and blue whales (Samsung).

Organizations using corporate advertising to enhance reputation must be prepared for their opponents to respond negatively to what they may perceive as the company's attempt to smooth over a history of corporate wrongdoing or to apply a "quick fix" to a serious image problem. For example, after increasing spending on positive corporate image building by a staggering 1,712 percent between 1998 and 2000, Philip Morris still ranked 59 out of 60 corporations in the 2002 Harris Interactive–Reputation Institute RQ Gold Study published in *The Wall Street Journal*.[19]

The company's aggressive image advertising campaign touting its philanthropic activities, coupled with its new identity program (see Chapter 4 for more on the Altria name change), actually worked to alienate critics further. Many viewed both as attempts to mask the company's true identity as a cigarette manufacturer responsible for thousands of cancer deaths. In fact, at Philip Morris's 2002 shareholder meeting, demonstrators waved a giant canvas banner depicting a skeletal Marlboro Man in a bandana marked "Altria."[20]

It is important, then, when using corporate advertising to enhance reputation that it is credible. Corporate advertising risks not being perceived as credible if, for instance, it ties closely to corporate vision, but that vision has not

[19] "Philip Morris Annual Meeting Draws Most Extensive Protest in Corporation's History," *PR Newswire*, April 25, 2002, Online Lexis-Nexis Academic, April 2002.

[20] Ibid.

been properly communicated to the organization's constituencies through other channels as well. This highlights the point made earlier that corporate advertising must be strategic and closely aligned with a company's overall communication strategy. In isolation, it will not have the power to change perceptions about the organization.

Recruit and Retain Employees

One of the most critical communication activities for any company is communicating with employees (see Chapter 7). If a corporate advertising campaign succeeds in explaining in simple terms what a large, complex organization is all about, this can be as helpful to employees as it is to the outside world. Corporate advertising is also an indirect way of building morale among employees. Trying to quantify this is very difficult, however. Garbett says that

> Putting a dollar figure on the savings attained by reducing employee turnover is difficult. Some say you should add recruitment and training costs, next multiply by the turnover rate, and then estimate the percentage of employees who might be persuaded to stay if they felt more positively about the company. Whatever the real figure, if corporate advertising can effect even a modest reduction in turnover, the savings to a large corporation is well worth the expense and effort of a campaign.[21]

Such advertising also helps companies attract the best and the brightest both at the entry level and for senior positions. A good corporate advertising campaign can create excitement among both potential and current employees. In 2002, GE launched a corporate print advertising campaign with four employee-related themes: diversity in leadership, the GE Fund, the GE Mentoring program, and volunteerism at the company. Many of the ads showed photographs of GE employees as children. In one ad, a girl is pictured holding a globe; the text reads, "Introducing Eugenia Salinas who has traveled throughout the world as GE's General Manager, Americas Marketing for GE Medical Systems. She's part of the group of minority and women leaders across GE responsible for over $30 billion in annual revenues."[22]

Other ads included more recent photos of GE employees who were involved in mentoring through the company-sponsored program or who participated in volunteer projects, along with members of their local community. Many such ads, ostensibly focused on employees, enhance a company's reputation with nonemployee constituencies as well. Consumers, for instance, may be impressed with GE's social responsibility programs or the caliber of their employees, which they read about in these print ads.

Conclusion Corporate advertising helps companies communicate their message to a wide audience quickly and efficiently, but at a rather high price. Some managers will shy away from it because of the costs involved and the difficulties in measuring its near-term effect on

---

[21] Garbett, *Corporate Advertising*, p. 120.

[22] GE company Web site, http://www.ge.com/campaign.htm (retrieved May 7, 2002).

sales. However, all the goals discussed for corporate advertising—increasing sales, enhancing reputation, and attracting and retaining employees—if met, will ultimately improve a company's financial situation.

The decision to run a campaign should be based, above all else, on a firm's overall communication strategy. Whether the company is changing its image, is suffering from erroneous perceptions in the marketplace, or simply wants to continue a successful, well-received campaign that solidifies its identity, corporate advertising can be a tremendous resource in positioning the organization for future success.

Corporate Ad Samples

EXERCISE QUESTIONS

Based on what you read in this chapter, evaluate the following eight advertisements (Exhibits 5.1 through 5.8) by answering these questions:

1. What is the purpose of each advertisement?
2. Are they corporate advertisements or product advertisements?
3. If corporate ads, what kind are they?
4. What constituencies are the ads aimed at?
5. Pick one of the ads and write a memo to the company's vice president of corporate communication explaining how you would improve the ad based on what you have just read.

EXHIBIT 5.1

Source: Under permission by V&S Vin and Sprit AB. ABSOLUT COUNTRY OF SWEDEN VODKA & LOGO, ABSOLUT, ABSOLUT BOTTLE DESIGN AND ABSOLUT CALLIGRAPHY ARE TRADEMARKS OWNED BY V&S VIN & SPRIT AB. COPYRIGHT 2002 V&S VIN & SPRIT AB. Photographer: Steve Bronstein.

EXHIBIT 5.2

Improving the world's food, water, shelter, and transportation.

It's not a UN conference. It's a company's mission.

Visit Dow's Web site and you'll see that our mission is, literally, *to constantly improve what is essential to human progress by mastering science and technology.* Visit any of the over 60 countries where Dow is working and you'll see the fruits of our labors: hardier, healthier crops; cleaner water; stronger building and transportation materials; more resilient and versatile fabrics; and smaller, energy-efficient electronics. Which isn't meant to say "mission accomplished" as much as "mission well worth accomplishing."

Health

Lifestyle

Communication

Transportation

Building

DOW*

Living.
Improved daily.

www.dow.com

*Trademark of The Dow Chemical Company

Source: Permission granted by The Dow Chemical Company.

EXHIBIT 5.3

Courtesy of GE.

EXHIBIT 5.4

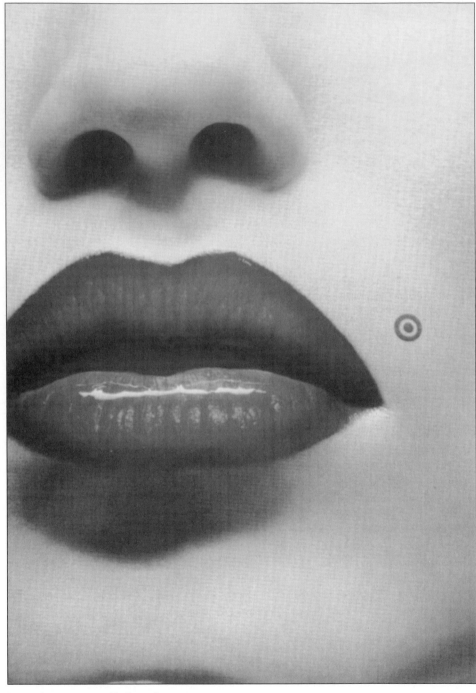

Source: Permission granted by Target Corporation.

EXHIBIT 5.5

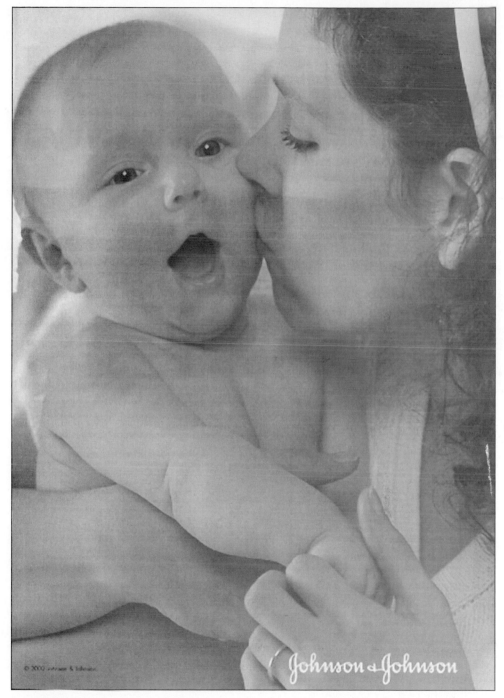

Source: Permission granted by Johnson & Johnson.

EXHIBIT 5.6

Courtesy of GE.

EXHIBIT 5.7

Courtesy of Evian.

EXHIBIT 5.8

A reputation is a fragile thing.

It all started with a simple idea: make a nutritious, high-quality, good-tasting flake of corn. Enter the one-and-only *Kellogg's Corn Flakes®* cereal.

Back in 1906, Mr. W.K. Kellogg never dreamed his delicate little creation would become the foundation upon which the Kellogg Company would grow to be the world's leading producer of cereal and a leading producer of wholesome snacks and other great-tasting foods.

Fifty years ago we were honored to have been counted among the original Fortune 500.

Today, we remain proud of our leadership position. And we think that through innovation and successful brand building our products will continue to excite consumers for the next 100 years.

Around the globe, over 25,000 Kellogg employees work diligently to make our company an example of consistency and reliability.

We continue to believe that over the long run our dedication to wholesome foods will lead not only to satisfied consumers, but healthy, dependable, long-term returns for our share-holders as well.

Like our founder, we believe that focus and attention to detail are what make a company truly great. That's why we'll never lose sight of Mr. Kellogg's original, simple idea.

And we'll stake our reputation on that.

Courtesy of Kellogg's.

CHAPTER SIX

Media Relations

One of the most critical areas within any corporate communication function is the media relations department. The media are both a constituency and a conduit through which investors, suppliers, retailers, and consumers receive information about and develop images of a company. Consumers, for instance, might see a *Dateline NBC* segment on a particular firm, or read an article about it in *BusinessWeek* or the *Wall Street Journal Online*. The media's role as disseminator of information to a firm's key constituencies has gained increasing importance over the years. Virtually every company has some kind of media relations department, whether it is one part-time consultant or a large staff of professionals.

In this chapter, we look at what media relations professionals do, and also how companies should approach increasingly sophisticated media. We examine who the media are, how firms communicate with the media through relationship building, and what constitutes a successful media relations program in today's changing environment for business.

The News Media

The news media are omnipresent in our society. With the advent of television in the late 1940s and early 1950s and the tremendous growth of the Internet in the 1990s, what had once been the domain of the print medium in newspapers increasingly has become part of the visual realm through television sets and computers.

The arrival of television moved the "headline news" that had formerly been found in newspapers to a new, nearly instantaneous medium. Newspapers adapted by taking over the kind of analysis that had previously appeared in weekly news magazines like *Time* and *Newsweek*. The news magazines, in turn, took over the feature writing that used to appear in older monthlies like *Look* and the *Saturday Evening Post*.

Referred to as "the press" in earlier times, the expanded media are a powerful part of society. The First Amendment of the Constitution guarantees the right of free speech in the United States, and over the years, the media have helped shape attitudes in this country on issues as diverse as gun control and hemlines, abortion and corporate pay. A free press also makes politicians accountable for their actions in both public and private life. Even politicians would argue that the media bring the distant world of politics into the home of the average citizen.

While most Americans feel strongly about the rights of a free press to say or print whatever it likes as long as it is not malicious, business has always had a more antagonistic relationship with the press. This stems in part from the privacy corporations enjoyed in the early part of this century. Unaccustomed to dealing with the news media, most companies simply acted as if they didn't matter. Later in the twentieth century, companies were forced to rethink this isolationist approach due to a number of developments, including laws governing the disclosure of certain information by public companies at regular intervals, a Supreme Court ruling in 1964 that required proof of malicious intent to win libel cases against the media, more public interest in business (see Chapter 1), and more media interest in business.

These last two events in particular—increased public and media interest—had a profound effect on business and its dealings with the media. Which came first? Although it is difficult to determine whether the media generated heightened interest in business or was simply responding to changes in public attitudes, what is certain is that sometime in the 1970s, business coverage started to change. Since then, the private sector has become much more public.

Part of what perpetuated this shift in attitudes was the public's realization that business had a tremendous effect on their lives. Incidents like the oil embargo, environmental problems at Love Canal, and questionable advertising on children's television programs all became enmeshed in other controversies in the 1970s such as Watergate and the Vietnam War. People began to see companies as controlling important parts of their lives but not having to answer to anyone in the way that government did to voters. Special interest groups emerged to deal with this problem and to make business more accountable.

Business leaders, on the other hand, were used to the privacy they had maintained for decades and were reluctant to admit that times had changed. Even today, some older business professionals resist accepting the importance of communicating through the media and would rather maintain little or no relationship with what they see as an institution that tries to tear down everything they build up. This kind of attitude is increasingly risky, and less common, however, as each industry—from oil and gas, to financial services, to pharmaceuticals—has found itself the subject of some level of scrutiny from the public and the media, and many companies have learned the hard way that having poor or nonexistent relationships with the media in these situations will only make them worse.

The Growth of Business Coverage in the Media

Before the 1970s, business news was relegated to a few pages toward the back of the newspaper (consisting mostly of stock quotations) and to a handful of business magazines; it received virtually no coverage at all in national and local television news broadcasts. As public attitudes changed, however, the business news sections in newspapers gained recognition and began to expand. Since the media are interested in satisfying the needs of readers and viewers, they had to meet the public's growing interest in the private sector and its participants.

Around the same time that the *New York Times* developed Business Day, a separate section published every day devoted to business issues, the *Wall Street Journal* became the number-one selling newspaper in the United States. Business magazines started to become profitable, and television networks and their local affiliates began to devote segments to business news.

Today, so many magazines and Web sites are devoted to business news that it is nearly impossible to find a topic not thoroughly covered by one media outlet or another. In recent years, news of corporations, the stock market, and business personalities has often become the lead story on national news television and radio broadcasts. With the 24-hour networks and all-day business coverage you can find on FOX, CNBC and CNN, corporate news is virtually impossible to ignore.

Compared to decades past, business news today is actually exciting. The large format *Fortune* magazine found in doctors' offices in the 1950s and 1960s was basically a dull vehicle for companies to express their points of view. *Fortune* was more successful than others, however, because it allowed executives to check its quotes—a practice then unknown anywhere other than this one magazine. Today its cover stories appeal to a wider audience. *Forbes* gains attention from a broad readership by publishing salaries of top entertainers, while *BusinessWeek* attracts an audience through features such as its widely read rankings of business schools and corporate boards.

As coverage of business increased, however, the media industry was consolidating. Fifty corporations controlled the vast majority of all news media in the United States in 1983. By 2004, only five corporations owned and operated 90 percent of this country's "mass media."[1] Thus, economics plays a big part in what gets covered, as major industrial companies worry more about the bottom line at their media subsidiary (for instance, General Electric and its NBC network).

In addition, buyouts and layoffs in the media industry have led to smaller newsrooms on tighter budgets. As a result, many reporters have to produce stories by themselves—the TV reporter who only did on-camera work is now responsible for the development of an entire story. Print reporters need to think more today about photos and graphics if they want to capture the attention of a public inundated with information.

Most executives today recognize that the media are typically not going to get very excited about the good things that companies do. Instead, the worse the news is about a company or its CEO, the more likely it is to become a major news story that will capture the media's (and the public's) attention, if only briefly. A 1997 study conducted by the Pew Research Center revealed that the public wanted more reporting on corrupt business practices by a margin of 60 to 28 percent.[2] By 2005, this impulse for more transparency and great reporting on business had morphed into a growing movement toward making journalism more transparent and treating the public as a partner in the process rather than a passive participant. The rise of online news from nontraditional sources in the form of bloggers is further proof of this trend and lends further support for corporations developing a thoughtful approach to its media relations with both traditional and nontraditional media.[3]

[1] Media Reform Information Center Web site, http://www.corporations.org/media (retrieved July 5, 2005).

[2] "Bad News: Another Study Finds Media Really Has Problems," *PR Reporter*, April 7, 1997, p. 1.

[3] Pew Charitable Trusts Survey, "Online Newspaper Readership Countering Print Losses: Public More Critical of Press, but Goodwill Persists," June 26, 2005, p. 17.

Building Better Relations with the Media

To build better relationships with members of the media, organizations must take the time to cultivate relationships with the right people in the media. This might be handled by employees within the company's media relations department (if one exists) or given to a public relations firm to handle. Either way, companies should be sure to avoid falling into some of the common pitfalls of what has historically been media relations "standard practice."

For example, most of the old-style public relations experts rely on a system of communication with the media that no longer works. That system is to send out press releases (or video news releases) to a mass audience and hope that someone will pick up the story and write about it. Why is this system no longer valid? The vast majority of press releases go unread by reporters in the United States—due to both the massive quantities of releases these reporters receive daily and the time constraints under which reporters work. The same is true for mail, e-mail, and voice mails from public relations agencies. Journalists who write about business for national publications such as *U.S. News & World Report* or *The Wall Street Journal* can receive hundreds of such releases in one day. "With all of the mail, faxes, and phone calls, it's really overwhelming," says Martha Groves, a staff reporter at the *Los Angeles Times*. "I'd guess I only use 10 percent of the mail I receive."[4]

When Federal Express and fax machines first came into daily use in the 1980s, many public relations professionals started overnighting and faxing releases to reporters, thinking that they would look more serious and thus get read. While this may have worked for a while, reporters caught on to what was happening and began screening overnight letters for the trash, just as they had done with regular mail for years. The analogy to what many people face each night when they come home to a mailbox stuffed with catalogs is appropriate here—people are now almost programmed to jettison anything in their mailbox that does not have first-class postage on it. This is true for e-mail as well—any e-mail that isn't personally addressed to the recipient is likely to be deleted or programmed to be automatically sent to the spam folder.

While they can be very effective, press releases are overused by public relations executives because they are relatively easy to write—even formulaic in terms of composition—and they can be widely distributed to certain segments of the media thanks to sophisticated computer programs that now allow companies to target specific audiences. There are even firms that will provide such services.

Many such service providers can be found on the Internet. eReleases, for instance, pulls from its database of over 30,000 journalists to target and submit a company's press release; they also will write the release for an additional fee.[5] Public relations agencies charge thousands of dollars for the same kind of service. In-house public relations professionals also create and send out hundreds of such

---

[4] Mark Ivey, "Pitching the Press," *Hemispheres*, August 1994, pp. 33–36.

[5] eReleases Web site, http://www.ereleases.com (retrieved July 5, 2005).

press releases to the same people over and over again for such mundane stories as the promotion of a midlevel executive.

With such wide distribution to an audience that is already saturated with information, how can anyone expect that this strategy could work? Yet public relations firms claim that the system is still quite valid and embrace the similarity to direct mail mentioned above. Response rates of 2 percent are considered a success in the direct-mail business, and public relations executives now get excited if their release gets picked up by a handful of publications.

Part of the problem is that the measure of success in the media relations business has for years been the amount of "ink" (or coverage) that a company gets, whether aided by in-house professionals or an outside consultant. Yet few companies try to figure out what value a "hit" (as it is called in the business) in a relatively unimportant publication has in terms of a firm's overall communication strategy. Getting lots of ink, which means lots of articles written about a company, may not have any value if it does not help the company achieve the communication objective (see Chapter 2) it started out with in the first place.

As discussed later in this chapter, most communication measures to date have focused on the quantity or efficiency of communication output, like the amount of media coverage generated or changes in audience attitudes. This information will always be important within the communications function; however, a new approach to measurement is being developed using traditional communication data in a new way to demonstrate the specific value communication adds to any organization. A BenchPoint survey of 1,040 communications professionals on the topic of measurement found that the movement toward measurement is being led from the top of organizations, with board directors and CEOs most likely to say, "Measurement is an integral part of PR" and "We will do more measurement in the future."[6]

The message to companies about press releases is: Use mass-mailed releases sparingly. Organizations should reserve this method for stories that they are sure will have a wide audience. In such cases, the same result can be achieved by placing the story on the *Public Relations Newswire* (*PR Newswire*) or convincing the Associated Press to put the story out on its wire if it is a major story that will have mass appeal. Most of the time, what works better is to find out who the right journalists are for a given story. Companies seldom use this tactic, however, because it takes more time to conduct such research, and senior executives outside the corporate communication function may be reluctant to pitch a major story to just one journalist at a time.

In a field cluttered with information coming from a variety of sources, however, this is actually the best approach. Ron Alridge, former publisher and editorial director of *Electronic Media*, makes this point in his article "A Few Tips for Having Good Media Relations." He emphasizes: "Understand the news organization you are dealing with. I wouldn't bother to list this seemingly obvious rule if so many media relations types didn't break it so often. . . Ignorance is always a turnoff."[7]

---

[6] BenchPoint Report on Measurement, 2004, http://www.benchpoint.com.

[7] Ron Alridge, "A Few Tips for Having Good Media Relations," *Electronic Media*, December 7, 1992, p. 48.

Conducting Research for Targeting Media

The way a typical media research operation might unfold for a company is as follows. First, senior managers working with the members of the corporate communication department determine what objectives they have for a certain story. Let's assume, for example, that the story is about a major company that is moving into a new foreign market. The managers' objective might be to create awareness about the move into the new market and also to discuss how the firm has changed its global strategy. Thus, this story is part of an overall trend at the company rather than a one-shot, tactical move. Given these considerations, the company would begin to search for the right place to pitch the story.

To do this, the corporate communication professionals look in their files to find out who covers their industry and the company specifically. This is relatively easy for most companies to do since the same reporters typically cover the same beat for a period of time and have established relationships with the company either directly or indirectly in that process. Some of these reporters—typically those from print journalism—would definitely be interested in the story. If the company is maintaining its records properly, it can determine at a glance which reporters will most likely cover the story and, more importantly, who will be likely to write a "balanced story" (code words for a positive piece) about this strategic move.

How do companies determine who is going to write a positive piece before rather than after pitching the piece? This is where ongoing research pays off. Each time a journalist covers a firm in the industry, corporate communication professionals need to determine what *angle* the reporter has taken. To continue with our example, suppose a look at the records shows that the *Wall Street Journal* reporter who covered the company's beat has recently written a piece about a competitor firm moving into a different market as part of its new global strategy. Chances are, this reporter will not be interested in writing the same story again about another company. Thus, the company should not pitch its story to this reporter.

By conducting this kind of research, companies can avoid giving reporters information that they are not interested in, and communications need only occur when a company's media audience is most likely to be receptive. While this system is not foolproof, it generally yields better results than sending out a story to 300 reporters hoping that four or five may pick it up, with no idea who they are or what angle they are likely to take on the story.

Today, most companies can easily access information about the journalists who cover them. Consultants generate computer analyses of reporters' articles, ask industry sources to provide critiques of writers they know, and even find out personal information about them. While earlier generations of PR professionals worked hard to get such information at long lunches with reporters, new technology allows CorpComm professionals to access such information through electronic databases, such as Bacon's MediaSource or the Bulldog Reporter's MediaBase.

In addition to figuring out who is covering a company's beat, the firm's corporate communication team needs to determine what kind of a reporter they are dealing with. For a television network, such as CNN, this means knowing who the producer for the piece will be. Then a communications professional from the company can call the head office in Atlanta and purchase the producer's last two or three stories. For a business magazine such as *Forbes*, electronic databases—such as LexisNexis or Factiva—contain stories that reporters have written over a period of time. Those written in the last two years are most likely to be useful to your company.

What can CorpComm professionals learn by looking at previous stories the producer at CNN has filed and earlier stories that the *Forbes* reporter has written? An individual tends to write about things or put together reports in a particular way. Very few reporters change their style from one story to the next. They have found an approach that works for them—a formula, so to speak—and they tend to stick with formulas that work.

What this kind of analysis usually reveals is that the journalist tends to write or present stories with a particular point of view. One such analysis performed for a company on a *Forbes* reporter's work showed that he liked to write "turnaround" stories. That is, he liked to present the opposite point of view from what everyone else had written about. So, if a company, for example, is trying to make a case for such a turnaround, this reporter would be more likely to write the kind of article that would be helpful for the company despite his negative tone.

Watching the CNN producer's work could help determine how this individual conducts interviews, how the stories are edited, whether he or she likes to use charts and graphs as part of the story, and so on. Let's say that the producer, for example, seems to present balanced interviews, as opposed to antagonistic ones, and likes to use charts and graphs. Again, this makes it seem as if such a producer could easily turn out a positive story for the company—a goal that should be pursued.

Corporate communication departments should perform the type of analysis discussed above for each call that comes in. Many executives complain about the amount of time such analysis takes, but the benefits of handling an interview with this kind of preparation make the effort involved well worthwhile.

Responding to Media Calls

In addition to doing their homework on reporters, companies can strengthen their relationships with the media through the way they handle requests for information. Many companies willingly spend millions of dollars on advertising but are unwilling to staff a media relations department with enough personnel to handle incoming calls from the media.

This can be a costly mistake, as responding to such requests carefully can make a powerful difference in how the company appears in the story. Let's say that a company has gotten negative press over the last couple of years because it has not kept up with the times, but it is now working on a campaign to change its reputation. A call comes in from a reporter at CNN and another call comes in from a reporter at *Forbes*. What should the communications staff do to ensure that both of these requests are met in a timely manner and one that will reflect best on the company?

To begin with, calls should come into a central office that deals with all requests for information from important national media. While this sounds like common sense, calls are often answered by an operator or electronic system who cannot distinguish between important and unimportant calls from the media. Many an opportunity has been lost because an operator or automated system failed to get the right message to someone in the corporate communication department.

Next, the person who takes the call should try to find out what angle the reporter is taking on the story. In our example, the CNN reporter may or may not have a particular point of view, but the *Forbes* reporter probably does, since that publication prides itself on taking a particular approach to its stories. The company needs to find out what that approach is before responding to their request. Let's assume that the CNN reporter wants to look at the company's activities as part of an industry trend toward more upscale positioning. The *Forbes* reporter, on the other hand, seems to imply from the conversation that she sees the company's new approach in a less-than-positive light.

The person responsible for that telephone call should try to get as much information as possible while being careful not to give in return any information that is not already public knowledge. The tone of the conversation should be as friendly as possible, and the media relations professional should communicate honestly about the possibilities of arranging an interview or meeting other requests. At the same time, he or she should find out what kind of deadline the reporter is working under.

This is often a point of contention between business and the media. Particularly with senior executives who are accustomed to arranging schedules at their own convenience, a call from the media at an inconvenient time can be an annoyance. But all reporters must meet deadlines. This means that they have to file their stories—whether on television or radio, in print, or on the Web—on a certain date, by a certain time. These deadlines usually have little flexibility, so knowing in advance what the deadline is allows you to respond within the allotted time. The conversation should end with the media relations professional agreeing to get back to the reporter within the allotted time. Being aware of deadlines is similarly critical when proactively pitching a story to avoid irritating reporters under deadline crunches and, by doing so, leaving them with a negative impression of the company.

Preparing for Media Interviews

Once the research and analysis are complete, the executive who will be interviewed needs to be prepared for the actual meeting with the reporter. If the interview is to be conducted by phone, as is often the case for print articles, a media relations professional should plan to sit in on the interview. The following approach works best.

First, the executive should be given a short briefing on the reporter or producer's prior work, using examples gathered in the research phase discussed earlier, so that he or she develops a clear understanding of the reporter's point of view. For example, if the reporter tends to write turnaround pieces, the appropriate passages from relevant stories should be shown to the executive.

One Fortune 500 CEO prepared for an interview with CNN by watching the last two or three major stories the producer had filed. Having done so, he was able to begin the conversation with the producer by saying how much he liked one of the stories. This positive beginning set the tone for the rest of the interview. Additionally, after learning that the producer always used a list of bullet points as part of each story, the CEO developed a list of points he wanted to communicate about the company in bullet-point form and handed it to him before he left. When the story was broadcast, it was positive on the company and the list of bullet points was right up there on the television screen, which delighted the CEO, who had worried for days about the interview.

Once the executive has been briefed on the reporter's background and likely angle, he or she should be given a set of questions that the reporter is likely to ask. These questions can be developed from what the communications staff member working on this interview has gleaned in previous conversations with the reporter, from an analysis of the reporter's work, and from what seem to be the critical issues on the subject. If possible, the communications specialist should arrange a trial run with the executive to go over answers to possible questions. The executive also should understand that the agenda for a news story is hard to change—once the reporter has decided to write or produce a particular kind of story, it is difficult to introduce a new topic into the discussion.

In preparing for a television interview, a full-dress rehearsal is absolutely essential. The interview should look as if it is totally natural and unrehearsed when it actually occurs, but the executive should be prepared well in advance. This means thinking about what to communicate to the reporter no matter what he or she asks during the interview. While the executive cannot change the agenda for the interview, as discussed earlier, he or she can get certain points across as the dialogue moves from one idea to the next.

In addition to thinking about what to say, the executive needs to think about the most interesting approach to expressing these messages. Using statistics and anecdotes can help bring ideas alive in an interview. What is interesting, however, depends on the audience. Many people mistakenly assume that the reporter is their audience, but it is the people who will watch the interview with whom they are really communicating. Communications professionals and executives must keep this in mind in determining the best approach for a television interview. (See Chapter 2 for more on communication strategy, especially analyzing constituencies.)

Finally, the executive needs to be prepared to state key ideas as clearly as possible at the beginning of the interview. Answers to questions need to be as succinct as possible. Especially in television, where sound bites of three or four seconds are the rule rather than the exception, executives need training to get complicated ideas into a compact form that the general public can easily understand. Andrew Grant, head of Tulchan Communications and a 10-year veteran of Brunswick Public Relations, advises: "A chief executive must distill the company into a story he or she can tell over lunch and a journalist should be able to walk away and write it down on the back of a cigarette packet."[8]

Gauging Success

As mentioned earlier, the amount of ink a company gets does not indicate whether it is achieving its communication objectives. Verizon keeps records of all of its hits, looking at not only where the ink has landed but also how well the company's key

[8] Dan Bilefsky, "Join the Sultans of Spin Media Relations," *Financial Times*, July 13, 2000, p. 19.

INTERVIEW TIPS

Communications expert Mary Munter suggests the following tips when preparing for a media interview:[1]

- Keep answers short; think in 10-second sound bites.
- Avoid saying "no comment"; explain why you can't answer and promise to get back to the reporter when you can.
- Listen carefully to each question; think about your response; only answer the question you were asked.

- Use "bridging" to move the interviewer from his/her question to your communication objective.
- Use anecdotes, analogies, and simple statistics to make your point.
- Keep your body language in mind throughout the interview.

[1] Adapted from Mary Munter, "How to Conduct a Successful Media Interview," *California Management Review,* Summer 1983, pp. 143–50.

messages are communicated. Nancy Bavec, former director of media relations at Verizon, explains, "My entire department's compensation is tied to our ability to elevate our media scores."[9] Part of elevating Verizon's media score is finding out where the media hits have landed (with what constituencies), not just determining that the media carried a story on the company.

AT&T also actively tracks its media score. In 1996, the company launched a new measurement initiative aimed at revealing how effective it was at communicating with the media. The research was focused on the organization's trouble spots and used clipping services to track media coverage. In addition, AT&T contracted research and consulting firm Yankelovich Partners to conduct an annual survey of business journalists to gauge perceptions of AT&T and its media relations staff.[10]

Not only was this information useful for improving the company's media relations within the company, but the information provided by all the measurement research also allowed AT&T to benchmark its results against those of its competitors. In the end, according to John Heath, a media relations manager at AT&T, "the media tracking ignited changes and improvements in AT&T's media relations department."[11]

In addition to this sort of media monitoring and analysis, the more sophisticated approach to measurement of media relations referenced earlier has the power to

- Identify which communications activities create the most value in terms of a specific business outcome.
- Evaluate how well an organization's various communications functions perform against an industry average.

[9] Quoted in "How Do Your PR Efforts Measure Up in the Wired World?" *Interactive PR and Marketing News,* November 26, 1999, p. 1.

[10] "Measurement Helps Telecom Giant Think Quicker," *PR News,* September 27, 1999, p. 1.

[11] Ibid.

- Demonstrate the total value created by a CorpComm department in terms of one or more business outcomes.
- Drive strategic and tactical decision making in the communications function, hedging reputational risk, and managing major events such as mergers and top management changes.
- Highlight actual corporate value created by communications activities.[12]

Maintaining Ongoing Relationships

By far the most critical component in media relations is developing and maintaining a network of contacts with the media. Building and maintaining close relationships is a prerequisite for generating coverage. A company cannot simply turn the relationship on and off when a crisis strikes or when it has something it would like to communicate to the public. Instead, firms need to work to develop long-term relationships with the right journalists for their specific industry. This usually means meeting with reporters just to build goodwill and credibility. The media relations director should meet regularly with journalists who cover the industry and also should arrange yearly meetings between key reporters and the CEO. The more private and privileged these sessions are, the better the long-term relationship is likely to be.

One example of a company's successful efforts to build strong media relations is Matalan Clothing Retailers in the United Kingdom. The company offers journalists tours of its headquarters, including opportunities to try on its clothing in changing rooms and, most surprisingly, to fully analyze its distribution network. Chris Lynch of Ludgate Communications, a representative of Matalan, explains, "We tactically avoid granting phone interviews in order to get journalists to meet us face-to-face. Otherwise it ends up being just about the numbers."[13] By taking such a personalized approach, Matalan quickly became a favorite company among journalists. This success has continued with Matalan recently winning "Home Retailer of the Year" in the National Home Awards sponsored by the *Daily Telegraph*.[14]

Many companies take a less "integrated" approach than Matalan and use the more typical venue of a meeting between a member of the media and a company executive. Since these meetings often have no specific agenda, they can be awkward for all but the most skilled communicators. Within organizations, people assigned to handle media relations should enjoy "meeting and greeting," should be tapped into the company's top-line strategic agenda, and should be able to think creatively.

Often these kinds of meetings occur at lunch or breakfast. They should be thought of as a time to share information about what is going on at the company, but with no expectation that a story will necessarily appear anytime soon. In the course of such a conversation, the skillful media relations professional will determine what is most

---

[12] Paul Argenti, "Demonstrating the Value of Communications through Measurement," July 2005.

[13] Bilefsky, "Join the Sultans of Spin Media Relations," p. 19.

[14] Matalan Web site, http://www.matalan.co.uk (retrieved July 5, 2005).

likely to interest the reporter later as a possible story. Without being blatant about it, he or she can then follow up at the appropriate time with the information or interviews that the reporter wants.

Media relations professionals should expect to be rebuffed from time to time. They may get turned down for lunch several times by reporters who are particularly busy, only to find them very receptive to a long telephone conversation. As is true with personal relationships, media relations professionals will find that they simply do not get along with every journalist they come into contact with. Unless the reporter is the only one covering a company's beat at an important national media outlet, this should not be an insurmountable problem. Where personality conflicts do occur, professionals can and should work around them to ensure that the overall relationship of the company with that media outlet is not jeopardized and media opportunities are not missed.

One hotel executive at a major chain didn't think that he needed to have any sort of relationship with the reporter covering his beat at *The Wall Street Journal*. After almost two years of being left out of nearly every major story on the industry, a consultant persuaded him to try again to establish a relationship with this reporter. The reporter was only too happy to make amends as well since she needed the company's cooperation as much as they needed her. Nonetheless, that attitude cost the company nearly two years of possible coverage that it would not get back.

Building a Successful Media Relations Program

What does it take, then, to create a successful media relations program? First, organizations must be willing to devote resources to the effort. This does not necessarily have to mean huge outlays of money; an executive's time can be just as valuable.

Jim Koch, brewmaster and president of the company that makes Sam Adams beer, brought his beer into the national limelight through the skillful use of media relations with the help of one outside consultant at a fraction of the cost of a national advertising program. More recently, on a much smaller scale, two sisters who started a greeting card company that specialized in cards that targeted a gay audience were interested in building a relationship with the media. Through their own efforts, writing letters, reading the newspapers to find out who the best reporters would be for their message, they were able to get hits in both the *New York Times* and *The Wall Street Journal*. In both cases, the media relations effort paid off in sales, which was the ultimate goal.

For many larger companies, the media relations effort will involve more personnel and often the use of outside counsel. What follows is what is needed, at a minimum, for the effort.

Involve Media Relations Personnel in Strategy

As one public relations executive at a large company put it, "They like to keep us in the dark, like mushrooms, and then they expect us to get positive publicity, usually at the last minute." Instead, companies need to involve someone, preferably the most senior corporate communication executive, in the decision-making process. Once a decision has been made, it is much more difficult to talk management out of it because of potential problems with communications.

While the communications point of view will not always win in the discussions that take place at top management meetings, having these individuals involved will at least allow everyone to be familiar with the pros and cons of each situation and decision. Communications professionals who are involved in the decision-making process also feel more ownership for the ideas that they need to present to the media.

Develop In-House Capabilities

While using consultants and public relations firms may be beneficial in some cases, by far the best approach for the long term is to develop an in-house media relations staff. As we have seen throughout this chapter, there is no magic to what communications professionals do, and the company can save thousands of dollars a month by using staff within the company and investing in the right databases to conduct research for analyzing the media.

One problem for many companies, however, is that they do not consider media relations to be important enough to hire professional staff in this area. Lawyers, executive assistants, and even accountants often handle communications because of the unfortunate assumption that, since "anyone can communicate," it doesn't matter who you put on this assignment. Companies must recognize that building relations with the media is a skill and that individuals with certain personalities and backgrounds are better suited to the task than others.

Companies also should not make the mistake of assuming that a former reporter will be the best person for the job. After all, if the reporter had been good at reporting, he or she probably would not be looking to change professions. Also, journalism graduates are likely to have been trained by people with doctorates but with little or no experience as reporters or editors.[15]

Use Outside Counsel Sparingly

Companies should hire outside counsel for advice or information (i.e., as consultants), to help out with a major story, or when a crisis hits. Otherwise, what you are typically hiring when you hire a major public relations firm is the time of a recent college graduate who is getting training to one day take the in-house job that you have waiting in your own company.

Another important use for outside firms is to help with the distribution of press releases and to create video news releases. This type of communication can be valuable for a company trying to get its message across to a wide audience. What these firms do is put together what looks like a real news story. It is then sent up via satellite for anyone to take down for their nightly news broadcasts. The better firms usually do a finished version of the story with a reporter, and then send "B-roll," which is backup tape, so that the local station or network can put together its own story.

---

[15] Iver Peterson, "Journalism Education Less Focused on the News," *New York Times*, May 5, 1996, p. D7.

Developing an Online Media Strategy

Until recently, media coverage—newspaper headlines or more in-depth profiles on television news shows like *60 Minutes*—has been the primary means for exposing corporate flaws. Accordingly, companies with well-managed media relations programs have had some leverage to get their own side of the story communicated to the public. Over the last two decades, however, wireless communication and the Internet have transferred an enormous amount of power into the hands of individuals. As Patricia Sturdevant, general counsel to the Washington-based National Association of Consumer Advocates, explains, "The Internet is a very effective new weapon for the consumer. Before the Internet, unless you had a lot of time or money, there wasn't any way to get the public's attention to a problem. Now, you can broadcast it to the entire world in an instant."[16] We will see in Chapter 10 that one disgruntled Dunkin' Donuts customer created a crisis situation for the company by launching his own anticompany Web site.

The Internet Age has many implications for business, including an expansion to individuals of powers that were previously concentrated in the hands of the organized media. Accordingly, companies' media strategies need to be augmented with tactics for dealing with this new dimension of coverage, including, for instance, establishing a forum for constituencies to share opinions, concerns, and complaints about the company, and a proactive effort to monitor information circulating about the company in various media channels including blogs.

As we discussed earlier in this chapter, the Internet has become a valuable tool that enables companies to get press releases out quickly and broadly. Unfortunately, however, the Internet does not discriminate between legitimate news and phony claims, and both are transmitted with equal speed and reach. In August 2000, a man in California e-mailed a phony press release about a company called Emulex to Internet Wire, posing as an employee of the company's PR firm. The press release stated that Emulex was revising its last quarter's profits to show a loss, that its CEO was stepping down, and that the company was being investigated by the Securities and Exchange Commission (SEC). Believing the release to be legitimate, Internet Wire posted it the following morning. The news about Emulex spread so rapidly that by 10:30 that same morning, when trading in Emulex shares was suspended on NASDAQ after the release was revealed to be fraudulent, Emulex's share price had fallen to $43 from $113.06 at the previous day's close.[17]

The perpetrator, a former employee of Internet Wire, had devised the scheme to drive Emulex's share price down so that he could recover money he was losing due to his own short position in the company's stock. His technological savvy had allowed him to create a phony e-mail account so that his message to Internet Wire looked as if it really came from the company's PR firm, and his familiarity with the terminology of Web-based releases gained during his own tenure at Internet Wire contributed to the seeming legitimacy of the press release. As the Internet is

---

[16] Rachel Beck, "Disgruntled Voices in Cyberspace Heard Loud and Clear," *AP Online*, May 4, 1999.

[17] Josh Meyer, "Suspect Held in Online Stock Market Fraud," *Los Angeles Times*, September 1, 2000, p. 1.

increasingly used as a tool to communicate company news to various constituencies, more care will have to be taken that sources are trusted and reliable. The Emulex case has surely promoted this kind of circumspection.

Because of the widespread reach of the Internet, a growing number of companies are paying more attention to the Web, realizing that bad publicity online can legitimately threaten their bottom line. Large corporations such as Verizon, Levi-Strauss, and Dell spend between $150,000 and $2 million annually on monitoring the Web.[18] Some firms assign employees or obtain external specialists to gather this kind of information. Search engines such as Google and Yahoo! are good places to start investigating. The "consumer opinion" section on Yahoo!'s site alone (http://dir.yahoo.com) lists over 300 consumer opinion sites—criticizing companies like American Express, Ford, Nike, Wal-Mart, and even Yahoo! itself.[19]

Extend Your Media Relations Strategy to the Blogosphere

Studies have shown that the public is often far more trusting of other consumers than it is of traditional institutions, including corporations.[20] This helps explain the phenomenal rise of the blog from the 1990s to the present. Blogs are publicly accessible personal Web sites that serve as sources of commentary, opinion, and information on a variety of topics. There were 10 million blogs in the United States at the end of 2005 and because of their speed, bloggers can and do alter the volume and tone of any conversation.[21] For example, bloggers played a role in the 2004 presidential election, with Howard Dean's *Blog for America* helping recruit volunteers and raise money. In January 2005, bloggers in Thailand, Indonesia, and India posted videos, photographs, and updates immediately and around the clock for weeks, outpacing more traditional news media who didn't have reporters in the area.

The most influential blogs, such as Instapundit and Daily Kos, attract more than 100,000 visitors as day—a number for any media relations professional to take seriously. In addition, blogs are an important tool for corporations to track consumer points of view and concerns. Many savvy media relations professionals have targeted lists of bloggers they contact because blogs are a growing and important media outlet.[22]

The following are some guidelines on blogs:

- Take blogs seriously. Find those that seem to be most interesting for your industry, bookmark them, and read them regularly.
- Act fast. If you need to respond to something on a blog, do so quickly and honestly. Similarly, if you are writing a corporate blog, make sure it is transparent and very up-to-date. Some corporations, such as McDonald's and Mazda, have

---

[18] "Cyber Snipers Underscore Need for PR Intelligence on the Web," *PR News*, September 20, 1999, Online Lexis-Nexis Academic, August 2001.

[19] Amelia Kassel, "Guide to Internet Monitoring and Clipping," CyberAlert White Paper, http://www.cyberalert.com/whitepaper.html.

[20] Lee Rainie, Pew Internet & American Life Project, "Data Memo: The State of Blogging," January 2005.

[21] Edelman and Intelliseek, "Trust 'MeDIA': How Real People are Finally Being Heard," White paper, Spring 2005.

[22] Ibid.

tried to tap into the power of the blogospere by creating fake blogs only to have this backfire when real bloggers exposed them.

- Don't dismiss requests for interviews and information from bloggers. Many are also established journalists, and if they are unhappy with your attitude, you may find your e-mail exchange published in full on their site.[23]

Just as the Internet can present problems for companies, it also can offer opportunities. Tapping into the information circulating on the Internet can give companies extraordinary access to information about customer needs and complaints. Monitoring Internet "chats" and blogs can enable companies to learn about current constituency needs and tailor actions to meet those that are most vital to the company's reputation and bottom line. By using the Internet proactively, companies can glean valuable insights about constituency attitudes, sentiments, and reactions to which they might otherwise not have access. In many ways, a company should view the Internet as an unprecedented and ideal survey group. Without a doubt, online monitoring can help companies gauge the sentiments of constituencies, allow them to respond effectively, and help them stay on top of today's information surge. However, companies should not become so consumed by the power of the Internet that they neglect other important media channels.

Handle Negative News Effectively

When a company does stumble upon bad news circulating about itself—be it a condemning attack in the blogosphere or a hostile op-ed article in a daily newspaper—the communications department should quickly assess the potential damage that the news might cause. Who is the person who has issued the complaint? Are the comments valid? Is the person speaking only as an individual, or does she or he represent a broader constituency, such as investors or employees? If a broader constituency, how widespread are the complaints? If a rogue Web site has been constructed, how many hits per day has it received, and how have people generally responded to the negative message? If an unflattering newspaper article has been printed, how wide is the paper's circulation?

Once these questions are answered, a company's task force or permanent crisis communication team—including members of senior management—must brainstorm some potential actions. Company lawyers should be consulted to discuss what legal stance the company might need to take. Lawyers will be able to offer advice about whether newspaper articles, Web sites, or blogs are defamatory, warranting a lawsuit against the perpetrator.

Conclusion

As technology develops new mechanisms for disseminating information, and as corporate communication professionals are able to develop databases through the use of more sophisticated software, the media relations function will continue to evolve away from the old PR flak model into a professional group that can help organizations get their message out quickly, honestly, and to the right media.

[23] Maja Pawinska Sims, "Monitoring the Web—Blogging, the Great Untapped Resource," *PR Week*, June 10, 2002.

Companies today are under constant scrutiny from many of their constituencies. A demand for instantaneous information accompanies this public watchfulness, and the pressure is increasing with each new technological innovation. Managers must be prepared to answer this demand by considering all constituencies—online or offline—in dealing with the media agents who inform them. By crafting messages with care and using proper media channels, companies can tap into this powerful "conduit constituency," the media, to ensure that their voices are heard.

Adolph Coors Company

Shirley Richard returned from lunch one April afternoon in 1982 and found a message on her desk that Allan Maraynes from CBS had phoned while she was out. "God, what's this?" was all she could say as she picked up the phone to discuss the call with her boss, John McCarty, vice president for corporate public affairs. Now in her second year as head of corporate communication for the nation's fifth-largest brewer, Richard was well aware of the Adolph Coors Company's declining popularity—a decline that she partially blamed on an ongoing conflict with organized labor. But the conflict was hardly breaking news, and she was almost afraid to ask why CBS was interested in the company.

Richard found out from her boss that Maraynes was a producer for the network's news program, *60 Minutes*. Reporter Mike Wallace had already phoned McCarty to announce plans for a *60 Minutes* report about the company. Program executives at CBS were aware of accusations of unfair employment practices that the AFL-CIO had raised against Coors and wanted to investigate the five-year battle between the brewery and organized labor.

Once McCarty explained the message from Maraynes, Shirley Richard sank into her chair. She had spent the last year working hard to understand organized labor and its nationwide boycott of Coors beer, and she was convinced that the company was being treated unfairly. She believed the union represented only a small subset of Coors's otherwise satisfied workforce. But Richard also doubted whether the facts could speak for themselves and was wary of the AFL-CIO's ability to win over the media. She was well aware of Mike

Wallace's reputation for shrewd investigative reporting and was reassured to some extent that the program would portray the company fairly.

On the other hand, *60 Minutes* was considered by many corporations as anti-big-business, and Richard had no idea how corporate officials would respond under the pressure of lights, camera, and the reporter's grilling questions. McCarty and Richard met with the two Coors brothers to discuss the network's proposal and to determine whether producer Maraynes should even be allowed to visit the Coors facility. Company president Joseph ("Joe") Coors and chairman William ("Bill") Coors were skeptical of the prospect of airing the company's "dirty laundry" on national television. But McCarty was interested in the opportunity for Coors to come out into the public spotlight. Richard had already calculated the enormous risks involved in granting interviews with Wallace and filming the Coors plant and employees and knew the Coors brothers' reservations were warranted.

Richard was frustrated by growing support for the boycott, and her own strategies to deal with the problem had been unsuccessful. She believed the interview with CBS might only exacerbate an already difficult situation. Her own public relations effort had been an attempt to portray the circumstances as she believed them to be: good management harassed by disgruntled labor organizers. She was convinced that her job was not an effort to cover up Coors's employment practices. "PR doesn't make you into something you're not," Richard stated. "You can't whitewash."

Richard debated how the company should handle the proposal from CBS, realizing that the communications strategy could seriously affect the corporation's public image. Any decisions

Source: This case was researched and written by Professor Paul A. Argenti in 1985 and revised in 1994, 1998, 2002, and 2005.

about approaching *60 Minutes* also would have to be approved by the Coors brothers. Richard felt uncertain about how much control she would ultimately have over the communications strategy. Joe Coors, an ardent conservative and defender of private enterprise, would undoubtedly resist an open-door policy with the network. At the same time, Richard wondered if she should attempt to convince the management of this traditionally closed company to open itself to the scrutiny of a *60 Minutes* investigation or whether the best defense would be a "no comment" approach. But with no comment from Coors, anything organized labor was willing to say on camera would go uncontested.

HISTORY OF THE ADOLPH COORS COMPANY

The Coors brewery was established in 1880 by Adolph Coors, a Prussian-born immigrant who came to the United States in 1868. Having trained as an apprentice in a Prussian brewery, 22-year-old Adolph Coors became a foreman at the Stenger Brewery in Naperville, Illinois, in late 1869. By 1872, Coors owned his own bottling company in Denver, Colorado. With his knowledge of brewing beer and the financial assistance of Joseph Schueler, Coors established his own brewery in Golden, Colorado. His product was an immediate success. In 1880, Adolph Coors bought out Joseph Schueler and established a tradition of family ownership that was maintained for almost a century.

The company continued to operate during Prohibition, switching to production of malted milk. During Prohibition the Coors Company also expanded with the development of new manufacturing operations. A cement manufacturing facility and a porcelain products plant were essential to the company's survival during the 17 years of Prohibition. Its brewing operations flourished again when alcohol was legalized in 1933.

Famous for its exclusive "Rocky Mountain spring water" system of brewing, the Adolph Coors Company soon became something of a legend in the beer industry. The Coors philosophy was one of total independence. A broad spectrum of Coors subsidiaries combined to create a vertically integrated company in which Coors owned and managed every aspect of production: The Coors Container Manufacturing plant produced aluminum and glass containers for the beer; Coors Transportation Company provided refrigerated trucks to haul the beer to its distribution center as well as vehicles to transport coal to fuel the Golden brewery; Coors Energy Company bought and sold energy and owned the Keenesburg, Colorado, coal mine, which was expected to meet the brewery's coal needs through the end of the 20th century; the Golden Recycle Company was responsible for ensuring a supply of raw materials for aluminum can production. By 1980, the recycling plant was capable of producing over 30 million pounds of recycled aluminum a year. Other subsidiaries fully owned by Coors included Coors Food Products Company, Coors Porcelain Company, and the American Center for Occupational Health.

THE COORS MYSTIQUE

A certain mystique surrounding the Golden, Colorado, brewery and its unique unpasteurized product won the beer both fame and fortune. Presidents Eisenhower and Ford shuttled Coors to Washington aboard air force jets. Actors Paul Newman and Clint Eastwood once made it the exclusive beer on their movie sets. Business magazines lauded Coors as "America's cult beer." As Coors expanded its distribution, the mystique appeared irresistible; Coors moved from twelfth to fourth place among all brewers between 1965 and 1969 with virtually no advertising or marketing.

Part of the Coors mystique was attributed to its family heritage. For over a century of brewing, company management had remained in the hands of Adolph Coors's direct descendants. Reign passed first to Adolph Coors Jr., then to his son William Coors. In 1977, Bill Coors turned over the presidency to his younger brother Joseph but continued as chairman and chief executive officer. The company's newest president, Joe Coors, was a well-known backer of right-wing causes such as the John Birch Society; a founder of a conservative think-tank, the Heritage Foundation; and a member of President Ronald Reagan's so-called Kitchen Cabinet. The family name was closely associated with strong conservatism by consumers, labor, and the industry.

The Coors Company was built on a tradition of family and, even after going public in 1975, remained an organization closed to active public relations. Bill Coors recalled that his father, Adolph Coors Jr., was a shy man, and throughout its history the company was reluctant to attract any public attention. In 1960, the sensational kidnapping and murder of brother Adolph Coors III focused the public eye on the family and the business, but Coors maintained a strict "no comment" policy.

THE NATURE OF THE BREWING INDUSTRY

From the mid-1960s through the 1970s and into the 1980s, the brewing industry was characterized by a shrinking number of breweries coupled with a growing volume of production and consumption. In 1963, Standard and Poor's Industry Surveys reported 211 operating breweries. Ten years later that number had dropped to 129, and by 1980 there were only 100 breweries in operation. On the other hand, per capita consumption of beer rose from 15 gallons a year in 1963 to 19.8 gallons in 1973. By 1980, per capita consumption had jumped to 24.3 gallons a year.

Until the mid-1970s, beer markets were essentially local and regional, but as the largest breweries expanded, so did their share of the market. Combined, the top five brewers in 1974 accounted for 64 percent of domestic beer production, up from 59 percent in 1973.

Previously strong local and regional breweries were either bought by larger producers or ceased operations.

A notable exception, however, was the Adolph Coors Company, which dominated the West. Until 1976, the company's 12.3-million-barrel shipment volume was distributed only in California, Texas, and 10 other western states. Coors's share of the California market alone was well over 50 percent in 1976. Coors dominated its limited distribution area, capturing at least 35 percent of the market wherever it was sold statewide. The Coors Company ranked fifth in market share nationally throughout the 1970s, trailing giants Anheuser-Busch, Joseph Schlitz, Phillip Morris's Miller, and Pabst, all of which had much broader distribution areas.

Competition for market share among the top five brewers was intense during the 1970s and led producers to more aggressive attempts to win consumers. According to compilations by Leading National Advertisers, Inc., advertising expenditures for the first nine months of 1979 were up 37 percent from the previous year for Anheuser-Busch, 18 percent for Miller, 14 percent for both Schlitz and Pabst, and 78 percent for Adolph Coors.

MARKETING AND DISTRIBUTION AT COORS

Industry analysts criticized the Coors Company's sales strategy for stubbornly relying on its product's quality and image rather than marketing. In 1976, the Coors mystique appeared to be losing its appeal to strong competitors—for the first time since Prohibition, Coors could not sell all of its beer. The company finally responded to competition by intensifying its marketing and development operations. Between 1976 and 1981, the company attempted to revive sales by adding eight new states to its distribution. In May of 1978, Coors began to market its first new product in 20 years: Coors Light. In 1979, Coors began the first major advertising campaign in its history to defend itself against aggressive competitors such as Philip Morris's Miller Brewing Company and Anheuser-Busch. The company's 1981 annual report pictured Coors's newest product—George Killian's Irish Red Ale—along with a newly expanded package variety designed to "keep pace with consumer demand."

The Coors Company went public in 1975, but investors did not fare well as stock prices declined for the rest of the decade. Coors entered the market at a share price of $31 but by 1978 had fallen to $16—a loss of about 50 percent for the first public stockholders. Net income, according to the company's annual report, was $51,970,000 in 1981, or $1.48 per share. That figure reflected a 20 percent drop from $64,977,000, or $1.86 per share, in 1980.

MANAGEMENT–LABOR RELATIONS AT COORS

During pre-Prohibition years, breweries, including Coors, were entirely unionized. In 1914, the first vertically integrated industrial union in the country established itself at Coors. When the country went dry, Coors remained viable through alternative operations, but the workforce still had to be reduced. Coors offered older workers employment but fired younger employees. A strike of union employees resulted and remained in effect until 1933, when Prohibition was repealed. The company, however, continued to operate without a union until 1937 when Adolph Coors Jr. invited the United Brewery Workers International (UBW) into the Coors Company.

In 1953, the company experienced an abortive strike by the UBW to which a frightened management immediately gave in. In 1955, Coors's organized porcelain workers struck because their wages were less than those of brewery workers. Although the plant continued to operate, all of Coors's unionized workers engaged in a violent strike that lasted almost four months. The union ultimately lost the battle 117 days after the strike, when workers returned to the plant on company terms.

Negotiations over a new union contract in 1957 ended in a stalemate between labor and management, and workers again decided to strike. For another four months, workers were torn between paternalistic and small-town personal ties to management and the demands of the union. Bill Coors, who was then the plant manager, recalled that during the strike, management had wanted to show the union it was not dependent on union workers. Coors hired college students during the summer of 1957 as temporary replacements for the striking brewers. When the students left, the picketers were threatened by management's vow to hire permanent replacements and returned to the plant. The strike was a clear defeat of the union's demands and ultimately left international union leaders with an unresolved bitterness toward Coors. Back in full operation by the fall of 1957, Coors management believed it had won complete control.

By the end of the 1950s, 15 local unions were organized at Coors. Management tolerated the unions, but claimed they did not affect wages or employment practices. The Coors family firmly believed that good management removed the need for union protection and that management could win workers' loyalty. In 1960, the plant's organized electricians went on strike but failed to garner the support of other unions, and the plant continued to operate with nonunion electricians hired to replace the strikers. Similar incidents occurred with Coors's other unions. A 1968 strike by building and construction workers ended with Coors breaking up 14 unions. By 1970, Coors's workforce was predominantly nonunion.

A contract dispute between Coors's management and UBW Local 366 erupted in 1976. Workers demanded a 10 percent wage increase and better retirement benefits. After more than a year of negotiations, union officials rejected management's compromise offer, which labor contended would erode workers' rights. In April of 1977, over 94 percent of UBW workers voted to strike. Production at the plant continued at 70 percent of normal capacity, however, and management boldly announced plans to replace striking workers. In defense of the union, AFL-CIO officials declared a nationwide boycott of the beer until a new contract settlement was reached. But within five days of initiating the strike, 39 percent of the union members crossed the picket lines to return to work.

In 1978, Coors management called an election for decertification of UBW Local 366. Because more than a year had passed since the strike began, National Labor Relations regulations restricted striking union members from voting. Only workers remaining at the plant, including "scabs" hired across the picket lines, could vote on whether to maintain the UBW Local. In December of that year, Coors employees voted a resounding 71 percent in favor of decertifying the Local UBW.

Since 1957, the Coors brewery had been a "closed shop," in which workers were required to pay union dues if they were to benefit from union action. But company officials called the 1978 decertification vote a victory for the "open shop," wherein workers could enjoy union benefits without paying dues as members. Union officials, frustrated over the lack of a new contract and the decertification vote, publicly charged Coors with "union busting."

In fact, according to AFL-CIO officials, the UBW was the 20th Coors union decertified since the mid-1960s. Management consistently argued that employees simply rejected union organization because they didn't require it; good management eliminated the need for a union to protect workers. But organized labor maintained that all 20 unions had been "busted" by votes called while members were on strike and scabs were casting the ballots. By the end of the decade, only one union representing a small group of employees remained active at Coors.

NATIONWIDE BOYCOTT

The AFL-CIO was determined not to be defeated by the ousting of the UBW Local from the Golden plant. In defense of the union, AFL-CIO officials declared a nationwide boycott of Coors beer until a new contract settlement could be reached and soon began to claim that their efforts had a significant effect on sales. In fact, 1978 figures reported a 12 percent profit decline for the brewery during fiscal 1977 and predicted that 1978 figures would fall even lower. Corporate officials conceded the boycott was one factor influencing declining sales but refused to admit the drop was consistent or significant.

The defeat of the Coors local brewers' union fueled the boycott fire, but the protest focused on issues beyond the single contract dispute begun in 1977. The other issues of protest related to Coors's hiring practices. Labor leaders claimed that a mandatory polygraph test administered to all prospective employees asked irrelevant and personal questions and violated workers' rights. In addition, the protesters claimed that Coors discriminated against women and ethnic minorities in hiring and promotion. Finally, boycotters argued that Coors periodically conducted searches of employees and their personal property for suspected drug use and that such search and seizure also violated workers' rights. The boycott galvanized organized labor as well as minority interest groups that protested in defense of blacks, Hispanics, women, and gays.

The boycott's actual effect on sales was the subject of dispute. Coors's sales had begun to fall by July 1977, just three months after the boycott was initiated. Some analysts attributed the drop not to protesting consumers, but rather to stepped-up competition from Anheuser-Busch, which had begun to invade Coors's western territories. Despite a decline, Coors remained the number-one seller in 10 of the 14 states in which it was sold. Labor, on the other hand, took credit for a victory at the end of 1977 when Coors's fourth-quarter reports were less than half of the previous year's sales for the same period. Dropping from $17 million in 1976 to $8.4 million in 1977, Coors was faced with a growing challenge. There was no doubt that management took the AFL-CIO protest seriously and began attempts to counter declining sales through more aggressive advertising and public relations.

FEDERAL LAWSUIT

The AFL-CIO boycott gained additional legitimacy from the federal government. In 1975, the federal Equal Employment Opportunity Commission (EEOC) had filed a lawsuit against Coors for discrimination in hiring and promotion against blacks, Mexican Americans, and women. The suit charged Coors with violating the 1964 Civil Rights Act and challenged Coors's hiring tests, which the EEOC said were aimed at revealing an applicant's arrest record, economic status, and physical characteristics. The lawsuit stated that the company used "methods of recruitment which served to perpetuate the company's nonminority male workforce."

In May of 1977, one month after the initiation of the AFL-CIO boycott, Coors signed an agreement with the EEOC, vowing that the brewery would not discriminate in hiring. But according to media reports, Coors still refused to admit any past bias toward blacks, Mexican Americans, and women. Coors said it would continue a program begun in 1972 designed to increase the number of women and minorities in all major job classifications. Striking brewery workers refused to sign the agreement, although the Coors's Operating Engineers Union entered into the agreement.

DAVID SICKLER AND THE AFL-CIO

The principal organizer of the AFL-CIO boycott against the Adolph Coors Company was the former president of the company's Local UBW. David Sickler had been employed by Coors for 10 years, acting as a business manager from

1973–1976. Sickler left the plant in 1976 to take a job with the AFL-CIO in Montana. In April of 1977, the AFL-CIO decided to put Sickler in charge of coordinating the national boycott against Coors. Sickler moved to Los Angeles, where he also served as director of the Los Angeles organizing committee and the subregional office of the AFL-CIO.

Sickler initially resisted the AFL-CIO's request to put him in charge of organizing the boycott. He believed that his past employment at the company made him too close to the situation to offer a fair position on the issues at stake. But the AFL-CIO felt that Sickler's tenure with Coors made him an ideal choice; according to Sickler, his personal reports of abuse by the company in hiring and employment practices were shared by numerous Coors employees and were the central issues of the boycott.

Sickler contended that when hired by Coors, he had been subjected to questions on a lie detector test regarding his personal life and sexual preference. In addition, he reported the company's practice of searching individuals or entire departments for suspected drug use. Despite corporate officials' insistence that the accusations were false, Sickler was convinced that Coors employees were generally "unhappy, demoralized."

Coors management was determined to fight back against the boycott, and filed a breach of contract suit against the Local 366. The company charged that any boycott was prohibited under contract agreements. Management also made clear to the public its outrage over the boycott, as chairman Bill Coors began to speak out in the national media. In a 1978 interview with *Forbes* magazine, Coors stated about the AFL-CIO: "No lie is too great to tell if it accomplishes their boycott as a monument to immorality and dishonesty." Earlier that year, Bill Coors defended the company against charges of being antiunion. A *New York Times* report on the dispute quoted the CEO as saying: "Our fight is not with Brewery Workers Local 366. Our fight is with organized labor. Three sixty-six is a pawn for the AFL-CIO; that's where they're getting their money."

CORPORATE COMMUNICATION AT COORS

The 1977 boycott forced company officials to reexamine the area of corporate communication. Because labor leaders set out to "destroy the company," Bill Coors, now chairman and chief executive officer of the company, believed management must relate its side of the story. "There was no lie they wouldn't tell," the CEO recalled. "No one knew about Coors, and we had no choice but to tell the story."

In 1978, John McCarty, a fund-raiser at Pepperdine University, was hired as the vice president for corporate public affairs. McCarty brought to Coors expertise in minority relations and set out to repair the company's damaged reputation among minority groups. McCarty established a staff of corporate communication officers. The division was organized into four branches under McCarty's leadership: corporate communication, community affairs, economics affairs, and legislative affairs.

In response to the boycott and declining sales, McCarty enlisted the expertise of J. Walter Thompson's San Francisco office to help the company improve its corporate image. Coors launched what analysts termed a strong "image building" campaign in 1979, with messages aimed at ethnic minorities, women, union members, and homosexuals. The theme throughout the late 1970s was clearly a response to labor's accusations against the company: "At Coors, people make the difference."

Another component of the new image campaign, according to media reports, was to condition company managers to project charm and humility in dealing with reporters. Coors executives participated in a training course designed to help them overcome a traditional distrust of the media.

SHIRLEY RICHARD

Shirley Richard was hired along with McCarty in 1978 to direct the company's legislative affairs function but was familiar with the Coors Company long before joining its staff. From 1974–1978, Richard worked on the Coors account as a tax manager for Price Waterhouse. One important issue for the Coors account, Richard recalled, was the deductibility of lobbying expenses and charitable donations. As part of her job, Richard became involved in the political arena, helping Coors set up political action committees. When Richard decided to leave Price Waterhouse in 1978, she asked Coors's vice president of finance for a job and was hired to head the legislative affairs department, a position she held until 1981.

Richard recalled her first year with the company as a time when Coors was "coming out of its shell"; Philip Morris's purchase of Miller Brewing Company meant increased competition for Coors and a demand for more aggressive advertising. In 1975, the company sold its first public stock. The bad publicity from the 1977 strike and its aftermath combined with greater competition led to a serious decline in sales and disappointed shareholders. Clearly, the Coors mystique alone could no longer speak for itself, and an aggressive public relations campaign was unavoidable.

One year before the *60 Minutes* broadcast of the Coors story, Richard became Adolph Coors Company's director of corporate communications. In that position, she managed 25 people, covering corporate advertising, internal communications, distribution communications, training programs, and public relations personnel.

CONFRONTATIONAL JOURNALISM

The challenge of CBS's *60 Minutes* to any company under its investigation was formidable. The 14-year-old program was consistently ranked in Nielsen ratings' top 10 programs throughout the 1970s. Media critics offered various explanations for the success of this unique program, which remarkably combined high quality with high ratings. A *New York Times* critic summarized the sentiment of many within the broadcast profession when he called *60 Minutes*, "without question, the most influential news program in the history of the media."

The program had earned its popularity through consistently hard-hitting, investigative reporting. Executive producer Don Hewitt proclaimed *60 Minutes* the "public watchdogs." In his book about the program, Hewitt recalled, "I became more and more convinced that a new type of personal journalism was called for. *CBS Reports*, *NBC White Papers*, and *ABC Closeups* seemed to me to be the voice of the corporation, and I didn't believe people were any more interested in hearing from a corporation than they were in watching a documentary." Stories revealing insurance executives taking advantage of the poor with overpriced premiums, companies polluting streams and farmlands by irresponsibly dumping, or physicians gleaning profits from unnecessary surgery had all worked to rally public support and faith in CBS as a sort of consumer protection agency.

The program's success in uncovering scandal was due in large part to the aggressive and innovative technique of Mike Wallace. Wallace had been with the program throughout its history and was responsible for shaping much of the *60 Minutes* image. His reporting was always tough, sometimes theatrical, and was commonly referred to within the media as "confrontational journalism." Wallace had a reputation in broadcast circles and among *60 Minutes* viewers for making the sharpest executives and politicians crumble.

But the program was not flawless. Hewitt admitted he had made mistakes, and one of the most glaring cases against *60 Minutes* was a story about the Illinois Power Company. In November of 1979, *60 Minutes* broadcast a story about cost overruns at a Clinton, Illinois, nuclear power plant, a story that included some obtrusive inaccuracies. Illinois Power was not

to be victimized by *60 Minutes* and produced a videotape about the program, portraying it as antibusiness and antinuclear. Hewitt admitted that the company's defense had worked. "Five years after Illinois Power took us over the coals for that story, the plant is now seven years behind schedule and more than two and a half billion over budget. Have we reported that? I'm afraid not. You see, their beanball worked."

Allan Maraynes was assigned to produce the Coors segment. His experience with *60 Minutes* was highlighted by some significant clashes with big business. He had produced stories on the Ford Pinto gasoline tank defects, Firestone tires, I. Magnin, and SmithKline. Maraynes was alerted to the Coors controversy when *60 Minutes* researchers in San Francisco told him they suspected bad things were happening at Coors. The research group told Maraynes that the AFL-CIO was calling Coors a "fascist organization," which sounded to the producer like good material for a story.

Maraynes first flew to California to interview David Sickler. "We said we were setting about to do a story explaining that a fascist state exists at Coors," Maraynes recalled about his conversation with Sickler. "If it's true, we'll do it." Maraynes wanted Sickler to give him as much information about the boycott as he had. Maraynes wanted the angle of the story to be a focus on case histories of the people who had experienced Coors's unfair treatment.

OPEN OR CLOSED DOOR?

With the phone call from Maraynes, all of the pressures from David Sickler, the AFL-CIO, and the boycott were suddenly intensified. Shirley Richard had worked hard in the last year to focus public attention away from the boycott, but now her efforts to project a positive corporate image were threatened. Thinking ahead to the next few months of preparation time, she felt enormous pressure in the face of such potentially damaging public exposure.

Shirley Richard was not naive about Mike Wallace or the power of television news to shape a story and the public's opinion. Richard, along with other Coors executives, believed that the company was not at fault, but that did nothing to guarantee that its story would be accurately portrayed in a *60 Minutes* report. Mike Wallace himself had voiced the reason for a potential subject to fear the program's investigative report. In a *New York Times* interview, Wallace stated: "You (the network) have the power to convey any picture you want."

Richard knew that a big corporation's abuse of employees was just the kind of story *60 Minutes* was built on, and she didn't want Coors to be part of enhancing that reputation, especially when she believed organized labor had fabricated the controversy about Coors. Given Mike Wallace's desire to get the story, Shirley Richard guessed the company would automatically be on the defensive.

60 Minutes was determined to do the story, with or without cooperation from Coors. Richard wondered, however, whether an interview with Mike Wallace would do the company more harm than good. On the other hand, she considered the possibility that the company could somehow secure the offensive and turn the broadcast into a final clarification of Coors's side of the boycott story.

Richard was clearly challenged by an aggressive news team, and she was uncertain about cooperation from the conservative Coors brothers. Even if she could convince them that an open door was the best policy, would corporate officials be able to effectively present the facts supporting Coors's position? The national broadcast would reach millions of beer drinkers, and Richard knew that the *60 Minutes* report could either make or break the future success of Coors beer.

CASE QUESTIONS

1. What problems should Richard focus on?
2. Should Shirley Richard encourage or discourage the Coors brothers to go on *60 Minutes*?
3. What kind of research should she do?
4. What would her communication objective be if Coors agreed to the interview? If the brothers did not do the interview?
5. What suggestions would you have for improving the corporate communication function at Coors?

CHAPTER SEVEN

Internal Communications

For years, managers have focused on "customer care." More recently, they have begun to dedicate the same kind of attention to their own employees, recognizing that employees have more to do with the success of a business than virtually any other constituency. A study by consulting firm Watson Wyatt found that companies with the highest levels of effective communication experienced a 26 percent total return to shareholders from 1998 to 2002, compared to a –15 percent return for firms that communicated least effectively. The same study concluded: "The bottom line is that employee communication is no longer a 'soft' function but rather a business function that drives performance and contributes to a company's financial success."[1] Internal communications in the twenty-first century is more than the memos, publications, and broadcasts that comprise it; it's about building a corporate culture and having the potential to drive organizational change.

In this chapter, we examine how organizations can strengthen relationships with employees through internal communications. We start by looking at how the changing environment for business has created the need for a stronger internal communication function. Then we explore ways to organize internal communications through planning and staffing and how to implement a strong program using various communication channels. Finally, we discuss management's role in internal communications.

Internal Communications and the Changing Environment

As discussed in Chapter 1, the environment for business has changed dramatically over the last half-century. Today's employee is a different person in terms of values and needs than his or her counterpart in earlier decades. Most of today's employees are well educated, have higher expectations of what they will get out of their careers than their parents did, and want to understand more about the companies they work for.

---

[1] Watson Wyatt & Company, "Connecting Organizational Communication to Financial Performance—2003/2004 Communication ROI Study," November 3, 2003, http://www.watsonwyatt.com.

The workplace of today is also different—tighter staffing, longer hours, greater workloads, and more emphasis on performance are the norm. In recent years, the increased outsourcing of jobs to foreign countries has filled many employees with feelings of fear, paranoia, and anger. And in the post-Enron era, many employees are functioning with a greater degree of cynicism or distrust of corporations and their senior managements. All of these factors are causing employees to look more critically at how senior management is communicating with them, what is being communicated, and whether or not they feel engaged in and aligned with the company's direction.

The increasingly complex and highly competitive nature of today's business environment puts greater pressure on employees and also calls for a more concerted effort in the area of internal communications. David Stum of the Loyalty Institute comments, "The American worker knows quite well that change is never-ending. How it's handled is what can lead the worker to be secure or insecure."[2]

For example, in 1996, just days after AT&T eliminated 40,000 jobs, the media reported then CEO Bob Allen receiving nearly $10 million in stock options. Juxtapose this with next AT&T CEO C. Michael Armstrong announcing another 18,000 job cuts in 1998—along with the freezing of executive salaries and the elimination of chauffeured limousines for senior executives. As Dick Martin, a now-retired public relations executive with AT&T for 32 years, explains: "[What Armstrong did] had little impact on the bottom line, but it demonstrated a spirit of shared sacrifice."[3]

Today's employees increasingly are demanding participation in the conversations that are driving organizational change. This participation is vital to keeping employees at all levels of the organization—regardless of job role or responsibility—tapped in, fostering a more genuine sense of community in companies large or small. In light of this, communication must be a two-way process. Employees today expect that when their opinions are solicited and they take the time to share feedback, senior management will listen—and act upon it.

At many companies, senior managers simply do not involve lower-level employees in most decisions. This tends to make these employees feel alienated and unwilling to accept changes within the company. According to a survey by market information company TNS, 40 percent of workers feel disconnected from their employers; two out of every three workers do not identify with or feel motivated to drive their employer's business goals and objectives; and 25 percent of employees are just "showing up to collect a paycheck."[4]

Managers need to recognize that, if they provide information to employees and also listen to them, those employees will be excited about their work, connected to the company's vision, and able to further the goals of the organization. A study by

---

[2] Sue Shellenbarger, "Workplace Upheavals Seem to Be Eroding Employees' Trust," *The Wall Street Journal*, June 21, 2000, p. B1.

[3] The Conference Board, "Your Good Name: Before You Lose It," *Across the Board*, November/December 2004.

[4] The Conference Board, "U.S. Job Satisfaction Keeps Falling, The Conference Board Reports Today," February 28, 2005, http://www.conference-board.org/utilities/pressDetail.cfm?press_ID=2582.

TEN TRUTHS ABOUT SKEPTICAL EMPLOYEES*

1. They're smarter than senior managers think they are.
2. They think senior managers are smarter than they actually are.
3. They hate it when you make them feel stupid.
4. They have short attention spans.
5. They have long memories.
6. They're desperate for direction.

7. They want to be able to think on their own.
8. They want the company to succeed.
9. They don't want to leave.
10. They want to believe in the company.

* Adapted from a speech given at the Tuck School of Business at Dartmouth by Rod Odham of Bell South's Small Business Services Division, October 1994.

Right Management Consultants revealed that the top area that managers and executives need to improve is their ability to engage employees in vision and strategy.[5]

As companies continue to focus on and strengthen their communication efforts, a further challenge will be ensuring employees believe in the sincerity of communications they are receiving. A 2004 study by management consultant Towers Perrin revealed only half (51 percent) of employees say their company is open and honest.[6]

The stakes could become even higher for companies who are not keeping their employees informed and genuinely engaged. The U.S. Bureau of Labor Statistics forecasts an expected labor shortage of 5 to 10 million workers by 2010.[7] In this environment, employees will have the luxury of becoming more discerning consumers in their job searches as the war for talent intensifies. Strong internal communications—fostering increased workforce loyalty and productivity—will thus continue to play a pivotal role in a company's employee retention and overall success.

Organizing the Internal Communication Effort

The best way to assess the effectiveness of a company's internal communication efforts is by determining what employees' attitudes are about the firm. This can be done through a *communication audit*. Based on audit results, communications professionals can design the right program for the organization.

For example, both Starbucks Coffee Co. and Kinko's Inc. hired outside consultants to conduct internal communication audits to identify strengths and weaknesses in those companies' existing communication practices. Detailed questionnaires

---

[5] Right Management Consultants, "30% of Managers & Executives Lack Necessary Management Skills," September 21, 2004, http://www.right.com.

[6] Towers Perrin, "Study Offers Insights on Effective Communication from the Perspective of Employees," January 2005, http://www.towersperrin.com.

[7] Michael Kinsman, "Most Workers Seem Ready to Change Jobs, Survey Finds," *San Diego Union-Tribune,* December 5, 2004.

HOW TO SUCCEED WITH EMPLOYEES

A Towers Perrin survey of 25,000 employees across multiple industries worldwide defines effective communication from an employee's perspective as including the following elements:

1. Open and honest exchanges of information.
2. Clear, easy-to-understand materials.
3. Timely distributions.
4. Trusted sources.
5. Two-way feedback systems.
6. Clear demonstrations of senior leadership's interest in employees.
7. Continual improvements in communication.
8. Consistent messaging across sources.[9]

[9] Towers Perrin, "Study Offers Insights on Effective Communication from the Perspective of Employees," January 2005, http://www.towersperrin.com.

uncovered precisely how employees viewed internal communications and helped management develop possible solutions to communication problems. In addition, Kinko's used in-person interviews and videoconferencing facilities to conduct nationwide employee focus groups and uncover the sentiments of employees from region to region.[8] In addition to conducting an overarching communication audit, regular "temperature checks" of employee opinions can be valuable in ensuring that communication channels and approaches continue to meet employees' evolving needs.

Once management knows how employees feel about the communications they are receiving internally and whether they understand its messages, it can implement an internal communication infrastructure to meet those needs. If an infrastructure is already in place, it can be adjusted or enhanced as necessary based on the audit results.

Goals for Effective Internal Communications

Now that we have seen how the changing environment affects the internal communication effort and the importance of collecting employee feedback through a communication audit, we need to explore how companies can organize the function so that it supports the overall mission of the firm. Let's begin by first defining some goals for effective internal communications.

Ultimately, effective internal communications should reinforce employees' beliefs that they are important assets to the firm. This can happen only if management believes that is true, and if the communication effort is handled by professionals.

Where Should Internal Communications Report?

In the past, internal communications reported to the human resources area, since traditionally this function dealt with all matters related to employees' welfare; but recent surveys show that over 80 percent of corporations in the United States place

[8] Boyd A. Vander Houwen, "Less Talking, More Listening," *HR Magazine,* August 1997, pp. 53–59.

the responsibility for internal communications in the corporate communication area.[10] Often, both areas have some involvement with internal communications. For instance, at Continental Airlines, responsibility for communicating messages from senior management is shared between human resources and corporate communication.[11]

Ideally, both the corporate communication and the human resources departments in large companies have someone in charge of internal communications. If the head of the internal communications department reports to the vice president in charge of CorpComm and the head communication for the human resources department to his or her respective vice president, each should have a dotted-line relationship with the vice president in the other area. Other companies situate communicators focused on human resources issues—including benefits and the new hire experience—in the corporate communication area to create continuity between both general and HR-related communication strategy and execution. These approaches also will help ensure that the goals of each department are fully met and that the lines of communication are kept open between these two critical functional areas.

Large, multidivisional companies often have internal communications representatives within each division who report jointly to the chief of staff for divisional management and to a firmwide corporate communication department. Ideally, each division shares best practices for delivering high-level messages to the employees in their respective areas—understanding the particular needs and nuances of their employee base, which, in turn, affects both the content and tone of communications. However, the channels may be different across divisions; for instance, some divisions may have a voice mail culture, while others may pay more attention to e-mail. In larger corporations, there might be vast differences in the online connectivity of employees; those working in production plants or call centers might have no e-mail access whatsoever, versus other office employees who are wholly reliant on e-mail access—whether in-office or remote—to get the job done.

In some cases, companies look outside their own organizations for help with internal communications. In January 2001, for example, General Motors announced that its employee communication professionals would report to a New York–based consultant specializing in management–employee relations.[12] The new reporting structure was implemented after surveys revealed that employees did not adequately understand management's key messages. The practice of relying on outside experts is becoming less restricted to times of crisis—in fact, by the mid-1990s, the Public Relations Society of America added an internal communications section to its organization.[13] As the importance of internal communication gains recognition, it is not surprising that PR and consulting firms have developed

[10] Michael Morley, "Corporate Communications: A Benchmark Study of the Current State of the Art and Practice," *Corporate Reputation Review,* Winter 1998, pp. 78–86.

[11] Lin Grensing-Pophal, "Follow Me," *HR Magazine,* February 2000, pp. 36–41.

[12] Thom Weidlich, "Getting the Corporate Point across to Employees," *New York Times,* July 25, 2001, p. C8.

[13] Ibid.

capabilities in the area of internal communications, or that companies are increasingly turning to them for assistance.

Regardless of where the internal communications is positioned and whether or not an outside consultant is used, it must work closely in conjunction with external communicators to integrate the messages disseminated to both internal and external audiences. Applebee's International, the largest chain of casual-dining restaurants in the world, integrated its public relations and internal communication functions in 2000 to keep messaging consistent across all audiences. Four of Applebee's five communicators handle press as well as employee relations.[14] This approach can help ensure that, when significant company news breaks, employees will not be the last to hear about it.

When news about a company hits the press or appears on the Internet, employees should already be equipped with the company's own version of the story so they feel they are being kept in the loop by their own team. This strategy also enables companies to maintain better control of their messages, without being at the whim of how the media position them.[15]

The lines between external and internal communications continue to blur as employees increasingly become members of various constituency groups. As David Verbraska, corporate communications general manager at Pfizer, explains: "Employees wear many hats—they're stockholders, recruiters, customers, and members of the community. . . Management must understand that the internal audience could be even more important to a company than external for all the right business reasons, and there are consequences in not aligning the areas."[16] This has caused some companies to view the label "internal communications" as archaic. The likelihood of memos or other communications leaking to the outside world with a click of the mouse means that internal communicators should always consider the ramifications of their messages being shared with external audiences, including reporters and investors.

Implementing an Effective Internal Communication Program

Once goals for an internal communication program are established and decisions made about where the function should report, the program is ready for implementation. In smaller organizations, internal communications may be a part of everyone's job since the ideal method of communicating with employees is one-on-one or in meetings with small groups of employees.

Even in larger organizations, however, this intimacy in the internal communication effort is a good start for building a more formal program. In this section, we will explore some of the key steps in implementing an effective internal communication program, from personal, one-on-one mechanisms to programs that use technology to distribute messages broadly and instantaneously.

[14] Richard Mitchell, "Closing the Gap: From the Inside out," *PR Week* (U.S.), November 22, 2004, p. 17.

[15] Ibid.

[16] Ibid.

Communicate Up and Down

Many large companies are perceived as being faceless, unfeeling organizations, an impression that is only reinforced when no upward communication exists from employees to management. When high-level managers isolate themselves physically and psychologically from other employees, effective communication cannot happen. Mass electronic communication can sometimes compound the "facelessness" of management.

A nationwide survey of over 5,000 employees in U.S. firms conducted by a major consulting firm showed that the greatest criticism employees have of companies is that they do not encourage upward as well as downward communication. Recent statistics also indicate that less than half (45 percent) of employees think senior leadership both talks and listens, creating an environment of two-way communication. In addition, less than half (49 percent) say there are existing systems to raise questions and issues with senior leadership or inform employees in a timely way about major decisions and developments.[17] Effective internal communications can generate a dialogue throughout the company, fostering a sense of participation that can make even the largest companies feel smaller in the hearts and minds of employees.

The best approach to communicating with employees is through informal discussions between employees and supervisors. Employees need to feel secure enough in their positions to ask questions and offer advice without fear of reprisals from top management. Continental Airlines CEO Gordon Bethune has been recognized for his high visibility among front-line employees and openness to communicating with them regularly. Each month, Bethune holds an "open house" in his office at which employees are invited to show up to speak with him about anything—issues, suggestions, or complaints. Several times a year, he travels to the airline's major hubs to meet with employees.[18] With this kind of open communication and care for employees as a hallmark of his leadership style, Bethune has been credited for a significant improvement in employee morale and overall corporate culture at Continental.

At another airline, JetBlue, it is not uncommon for employees to be on a first-name basis with senior executives. Each employee spends his or her first day at an orientation, including an hour with president and COO Dave Barger, CEO Dave Neeleman, and vice president of people Vincent Stabile to talk about the JetBlue brand, airline economics, how to interact with customers, as well as the fundamentals of the company's culture and values.[19] Many credit this highly personal training and management style with JetBlue's low annualized employee turnover rate of between 10 and 12 percent versus the industry average of approximately 20 to 24 percent.[20]

---

[17] Towers Perrin, "Study Offers Insights on Effective Communication."

[18] Brian O'Reilly, "The Mechanic Who Fixed Continental," *Fortune,* December 20, 1999, pp. 176–86.

[19] Eve Tahmincioglu, "True Blue," *Workforce Management,* February 1, 2005, p. 47.

[20] Ibid.

Conversations with management promote feelings that employees themselves are serving as catalysts for organizational change. As Peter Senge highlights with a quote from the ancient Chinese visionary Lao Tsu:

> The wicked leader is he who the people despise, the good leader is he who the people revere, the great leader is he who the people say, "We did it ourselves."[21]

Respecting employees as well as listening and interacting with them form the basis for an effective internal communication program. John Horne was able to achieve this at Navistar by talking to small groups of employees and simply asking them what was on their minds. This created an atmosphere of trust and paved the way for a remarkable turnaround at Navistar.

Make Time for Face-to-Face Meetings

One means of ensuring that employees have access to senior management is to hold regular, in-person meetings with fairly large groups of employees. Such meetings should take place frequently (at least quarterly) and should be used as opportunities for management to share company results and progress on key initiatives and to demonstrate responsiveness to prior employee feedback. Most importantly, such meetings should provide employees with an opportunity to ask questions of management in an open forum. If size and geography prevent employees from participating in person, video or telephone conferencing should be used to facilitate their inclusion.

Topics for these types of gatherings should be limited; rather than trying to tackle everything that is going on at the company, managers should survey employees beforehand to find out what is most important to them. Then a presentation can be built around one or two critical issues from the employee perspective, plus one or more messages that management wants to share. Too often, management only sets up such meetings when the company has an important pronouncement, reducing the likelihood of relevant dialogue.

Starbucks supplements an online idea program that encourages employees to e-mail ideas to their managers with a program known as "Open Forum." Open Forum sessions are held quarterly at 14 different venues nationwide, comprising three hours of senior management presentations, updates on critical issues, an informative videotape, and extensive Q&A. While the sessions are not mandatory, attendance rates are high as employees take advantage of opportunities to interact with senior management and hear firsthand about company strategy and goals.[22] In some cases, offering employees an online dialogue appeals to those not comfortable standing up in front of colleagues and speaking in a public forum.

Certainly, large-scale events are an effective means to reach out to the greatest number of employees at one time, but managers should not overlook the importance of also meeting with employees in smaller groups. If they are seeking feedback

[21] Peter Senge, "The Leader's New Work: Building Learning Organizations," *Sloan Management Review* 32 (Fall 1990), pp. 7–23.
[22] Vander Houwen, "Less Talking, More Listening."

or opinions about key initiatives, managers may find that employees are more forth-coming when not in a large group setting. Smaller groups are also more conducive to resolving specific problems.

When Rob Frazier was hired by Colgate Palmolive to take over operations of its Mennen deodorant plant in Morristown, New Jersey, and turn the plant profitable within a year, he faced a number of challenges. "There was no communication going on in the plant, and what was being sent across the transom was inaccurate," said Frazier. "We were losing over $10 million a day, and morale was at an all-time low."[23]

One of the first things Frazier did after arriving on the scene was to meet with plant employees in groups of 10 to understand their challenges. Shortly thereafter, he began a tradition of daily morning "check-ins." In these brief meetings, employees lined up against the wall all the way around the room, making a circle. They talked about what had happened on the line the previous day and what was likely to happen that day. Issues were raised, questions answered, and problems solved. Aware that their voices had been heard and their concerns recognized, the Mennen employees filed out of the room ready to get to work and to contribute to the plant's success. They realized their contributions counted, and all it took was 15 minutes of Rob Frazier's day.

Communicate Online

While meetings are an important way to communicate with employees, the advent of company intranets in the late 1990s provided a new channel through which companies could reach their employees quickly and broadly with important news on events and key management initiatives. Many company intranets also serve as interactive platforms where employees can rally together and share their views on company programs, activities that contribute to building trust.

IBM has received much attention and praise for using its corporate intranet, dubbed "W3," as a means to host a global internal conversation and tap into the collective knowledge of its almost one-third of a million employees who serve clients in 170 countries. IBM's "Jam" technology enables employees to log in and type real-time comments in a discussion forum that tracks thousands of discrete conversational threads during a companywide "Jam" event.[24] With the discussion topics predetermined, employees can contribute a one-off idea in a matter of seconds, or can commit hours to the Jam, reacting to comments submitted by colleagues or vocalizing detailed opinions or suggestions.

While IBM held its first employee Jam in 2001 to help promote intranet use, the 72-hour "ValuesJam" hosted in July 2003 effected especially significant organizational change. Under the leadership of CEO Sam Palmisano and following a six-month review of IBM's management organization, the topic of this Jam was the values underpinning IBM's culture and how those values would drive

---

[23] Interview with Rob Frazier, October 15, 1999. All direct quotes from Rob Frazier came from this interview.

[24] Paul Hemp and Thomas A. Stewart, "Leading Change When Business Is Good: The HBR Interview—Samuel J. Palmisano," *Harvard Business Review*, December 1, 2004, pp. 1–10.

innovation and industry leadership going forward. Throughout the three days of the ValuesJam, more than 50,000 employees joined in to contribute close to 10,000 comments to the discussion. Following the ValuesJam, Palmisano announced to his executive committee: "You guys ought to read every one of these comments, because if you think we've got this place plumbed correctly, think again."[25]

Following detailed analysis of all the Jam postings, IBM distilled the major themes defining what employees think IBM is and should be. In November 2003, Palmisano announced IBM's new set of corporate values, essentially written by the employees themselves through the ideas expressed via the Jam. Employees were hungry for the new values that they authored: in the 10 days following the announcement of the new values, more than 200,000 people downloaded the document on the intranet.[26] Since the ValuesJam, IBM continues to host global and more targeted Jams, and Palmisano considers the technology to be a crucial part of his management approach.

Internet technology, while extremely powerful, must be used thoughtfully if it is to enhance communication rather than detract from the impact of management's messages. Employees are bombarded by information, especially given the near ubiquity of e-mail and voice mail. In fact, information overload was one of the primary complaints cited in every corporate employee survey conducted in 1997 by Vander Houwen Public Relations.[27] The trend continues today: a 2005 survey by Forrester Research revealed that while 69 percent of company intranet users classified their company intranet as "very important," only 44 percent feel that it's easy to find what they're looking for, with improved search capabilities ranking as the area requiring the most improvement.[28]

Consequently, companies need to invest a considerable amount of thought into ensuring their messages are getting through to employees and that information is easy to find. Portal technology is being used more frequently to help employees more readily locate and manage online information. Portals combine links to key intranet pages, headlines, and applications on a single screen, similar to a Google or Yahoo! home page. Bank of America began using a portal technology to whittle its nearly 2,000 internal sites down to 200, a much more reasonable number for employees to navigate.[29]

A company intranet should be dynamic and engaging, with the home page regularly refreshed, so it becomes an employee's go-to resource for the latest company information. Ideally, it should be integrated into an employee's workday, so that he or she checks it continuously throughout the day. As a senior vice president at Ketchum public relations explains: "We treat our intranet as if it were a journalistic vehicle. We change the home page every day." The end result: employees

---

[25] Ibid.

[26] Ibid.

[27] Vander Houwen, "Less Talking, More Listening."

[28] Forrester Research, "Employees Tell Forrester Research What They Really Think of IT," May 27, 2005, http://www.forrester.com.

[29] John Goff, "Cutting through the Clutter," *CFO Magazine,* November 2, 2004.

check the intranet each morning "just like they would check the front page of their daily newspaper."[30]

Managers should resist the impulse to move *all* communication online unless sure that all employees will use this medium. Surveys can reveal how employees would like to receive different types of information, which helps determine what types of information a company's intranet will be the best channel for. An effective internal communication strategy should focus on both content and channel, recognizing that use of multiple channels (some traditional and some more innovative) offers the best potential for success.

And while video and online communication channels are often expedient and engaging, they should not be used as a substitute for personal, face-to-face communication between all levels of management and employees.

Create Employee-Oriented Publications

In addition to online communications, another common form of information sharing in many companies is through the print medium. (Print communications are particularly important to prevent employees without e-mail access from feeling marginalized.) Unfortunately, most internal company publications are unexciting. How can companies make monthly newsletters or magazines more interesting to employees?

Companies need to realize that their publications are competing with the national and local media for their employees' attention. Today's employee is a sophisticated consumer of information more interested in seeing something akin to *USA Today* than a list of bowling scores or a photo of the "employee of the month." Ideally, the publication should connect employees with goings-on beyond their local surroundings; it should discuss important happenings and accomplishments across the company and give employees a clear sense of the company's overarching direction and strategy.

Creating an employee publication is an ideal job for a former journalist. The most senior communication official and the CEO also should take an interest in company publications to ensure that employees are getting the real story about what is happening to the company and the industry in the most interesting presentation.

Rob Frazier personally took over the Mennen plant's internal newsletter to communicate directly with his employees. His front-page articles soon became one of the most valuable sources of information for employees. A few months after his arrival in Morristown, Frazier decided to write about the 12 characteristics of an excellent manufacturing operation. Number 4 on his list (after "zero accidents," "neat and orderly at all times," and "people are important") was excellent communication. Here is an excerpt:

> Excellent communication is very difficult and will not be achieved unless we work very hard to make it happen. I am referring to communication between functions (planning, manufacturing, finishing, warehouse, engineering, etc.),

---

[30] Scott Kirsner, "Building an Intranet Is One Thing, Getting People to Use It Is Another," *CIO*, December 21, 1999.

communication on our results, communication on jobs well done, communication on how we can improve our performance, and communication on how the business is doing.

Please make a note to yourself to do something to improve communication this week. I will be installing a white board near the entrance and writing a piece of information on that board each day in an effort to improve communication. What will each of you do?

Another way to reach employees through company publications is to send the magazines to their homes rather than distributing them at the workplace. Although this is more expensive, it helps make the company a part of the family, something that will be a source of pride for the employee and his or her spouse.

Above all, every publication—just as with any other online or print communication—must be honest about anything that might affect employees. The goal is to make employees feel like a part of the team, and on the cutting edge of what is happening within the firm and its industry. The tone of publications also should be realistic as many employees will see through and distrust anything that seems more like propaganda than a genuine communication.

The messages that go into these periodicals will vary by industry and company, but managers must strike the right balance between what employees are interested in and what they really need to hear from top management. Employees should look forward to the next issue of the company publication in the same way they do their university's alumni magazine. In fact, alumni magazines are excellent models in terms of style and tone for company publications.

Other print materials also are produced from time to time in response to important events that directly affect employees. For example, the health or retirement benefits areas need a special set of publications. If a company is gearing up for a reduction in health benefits, it may start communicating with employees months before the actual changes take place to put these changes in context for employees. In this situation, the corporate communication staff would likely work with human resources to craft a communication strategy for what could be a year-long communication process. Special welcome publications and materials also must be produced for new employees to create a positive and seamless new hire experience.

Management also can use memos and letters to communicate to employees about internal changes, such as management succession, new group structures, or important deals or contracts. These written communications should come out frequently enough so that employees do not feel that it is unusual, but not so often that they stop hearing management's messages. Certainly in the case of major events such as a takeover or merger, employees need to be informed ahead of external constituencies.

The timing gap between internal and external communications about such events must be narrow, however, as it can be damaging to the company if employees communicate sensitive information haphazardly to external constituencies before the company can make an official statement to the media or its client base. Similarly, as discussed earlier in the chapter, if employees hear critical company news from external sources prior to receiving an internal communication, the impact on morale and trust can be damaging.

Communicate Visually

We saw earlier that Americans are increasingly turning to television and computers as opposed to newspapers to get their news. Similarly, employees are becoming more visually oriented in their consumption of information, particularly given increased use of company intranets. As a result, many companies have developed ways to communicate with employees through this powerful medium, now including everything from basic Webcasts to multimedia presentations allowing for employee interaction.

Most large corporations have elaborate television studios with satellite capabilities staffed by professionals. Such sophisticated systems are the best mechanisms for communicating with employees through visual channels. Even if your company does not have its own studio, outside vendors can provide these services as needed.

These studios are often used to create "video magazines" that can be made available to employees in outlying areas, helping them feel part of the organization even when company headquarters is 1,000 miles away. Companies are now broadcasting programs across the Web for employees to view over the company intranet with increased frequency. Employees without e-mail access can convene in spaces such as cafeterias to view Webcasts in large groups, creating a communal experience and encouraging interemployee discussions.

JetBlue holds meetings on the last Friday of each month, when the president spends two hours discussing industry happenings and hosting a live Q&A session. While 200 employees typically attend in person, the video is also posted and broadcast on the intranet, generating thousands of hits from those not able to attend.[31] Citigroup hosts the longest-standing quarterly employee broadcast, held the morning the company's quarterly earnings are released. The broadcast—reviewing financial performance, other key company initiatives and accomplishments, and, more recently, a historical feature about one of Citigroup's legacy businesses—began in the late 1970s under the leadership of Walter Wriston as chairman and CEO of Citicorp and has not missed a quarter since. Thousands of employees watch the broadcast live or on video rebroadcast, and all have the opportunity to order DVD or VHS copies to view at home.

Managers should not see expenditures on such communication as frivolous or wasteful but rather as an investment in the firm, a way to make each employee feel more connected, while also "humanizing" senior management. In contrast to the sometimes impersonal nature of e-mail communication, these communications can offer employees a personal touch—literally bringing a company's leaders and vision to life without the time and expense of traveling.[32] If such a production is well done, it can be a tremendous morale booster as well as a visual history of the company that can be used for years to come.

And visual communication does not always have to be high-tech. At Colgate-Palmolive's Mennen plant, for example, ubiquitous white boards revealed details about breakdowns, production goals, sick leaves, birthdays, vacation schedules,

---

[31] Tahmincioglu, "True Blue."

[32] Julie Flower, "Seeing You Loud and Clear: Will Visual Technology Ever Make a Real Impact on Business Communication?" *Communication World*, December 1, 2002, p. 18.

and numbers of units coming off each line. A special racecar billboard depicted the productivity of each line relative to the others—a visual measure of success and a source of motivation and pride. And recall plant manager Rob Frazier's request that employees write each day on a white board what they were doing to improve communication: What better way to share ideas? Such visual communication is inexpensive, easy to implement, and virtually impossible for any employee on the plant floor to miss.

Focus on Internal Branding

In this chapter, we have discussed the importance of clear, two-way communication about strategy and direction. Internal branding is also important to building morale and creating a workplace where employees are "engaged" with their jobs. While communicators do inform employees about new advertising campaigns, they seldom recognize the need to "sell" employees on the same ideas they are trying to sell to the public.[33]

Internal branding is especially critical when an organization is undergoing changes such as a merger or a change in leadership. When British Petroleum merged with Amoco and then ARCO, it rebranded itself as BP and launched an internal branding campaign simultaneously with an external program. Proclaiming that the merged entity was going "beyond petroleum," the campaign reinforced the rebirth of an oil company into an energy company with an open, collaborative, "new-economy" culture. Employees of the three companies that merged to become BP now have a solid identity to relate to.

The launch of a new advertising or rebranding campaign is also an appropriate time to think of internal branding. Nike links internal and external marketing by granting numerous senior executives the second title of "Corporate Storyteller"—tasking them to share stories with Nike employees that echo the company's ad campaigns, instead of focusing solely on financial results.[34] Volkswagen took a similar approach when it introduced its "Drivers wanted" advertising campaign. In lieu of electronic communications and PowerPoint presentations, staff and dealers watched a creative film that brought the campaign's slogans and essence to life, instilling in them the spirit of the relaunched brand they would be selling to customers around the world.[35]

Internal branding campaigns also can be launched when results of internal audits reveal that employees are not connecting with a company's vision or when morale is low. When internal and external marketing messages are misaligned, the customer experience will suffer, with adverse effects on the company. For example, one health care company marketed itself as putting the welfare of its customers as its number-one priority, while telling employees that the number-one priority was cutting costs.[36] And amid numerous labor lawsuits, retailing giant

---

[33] Colin Mitchell, "Selling the Brand Inside," *Harvard Business Review,* January 2002, pp. 5–11.

[34] Ibid.

[35] Ibid.

[36] Ibid.

Wal-Mart based an entire advertising campaign on its employees to boost morale. A national ad campaign profiling individual Wal-Mart workers and highlighting benefits and opportunities for professional development and advancement at the company has been credited for helping instill a sense of belonging and pride among many employees.[37]

Even when employees *understand* the company's brand promise or key customer deliverable, it is not until they *believe* it that they can really help the company carry it out. Just as external branding campaigns aim to create emotional ties among consumers to your company, internal branding's goal is to do the same with employees. Focusing attention on this important area will generate improved employee morale and, ultimately, better results for the company.

Consider the Company Grapevine

In considering the formal channels of internal communications discussed in this chapter so far, we cannot neglect the importance of their informal counterparts. The company grapevine—an informal communications network including everything from private conversations between two employees to the latest anecdotes shared in the cafeteria—should be considered as much of a communication vehicle as a company's house organ or employee meetings. In fact, given that nearly half of all employees credit the grapevine with bringing them word of major corporate changes,[38] distributing messages faster and in more credible forms than formal channels, it is even more crucial that managers tap into it. Yet many employers downplay the grapevine's importance, with only 17 percent thinking workers rely on it for information.[39] In fact, statistics reveal that over 90 percent of companies do not have a policy for dealing with the grapevine or for managing any other informal communications network.[40] Ultimately, if employees do not receive complete or timely information from their employers, they will have no choice but to rely on one another—as well as external sources—to fill in the gaps.

Managers can find out what employees think by simply asking questions. Union Carbide, for example, uses overnight polling to gauge employee reactions to its programs. In one study, 89 percent of managers conceded that the grapevine transmits negative information indicative of a lack of trust concerning other employees, supervisors, or organizational policies.[41] Broader surveys can help pinpoint what employees are hearing from management and how they are perceiving things. GM conducts a "Global Employee Census" every two years or so, asking employees to complete a 100+-item survey to gauge their understanding of

---

[37] Eve Tahmincioglu, "Employing Workers in Ads to Polish Image, Boost Internal Morale," *Workforce Management,* April 1, 2005, p. 61.

[38] Jared Sandberg, "Ruthless Rumors and the Managers Who Enable Them," *The Wall Street Journal,* October 29, 2003, p. B1.

[39] Ibid.

[40] Sheri Rosen, "Carry on the Conversation: Helping Employees Make Sense of What Happens at Work," *Communication World,* March 1, 2005, p. 24.

[41] Suzanne M. Crampton, John W. Hodge, and Jitendra Mishra, "The Informal Communication Network: Factors Influencing Grapevine Activity," *Public Personnel Management* 1 (December 22, 1998), p. 569.

corporate goals, priorities, and other defining elements of the organization.[42] Other companies conduct such all-employee surveys on an annual basis, such as Citigroup's "Voice of the Employee" survey. The stronger the sense of trust, commitment, and engagement between employees and management, therefore, the less often employees will resort to the grapevine as the chief means of expressing their voice and hearing those of fellow employees.

Management's Role in Internal Communications

A common thread in the company examples discussed in this chapter is the involvement in internal communications of CEOs and other senior leaders within organizations. This is critical because these individuals are the "culture carriers" and visionaries within a company, and all communications relating to organizational strategy start with them. Increasingly, CEOs and senior managers—in the tradition of J.P. Morgan's desk on the trading floor—are even positioning themselves in the midst of their employees physically, working at standard desks and in cubes, to boost camaraderie, engage employees more directly, and create a sense of shared culture and responsibility among employees from the bottom to the top of the ladder.[43]

Robert Dilenschneider, founder of corporate strategic counseling and public relations firm The Dilenschneider Group, describes the type of leader the twenty-first century corporate landscape demands: "What's needed now is a different kind of CEO: Men and women who shed the trappings of imperial power, work with their boards of directors in new, dynamic relationships and find fresh ways to unleash the creative potential of their people, from middle managers to front-line workers. This will require a big shift in attitude from change-averse managers. They'll need to get off their private jets and fly with everyone else, shed the large personal staffs that coddle and isolate them and spend real time with the workers who are on the factory floors, behind the sales counters or in the office cubicles."[44]

Physical presence and interaction are an important start. Senior managers, however, also need to work closely with internal communications professionals to ensure their messages are received and, most importantly, understood by all employees. The "understanding" component is crucial but sometimes overlooked. Donald Sheppard, CEO of Sheppard Associates, an independent consulting agency specializing in internal communication strategy, says, "You can have a vision of 'we want to be this'—that's nice, but the person out there in the plant in Michigan or in India needs to understand how that applies to him or her and what he or she needs to do differently. That can't be done at any macro level."[45]

---

[42] Bruce Jeffries-Fox, "Engaging Employees Leads to Self-Enlightened Interest," *PR News* 61 (April 6, 2005).

[43] Jared Sandberg, "The CEO in the Next Cube—Bosses Who Abandon Offices Win Kudos for Collegiality, but Make Neighbors Nervous," *The Wall Street Journal,* June 22, 2005, p. B1.

[44] Robert L. Dilenschneider, "When CEOs Roamed the Earth," *The Wall Street Journal,* March 15, 2005, p. B2.

[45] Pophal, "Follow Me."

To achieve this "micro" level understanding of what strategic goals or initiatives mean to individuals, internal communications professionals should work with front-line managers to help make messages relevant to the employees who report directly to them. KPMG LLP in Montvale, New Jersey, introduced a program called "The Power of One"—an annual event where key messages and information about firm strategy are shared first with the firm's partners, and then subsequently "cascaded" down through the other layers of the firm. FedEx also focuses development efforts on front-line managers, including work in the area of communication.[46] These individuals, after all, have the greatest potential to help relate management's "vision" to employees' individual business units, and, importantly, to their day-to-day activities.

Conclusion

Over the last several years, "management by walking around" and other management philosophies basically have come to the same conclusion: managers need to get out from behind their desks, put down their cell phones, get away from their computers, and go out and get to know the people who are working for them. No other method works as well, and no "quick fix" will satisfy the basic need for interaction with other employees.

With all the sophisticated technology available to communicate with employees today, such as e-mail, intranets, blogs, and satellite meetings connecting distant offices, the most important factor in internal communications begins with the manager who has a basic responsibility to his or her employees. That responsibility is to listen to what they have to say and to get to know who they really are as individuals. We have come a long way from Upton Sinclair's *Jungle* to the modern American corporation. Today's employees do want high-tech and sophisticated communications, but they also want personal contact with their managers. Understanding this fact is the cornerstone of an effective internal communications program.

[46] Ibid.

Westwood Publishing

Dan Cassidy, a 2005 graduate of the Tuck School of Business at Dartmouth, was driving home from work listening to more depressing news on the radio about layoffs at another large media company. He had just left a meeting with his boss, Catherine Callahan (see Exhibit 1), the vice president of human resources at Westwood Publishing. "Dan, we are going to have to let some of the old-timers go. I'm hoping that the CEO will buy my plan for a voluntary severance and early retirement package. We should be able to move out some of the deadwood in this company as well."

Westwood Publishing had never laid off anyone in the 10 years of its existence. As the director of employee relations, Dan would be responsible for telling employees about the new policy within the next couple of days.

As he looked at the beautiful southern California hills surrounding the freeway, many thoughts were going through his head. How should he identify the issues involved for all employees? Should he get the people in corporate communication involved? Who would be the best person to release the information? What about communication with other Westwood constituencies? And what would be the long term effects of what would be reported in the media as a "major downsizing"?

WESTWOOD PUBLISHING BACKGROUND

Westwood was started by Linda Bosworth, a brilliant UCLA graduate, following her graduation from college in 1990. With only $10 thousand in

EXHIBIT 1 The People in the Case

Linda Bosworth	CEO of Westwood Publishing
Catherine Callahan	Vice president of human resources
Eric Ridgway	Vice president of corporate communication
Dan Cassidy	Director of employee relations
Craig Stevens	Outside public relations consultant

capital borrowed from her father, Bosworth had built the firm up to a multimillion-dollar trade magazine publisher with hundreds of titles and a broad subscriber base. Beginning in the mid-1990s, Westwood began to focus strategically on high-tech trade publications.

As the business grew, Bosworth gradually turned the day-to-day operation of Westwood over to professional managers, preferring young MBAs from top business schools. But the original group of employees, mostly men in their mid-50s, still represented the bulk of senior management at Westwood.

By the turn of the century, analysts were predicting that the publishing industry in general and Westwood in particular were ready for consolidation. Many of Westwood's competitors had trimmed their workforces repeatedly after the dot-com bubble burst in early 2000. By this point, half of Westwood's titles were for high-tech and Internet companies. But Bosworth felt that keeping all of her employees happy through good times and bad was more important than anything else.

In a speech that Bosworth delivered to all of Westwood's employees in 2003, she outlined the company's philosophy toward employee turnover: "You, the employees of Westwood, are the most important asset that we have.

Source: This case was written by Professor Paul A. Argenti in 2005. It is a fictionalized version of an actual case, but the industry and characters have been disguised.

Despite the difficult times this company now faces, you have my assurance that I will never ask any of you to leave for economic reasons. This is not General Motors!"

CORPORATE COMMUNICATION AT WESTWOOD

The company relied on a small staff of public relations professionals to handle its communication efforts. All of the various activities that could be decentralized (such as internal communications, investor relations, etc.) were housed in the appropriate functional areas. This developed naturally as the company grew to become one of the largest independent trade magazine publishers in the United States.

The young owner/CEO enjoyed much attention from the press as a result of her meteoric rise in the business world. She relied on an outside consultant, Craig Stevens, to handle her own public relations. Stevens also had a tremendous amount of influence over the communications department at the company itself.

The vice president of corporate communication, Eric Ridgway, was actually one of the several employees who would be affected by the current plan to trim the workforce. He had been hired early on as a favor to Bosworth's father. Ridgway had spent 25 years at the *Los Angeles Times* before signing on at Westwood, and while he had a media background, he did not know much about the trade magazine business or the industries that made up Westwood's primary subscriber base. The problems associated with Ridgway made the communications effort more difficult for both Dan Cassidy and the outside counsel advising him through the process.

THE VOLUNTARY SEVERANCE AND EARLY RETIREMENT PROGRAM

Although the CEO was very much against the two programs that were about to be implemented, she had been convinced by both Callahan, the head of human resources, and her board of directors that something had to be done immediately or the company itself would be at risk.

The way the programs would work, several senior managers would be told about the generous voluntary severance or early retirement packages and asked to avail themselves of the appropriate plan. Thus, a director who had received less than excellent performance appraisals for two consecutive years would be a prime candidate for voluntary severance while a vice president approaching 60 would be offered the retirement package. Although both of these programs were "voluntary," the supervisors responsible for identifying candidates were urged to get the weaker people to agree as soon as possible.

COMMUNICATING ABOUT THE PLANS

Cassidy reported to work the following day and was asked to attend a meeting with his supervisor, Catherine Callahan; Bosworth; and Craig Stevens. "Well, Dan, how are you going to pull this one off?" joked Bosworth. Cassidy responded, "Quite honestly, Linda, given your position on this issue, my feeling is that you need to get involved with the announcement tomorrow."

As the discussion progressed, however, it was obvious to Dan Cassidy that he was the one that his boss and the head of the company wanted to take the heat. After two hours, Bosworth looked at Dan squarely in the eye and said: "This was not my idea in the first place, but I know we have no choice but to adopt the voluntary severance packages and early retirement plans for Westwood Publishing. Unfortunately, I need to leave for a conference in New York the day after tomorrow. You and Catherine are going to have to take responsibility this time."

Dan looked over at Catherine. She was gazing at a drawing on Bosworth's wall. It was a picture of someone about to lose his head by guillotine during the French revolution. Somehow the picture seemed very appropriate to their situation.

CASE QUESTIONS

1. Create a strategy for communicating change at Westwood Publishing that you could give to Bosworth.

2. How do changes in the workforce affect how Cassidy ought to think about communicating the new policy?

3. What advice would you give Cassidy about how communications to employees are structured at Westwood?

CHAPTER EIGHT

Investor Relations

As companies strive to maximize shareholder value, they must continually communicate their progress toward that goal to the investing public. Accordingly, investor relations is an essential subfunction of a company's corporate communication program. While explaining financial results and giving guidance on future earnings are critical investor relations activities, companies today need to go "beyond the numbers"—as Collins and Porras explain in their book *Built to Last:*

> Visionary companies pursue a cluster of objectives, of which making money is only one—and not necessarily the primary one. Yes, they seek profits, but they're equally guided by a core ideology—core values and sense of purpose beyond just making money. Yet, paradoxically, the visionary companies make more money than the more purely profit-driven comparison companies.[1]

Investor relations professionals therefore need to link communications to a company's strategy and "vision" as frequently as possible. Increasingly, the investor relations (IR) function is getting involved in activities traditionally handled by PR and media relations professionals and communicating with many of the same constituencies. In addition to a solid understanding of finance, then, IR professionals also need strong communication skills.

In this chapter, we begin our examination of this important subfunction with an overview of investor relations and a brief look at its evolution over the years. We then turn to the goals of investor relations and provide a framework for IR. After discussing important investor constituency groups and how IR reaches them, we look at how the function fits into an organization, and conclude with a discussion of investor relations in the changing business environment.

Investor Relations Overview

The National Investor Relations Institute (NIRI) defines investor relations as "a strategic management responsibility that integrates finance, communication, marketing and securities law compliance to enable the most effective two-way communication between a company, the financial community, and other constituencies, which ultimately contributes to a company's securities achieving fair valuation."[2] The chief

---

[1] James C. Collins and Jerry I. Porras, *Built to Last* (New York: Harper Business, 1994), p. 8.

[2] NIRI corporate Web site, http://www.niri.org (retrieved July 30, 2005).

financial officer of one corporation explained the task of the IR professional as follows: "You're competing for the investment dollar. Your company's story must appeal to the investment world more than the next guy's, or you can't expect to win the coveted shelf space for which everyone is fighting."[3]

As these descriptions illustrate, investor relations is both a financial discipline and a corporate communication function. Changes in the business and regulatory environment over the past decade have affected the way corporations decide how, to whom, and to what extent they convey financial and operating results.

Investors want understandable explanations of financial performance as well as nonfinancial information about companies. According to a report from Ernst & Young's Center for Business Innovation, investors give nonfinancial measures, on average, one-third of the weight when deciding to buy or sell a stock.[4] Examples of nonfinancials include the credibility of management, the company's ability to attract top talent, and the quality and execution of corporate strategy. A survey by McKinsey & Co. found that three-quarters of institutional investors from the United States, Europe, Latin America, and Asia said that board practices are as important as financial results when considering investing in a company.[5]

To ensure that a company presents itself clearly and favorably on all these fronts, then, IR professionals must have both financial acumen and solid communication skills. Access to senior management is also necessary so that the IR function is connected to the company's strategy and vision. An IR department organized in this way is positioned to instill investors' confidence in both good times and bad.

The Evolution of Investor Relations

In the early part of the twentieth century, corporate secrecy was a great concern for companies. Disclosure of any kind was seen as potentially harmful to the interests of the corporation. This all changed in the 1930s with the passage of two federal securities acts that required public companies to file periodic disclosures with the U.S. Securities and Exchange Commission (SEC). Despite the new reporting responsibilities brought about by the enactment of the Securities Act of 1933 and the Securities Exchange Act of 1934, corporations were interested only in mandatory disclosure, which required little in the way of an investor relations function.

Investor relations did not begin to resemble the discipline we know today until the 1950s. A decade later, the National Investor Relations Institute officially recognized the IR function. NIRI was established as a professional association of corporate officers and investor relations consultants who were responsible for communicating with corporate management, the investing public, and the financial community. Around the same time, the Chicago-based Financial Relations

---

[3] Brett Nelson, "So What's Your Story?" *Forbes*, October 30, 2000, p. 274.

[4] David A. Light, "Performance Measurement: Investors' Balanced Scorecards," *Harvard Business Review*, November–December 1998, pp. 17–20.

[5] Editorial Staff, "2000: A Look Back at the Year That Was: The Advent of Regulation FD Made Last Year a Year IROs Will Not Soon Forget," *Investor Relations Business*, January 8, 2001, pp. 12–13.

Board, now a unit of The Interpublic Group, became the first public relations firm dedicated to helping its clients develop relationships with investors.

By the 1970s, FRB had pioneered the distribution of investment profiles that laid out a company's long-term financial goals and strategies. Prior to this innovation, information reached potential investors through presentations by company representatives to local stockbroker clubs or analysts' societies.

Further regulatory changes altered the landscape for IR in the 1970s. With the enactment of the Employee Retirement Income Security Act (ERISA) in 1974, pension fund managers were legally held responsible for acting in the best interests of their beneficiaries. This new responsibility made pension fund managers more demanding of their portfolio companies. For instance, they sought more detailed explanations of company results, particularly when companies underperformed.

In the 1980s, state and local laws enabled pension funds to increase the equity allocation in their portfolios. That share rose to 36 percent in 1989 from 22 percent in 1982, making institutional investors an even more important constituency for the IR departments of corporations. At the same time, inflation caused many individual investors to flee the stock market, and by the end of the 1980s, institutional investors represented 85 percent of all public trading volume.

The first conference calls were held for hundreds of institutional investors at a time in the 1980s. Soon thereafter, quarterly conference calls were standard practice at many companies. A decade later, the Internet provided yet another channel for communicating company financials to large numbers of investors. Organizations began to create investor relations areas within their corporate Web sites to post information such as news releases, annual reports, 10-Ks (SEC required annual filing) and 10-Qs (SEC required quarterly filing), and stock charts.

Even with mass communications such as conference calls and Webcasts, however, IR professionals still arranged for periodic private meetings between large institutional investors or sell-side analysts with the chief financial officer (CFO) or the chief executive officer (CEO). This allowed the analysts to ask specific questions and get management's feedback on their own earnings models and projections.

These practices changed with the enactment of legislation designed to put individual investors on a level playing field with large institutions. The 1990s saw a resurgence of individual investor participation in the stock market and, at the same time, deepening concerns that these individual players were not afforded the same access to company information as their institutional counterparts. This theory was supported when two studies showed that volatility and trading increased immediately after quarterly conference calls (which were only open to institutional investors).[6]

In response to this, in late 2000, the SEC passed Regulation Fair Disclosure, commonly referred to as "Reg FD," prohibiting companies from disclosing "material nonpublic information" to the investment community (e.g., institutional investors, analysts) that has not already been disclosed to the general public. One of the

---

[6] Steve Davidson, "Understanding the SEC's New Regulation FD," *Community Banker*, March 2001, pp. 40–42.

immediate effects of this legislation was the opening up of conference calls to *all* investors, inviting individuals into a previously closed forum that allowed them to hear about company results and strategy directly from senior management. Generally, it set a more formal and coordinated tone for guidance—companies could no longer give "selective guidance"; that is, they could no longer provide some investors with information on earnings projections before others. Some of the other implications of Reg FD for IR will be discussed later in this chapter.

Over the last 50 years, IR has gained the respect and attention of senior management, who increasingly acknowledge it as a vital corporate communication function. The majority of the largest publicly held corporations in the United States and a growing number of small and mid-sized companies are now members of NIRI; by 2005, NIRI had over 4,600 members in 35 chapters in the United States.[7]

Given that investors today demand more communication, more transparency, and more access to companies than they have in the past, corporations competing for their investment dollars need to create IR programs that deliver on these requirements. In the next section, we will explore how organizations can accomplish this.

A Framework for Managing Investor Relations

How do companies attract and retain investors? When you consider that 76 percent of the average U.S. company shares listed on the New York Stock Exchange turn over each year, you begin to appreciate the challenges facing investor relations officers (IROs). The following section addresses the key objectives of investor relations and also provides a framework for the implementation of a successful IR program.

The Objectives of Investor Relations

While the structure of an investor relations program will vary from one organization to the next based on the size of the company, the complexity of its businesses, and the composition of its shareholder base, the main goal of any IR program is the same: to position the company to compete effectively for investors' capital. To achieve this goal, companies need to focus on the following objectives:

1. *Explain the company's vision, strategy, and potential to investors and "conduit constituencies" such as analysts and the media.* One of the most critical duties of an IR professional is to get messages about company results and potential future results across as understandably as possible to the investing public. We will further examine the various investor constituencies later in this section.

2. *Ensure that expectations of the company's stock price are appropriate for its earnings prospects, the industry outlook, and the economy.* IROs need to understand investor concerns and expectations for their organizations and relay this information to management so that there is a high-level understanding of what the market anticipates from the company. If management does not see the company being

---

[7] National Investor Relations Institute Web site, http://www.niri.org/about/mem_profile.cfm.

able to meet market expectations, it needs to work with IR to craft a communication plan to explain why and to manage expectations appropriately. Conversely, if management feels that the company's potential is not reflected in its stock price (that the stock is undervalued), an IR strategy should be developed to help investors see that potential and, accordingly, drive the stock to appropriate levels.

3. *Reduce stock price volatility.* Particularly in a "sell-now-ask-questions-later" environment, having strong IR capabilities is critical to maintaining a stable stock price and shareholder base. This can be accomplished through the related goal of optimizing the company's shareholder structure to include primarily long-term owners of the stock. Companies with stable share prices typically enjoy a lower cost of capital and thus can issue new equity more economically. In addition to the more strategic goal of stabilizing share price over the long term, IROs often have to respond to market news or events that have the potential to affect stock price negatively in the short term. We will cover some examples of this later in this chapter.

Now that we understand what investor relations is designed to accomplish, let's look at how it achieves these objectives. Figure 8.1 depicts how the IR function communicates both directly and indirectly with investors. The indirect communication occurs through "intermediaries" such as analysts, the media, and rating agencies. Communication with these constituencies influences stock price, volatility, and, in turn, the firm's cost of capital and reputation.

Types of Investors

A company's IR strategy should address both retail investors (individual shareholders) and institutional investors (pension funds, mutual funds, insurance companies, endowment funds, and banks). These constituencies, however, place

FIGURE 8.1

Investor Relations Framework.

Source: Adapted from Markus Will and Anna-Lisa Wolters, "Interdependencies of Financial Communications and Corporate Reputation," *Proceedings of the 5th International Conference on Corporate Reputation, Identity, and Competitiveness*, Paris, France, May 17–19, 2001, p. 14.

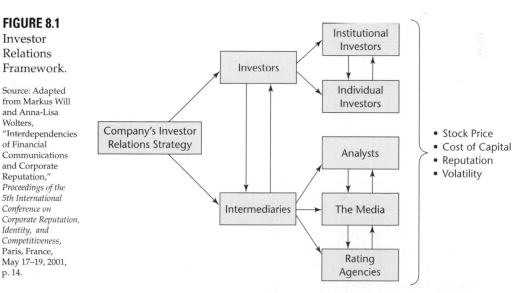

different demands on the IR department and require the use of different communication channels. For example, individuals often require substantially less detailed information due to their relative lack of sophistication but require more hand holding with respect to routine matters such as stock split transactions. In addition, compared to individuals, institutions provide companies with access to larger, fairly concentrated pools of capital, affording them greater efficiencies in message delivery and market impact (defined as the combination of trading volume and price movement).

Institutional Investors

U.S. institutions now own $7.5 trillion of the approximately $13.8 trillion U.S. equity market.[8] Institutional investors have larger holdings than individuals and trade more actively, and thus can have a greater effect on stock price volatility. Their block trading activities can have a tremendous short-term effect on a company's stock price performance, particularly for small- to medium-sized companies.

IR departments can identify and target multiple categories of institutional investors. For instance, institutions can be broken down into groups based on portfolio turnover (high, moderate, and low) as well as investment styles (e.g., growth, value, income, and index). By grouping investors into smaller constituencies with similar characteristics, IROs can efficiently communicate their message to appropriate target audiences. For example, explaining a company's vision and outlook to index investors will yield little benefit because index fund managers do not have the discretion to change portfolio holdings away from index weightings.

IR professionals (or their agencies) can use databases to gather information on institutional stock holdings, turnover rates, and basic portfolio characteristics to identify institutions whose portfolio characteristics closely coincide with their company's price/earnings (P/E) ratio, yield, market capitalization, and industry classification. A company with a low price/book ratio, for instance, might focus on marketing itself to mutual fund managers who specialize in "value" investments. A small company will similarly target small-cap managers, and possibly start raising awareness among mid-cap managers if it is approaching a larger capitalization. This kind of research will prevent the company from spending too much time communicating with uninterested investors.

Having identified those institutions whose investing criteria match its characteristics, the company should develop a plan to interest them in investing for the long term. IROs can then reach those institutions in a variety of ways, including day-to-day phone contact and one-on-one meetings with analysts. For meetings with representatives of large, influential institutions the company would like to have a relationship with, the CEO and/or CFO are often involved.

More formal gatherings are another way to access large groups of institutional investors. For example, CEOs often address analyst or brokerage societies, industry conferences, and conferences geared toward particular kinds of organizations (such as small cap, high-tech firms, for example). Companies also host their own

---

[8] "Flow of Fund Accounts of the United States," Board of Governors of the Federal Reserve, p. 90, http://www.federalreserve.gov/releases/z1/Current/z1.pdf (retrieved July 30, 2005).

meetings in major financial centers such as New York and Boston and invite institutional investors who either own or might want to buy the company's stock.

Individual Investors

Individual investors in the United States own approximately $6.3 trillion in equities.[9] Like institutions, individual investors are not a monolithic constituency group. They may own stock directly, or through mutual funds, company stock plans, or 401(k) plans. They may actively trade securities to generate trading profits on an intraday basis, apply "buy-and-hold" strategies to save for retirement, or anything in between.

Compared to institutions, individual investors have smaller account sizes and generate lower trading volume. In addition, as mentioned earlier, they tend to require different types of information than institutional investors.

We talked in Chapter 2 about the blurring lines between a company's constituency groups. As an example, individual investors also can be employees of the company whose stock they are investing in, through either a 401(k) program, bonus compensation in the form of company stock, or options. Employees read about the financial performance of their own companies in the media and expect to see information that is consistent with what they are hearing internally. Companies thus should be prepared to respond to employees' concerns about depictions of their organization appearing in the press that are inconsistent with management's own messages to them.

Reaching individuals is more difficult than connecting with institutions, as they are more numerous and harder to identify. The channels companies use to communicate with individual investors include direct mail to affinity groups (e.g., current shareholders, employees, customers, suppliers), the brokerage community to promote their stocks with individuals, and visibility generated through the media and advertising (see Chapter 5 for more on financial advertising).

In recent years, the Internet also has proved to be a powerful channel for providing investors with real-time information about companies. A Roper Starch Worldwide study revealed that 25 percent of Web users use the Internet to access corporate information, while 18 percent use it to access information on finance and investments.[10]

The Internet is certainly used by institutional investors as well as individuals—portfolio managers and analysts can now use it to obtain baseline information quickly and easily about a company's financials and see up-to-date press releases—but for individuals who do not also have relationships with company IROs or CFOs, it has provided previously unparalleled access to company information.

Intermediaries

Investors often learn about corporations through sources other than the company itself. In particular, the media and the analyst community are key conduits.

---

[9] Ibid.

[10] Richard W. Wertheim, "Investor Relations and the Internet: A Revolution in the Making," *Executive Speeches* 14, no. 4 (February 1, 2000), pp. 27–32.

Companies provide information to them through conference calls highlighting quarterly achievements, press conferences announcing annual financial results, and face-to-face meetings to discuss company developments and strategy. Reporters and analysts often present management with probing and difficult questions and report the company's responses to the investing public. Accordingly, management should present honest answers and messages that are consistent with what the organization communicates to investors directly.

The Media

We learned in Chapter 6 that the business world increasingly attracts print, television, and online media coverage. Business network news hosts regularly discuss earnings announcements on their programs and often invite equity research analysts to appear and comment on developments within companies they follow.

Media coverage of business can have a dramatic effect on a company's stock price. As an example of this, in early 2002, shares of Krispy Kreme Doughnuts fell nearly two points after a *Forbes* article pointed to an "off-balance-sheet trick" in the company's financial statements. Unfortunately, the reporter had read the wrong line of the balance sheet to come to this conclusion. After Krispy Kreme's chief operating officer (COO) drafted a letter to the editor of *Forbes* and spoke with wire services so that they could issue articles the next day pointing out the error, the stock price returned to prior levels.[11]

As further evidence of the power of the media in the realm of investor relations, about one in two retail brokers surveyed by the Financial Relations Board stated that what they read in the media influenced them and their clients in making investment decisions. Certainly, having a strong media relations function coordinated with the IR department will be beneficial to a firm's investor relations effort by maximizing access to media outlets and ensuring consistency in the messages each group sends to the media.

Additionally, for low-visibility companies looking to attract investors, obtaining the right kind of media coverage can be a critical component of an IR strategy. In response to the rising influence of the financial media, some IR and PR consulting firms offer "financial media relations" programs to help companies target media strategically.

As will be discussed in the next section, the media also play an important role in bringing the views of prominent analysts to the investing public as well, giving a voice to this other very influential intermediary.

Sell-Side Analysts

IR functions target the financial community through "buy-side" and "sell-side" analysts. Buy-side analysts typically work for money management firms (mutual funds or pension funds, for example) and research companies for their own institutions' investment portfolios. They sometimes use sell-side research in their

[11] Robin Londner, "Investment Insiders Grow Skeptical of Financial Data," *PR Week*, February 11, 2002, p. 3.

analysis, but many perform proprietary analysis, including company visits and their own review of company financials. As such, for the purposes of our investor relations framework, buy-side analysts belong in the institutional investor constituency group and are not intermediaries.

Sell-side analysts, however, cover stocks within certain industries and generate detailed research reports that offer "buy," "sell," or "hold" recommendations. This research is then provided to clients of investment banks such as Merril Lynch or retail brokerages such as Charles Schwab. Thus, sell-side analysts are intermediaries between a company and existing and potential investors.

In the late 1990s and with the crash of the Internet bubble in 2000, sell-side analysts came under fire for continuing to issue "buy" recommendations on severely underperforming stocks. The media raised awareness of the inherent conflicts of interest in the job of a sell-side analyst working for an investment bank. Traditionally, companies covered by a firm's research team were also important banking clients who could take their business elsewhere or cut off the analysts' access to information if offended by an unfavorable rating.

As the Internet economy was thriving and stock prices seemed to be on an unstoppable upward trajectory, many of these sell-side analysts enjoyed near-celebrity status. Merrill Lynch entertainment analyst Jessica Reif Cohen could, in her own words, "instantly add—or subtract—billions in market value."[12] Salomon Smith Barney telecommunications analyst Jack Grubman was viewed with similar awe. As business coverage received increasing attention in the media, these analysts became household names. At the height of the dot-com boom, Morgan Stanley's Mary Meeker was even profiled in the *New Yorker* magazine.

This kind of visibility meant that analyst recommendations carried tremendous weight. According to Zacks Investment Research, between 1985 and 2000, stocks that attracted coverage by three or more analysts fared 37 percent better over the ensuing six months than stocks that did not receive the same coverage.[13] However, when that period is viewed from 1996 to 2003, buy recommendations by independent securities firms (those that have no investment banking business) outperformed the buy recommendations issued by analysts at investment banks, by an average of 8 percent annually. In the period following the NASDAQ market peak, buy recommendations underperformed by 17 percent annually.[14]

Even when the Internet bubble burst in early 2000, many analysts maintained sky-high valuations on companies whose stocks were simultaneously plummeting. Investors, who had come to view these analysts as trusted advisors, felt betrayed and misled. Media coverage of these "star analysts" was just as prevalent as it had been in the dot-com heyday, but its angle on the analysts was decidedly changed. A *Vanity Fair* article characterized the group as "superstar analysts who were no longer objective observers of the market: they were insiders with inherent

---

[12] Nina Munk, "In the Final Analysis," *Vanity Fair*, August 2001, p. 100.

[13] Brett Nelson, "So What's Your Story?" *Forbes*, October 30, 2000, p. 274.

[14] UCLA Anderson School of Management, http://www.anderson.ucla.edu/x5046.xml. Retrieved May 9, 2005.

conflicts of interest."[15] Mary Meeker, once dubbed "Queen of the Net," appeared on the cover of *Fortune* magazine in a feature article entitled "Can We Ever Trust Wall St. Again?"[16]

The burst of the bubble ushered in an era of analyst regulation that changed the landscape for communicating with the sell-side analyst community.

In October 2000 the SEC-proposed Regulation Fair Disclosure (Reg FD) took effect. Previously, corporations had communicated with analysts through many of the same channels they used for institutions. One-on-one meetings or lunches with the CEO or CFO were common. On a day-to-day basis, IR professionals spent a great deal of time on the phone with analysts, going over specific inquiries or providing feedback on their models. Reg FD sought to eliminate this standard practice of company executives sharing nonpublic information with security analysts by requiring parallel public disclosure of this information. It had been alleged that executives would reveal material financial and operational information to analysts of investment banks with which their companies had business relationships. And, as a result of Reg FD, corporations were no longer free to give specific feedback on analysts' earnings models beyond corrections to factual data—much to the dismay of the analyst community.[17] This had long been standard practice and a key mechanism for use by analysts in formulating their own estimates for companies. Many companies responded to the new rule by providing their own models to analysts instead of providing specific feedback on models the analysts created.

In April 2003, the Securities and Exchange Commission, the New York Stock Exchange (NYSE), the National Association of Securities Dealers (NASD), and the New York attorney general announced the $1.4 billion Global Analyst Research Settlement with 10 of the largest U.S. investment banks. The Global Settlement was the result of a long investigation by the New York district attorney that found evidence of investment banks inappropriately influencing the work of research analysts. The settlement sought to eliminate the inherent conflicts of interest in the job of a sell-side analyst working for an investment bank. The settlement imposed $1.4 billion in fines and penalties on 10 of the largest U.S. investment banks and mandated structural changes to ensure research and coverage decisions were independent and prohibiting improper interactions between a firm's investment banking and research functions. In particular, analyst compensation could no longer be based directly or indirectly on investment banking revenues and research analysts are now prohibited from participating in investment banking sales efforts, such as pitches and roadshows.[18]

Several changes have occurred in the IR environment post–Reg FD and the Global Settlement. The strict regulations surrounding research on stocks have

[15] Robin Londner, "Street Cleaning," *PR Week*, July 23, 2001, p. 17.

[16] Peter Elkind, "Can We Ever Trust Wall St. Again?" *Fortune*, May 14, 2001, p. 69.

[17] Tommye M. Barnett, "To Speak or Not to Speak," *Oil and Gas Investor*, September 2001, pp. 73–75.

[18] SEC Fact Sheet on Global Analyst Research Settlement, http://www.sec.gov/news/speech/factsheet.htm (retrieved July 27, 2005).

made it more difficult and costly for investment firms to maintain research coverage of as many stocks as they used to. Major broker-dealers are concentrating research on large-capitalization stocks. Thirty-eight percent of all NASDAQ-listed companies and 17 percent of NYSE companies have no analyst coverage and 50 percent of all publicly listed U.S. companies have two or fewer research analysts covering them.[19] As a result of regulation, there are now fewer analysts and therefore fewer channels for public companies to communicate with the investor community.

The settlement also has meant that analyst coverage has become less optimistic. In 2000, at the height of the boom, 95 percent of stocks in the S&P500 had no "sell" ratings and no stock had more than one sell rating.[20] Since the settlement, however, according to research from Washington University in St. Louis, analysts have become more cautious in issuing forecasts and recommendations.[21] Among investment firms that had both research and investment banking practices, "strong buy" recommendations were made on stocks 37 percent of the time in the period prior to the Global Settlement, versus 21 percent of the time following the settlement; "buy" recommendations were made 40.6 percent of the time before versus 32.2 percent of the time after; and "hold" recommendations, which have traditionally been seen as bad news by the market, were made 19.9 percent before and 43.3 percent after by affiliated analysts.

One certainty is that the relationships between analysts and the companies they cover can be fraught with tension if not handled strategically. Consider the story of Tad LaFountain, a long-time analyst at Wells Fargo Securities, who announced in July 2005 that he was dropping coverage of semiconductor giant Altera Corporation because company management would not take his calls or provide adequate information to analyze the business. According to Mr. LaFountain, who had a "sell" rating on the stock, the company objected to his negative opinion. One of 31 analysts covering Altera, Mr. LaFountain says he was told by Altera's VP of investor relations Scott Wylie and CFO Nathan Sarkisian that "it was not in the shareholder's interest to facilitate" his analysis.[22]

Media coverage of this decision was fast and negative, with many seeing the move as an attempt to manipulate opinion. A few days later, Altera was forced to apologize, saying, "In retrospect, our decision to disengage was in error, and (we) apologize to Mr. LaFountain, our investors and the investment community."[23]

Clearly, analyst reports contain much more than a simple buy or hold recommendation, and despite the recent crisis of confidence in the objectivity of these ratings, other information about companies contained in these reports is often used by institutional investors to help them with their investment decisions.

---

[19] NASDAQ Corporate Services Network, https://www.nasdaq.net/pbpubnisn/IRN.htm (retrieved July 23, 2005).

[20] William H. Donaldson, "Speech by SEC Chairman: CFA Institute Annual Conference," Philadelphia, PA, May 8, 2005, http://www.sec.gov/news/speech/spch050805whd.htm (retrieved July 29, 2005).

[21] Stephen Taub, "Spitzer Pact Cut Analyst Bias: Study," CFO.com, November 10, 2004.

[22] Gretchen Morgenson, "An Analyst Receives a Time Out from Altera," *New York Times*, July 27, 2005.

[23] Gretchen Morgenson, "With Apology to an Analyst, Altera Seeks to Repair a Rift," *New York Times*, July 29, 2005.

Analysts remain an important conduit constituency for a company's IR strategy. IROs also should be prepared to communicate strategically with and handle downgrades from analysts with a communication plan.

Rating Agencies

In the United States, examples of rating agencies include McGraw-Hill's Standard & Poor's (S&P), Moody's Investors Service, and Fitch Ratings. These agencies analyze companies in much the same way that buy-side and sell-side analysts do, but with a specific focus on their creditworthiness. The ratings that these agencies assign to a company reflect their assessment of the company's ability to meet its debt obligations. This, in turn, determines the company's cost of debt capital (the interest rates at which it borrows).

These agencies make their ratings available to the public through their ratings information desks and published reports. The highest ratings are AAA (S&P, Fitch) and Aaa (Moody's), and the lowest are D (S&P) and C (Moody's), representing companies that are in default of existing loan agreements. Companies rated BBB/Baa or above are considered "investment grade," and those below are considered not investment grade, or "high yield." The term *junk bonds* also refers to below-investment-grade bonds. The lower the rating, the higher the agency's assessment of the company's potential to default on its loans, thus making it more expensive for the company to raise capital by issuing debt.

Debt ratings affect more than a firm's cost of capital. Senator Joseph Lieberman, chair of the Senate Committee on Governmental Affairs, put it this way:

> The credit raters hold the key to capital and liquidity, the lifeblood of corporate America and of our capitalist economy. The rating affects a company's ability to borrow money; it affects whether a pension fund or money market fund can invest in a company's bonds; and it affects stock price. The difference between a good rating and a poor rating can mean the difference between success and failure, prosperity and bad fortune.[24]

As a recent example of the ripple effects that debt ratings can have on a company, when U.S. telecom giant WorldCom Inc.'s debt went under review by S&P and Moody's for possible downgrade to junk status, the company's stock price plummeted 28 percent in one day in late April of 2002. Investors knew that WorldCom's drop to junk status would trigger provisions in some of the company's debt covenants that would force it to repay $2 billion in loans within 90 days, creating a liquidity crisis.[25]

Credit rating analysts are similar to equity research analysts when it comes to their relationship with a company, with the obvious exception that they will focus

---

[24] Statement by Chair Joseph Lieberman, "Rating the Raters: Enron and the Credit Rating Agencies," U.S. Senate Committee on Governmental Affairs Web site, March 20, 2002, http://www.senate.gov/~gov_affairs/03202002lieberman.htm (retrieved April 30, 2002).

[25] James S. Granelli and Elizabeth Douglass, "WorldCom Shares Dive on Debt Worry; Telecom Firm's Stock Falls 28% to a Record Low of $2.20. Bondholders Fear It Will Be Reduced to Junk-Bond Status," *Los Angeles Times*, April 30, 2002, p. 1.

a great deal more on the company's debt structure. Additionally, many buy-side and sell-side analysts rely on the research and ratings of credit analysts as a component of their own assessment of the company overall, especially for firms within capital-intensive industries characterized by heavy debt loads.

For these reasons, rating agencies are an important intermediary constituency for a company's IR efforts.

Developing an Investor Relations Program

Now that we understand who the key investor constituencies are, let's look at how IR functions are structured to communicate with them: in-house, delegated to an agency, or some combination of the two. This section also will take a closer look at some of the activities that make IR such an important function within a company.

How (and Where) Does IR Fit into the Organization?

A company's IR function can be structured in a number of ways, from fully in-house to fully outsourced. In-house IR teams are typically small: According to NIRI, the average size of a corporate IR department is between one and two people. At smaller organizations, the CFO might handle IR responsibilities directly and use an agency to perform some of the more routine report-writing tasks.[26]

When companies do turn to agencies for assistance, they can choose from agencies that specialize in IR work, such as Kekst & Company, Abernathy MacGregor, and the Financial Relations Board, or full-service PR firms that have strong IR specialty groups, such as Fleishman-Hillard or Burson-Marsteller. Agencies can help with projects and activities across the spectrum of IR, from report-writing and arranging analyst conferences to higher-end services such as bankruptcy and litigation communications, mergers and acquisitions, and initial public offerings. More recently, agencies also have focused on fully understanding Reg FD so that they can help companies with disclosure policy given the new regulation.[27]

The division of responsibilities between what is done in-house versus what is handled by the agency depends on several factors, including the size of the firm and its IR objectives. However it is arranged, the individuals responsible for a company's IR efforts should have access to senior management, including the CEO and CFO. This appears to be the case for in-house IR professionals—two-thirds of corporate NIRI members report to the CFO.[28]

Given the increasing overlap in IR and areas like media relations, in some organizations IR and corporate communication are linked or part of the same

---

[26] "Investor Relations: Corporate," *PR Week*, September 24, 2001, p. 19.

[27] Ibid.

[28] "Understanding IR," *PR Week*, September 24, 2001, p. 17.

ANNUAL REPORTS: MORE THAN JUST THE NUMBERS

SEC reporting requirements create the need for a number of documents to be produced periodically, such as the annual report, the form 10-K, and form 10-Q, for example. Companies can file these reports electronically with the SEC and investors can download them from the SEC's online database, EDGAR, or the company's own Web site in addition to, or instead of, receiving hard copies.

Among all these documents, the annual report is the most time-consuming, expensive, and high-profile. An annual report is a company's equivalent to a "coffee table piece," and is now being used by companies as much as an image vehicle as a reporting tool. Sid Cato has been ranking annual reports since 1983 and providing "best and worst" lists that appear in magazines like Fortune.[1] Though investors can obtain the financial information contained in a printed annual report faster online, there is still great demand for the printed piece. Though 82 percent of the Fortune 500 companies surveyed by Roper Starch in its worldwide "Annual Reports in the New Economy" stated that they post their annual reports on their corporate Web site, their annual report press runs (on average) actually rose in 1999 over the previous year.[2]

Executives surveyed by Roper Starch ranked the printed annual report as the single most important document their company produces. One executive said that the annual report "should be the face of the firm."[3] An annual report gives a company the opportunity not only to share and explain results for the prior year but also to communicate the company's vision.

Annual reports typically have themes that are carried through the piece in graphics and text. Ford Motor Company's 2000 annual report, ranked number one by Sid Cato, had the theme "Connecting with Customers." The theme was picked up in then-chairman Jacques Nasser's shareholder letter, as well as through a series of photos of satisfied customers. Ford produced eight different covers for the report, each showing a real customer family.

In 2001, Ford ranked number one again in Mr. Cato's list, with the theme "Building Our Future." Chair and CEO Bill Ford's letter to shareholders began, "Our results in 2001 were unacceptable," and goes on to acknowledge that the company lost sight of what was important in 2001—its products and people—in the midst of the Ford Explorer tire recalls and a bleak economic environment.

Ford pledged a "back-to-basics" approach for the future that was echoed in the imagery throughout the report. Photos of shiny new Ford cars and trucks were superimposed on sepia-toned prints of cars, assembly lines, and employees of years past. The last section of the report, titled "What We've Learned in the Last 100 Years," included lessons such as "Be Courageous" and "Show Passion," each supported with quotes from founder Henry Ford, his son Henry Ford II, Edsel Ford, and now-Chair Bill Ford. The report clearly delivered more than financial results: It was an articulation of the company's vision.

Today, annual reports are used as reporting vehicles, brand builders, recruiting pieces, marketing brochures, corporate image books, and strategic positioning tools.[4] Even as more companies post their annual reports online, it doesn't appear that the hard-copy version will go away.

[1] Julie Schlosser, "He Ranks and Files," *Fortune,* April 15, 2002, p. 58.
[2] "Are Annual Reports Still Relevant?" @ *ISSUE, The Journal of Business and Design* 6, no. 2 (2001), pp. 26–31.
[3] Ibid.
[4] Ibid.

group. The advent of Regulation Fair Disclosure also has made many companies consider the merits of combining these areas—or at least ensuring that they are closely coordinated—to avoid inadvertent selective disclosure.[29] If companies applaud the idea of a closer partnership between IR and corporate communication, however, this is not yet broadly reflected in corporate structure. According

[29] Robin Londner, "IR-PR Link Not Seen in Chain of Command," *PR Week,* March 4, 2002, p. 3.

to a recent survey, corporate communication and marketing departments still report independently of IR at over 70 percent of companies.[30]

Using IR to Add Value

As mentioned earlier, the investor relations function assumes a marketing role with respect to a company's stock, which involves much more than producing and distributing annual and quarterly reports, responding to shareholder inquiries, and sending information to securities analysts. IR plays both proactive and reactive roles within an organization.

Proactively, IR targets investors to market the company's shares to and provides regular informational updates and explanations of performance to the marketplace. Proactive communications can go beyond traditional analyst calls and include activities such as "field trips" for analysts and portfolio managers. Plant tours and meetings or lunches with key company executives can provide investors and potential investors with a true feel for the company and its management.

IROs also craft communication strategies in response to certain internal or external events. Internal events such as mergers, acquisitions, or the sale of a part of the business allow time to confer with the CEO and CFO, develop a communication strategy around the event, and script answers to anticipated questions and concerns. External events, however, such as an unanticipated crisis (see Chapter 10) require much more rapid damage control.

Charles C. Conaway, former president of the drugstore chain CVS Corp., explained: "Unless you have a very targeted investor-relations program that communicates your message, you're going to get in trouble."[31] CVS underwent a restructuring in 1995 that resulted in a complete turnover of its shareholders in the course of one year. To resolve this instability, CVS bolstered its investor relations program and began actively recruiting longer-term institutional investors to suit its new growth profile.[32] In 2004, CVS won the Interactive Investor Relations Award from the Web Marketing Association.

Companies with extensive IR resources can conduct research to identify their most influential shareholders and seek to understand what motivates them, allowing management to predict more accurately the effect on share price of various events or announcements. Research on the changing stock prices of large U.S. and European public companies over a two-year period showed that a company's share price is significantly influenced by a maximum of 100 current and potential shareholders.[33] By identifying these investors and creating profiles on each of them that detail how they make decisions and what motivates them,

[30] "Business Wire Announces Survey Results on the Consolidation of Communications in IR and PR," *Business Wire*, March 21, 2002, Online Lexis-Nexis Academic, April 2002.

[31] John A. Byrne, "Investor Relations: When Capital Gets Antsy," *BusinessWeek*, September 13, 1999, p. 72.

[32] Ibid.

[33] Kevin P. Coyne and Jonathan W. Witter, "What Makes Your Stock Price Go Up and Down," *McKinsey Quarterly*, no. 2 (2002), p. 28.

companies can better perform scenario analysis on the potential effect on the stock price of certain announcements. If necessary, management can modify plans to bring them in line with the desires of key shareholders and minimize negative effects on stock price.[34]

Management also must be careful, however, not to become beholden to investor demands in the short term. The bull markets of the 1980s and 1990s were a major cause for the short-term orientation of the investment community. As Darrell K. Rigby, Bain & Company director, has commented: "I've seen so many senior executives saying and doing things to deliver short-term news lately that it's a little frightening. . . Their time horizons are shortening. They're thinking more about retiring rich at 45 or 50 and less about the institution they will leave behind."[35] Perhaps a certain corporate strategy will not deliver the earnings that investors and analysts are expecting in the short term, but if the strategy is one that the company believes is right for the long term, management must clearly explain the reasons for this to the investment community. Indeed, as former SEC Chairman William H. Donaldson said in a 2005 speech, "The focus on short-term results has had a counter-productive influence on companies, on investors and on analysts themselves."[36]

NIRI's Lou Thompson maintains that the 19 percent drop in Hewlett-Packard (HP) shares and nearly 10 percent decline in Compaq shares that occurred the day the HP-Compaq merger was announced in 2004 could have been mitigated by stronger IR efforts. If Compaq and HP had identified market skepticism over the merger, Thompson argued, the companies could have addressed these concerns before investors "voted with their feet" and took a toll on both companies' stock prices.[37]

When a crisis hits, or a company undergoes some structural change that the market reacts to negatively, investors have already lost money, as the stock price usually adjusts downward nearly instantaneously. Either shareholders can join in the selling, or they can continue to hold the company's stock hoping that it will recover. To ensure that shareholders do not sell, companies must be prepared with swift, honest communications to investors when the stock price starts spiraling downward.

Management must identify the problem (or perceived problem), what caused it, and, importantly, what it is doing to address it. In these types of "damage control" situations, channel choice matters: a Webcast or conference call with the CEO or CFO will carry much more weight than a press release posted to the company Web site.

Similarly, when a company is not performing as well as it should, IR professionals should communicate to analysts and investors what management is doing about the situation. Such candor is definitely in the company's best interests. As author Thomas Garbett says:

---

[34] Ibid.

[35] Byrne, "Investor Relations."

[36] Donaldson, "Speech by SEC Chairman."

[37] "Understanding IR," *PR Week*, September 24, 2004, p. 17.

Information reduces risk. The stock market, as a process, arrives at a stock price based upon all known elements relating to the company. Some of the unknown factors add to the price, others subtract. Areas about the company that are unknown usually contribute to the minus side of the price equation.[38]

Investor Relations and the Changing Environment

In this chapter, we have discussed the evolution of the IR function over the years and some of the external developments that have shaped it. Over the past decade, technological advances and the changing business environment have been significant influences on the field of investor relations.

As mentioned earlier, many companies are creating investor relations areas on their corporate Web sites that make stock quotes and charts, news releases, and company financial statements available to anyone with Internet access. Investors find this kind of instantaneous access to information reassuring, particularly during periods of market volatility and uncertainty. Earnings Webcasts also are becoming popular. These events enable participants to witness firsthand how companies' top executives handle themselves, and can bring an otherwise two-dimensional upper management to life for current and potential investors.

Web-based IR is becoming increasingly prevalent and is supported by external vendors and agencies that can help a company create effective sites. Jeffrey Parker (who founded First Call) and Robert Adler established Corporate Communications Broadcast Network (CCBN) in 1997, recognizing that "the concept of 'Internet time' has created pressure on corporations to do everything better, cheaper, sooner and faster."[39] CCBN (acquired by Thomson in 2004) now builds and manages the IR portions of the Web sites of over 2,500 publicly traded companies. Shareholder.com also emerged in the 1990s to provide an array of online IR services—including Web site hosting, Webcasts, and integrated e-mail broadcasts—and now works with over 750 companies, including Coca-Cola Enterprises, Delta Air Lines, and Tiffany & Co.[40]

The Internet enables greater transparency by providing nearly real-time information about companies to a wide audience, and this transparency is especially valued in the current business environment. Indeed, see Chapter 9 for more information on the Sarbanes-Oxley legislation and the effect it has had on the need for transparency in business.

Considering that seven of the 15 largest business bankruptcies since 1980 occurred in 2001, investors have witnessed previously unimaginable corporate events over a short period of time. Energy giant Enron went from No. 7 in the Fortune 500 to the

---

[38] Thomas F. Garbett, *How to Build a Corporation's Identity and Project Its Image* (Lexington, MA: Lexington Books, 1988), p. 99.

[39] From CCBN company Web site, http://www.ccbn.com/about/faqs.html (retrieved April 11, 2002).

[40] Business/technology editors, "Shareholder.com Clients Showcase Strength at *IR Magazine* U.S. Awards," *Business Wire*, April 3, 2002, Online Lexis-Nexis Academic, April 2002.

single largest bankruptcy in history.[41] In fact, BankruptcyData.Com revealed that public company bankruptcies reached a record 257 in 2001—increasing from the 176 occurring in 2000.[42] Consequently, investors are keeping a watchful eye on Wall Street using both traditional and online media tools. As William Allen, director of New York University's Center of Law and Business, remarks: "There has not been such widespread scrutiny into the techniques employed in the financial markets since the 1920s."[43]

Many assessed the fall of Enron as a greater detriment to investor confidence than the bursting of the dot-com bubble. Additionally, as sell-side analysts came under fire for biased recommendations and conflicts of interest, investors became more uncertain of where they could turn to for objective information about the companies whose stock they owned. Consequently, many retreated from the market altogether.

Even America's most admired corporations have felt the ripple effects of investor insecurity. General Electric, for example, saw its shares plummet to $35 in February 2002, even though the company had not—unlike an increasing number of companies in today's media spotlight—been accused of any sort of misdeed. However, GE's financing subsector, GE Capital, came under fire for not offering substantial earnings information to the public, forcing the company to make reporting changes that increase transparency.[44]

Cendant, one of the foremost providers of travel and real estate services in the world, was created by the merger of HFS Inc. and CUC International in December 1997. In April 1998, Cendant was hit hard when it was discovered that CUC's financial statements had been overstated by hundreds of millions of dollars in both revenues and profits. Following this discovery, the market value of Cendant dropped more than 40 percent, threatening the credibility of both the company and CEO Henry Silverman. It also brought a barrage of questions from numerous constituencies. How could the company and its CEO not have conducted adequate "due diligence" to uncover CUC's fraudulent reporting before the transaction was completed? Silverman realized that, to regain credibility, complete honesty and financial transparency were the only viable course of action. He established the mantra, "Tell the truth. Tell it all. Tell it now," insisting that all the accounting irregularities be acknowledged as soon as they were known. Silverman and the company's head of corporate communication and investor relations, Sam Levenson, continue to tell the Cendant story as frequently and as clearly as possible to restore investor confidence in the company. "I can never be far away from investor relations or public relations. At the end of the day, I'm accountable," says Silverman. "You can never over-communicate. There is no such thing."[45]

---

[41] Susan Scherreik, "Finding Stocks You Can Trust," *BusinessWeek*, March 25, 2002, p. 128.

[42] Ibid.

[43] Stephen Gandel, "Posse Pursues Wall St.," *Crain's New York Business*, April 12, 2002.

[44] Ben White, "Enron-Related Fears Take Toll on Other Firms' Stocks," *Washington Post*, February 13, 2002, p. E01.

[45] Paul A. Argenti, Robert A. Howell, and Karen A. Beck, "The Strategic Communication Imperative," *MIT Sloan Management Review* 46, no. 3 (Spring 2005), pp. 83–89.

As seen from the above examples, investor relations is even more important to companies against this backdrop of uncertainty and mistrust. Clear, full disclosure of business results will put companies in a strong position in the competition for investor capital.

Conclusion

Many activities fall under the IR function, from planning and running annual meetings and putting together reports for SEC filings to targeting and marketing the company's shares to investors. The way all these should be approached is no different from any other communication activity: Companies need to follow a communication strategy that includes a clear understanding of the company's objectives and a thorough analysis of all of its constituencies so that appropriate messages can be crafted and delivered.

Unfortunately, efforts to quantify IR's direct effect on stock price and/or a company's cost of capital have yielded little in the way of results. Today's equity markets are influenced by many factors beyond companies' control, and thus, while it is still used as a broad indicator, stock price does not single-handedly signal an IR success or failure. Anecdotal evidence, however, does provide a basis for the simple conclusion that IR is a required communication function in today's marketplace.

No company can afford to deal with the current investment community without developing an effective investor relations function, whether it is fully in-house, fully contracted to an outside agency, or a combination of the two. The price paid for overlooking this advice is far greater than the investment made in the personnel that staff this important function.

Steelcase, Inc.

Perry Grueber sat at his desk at Steelcase, Inc., on a bright day in July 2000, thinking about the work that lay ahead for him. Grueber had just joined Steelcase, a maker of office furnishings and workspace solutions, as Director of Investor Relations. Steelcase was dedicated to improving IR at the company and had promised Grueber the resources he required to make the department an effective tool for communicating to key constituencies.

When Grueber accepted his job in May, Steelcase was trading at $11.56 per share, just above its all-time low of $10.38 per share and down 70 percent [from] a high of $37.94. Steelcase's operating performance was mostly to blame for the declining share price; however, the company's communications with its investors also had played a role. The company had high turnover in its institutional shareholder base and, since the time of its IPO, had not actively marketed itself to sell-side analysts. These analysts, in return, expressed little interest in the company. At the same time, insider sales were increasing, sending more shares into the market amid soft demand. Grueber needed a new IR strategy to help Steelcase turn its situation around. As he settled into his new office at the company's headquarters in Grand Rapids, Michigan, he began to assess the challenge that lay before him objectively.

HISTORY OF STEELCASE, INC.

Steelcase was founded in 1912 by Peter Wege, Henry Idema, and 12 other investors under

Source: This case was prepared by Thomas Darling under the supervision of Professor Paul A. Argenti at the Tuck School of Business at Dartmouth. Information was gathered from public and corporate sources, including interviews with Perry Grueber at Steelcase in May 2002.

the name Metal Office Furniture. Wege hoped to capitalize on the benefits of metal furniture over its more flammable wooden counterparts. This original vision found success early on, as government architects began to specify metal in their designs and turned quickly to Metal Office Furniture to fill their demand. Early company successes included the development of the metal wastebasket and the later invention of the suspension cabinet, which became the foundation for all modern filing cabinets.

Company sales in 1913, the first full year of operations, were at $76,000. As revenues began to increase, Metal Office Furniture hired a media consultant, who created the trademark Steelcase name in 1921. World War II and the resulting war material contracts benefited the company, and the boom years of the 1950s and 60s catapulted Steelcase further forward in terms of revenues and profits. By the late 1960s, Steelcase had become the largest manufacturer in the office furniture industry. It retained that status through the year 2001, when the company reported revenues of $4.1 billion.

Steelcase's founder, Peter Wege Sr., died in 1947. Wege's partner Henry Idema died four years later in 1951, and control of the company fell to Henry Idema's son Walter. The Idemas began a tradition of family stewardship over the company that continued when Walter Idema's son-in-law Robert Pew II assumed leadership in 1966. Pew became executive chairman in 1974 and retained that title until his retirement in 1999, although James P. Hackett became president and CEO in 1994. By 2000, Steelcase as a company retained the imprint of the vision and the direction it had received through the founding families' descendants.

IDENTITY, VISION, AND REPUTATION

Steelcase built its image from the set of values held by founders Peter Wege and Henry Idema, clearly articulated in its organizational goals: "Steelcase aspires to transform the ways people work . . . to help them work more effectively than they ever thought they could."[1] Every employee read the company's core values statement:

> At Steelcase, We:
>
> Act with integrity
>
> Tell the Truth
>
> Keep commitments
>
> Treat people with dignity and respect
>
> Promote positive relationships
>
> Protect the environment
>
> Excel[2]

Steelcase had a history of "putting people before profits"[3] and dealing fairly with its employees. As Grueber explained, "There is very much a family atmosphere . . . I've never seen a better benefits package and it is not just executive benefits; it's all the way down the line." Tenure with the firm averaged nearly 18 years. The values embodied in Steelcase's treatment of its employees applied to other constituencies as well, including dealers, vendors, and the communities in which Steelcase operated.

As Grueber described it, Steelcase prided itself in "communicat[ing] values through actions. It's not just the corporate line." For example, shortly after becoming CEO, James Hackett voiced his concern that Steelcase's offices did not communicate the company's goal of transforming the way people work to be more effective. Outdated headquarters designs from the 60s and 70s isolated executives in their offices. When company management wanted to conduct brainstorming or other creative sessions, they often "fled headquarters."[4]

James Hackett challenged senior management to trade their traditional offices for a new office environment one floor below. This office overcame the existing separation and used a quarter less space. The offer contained an escape clause, allowing management to move back to the traditional offices after a trial period. But the redesigned offices proved to be an unmitigated success, increasing workplace effectiveness and becoming the prototype for a new line of systems furniture called Pathways.[5]

Internally, all members of Steelcase acted in a way that reinforced the company's message of open communication at every level. As Grueber explained, "Executives all have an open-door policy. If you came to visit our offices, you would see that our senior executives reside in an open-plan environment. They don't have enclosed offices and so, we go to great lengths to live our vision."

Externally Steelcase's strong values helped create a dealership network that was the envy of the industry and demonstrated the extent to which Steelcase's values shaped its business. Steelcase relied heavily on its dealers to support its "made to order" business model, and made a point of treating them with respect, as primary purchasers of their products and as fellow businessmen whose own businesses would prosper as Steelcase's prospered.

THE INITIAL PUBLIC OFFERING

During its time as a private company, Steelcase had developed a much-admired reputation stemming from its well-articulated identity, vision, strategy, and culture. While Steelcase intended to continue its focus as defined by the

---

[1] Steelcase, Inc., Web site, "Our Company: Overview," http://www.steelcase.com/servlet/OurCompany (retrieved May 24, 2002).

[2] Ibid.

[3] Conversation with Perry Grueber.

[4] Marc Spiegler, "Changing the Game," *Metropolis Feature*, July 1998, http://www.metropolismag.com/html/content/0798/jl98game.htm (retrieved May 16, 2002).

[5] Ibid.

original families into the future, the company also believed that it had reached a point where it would benefit from a changeover to public ownership. This change would provide increased liquidity to the company's founding families and give them the ability to diversify their holdings. As the list of Steelcase heirs grew, liquidity became more important to these private owners. Many of the family members wanted to diversify their long-term holdings and allow for distributions to charities and other philanthropic activities. During its 90 years as a private company, Steelcase had grown to become a member of the Fortune 500 and the largest manufacturer of office solutions in the United States. By 1998, the private ownership structure for this organization was simply too inflexible.

The economic environment at the end of the 1990s was prime for Steelcase's initial public offering. Data from the Business and Industrial Furniture Manufacturer's Association (BIFMA) forecast double-digit increases in office furniture shipments throughout the first three quarters of 1997.[6] Steelcase was the leader in this growing furniture shipment industry, which was already worth $10 billion in 1996. Furthermore, the U.S. economy overall was still growing at an impressive pace (although the Asian crisis had sparked some doubt in late 1997), white-collar job growth remained strong, and companies were flush with cash from the booming stock market.

Steelcase came to market on February 18, 1998, with a 12.5-million-share offering priced at $28 per share; the proceeds went entirely to family stakeholders. The offering proved very popular with money managers and was oversubscribed to such a degree that the number of shares was increased from 9.4 million to 12.5 million and the IPO price quickly exceeded the originally projected range of $23–$26 per share. On the first day of trading, Steelcase shares rose from the opening offer to close at $33.63, up approximately 20 percent.

After the IPO, 156 million total shares were outstanding, with 12.5 million in public hands, and the balance owned by the founding family. Employees received a gift of 10 shares each and options allowing them to purchase shares at below-market rates. One-third of the IPO shares went to employees. Institutions were the largest purchasers of the 12.5 million shares sold to the public.

STEELCASE AS A PUBLIC COMPANY (IPO TO JUNE 2000)

Steelcase hit an all-time closing high of $37.94 per share on March 13, 1998, less than one month after the IPO. Almost everything that followed with respect to the company's stock price, however, was disappointing. Uncertainty caused by the 1997 Asian crisis and the 1998 Russian default significantly disturbed many companies' capital expenditures. In addition, as the year 2000 approached and "Y2K" fears loomed, corporate spending was focused almost solely on technology and information systems. Although traditional indicators of furniture system demand remained strong, those indicators did not translate into end demand for Steelcase's products.

In 1999, just as the company's profitability started to weaken, Steelcase purchased the remaining 50 percent of Strafor, a previous joint venture interest in Europe and Africa with annual sales of $500 million. Because the two companies concentrated on different aspects of the furniture business, the addition of Strafor's business to the balance sheet had a material effect on several of Steelcase's financial ratios. All of Steelcase's products were "made to order." This business model had allowed it to carry only a small amount of inventory, and Steelcase's dealers typically paid for purchases in less than 30 days. Strafor did not have the same inventory constraints. Also, many of Strafor's customers, by contrast, were accustomed to paying closer to 90 days after receiving an order. With the Strafor acquisition, inventory at Steelcase rose and inventory

[6] Mahua Dutta, "Steelcase Builds IPO," *IPO Reporter*, February 16, 1998.

turnover fell. At the same time, however, a new customer base increased Steelcase's collection risk. The softness in the balance sheet reinforced investor concerns over deteriorating earnings performance.

Steelcase performance in 1999–2000 was mediocre. Sales slumped or, at best, remained flat. Cost control initiatives and a cut in bonuses brought earnings up in 1999, but gains were erased by a significant fall in earnings reported in 2000.[7] Steelcase had expected a certain amount of business in 1999 that never materialized, throwing off the company's cost structure and causing the gross margins to drop.

Sagging sales turned into a flood of orders in early 2000, coming in from companies that had delayed renovation projects until after Y2K. Investors expected Steelcase to bounce back quickly. Unfortunately, the company had underestimated the costs associated with serving a rush of new orders. According to Grueber, "As the surge in business came in 2000, when our system should have been there to meet the needs without any difficulty, the customer service requirements were so rigorous in terms of delivering product, getting it there on time, and the pricing environment so tough that we had further erosion of our gross margins and operating margins." Profitability and operating margins continued to slump.

At the time of the IPO, Steelcase had no debt on its balance sheet. It had positive earnings of $1.40 per share (including shares issued through the IPO) and an overall strong demand for its product. Two years later, Steelcase faced increasing volatility in end demand and a weaker balance sheet. The company was unsure of what strategy to communicate to investors. "The market just didn't understand what was happening," said Grueber, "and we were not in a position to articulate a great strategy."

[7] Note that Steelcase operates on a fiscal year ending in February and all references to financial statements are for the year ending in February.

THE INVESTOR RELATIONS EFFORT (1998–2000)

STRUCTURE

Because of its large size and market-leading position, Steelcase had the potential to be a credible, attractive investment for multiple types of institutional investors. But institutions didn't flock to Steelcase shares. The company was large enough to be included on several indices; however, its percentage weighting was often adjusted to reflect its small float (the number of shares owned by the public, not including insiders). Many institutional investors chose to steer clear because of its relative illiquidity. SEC filings showed only 28 institutional holders of Steelcase in 2000, representing between 5 and 8 percent of the shares available to the public. With the exception of several small index players, turnover among institutions was well over 50 percent, meaning that the institutional shareholder base changed every two years.

When Perry Grueber arrived at the company to take over as Director of Investor Relations, he replaced Gary Malburg, who was both the Vice President of Finance and Treasurer and head of IR. Malburg had been responsible for communicating with investors, answering questions, and assisting with the financial statements. However, because of significant and growing responsibilities in the Treasury department, only about a quarter of his time was available for investor relations activities. The company's Corporate Communications Director, Allan Smith—who reported to the Vice President of Global Marketing and Communications, Georgia Everse—also assisted the IR effort, crafting and disseminating press releases and creating the company's annual report. The staff in these two divisions had few formal channels for interaction. Steelcase's internal structure lacked a clear conduit for IR staff to respond to the concerns of its shareholders.

Although IR had not been a priority at Steelcase, the company had not remained inactive in its attempts to communicate with existing shareholders following its IPO. It engaged the services of Genesis, Inc., a highly respected investor relations consulting company. According to Deborah Kelly, a partner at Genesis, "The good news was that Steelcase was widely respected by its core constituencies as the dominant force in the office furniture industry and as being guided by people with strategic vision and a solid grasp of trends."[8] Nonetheless, she continued, "there was frustration among investment analysts regarding performance."

Genesis's main responsibility was advising Steelcase in the creation of the company's annual report. Genesis also helped plan Steelcase's first "analyst day" in November 1999, an event hosted by the company for buy- and sell-side analysts and portfolio managers. Leading up to this "analyst day," Steelcase hired another outside consultant to perform a perception study of investors' opinions about company communications. The report produced from the study, according to Kelly, revealed that "investors were looking for a more proactive IR program that could help them better understand strategic objectives and they wanted to have greater access to management, so they could get more than just the phone answered." Analyst day helped open up the decision-making process to many analysts and portfolio managers, but this important first step lacked the vital follow-up that additional proactive communications might have provided. As he entered the company, Grueber had the opportunity to launch a renewed and sustained effort to implement strong IR strategies at Steelcase.

GUIDANCE AND REPORTING

In some ways, Steelcase resembled a public company even before its IPO in 1998; it had a board of directors, audited financial statements, and a large shareholder base. Once Steelcase became a public company, however,

the previous shareholder makeup led to an "inner circle" mentality that proved difficult to change. Management was not used to the additional requests for information and sometimes assumed a defensive posture toward inquisitive analysts or investors. "Once we had come public," said Grueber, "we were providing the required elements but not a great deal of insight into decision making at the company or the strategic direction of the company."

Steelcase's reluctance to share publicly its inner decision-making processes extended a company approach to communications that had developed during its decades of heavy reliance on the controlling families' leadership. The families chose board members as their representatives, who then hired and supervised the management team. The company under this system earned a strong level of trust both in its direction and in the quality of the reported information. Very little information was ever questioned or requested by non–board members. Along with this trust, though, came a highly conservative outlook from company leadership with regard to the amount of information shared and prospective statements regarding business performance.

In each earnings release, Steelcase typically disclosed very specific guidance for the upcoming year or quarter. Grueber noted, "The company, due to its conservative nature, has been very cautious about selective disclosure throughout its public life. The way they communicated to the Street was through a press release." Due to advice from internal counsel and a desire to prevent selective disclosure, management never "walked the Street up or down" with its estimates.[9] Another major factor in Steelcase's conservative approach to

---

[8] This and all quotes are from interviews with Deborah Kelly in May 2002.

[9] "Walking the Street" is a practice that includes providing material information to analysts during conversations, making excessive statements concerning future earnings prospects, or blatantly encouraging analysts to raise a lower earnings estimate. Some of these tactics have since been prohibited through the Regulations for Fair Disclosure, enacted in 2000.

its disclosures after it became public was the lack of incentives to develop a strong quarterly forecasting discipline during its years as a private company. In addition, the company did not strive to build and maintain relationships with its analysts, so when it came time to disseminate information, it didn't have a receptive ear through the sell-side analysts.

Steelcase's inexperience with releasing company information to the analyst community cost it credibility in the years immediately following its IPO. Press releases assumed relatively high importance at Steelcase in a company environment that both lacked a strong channel for adjusting guidance and reflected the company's inherently conservative attitude toward providing information to outside parties. Unfortunately, if the information published in a current press release was inconsistent with earlier guidance, Steelcase could do very little to minimize the surprise the information caused investors. Several pre-announcements in 1998 and 1999 damaged Steelcase's reputation with investors and increased the perceived risks associated with owning the stock. As Genesis's Deborah Kelly explained, "They kept missing quarters and it was an unusually large number. For a company that has just gone public, usually you want to have 4–5 quarters in the bag . . . Not here."

NEXT STEPS FOR STEELCASE

Overall, Steelcase put a tremendous amount of effort into its IPO and into readying itself for the rigor of being a public company. Unfortunately, assumptions about public company communications that Steelcase made based upon past experiences as a private company often led to disappointment for investors. In addition, the equity markets entered into an extremely turbulent period after the IPO, which caused significant shocks to equity values and corporate capital spending and also created a harsh environment for a newly public company to develop

its investor relations acumen. Deborah Kelly summed up Steelcase's situation as follows:

I think they put a lot of effort into getting a grasp for what being a public company meant from a communications perspective. They are such good people. They are a terrific management team in terms of doing the right thing, integrity, and caring about what happens. The shock was that they had spent so many years communicating with owners that I don't think they realized there might be a difference when you go public. It was kind of a shock that you had to do things a little differently and have a different sensitivity with this group.

As part of Steelcase's effort to readdress its corporate communication to investors, the company had hired Grueber, and now it was up to him to outline his goals and strategy for the IR department.

CASE QUESTIONS

1. As part of creating the full-time IR position, Steelcase had to decide where to place Grueber in the company hierarchy. Given the issues facing Steelcase when Grueber arrived, what are the strengths and weaknesses of placing Grueber under the CFO versus the corporate communication department?
2. What resources should Grueber ask for? How should he organize the function (reporting lines, internal staff versus agencies, etc.)?
3. What investor constituencies should Steelcase try to interest in the company's stock? What channels should Grueber use to attract them? What message would Steelcase deliver to them?
4. What mistakes did Steelcase make in its past IR efforts?
5. What are the biggest challenges facing Steelcase in mid-2000 and beyond? How would you position the IR function to handle those challenges?

CHAPTER NINE

Government Relations

Government and business in the United States tend to have an adversarial relationship as business attempts to minimize government involvement in the private sector and Washington attempts to manage the needs of all citizens by exerting its power over the corporate realm.

Government influences business activities primarily through regulation. Originally, government regulation managed market competition. The first government regulations applied to industries such as telecommunications where high barriers to entry facilitated the emergence of monopolies that could hurt the consumer. In these cases, regulation replaced Adam Smith's "invisible hand" to protect citizens from high prices, bad service, and discrimination.

Governmental regulation of monopolies has not prevented large corporations, however, from wielding impressive political and social power. The predominance of global corporate giants such as Nike, Coca-Cola, and McDonald's transcends voting districts and political borders. Some of the most politically active organizations in the United States are, in fact, domestic or multinational corporations and trade associations.[1] Political largesse on the part of big business has made many Americans cynical about the integrity of the political process in Washington and its ability to govern the corporate world properly.

On the list of trustworthy professions, many voters rank politics below business. However, 90 percent of incumbents still return to Congress each election, indicating that if this distrust does exist, Americans are not translating their dislike of politicians in general into action against particular office holders by voting them out.[2] At the same time, as Chapter 1 has shown, action against particular corporations that the public perceives as corrupt is increasingly prevalent. Anticorporate campaigns range from boycotts and demonstrations, to support of legislation to restrict corporate influence on Capitol Hill. When Congress responded to scandals at Enron, Tyco, and WorldCom with a wave of reforms aimed at curbing corporate misdeeds and enforcing tougher standards on transparency of reporting, the government appeared to take the protestors' side.

In this chapter, we first examine the nature of the relationship between government and business. Then, we discuss the importance of government relations departments within companies and how the function itself has developed over the

---

[1] Wendy L. Hansen and Neil J. Mitchell, "Disaggregating and Explaining Corporate Political Activity: Domestic and Foreign Corporations in National Politics," *American Political Science Review*, December 1, 2000, p. 891.

[2] Douglas G. Pinkham, "How'd We Get to Be the Bad Guys?" *Public Relations Quarterly*, July 22, 2001, p. 12.

past few decades. After seeing how businesses today manage internal and external government affairs, we highlight some of the political activities that companies use to advance their agendas in Washington.

Government Begins to Manage Business: The Rise of Regulation

Government regulation began over 100 years ago with state regulation of the railroad companies. By the mid-nineteenth century, trains had triumphed over rival forms of land transportation. Railroad systems opened travel opportunities to people all over the United States and drove the growth of industry, shipping goods quickly across long distances. However, the railroads also presented the country with enormous problems. While proponents of a laissez-faire approach to the markets maintained that competition would regulate business, it failed to regulate the railroads and corruption ensued.

The federal government's regulation of business began in 1887, with the Act to Regulate Commerce and the establishment of the Interstate Commerce Commission (ICC). Then, in 1890, another critical piece of legislation was passed: the Sherman Antitrust Act. This established a legal framework to prevent trusts from restricting trade and reducing competition, and remains the main source of antitrust law in the United States. From the ICC and the Sherman Antitrust laws to the hundreds of regulations currently in place, covering topics that range from the environment to pornography to food quality, the government is actively engaged in business affairs. Each year the federal government passes laws, and even creates new agencies, to correct what it perceives as market externalities produced by private business.

Some examples of past bills that affected business include the Cigarette Labeling and Advertising Act (1965), which requires all cigarette packages to carry warnings about the hazards of smoking; the Clear Air Act Amendments (1970), which outlined procedures for monitoring air quality; and the Employee Retirement Income Security Act of 1974 (ERISA), which set new federal standards for employee pension programs.

One of the most significant acts to affect business was the Sarbanes-Oxley Act of 2002, officially titled the Public Company Accounting Reform and Investor Protection Act. It came in the wake of a series of corporate financial scandals, including those affecting Enron, Arthur Andersen, and WorldCom.

The act was designed to review dated legislative audit requirements and, by doing so, protect investors by improving the accuracy and reliability of corporate disclosures. The act covers issues such as establishing a public company accounting oversight board, auditor independence, corporate responsibility, and enhanced financial disclosure. It also eliminated some of the most egregious practices in the accounting world, such as using auditing as a loss leader to encourage companies to buy their higher-profit consulting services. It also mandated that companies test their internal financial controls to help ensure that fraud doesn't happen.[3]

---

[3] American Institute of Certified Public Accountants Web site, http://www.aicpa.org (retrieved June 27, 2005).

Historically, business has resisted new regulations, especially laws that mandate costly additions to existing procedures. One example of these regulations is the "best available technology" clauses of many environmental laws, which demand that polluting companies maximize investment in "clean" equipment when they update their facilities. American industry has complained that regulations hurt American businesses and their efforts to compete with foreign rivals. Regulatory bills, they argue, add costs to American companies not incurred by foreign competitors. These costs could drive up the price of American products, making them comparatively less attractive than foreign substitutes. Corporate America has especially been hit by the costs associated with complying with Sarbanes-Oxley. The amount and extent of government involvement in the market has fluctuated with changes in White House administrations, but in spite of these fluctuations, and the arguments against regulation, business will always have to deal with a baseline level of government regulation.

The Reach of the Regulatory Agencies

Through the years, regulatory agencies have evolved into sophisticated organizations. Franklin D. Roosevelt's New Deal gave government incredible power to regulate business. The Securities and Exchange Commission (SEC) was created to stabilize financial markets, and the National Labor Relations Board to remedy labor problems. The Federal Communications Commission (FCC) regulated radio, television, and telephones, and the Civil Aeronautics Board (CAB) regulated the airlines. The safety rulemaking powers would later be transferred to a new agency, the Federal Aviation Administration (FAA), and then undergo yet another restructuring as part of Homeland Security after the terrorist attacks of September 11, 2001. More recently, Sarbanes-Oxley (SOX) increased the power of the PCAOB, a congressionally created private-sector, nonprofit corporation. The PCAOB has sweeping powers over the nation's external auditors with respect to their auditing of publicly held companies. This is only a small selection of the regulatory agencies that have emerged over the last century.

Government is involved in virtually all stages of business development. Many enterprises cannot begin operations until they receive a license from a regulatory agency such as the Interstate Commerce Commission (ICC), the FCC, or the Food and Drug Administration (FDA). Once an enterprise has its license to operate, the same government agencies must then inspect and approve its products. The Consumer Product Safety Commission (CPSC) helps set safety standards for consumer products, and most products must pass its "tests" before they ever reach the market.

Beyond approving which products become available to the public, the government also can influence the prices of goods and services. Agricultural goods, forest products, and metals are examples. Using congressionally approved formulas, federal agencies set floor prices, volume-based subsidies, and quota systems that shape the prices in these markets. The government also heavily influences the prices set by transportation, communications, and utility companies—industries that provide the basic infrastructure for society.

Since the days of the Sherman Antitrust Act, the US government has continued its efforts to prevent monopolies and other anticompetitive business practices. One example is the Federal Trade Commission's (FTC) rejection of a merger between Staples and Office Depot. The FTC argued that, if they merged, each superstore would lose its largest competitor. Without the check that direct competition between Staples and Office Depot had placed on prices, the merged office supply store would gain considerable control over what it charged its customers. The FTC viewed the joining of Staples and Office Depot as more of a threat to consumers than a benefit, and so prevented the merger.[4] A more recent example of the power of the FTC is Blockbuster Video dropping its hostile takeover bid for Hollywood Entertainment, another video rental company, citing the probability of not getting regulatory clearance.[5]

In the next section, we will look at how business has responded to government regulation and ways in which companies work with lawmakers to ensure their own voice is heard when drafting business-specific legislation.

How Business "Manages" Government: The Rise of Government Relations

In light of the government's heavy involvement in commercial affairs, business eventually realized that, instead of fighting regulation, a more effective approach would be advocating their own positions to key political decision makers. Companies began to protect their interests with well-crafted lobbying and negotiating tactics, particularly when they were facing substantial opposition from consumer and community groups whom politicians were eager to appease.

Philip Morris, a company operating in the controversial tobacco industry, is a good example of a politically active corporation. The tobacco giant was the largest political action committee contributor in the 1987–1988 election cycle—distributing a total of $623,380. In the 2002 election cycle, Philip Morris's parent company's PAC, Altriapac, made $1,702,467 in political contributions.[6] During this time, the company maintained its political momentum by having the second largest number of lobbyists on Capitol Hill (behind General Electric) with 28 representatives in its Washington, D.C., office.[7] In 2004 Altria ranked second in the Center for Public Integrity's annual ranking of corporate spending on lobbyists, spending some $13,240,000 on 24 internal staffers and 74 external consultants.[8]

An article published in the *American Political Science Review* in December 2000 revealed that in a survey of the 565 Fortune 1000 firms, 72.6 percent engage in some

---

[4] John M. Broder, "FTC Rejects Deal to Join Two Giants of Office Supplies," *New York Times*, April 5, 1997, p. 7.

[5] CNN Money.com, "Blockbuster Throws in the Towel," March 25, 2005, http://money.cnn.com/2005/03/25/news/midcaps/blockbuster_offer/?cnn=yes (retrieved June 27, 2005).

[6] Federal Election Commission Web site, http://www.fec.gov/ (retrieved June 19, 2005).

[7] Hansen and Mitchell, "Disaggregating and Explaining Corporate Political Activity," p. 891.

[8] Center for Public Integrity Web site, http://www.publicintegrity.org (retrieved June 27, 2005).

form of measurable political interaction with the federal government, 56.4 percent of the domestic Fortune 500 engage in lobbying activities, and 54.6 percent have political action committees (PACs). Virtually all of the top 200 Fortune 500 companies are politically active.[9]

In the interaction between business and Capitol Hill, powerful lobbies and trade unions are prevalent—subjecting the government to a multitude of pressures. As Alfred D. Chandler Jr., an economic historian, wrote, "the visible hand of management [has] replaced what Adam Smith referred to as the invisible hand of market forces. . . [Business has] acquired functions hitherto carried out by the market, it [has become] the most influential group of economic decision makers."[10]

Businesses use a number of tactics to further their own agendas in Washington. In this section, we look at the rise of the government relations function within companies.

The Government Relations Function Takes Shape

In the late 1960s and early 1970s, government regulations placed on certain industries significantly raised the cost of doing business. "It became apparent to American business leaders that in order to win in Washington, they would have to adapt the rules to their advantage, and that meant playing Washington's game."[11] "Playing the game" became the job of a company's government relations, or government affairs, department. This function concentrated specifically on the positive and negative effects of policy and policy changes, as well as monitoring shifts in ideology and agendas on Capitol Hill and accurately identifying emerging trends. By being knowledgeable about government and getting involved in the development of regulatory policy, business could better protect itself from damaging regulations while taking advantage of any positive opportunities that governmental regulation created.

Since the 1980s, government relations departments have improved their effectiveness by studying the methods of other companies, hiring consultants, organizing popular support, learning to use the media properly, making alliances, creating political action committees, and establishing connections with influential Washington insiders. By applying business and marketing techniques to politics, and combining traditional organizational tools with advanced technology (i.e., computerized association memberships, the Internet, electronic and paper newsletters), business has increased its influence over Washington's policymakers. Over 50 percent of Fortune 500 corporations had representatives in Washington or retained counsel there.[12]

Many companies, such as Bridgestone/Firestone and Wal-Mart, have learned the costs associated with *not* having a Washington presence. When the National

[9] Hansen and Mitchell, "Disaggregating and Explaining Corporate Political Activity," p. 891.

[10] Walter Adams and James W. Brock, *The Bigness Complex: Industry, Labor, and Government in the American Economy* (New York: Pantheon Books, 1986).

[11] Sar A. Levitan and Martha R. Cooper, *Business Lobbies: The Public Good and the Bottom Line* (Baltimore, MD: Johns Hopkins University Press, 1984), pp. 4–5.

[12] Hansen and Mitchell, "Disaggregating and Explaining Corporate Political Activity," p. 891.

Highway Traffic Safety Administration forced Bridgestone/Firestone to recall millions of tires, the company had no Washington office in place and had lost most of its outside consultants. The company needed to seek out new representation in the midst of a highly publicized crisis. Bridgestone/Firestone learned from this mistake and now has a dedicated Washington office and several consultants.[13]

In the 1990s when China entered the World Trade Organization, Wal-Mart executives discovered a problem: U.S negotiators had agreed to a 30-store limit on foreign retailers operating in China—a major roadblock for Wal-Mart's expansion plans. So, in 1998, Wal-Mart hired its first lobbyist in an attempt to build a Washington presence for a company that had traditionally shunned political involvement but found itself facing legal challenges from unions, workers' lawyers, and federal investigators. Today Wal-Mart has five lobbyists on its payroll and its political action committee was the biggest corporate donor to federal parties and candidates in 2003, giving more than $1 million, up from $182,000 in the 1997–1998 election cycle.[14]

The Foundation for Public Affairs (FPA) conducted a survey in 2000 to define the responsibilities of public affairs executives. Two-thirds of the 223 executives polled reported that they provide senior management with political and social trend forecasts as one of their duties, with over half reporting directly to the company CEO, president, or chairman.[15] Sixty percent of respondents reported a direct correlation between this trend monitoring and the company's overarching strategy. The duties for government affairs executives revealed in the Foundation for Public Affairs statistics point to a greater interaction between this department and public affairs, two functions that were once separate within companies.[16] A more recent survey by the FPA found that six professionals and two administrative staff people comprise the median corporate public affairs department and the median annual budget is $2 million to $3.5 million.[17]

Along with a strong internal team for government relations, a number of businesses today outsource certain functions to external firms in a "divide and conquer" strategy. In responses to a recent survey, half of the public affairs executives reported an increase in outsourcing from 1997 to 2000.[18] Not surprising then is the fact that the number of registered lobbyists in Washington has more than doubled since 2000 to more than 34,750, while the amount that lobbyists charge their new clients has increased by as much as 100 percent. This increase has been caused by rapid growth in government, Republican control of both the White House and

[13] Shawn Zeller, "Lobbying: Saying So Long to D.C. Outposts," *National Journal*, December 1, 2001, http://www.nationaljournal.com (retrieved June 2002).

[14] Jeanne Cummings, "Joining the PAC: Wal-Mart Opens for Business in a Tough Market: Washington," *The Wall Street Journal*, March 24, 2005, p. A1.

[15] "Survey Shows Public Affairs Emerging as Top Management Function," *Public Relations Quarterly*, July 22, 2000, p. 30.

[16] Ibid.

[17] "CEOs More Politically Involved, but Many Shrug Off Value of Crisis Planning," *Executive Update Magazine*, February 2003.

[18] "Survey Shows Public Affairs Emerging as Top Management Function," p. 30.

Congress, and wide acceptance among corporations that they need to hire professional lobbyists to secure their share of federal benefits.[19]

The external lobbying consultants in Washington to whom companies often turn for advice and guidance on political activities can command rates of $15,000 to $25,000 per month. Hewlett-Packard Co., the California computer maker, nearly doubled its budget for contract lobbyists to $734,000 in 2004 and added the elite lobbying firm of Quinn Gillespie & Associates LLC. Its goal was to pass Republican-backed legislation that would allow it to bring back to the United States at a dramatically lowered tax rate as much as $14.5 billion in profit from foreign subsidiaries. The extra lobbying paid off. The legislation was approved and Hewlett-Packard will save millions of dollars in taxes. "We're trying to take advantage of the fact that Republicans control the House, the Senate and the White House," said John D. Hassell, director of government affairs at Hewlett-Packard. "There is an opportunity here for the business community to make its case and be successful."[20]

These steep costs make relying entirely on outside counsel to oversee all government affairs activities unrealistic for most companies. For example, after closing its Washington office in 2000, Lucent Technologies soon discovered that depending on external consultants can be just as expensive as operating a small-scale Washington office.[21] Microsoft has successfully built a strong in-house government relations function. After the Justice Department filed an antitrust suit against the company in 1998, Microsoft initiated a government relations overhaul of unprecedented magnitude. The end result was a team of 15 savvy government affairs staffers in Washington—a presence three times larger than the average corporation's lobbying presence in D.C.—as well as lobbying representatives in every major state nationwide.[22] Microsoft also implemented a number of less conventional strategies, including constructing a Web site tailored to generate nationwide support for the company from individuals. The company has spent more than $61 million on lobbying since 1998, according to the Center for Public Integrity, a political watchdog group. The majority of Microsoft's 20 registered lobbying companies are law firms dealing with legal and tax issues.[23]

As with all other corporate communication functions, companies must measure the impact of their government affairs program to gauge whether it is properly tailored to the existing political environment. Today, businesses use a range of methods to track and evaluate their efforts. A 1999 survey by the Foundation for Public Affairs revealed that 94 percent of companies use objectives set and achieved, 69 percent use legislative wins and losses, and 64 percent use costs reduced or avoided as measuring sticks for their performance in government affairs.[24]

---

[19] Jeffrey H. Birnbaum, "Lobbying Firms Hire More, Pay More, Charge More to Influence Government," *Washington Post*, June 22, 2005.

[20] Ibid.

[21] Zeller, "Lobbying."

[22] Jeffrey H. Birnbaum, "How Microsoft Conquered Washington," *Fortune*, April 29, 2002, pp. 95–96.

[23] Alicia Mundy, "Consultants for Microsoft Aren't Such Odd Couples," *Seattle Times*, May 4, 2004.

[24] Pinkham, "How'd We Get to Be the Bad Guys?"

A results-focused approach will help ensure that a government affairs program stays strategically on track.

The Ways and Means of Managing Washington

An internal staff of government relations professionals and senior leaders who are engaged in the issues that affect their companies are two important components of any business's strategy to stay tapped into Washington. In this section, we look at some of the specific activities that companies use to advance their positions with lawmakers.

Coalition Building

The 1970s saw a great "political resurgence of business." Many of the methods used by government relations departments today became established or perfected during this period. In particular, coalition building emerged as a popular form of political influence. Many businesses previously acted to defend only their individual interests when faced with legislative problems, without considering the ways in which their own concerns might coincide with those of other groups or organizations. When a particular company was in trouble, it often battled Washington alone, even when the same issues applied to many other corporations within its industry.

The times of each business standing alone in Washington ended when legislation that affected most, if not all, businesses became more common than the earlier regulations that had affected one or a small collection of industries. Laws concerning consumer safety and labor and wage reform led the wave of these broader regulations. Companies soon learned the benefits of working together. When one company was affected by new regulations, it would now find other firms in a similar position to form ad hoc committees. In these committees, the companies forged alliances of support on the business level, which then translated into channels for expressing their views in a greater number of congressional districts and states.

While loosely formed ad hoc coalitions are still common, companies also often join established industry associations that pool financial and organizational resources for representing their positions in Washington. The Consumer Electronics Association (CEA), for example, advocates that industry's collective viewpoint on issues that include government regulation of broadband, consumer home recording rights, and copyright protection. The National Cattlemen's Beef Association (NCBA) is a similar organization presenting the unified views of thousands of ranchers and beef producers with respect to public policy affecting the cattle industry.

By joining forces through either ad hoc coalitions or more formalized industry associations, companies can assert greater power and have a better chance of affecting legislative outcomes than they would have acting alone.

CEO Involvement in Government Relations

Large and small companies alike strengthen their government relations programs through actively involving senior management in political activities. As they have recognized the importance of gaining a seat at the policy discussion table for their companies, an increasing number of CEOs are stepping into the policy debate. This trend does not surprise most executives. As John de Butts, former chairman of AT&T, remarked, "So vital . . . is the relationship of government and business that to my mind the chief executive officer who is content to delegate responsibility for that relationship to his public affairs expert may be neglecting one of the most crucial aspects of his own responsibility."[25]

Indeed, 98 percent of the chief executives of the 115 major companies surveyed took part in some form of political involvement activity in 2002, including extensive government relations work for trade or business associations. Other activities drawing CEO participation were correspondence to federal legislators or regulators, endorsement of the company's political action committee, direct lobbying of federal legislators, and attendance at candidate fundraisers.[26]

Frederick W. Smith, founder, chair, and chief executive officer of FedEx, exemplifies the benefits of CEO involvement in government relations. Since FedEx's inception in 1973, Smith has advanced his company's interests by using ingenuity, networks of personal alliances, and strategic charitable contributions. Examples of his creative political outreach range from FedEx's maintenance of a small corporate jet fleet ready to fly members of Congress across the country at a moment's notice to Smith's preservation of his longstanding relationship with former Yale fraternity brother George W. Bush.[27] As Wendell Moore, chief of staff to Tennessee Governor Don Sundquist, explained: "The fact that Smith knows his members of Congress on a first-name basis is a significant reason that the company has been so successful."[28]

FedEx continues to reap the rewards of its CEO's notable presence on Capitol Hill. For example, during the Clinton administration, Smith's rapport with the President undoubtedly led to his place as part of the official delegation on a trade mission to China. In 2002, the U.S. Postal Service announced a seven-year partnership with FedEx worth up to $7 billion, in which FedEx planes provided the postal service an air-delivery network in exchange for having its branded drop boxes installed at 10,000 post offices nationwide, a major accomplishment for Smith's well-positioned company.[29]

Lobbying on an Individual Basis

When business leaders realized the importance of having a say in the activities on Capitol Hill, they turned to lobbying groups to help them successfully advance their viewpoints with congressional decision makers. (Lobbying is any activity aimed at promoting or securing the passage of specific legislation through coordinated communications with key lawmakers.) In recent decades, as government intervention has grown, so has the number of organizations in Washington that present the views of business to Congress, the White House, and the regulatory agencies.

[25] James W. Singer, "Business and Government: A New 'Quasi-Public' Role," *National Journal*, April 15, 1978, p. 596.

[26] "CEOs More Politically Involved."

[27] Michael Steel, "FedEx Flies High," *National Journal*, February 24, 2001, http://nationaljournal.com (retrieved June 2002).

[28] Ibid.

[29] Ibid.

Using individuals in lobbying (which typically consists of activities such as letter writing, editorials or op-ed pieces in print news media, and office visits to lawmakers) can have a significant impact in Congress. The U.S. Chamber of Commerce, for one, has conducted very effective and sophisticated grassroots campaigns to increase its influence. With state and local chapters that contain thousands of members, the Chamber of Commerce has a wide base from which to work. By 1980, it had established 2,700 "Congressional Action Committees" that consisted of executives who were personally acquainted with their senators and representatives. These executives received information about events in Washington through bulletins from the Chamber's Washington office and remained in touch with their representatives so that they might contact them when called upon to do so.

This method of lobbying through far-reaching constituencies has produced good results: "within a week [the Chamber of Commerce] . . . can carry out research on the impact of a bill on each legislator's district and through its local branches mobilize a 'grassroots campaign' on the issue in time to affect the outcome of the vote."[30] Today, the Chamber of Commerce—once poorly regarded in Washington—has a grassroots network of 50,000 business activists, an expansive membership of 3 million businesses, 830 business associations, and 102 American Chambers of Commerce abroad.[31]

Returning to our earlier Microsoft example, this company's lobbying efforts, which included its "grassroots" Web site campaign, clearly have paid off as well. In 2001, Microsoft's lobby against copyright violators resulted in a government crackdown on software piracy. Later that year, in the wake of the September 11 terrorist attacks, Microsoft led the charge in persuading the Bush administration to allot over $70 million to improve "cybersecurity" in America.[32]

Success stories like Microsoft and the U.S. Chamber of Commerce have prompted many major corporations to establish campaigns that target individuals. In addition to achieving desired legislative outcomes, "a prudently managed grassroots program can be a team-building exercise. Providing information about legislation that will affect current and future company activities will be of interest to many employees at all ranks. . . [B]uilding a grassroots program with employees makes them part of the team."[33] Using individuals in lobbying is one of the most popular methods for companies and their employees to get involved in politics. Blogs have become an important part of these grassroots campaigns, as they can be targeted to niche groups of constituents very easily.

Political Action Committees

Another popular method of getting involved in government is the formation of political action committees. The idea for this movement came from organized labor,

---

[30] Graham Wilson, *Interest Groups in the United States* (New York: Oxford University Press, 1981).

[31] American Chamber of Commerce Web site, http://www.uschamber.com (retrieved June 27, 2005).

[32] Birnbaum, "How Microsoft Conquered Washington."

[33] Gerry Keim, "Corporate Grassroots Program in the 1980's," *California Management Review* 28, no. 1 (Fall 1985), p. 117.

which created official committees responsible for raising and dispersing money to support political campaigns. In 1980, 1,200 companies had their own PACs; today there are 4,700.[34] Approximately 58 percent of Fortune 500 companies currently have a PAC.[35] Industry leaders such as Wal-Mart, UPS, and SBC have some of the largest and most active PACs, giving between $1 and $1.8 million to candidates in 2003.[36] Nineteen percent of Wal-Mart's 60,000 domestic managers contribute to its PAC, mostly through payroll deductions that average $8.60 a month.[37]

To target their funding efficiently, PAC administrators need to have access to information about each political candidate and the races they support. The Business-Industry Political Action Committee (BIPAC) was formed to meet these information needs. While this group does contribute directly to candidates, its most important role is to research candidates and identify close races. During each election year, BIPAC holds monthly information briefings for PAC managers, along with providing daily updates on congressional races through a BIPAC telephone service. By using their national organization, individual PACs remain well informed and are able to direct their funds intelligently.

PACs have arisen out of an increased political awareness in corporate managers. They provide a simple framework for getting employees involved in political issues that could determine their employers' well-being into the future. Employee involvement is key, as federal election law prevents direct corporate contributions to party committees and candidates. According to one executive, "PACs are one of the most effective vehicles to generate individual participation in the political process to come along in a long time." Another executive further commented, "Our first goal is to involve our people in the political process. Only about five percent of our time is devoted to fund raising and the distribution of funds; ninety-five percent is devoted to political education. Our philosophy is to encourage long-term understanding and continuing involvement in the political process."[38]

The Public Affairs Council estimates that PAC contributions currently account for between 1 and 10 percent of political donations.[39] The amount of money that businesses contribute to politicians in any given election cycle is staggering. According to the Center for Responsive Politics, business interests contribute far more money to candidates and political parties than do labor unions or ideological groups. In the 2002 election cycle, business interests contributed some $1,008,400,000.[40] The flow of money from business interests to political campaigns has alarmed some sectors of the American public, who fear that businesses' ability

---

[34] Federal Election Commission Web site, http://www.fec.gov (retrieved June 17, 2005).

[35] Tim Reason, "Campaign Contributions at the Office," *CFO Magazine*, July 12, 2004.

[36] Wesley Bizzell, "Office Politics," *Corporate Counsel*, March 2004.

[37] Cummings, "Joining the PAC," p. A1.

[38] Edward Handler and John R. Mulkern, *Business in Politics* (Lexington, MA: Lexington Books, 1982).

[39] Jeffrey H. Birnbaum et al., "The Influence Market: Capitol Clout: A Buyer's Guide: Access in Washington Comes at a Price," *Fortune*, October 26, 1998, p. 177ff.

[40] Center for Responsive Politics Web site, http://www.crp.org (retrieved June 27, 2005).

to back their agenda with large sums of money gives them an unfair advantage in having their voice heard in Congress. A recent *BusinessWeek*–Harris Poll revealed that three-quarters of Americans think large companies are too influential in Washington. The same poll concluded that 84 percent of the public believes campaign contributions made by big business have too much influence on American politics.[41] Clearly, not everyone views business political spending as a positive trend.

Conclusion

Corporate America's relationship with various levels of government extends far beyond licenses, safety standards, and product prices. Today, the influence of private business on public affairs, and vice versa, has become so established that we often assume changes in one arena will lead to changes in the other. Democratic reform in Latin America and Eastern Europe came hand in hand with market reform, and upon China's acceptance into the World Trade Organization (WTO), President George W. Bush declared, "I believe a whiff of freedom in the marketplace will cause there to be more demand for democracy."[42]

In America, defining the roles of government and business with regard to each other is an ongoing process. In the summer of 2002, a crisis of confidence in business ethics and corporate governance compelled President Bush to address Wall Street leaders, saying, "We must usher in a new era of integrity in corporate America."[43] Congress moved rapidly to negotiate a raft of bills and proposals that would regulate not only how businesses are run, but also how they report their activities to the public. Several years later, government and business are still struggling to find a balance, with business claiming that the cost of complying with Sarbanes-Oxley is too high.

On the technology front, the Internet has significantly shaped companies' approaches to government affairs. Companies may rely heavily on Web monitoring, issues-focused Web sites, and online networks of grassroots lobbyists to track important legislation and broaden the reach of their own coalitions.[44] At the same time, as we learned in Chapters 1 and 4, the speed at which information flows over the Internet means news of corporate wrongdoings or legal violations has the potential to reach many constituencies before senior management can prepare for the crisis at hand.[45]

With the complexities of globalization and the ever-increasing speed of information flows, businesses must devote attention and resources to actively manage their relationships with the government and its lawmakers. Successful

---

[41] Pinkham, "How'd We Get to Be the Bad Guys?" p. 12.

[42] Lawrence F. Kaplan, "Why Trade Won't Bring Democracy to China," *New Republic*, July 9, 2001, p. 23.

[43] Randall Mikkelsen, "Update 4: Bush Seeks 'New Era of Corporate Integrity,'" Reuters, July 9, 2002, http://www.Forbes.com (retrieved July 12, 2002).

[44] Pinkham, "How'd We Get to Be the Bad Guys?" p. 12.

[45] Douglas G. Pinkham, "Corporate Public Affairs: Running Faster, Jumping Higher," *Public Relations Quarterly*, no. 5 (Summer 1998), pp. 33–37.

companies recognize the importance of staying abreast of what happens on Capitol Hill. "It is essential we have a very strong presence," said Robert L. Garner, president of the American Ambulance Association. "It's pricey, but it's the cost of doing business in the federal environment."[46] Critical to this effort to keep connected with Washington is the government relations function, which, whether entirely internal or partially outsourced, must be an integrated function of a company's overall communication strategy.

[46] Birnbaum, "Lobbying Firms Hire More."

Case 9-1

Disney's America Theme Park: *The Third Battle of Bull Run*

When you wish upon a star, makes no difference who you are. Anything your heart desires will come to you. If your heart is in your dreams, no request is too extreme . . .

—*Jiminy Cricket*

On September 22, 1994, Michael Eisner, CEO of the Walt Disney Company, one of the most powerful and well-known media conglomerates in the world, stared out the window of his Burbank office, contemplating the current situation surrounding the Disney's America theme park. Ever since November 8, 1993, when *The Wall Street Journal* first broke the news that Disney was planning to build a theme park near Washington, D.C., ongoing national debate over the location and concept of the $650 million park had caused tremendous frustration. Eisner thought back over the events of the past year. How could his great idea have run into such formidable resistance?

THE CONTROVERSY COMES TO A HEAD

Eisner's secretary had clipped several newspaper articles covering two parades that took place on September 17. In Washington, D.C., several hundred Disney opponents from over 50 anti-Disney organizations had marched past the White House and rallied on the National Mall in protest of the park. On the same day in the streets of Haymarket, Virginia, near the proposed park site, Mickey Mouse and 101 local children dressed as Dalmatians had

Source: This case was written by Elizabeth A. Powell, assistant professor of business administration, and Sarah Stover, MBA 1997. It was written as a basis for class discussion rather than to illustrate effective or ineffective handling of an administrative situation. Copyright © 2001 by the University of Virginia Darden School Foundation, Charlottesville, VA. All rights reserved. To order copies, send an e-mail to dardencases @ virginia.edu.

appeared in a parade that was filled with pro-Disney sentiment. Eisner was particularly struck by the contrast between the two pictures: one showing an anti-Disney display from the National Mall protest and another of Mickey and Minnie Mouse being driven through the streets of Haymarket during the exuberant community parade.

Despite the controversy depicted in the press, on September 21, Prince William County, Virginia, planning commissioners had recommended local zoning approval for Disney's America, and regional transportation officials had authorized $130 million in local roads to serve it. It appeared very likely that the project would win final zoning approval in October. At the state level, Virginia's Governor George Allen continued his strong support of the park's development.

Over the past three weeks, however, Eisner had been ruminating over a phone call he received in late August from John Cooke, president of the Disney Channel since 1985. While Cooke had no responsibility for Disney's America, he had more experience in the Washington, D.C., political scene than any other of Disney's highest-ranking managers and was one of Eisner's most trusted executives. Cooke was not encouraging about the park's prospects. Quite familiar with many of the park's opponents, he believed they would not give up the fight under any circumstances. Given the anti-Disney coalition's considerable financial resources, the nationally publicized anti-Disney campaign could go on indefinitely, inflicting immeasurable damage on Disney's fun, family image. Cooke advised Eisner to think very seriously about ending the project.

Eisner's thoughts drifted to the many other problems he had encountered in 1994. In April, Eisner's good friend and number-two executive at Disney, Frank Wells, had been killed in a helicopter crash during a backcountry ski trip. In July, Eisner himself had been rushed to the hospital with chest pains and had undergone quadruple bypass surgery. In August, Jeffrey Katzenburg, the executive credited with several Disney blockbusters and Disney's increased financial success since Eisner took over leadership in 1984, had resigned when Eisner did not promote him to Wells's job. Considerable media coverage had followed, with journalists discussing a "leadership crisis" at Disney.

Since the mid-1980s, Eisner's business strategy was to revitalize Disney by broadening its brand into new ventures. While promising at first, now the wisdom of some of the ventures seemed less certain. The worst example, EuroDisney, the new Disney park located outside Paris, continued to flounder. The numbers for fiscal year 1994, due in just a couple of days on September 30, didn't look promising. Estimates said net income would be down to $300 million from $800 million the year before, mostly because EuroDisney lost $515 million from operations and $372 million from a related accounting charge.[1]

The good news was that due to cost cutting, EuroDisney's losses were actually less than in the previous year, while the bad news was that attendance was also down. Prince al-Waleed bin Talal bin Adulaziz of Saudi Arabia had agreed to buy 24 percent of the park and build a convention center there, thus relieving some of the financial pressure, but it seemed that the negative press coverage of that park's troubles would never end.

The Disney's America problem was particularly bothersome, however. Eisner realized that the controversy surrounding the park, coupled with the many other highly publicized problems of 1994, was damaging Disney's image. Due to publicity about its highly visible corporate problems, Disney's image as a business threatened to tarnish its reputation for family-friendly fun and fantasy.

Personally, Eisner was particularly fond of the Disney's America concept. He had helped develop the original idea and had personally championed it within the Disney organization. He recalled the early meetings during which several Disney executives, including himself, had brainstormed an American history concept. He and the other executives had strongly believed that Disney had the unique capability of designing an American history theme park that would draw on the company's technical expertise and offer guests an entertaining, educational, and emotional journey through time. They envisioned guests, adults and children alike, embracing a park dedicated to telling the story of U.S. history. Eisner had hoped the park would be part of the personal legacy he would leave behind at Disney. As he told a *Washington Post* reporter, "This is the one idea I've heard that is, in corporate locker room talk, what's known as a no-brainer."[2]

THE DISNEY'S AMERICA CONCEPT AND LOCATION

The idea of building an American history theme park originated in 1991 when Eisner and other Disney executives attended a meeting at Colonial Williamsburg in southeastern Virginia. The executives were impressed by the restored pre-Revolutionary capital. Disney had already been thinking about locations for theme parks that were on a somewhat smaller scale than the company's massive ones. Visiting Williamsburg helped Disney make the connection to a new park based on historical themes.

Disney's attention soon shifted focus to Washington, D.C. As the third-largest tourist market in the United States and the center of

---

[1] The Walt Disney Company Annual Report, 1995. See also Kim Masters, *The Keys to the Kingdom* (New York: William Morrow, 2000), p. 299.

[2] William M. Powers, "Michael in Eisnerland: Disney's Chairman's Sense of Wonder, Will to Win Drive for Virginia Theme Park Plan," *Washington Post*, January 23, 1994, p. H1.

American government, the nation's capital seemed a natural location for an American history park. The abundance of historical sites in the area broadened its appeal as a center of American history. Disney's other parks were located on the fringes of developed urban centers (Anaheim, Orlando, Tokyo, and Paris). The parks gained advantages from their proximity to urban centers, but due to their peripheral locations, Disney was able to acquire lower-priced land and ensure a safe environment for visitors, far from inner-city congestion and crime.

Disney needed a location with easy access to an airport and an exit off an interstate highway. Executives hoped to find land that had already been zoned for development as well as local and state politicians who would be open to economic growth. In Prince William County, located in the heart of Virginia's Piedmont region, Disney found all these things. Dulles International Airport was located just east of Prince William County. U.S. Interstate 66 (I-66), the main traffic artery connecting Washington, D.C., with its western suburbs, could transport tourists straight from Washington's monuments and museums into Prince William County, a distance of about 35 miles.

The political and economic context also made Prince William County attractive to Disney. Virginia had long been a pro-growth state, and its governors were constantly under pressure to bring in new business. Democratic Governor Doug Wilder would leave office in November 1993, having lost some notable campaigns to bring growth to Virginia's economy. Polls showed that he would likely be replaced by Republican George Allen, the son of a former Washington Redskins American football coach and a graduate of the University of Virginia. If elected, Allen would be under instant pressure to create state economic growth. Most Prince William County officials were also "pro-growth," though not well prepared for it. The county's growing population of middle-class residents (up 62 percent since

1980) paid the highest taxes in the state of Virginia due to a dearth of economic development within the county. The Virginia legislature set an ambitious goal in 1990 to attract 14,000 jobs and $1 billion in nonresidential growth to the county to fund more and better schools and county administrative services, in addition to reducing residential taxes paid by each family.

In the spring of 1993, Peter Rummell, president of Disney Design and Development, which included the famous Imagineering group, as well as the real estate division, identified 3,000 acres in Prince William County near the small town of Haymarket (population 483). The largest property was a 2,300-acre plot of land, the Waverly Tract, owned by a real estate subsidiary of the Exxon Corporation. Waverly was already zoned for mixed-use development of homes and office buildings, yet due to a weak real estate market, Exxon had never broken ground on the undeveloped farmland. For a modest holding price, Exxon was willing to option the property. Using a scheme that had worked years before in Orlando, the Disney real estate group bought or put options on Waverly and the remaining 3,000 acres without revealing the company's corporate identity in any of the transactions.

THE VIRGINIA PIEDMONT

The northeast corner of Virginia comprises the Piedmont region. The region contains countless significant sites related to U.S. history, including, for example, the preserved homes of four of the first five U.S. presidents: Washington, Jefferson, Madison, and Monroe. According to Pulitzer Prize–winning historian David McCullough, "This is the ground of our Founding Fathers. These are the landscapes—small towns, churches, fields, mountains, creeks, and rivers—that speak volumes."[3]

---

[3] Richard L. Worsnop, "Historic Preservation," *The CQ Researcher*, October 7, 1994, p. 867.

Thomas Jefferson loved the agrarian life he found on the farms east of the Blue Ridge Mountains. In his letters, he exulted over the region's "delicious spring," "soft genial temperatures," and good soil.[4] In all the world, Jefferson said, he knew of no happier condition than that of a Virginia farmer in the Piedmont.[5]

The region is also home to more than two-dozen Civil War battlefields. The U.S. Civil War was fought largely over the issue of slavery, pitting northern states against the southern states that had seceded from the union. Just a few miles from the Waverly tract is Manassas National Battlefield Park, land that is protected and preserved by the U.S. National Park Service, commemorating two major Civil War battles. The first battle in 1861 was the Civil War's first major land engagement. The second, in 1862, marked the beginning of Confederate General Robert E. Lee's first invasion of the North. On what would become some of the bloodiest soil in U.S. history, Lee reflected at Bull Run in 1861, "The views are so magnificent, the valleys so beautiful, the scenery so peaceful. What a glorious world the Almighty has given us. How thankless and ungrateful we are, and how we labor to mar His gifts."[6]

While largely rural and predominantly middle class, the region was also notable as home to some of America's most wealthy and influential citizens. In 1905, a group of millionaire sportsmen from New York chose the area as a warm-weather location to indulge their enthusiasm for fox hunting. By 1993, the Piedmont was one of the nation's most concentrated horse farming regions outside Kentucky. The largest estates suggested the presence of privilege at every turn: perfect fences built from stone or wood, carefully manicured pastures, large barns requiring lots of hired help, a

EXHIBIT 9.1

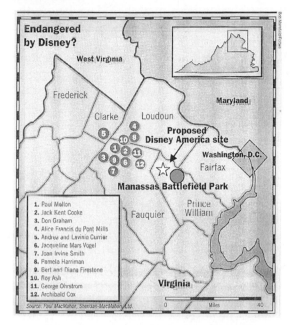

The Third Battle of Bull Run: The Disney's America Theme Park. Proximity of Disney's America Site to Several Wealthy Residents. Design: Bob Mansfield/Forbes. Source: Lisa Gubernick, "The Third Battle of Bull Run," *Forbes 400*, October 17, 1994, p. 72. Reprinted by permission of *Forbes* Magazine, copyright 2002, Forbes, Inc.

few private landing strips, and long private lanes lined with boxwood or dogwood that led to magnificent private homes. Exhibit 9.1 provides a map showing the locations of some of the area's most wealthy homeowners.

The Piedmont also had a history of successfully fighting local development projects. In the late 1970s, the Marriott Corporation had proposed building a large amusement park, and, in the late 1980s, a development group had planned to develop a major shopping mall in the area. Both projects were defeated by local opposition.

DISNEY'S PLANS REVEALED

To keep its land acquisition secret, Disney had done little to work with local government and communities, but by late October of 1993, Eisner

[4] Rudy Abramson, "Land Where Our Fathers Died," *Washingtonian Magazine*, October 1996, p. 62.

[5] Ibid.

[6] "Making a Stand," *Conde Nast Traveler*, September 1994, p. 148.

learned that Disney's plans had begun to leak.[7] It would only be a matter of days before the news would hit the media, so in the meantime Disney had to act quickly. Behind the scenes, Eisner contacted outgoing Governor Wilder and Governor-elect Allen. Both gave their immediate support and agreed to attend a public announcement scheduled for November 11. The company hired a local real estate law firm, and also retained the services of Jody Powell, former press secretary to President Jimmy Carter, who ran the Powell Tate public relations firm. Powell was an interesting choice because he had taken a high-profile role in opposing the defeated shopping mall project.

On November 8, 1993, a brief item appeared in *The Wall Street Journal* stating that Disney was planning to build a theme park somewhere in Virginia. That same day, Disney officials confirmed the story but provided no additional details. The next day, a *Washington Post* reporter identified Prince William County as the targeted area. Disney spokespeople confirmed the location and added some details. Disney officials briefed reporters and legislators, stating that they had investigated possible obstacles to the project, including environmental and historic preservation concerns, and believed there would be no serious problems.[8] They also stated that they had studied traffic patterns on I-66 and believed additional theme park traffic would not exacerbate rush hour congestion.[9] Because 65 percent of Prince William County residents commuted to jobs in other Northern Virginia counties, traffic congestion was a primary concern. On November 10, the *Post* ran the first full news story, headlined "Disney Plans Theme Park Here; Haymarket, VA: Project to Include Mall, Feature American History."

As local discussion increased, Disney held an upbeat news conference on November 11 and also issued a press release. Rummell, flanked by the governors and local officials, revealed an architectural model of the theme park and the surrounding development plans. The park logo featured a bold close-up of a stylized bald eagle rendered in navy blue, draped in red and white striped bunting, and with the words, "Disney Is America" emblazoned in gold across the eagle's chest.

Disney's America was presented as a "totally new concept . . . to celebrate those unique American qualities that have been our country's strengths and that have made this nation the beacon of hope to people everywhere." Disney would draw upon its entertainment experience in multimedia and theme park attractions. Disney officials emphasized the park's focus on the Civil War. Guests would enter the park through a detailed Civil War–era village and then ride a steam train to explore nine areas, each devoted to an episode from American history. One of these included a Civil War fort, complete with battle reenactments. Other exhibits included "We the People," depicting the immigrant experience at Ellis Island, and "Enterprise," a factory town featuring a high-speed thrill attraction called "The Industrial Revolution."

Disney officials predominantly sold the park on its economic benefits to the local area, stating that the park would directly generate about 3,000 permanent jobs[10] along with 16,000 jobs indirectly.[11] Around the park, the company would develop resort hotels, an RV park, a 27-hole public golf course, a commercial complex with retail and office space, and 2,300 homes.[12] Disney projected $169 million in tax revenues for the first 10 years after the park

[7] Michael D. Eisner, *Work in Progress* (New York: Random House, 1998), p. 323.

[8] Kirsten Downey and Kent Jenkins Jr., "Disney Plans Theme Park Here; Haymarket, VA.: Project to Include Mall, Feature American History," *Washington Post*, November 10, 1993, p. 59.

[9] Ibid.

[10] Spencer S. Hsu, "Disney Project Runs into Concern about Traffic Pollution," *Washington Post*, November 12, 1993, p. A18.

[11] Lisa Gubernick, "The Third Battle of Bull Run," *Forbes 400*, October 17, 1994, p. 68.

[12] Ibid.

opened in 1998 and nearly $2 billion over its first 30 years.[13] In addition, Disney would donate land for schools and a library, and reserve up to 40 percent green space as a buffer around the core recreational area.[14]

In part, the announcement came off better in print than at the conference. In the press release, Bob Weis, senior vice president of Walt Disney Imagineering, was quoted as saying, "Beyond the rides and attractions for which Disney is famous, the park will be a venue for people of all ages, especially the young, to debate and discuss the future of our nation and to learn more about its past by living it." In the conference, however, Weis said of the attractions, "We want to make you a Civil War soldier. We want to make you feel what it was like to be a slave, or what it was like to escape through the Underground Railroad." Weis's intended meaning was to refer to the new technology of virtual reality that would be used, but critics quickly jumped on the statement. *Washington Post* columnist Courtland Milloy contrasted the description to "authentic history" that would have to portray atrocities like slave whippings and rape.[15] Author William Styron wrote that he believed the comment suggested that slavery was somehow a subject for fun or that the escape route used for slaves was similar to a subway system.[16]

PIEDMONT OPPOSITION

Almost immediately after Disney confirmed its plans to build a park in Prince William County, anti-Disney forces began organizing their opposition. To many who were alarmed, the plans seemed already so well-developed that they gave the impression of a *fait accompli*. Just days after Disney's formal announcement, a meeting was held at the home of Charles S. Whitehouse, a retired foreign service officer who had owned property in the Virginia hunt country since the early 1960s. The dozen guests included William D. Rogers, former undersecretary of state under Henry Kissinger and now a senior partner in a powerful Washington law firm; Joel McCleary, a former aide in the Carter White House and former treasurer of the Democratic National Committee; and Lavinia Currier, great-granddaughter of Pittsburgh financier Andrew Mellon. William Backer, a former New York advertising executive who had created slogans for Coca Cola ("Coke—It's the Real Thing") and Miller Beer ("If you've got the time, we've got the beer"), also attended. The group worried that the proposed development would undermine the upper Piedmont's "traditional character and visual order."

The phrase came from the charter of the Piedmont Environmental Council (PEC), a rural-preservation group co-chaired by Whitehouse. Many of Whitehouse's guests had donated considerable amounts of time and money to the organization, which fought development and bought land and easements to preserve the area. The PEC was originally founded in 1927 by a group of prominent landowners. Over the years, it fought successfully against uranium mining and plans for a "western bypass" highway. The group was currently working to expand state programs allowing tax reductions for landowners who promised to use their land for farming rather than for subdivisions. To date, the effort had protected 400,000 acres of farmland from development.

The group discussed the options for stopping Disney's encroachment upon the hunt country. There was the possibility of derailing the project during the Virginia legislature's next session. Rogers discussed some of the legal options. Backer suggested a negative publicity campaign, possibly at a national level, to force an image-conscious company like Disney

[13] Ibid.

[14] Park Net, National Park Service, "More Battles: The Horse and the Mouse, Battling for Manassas," http://www.cr.nps.gov/ history/ online_books/mana/adhi11b.htm (last modified August 8, 2001).

[15] Ibid.

[16] Chris Fordney, "Embattled Ground," *National Parks*, November/ December 1994, p. 28.

to retreat. He argued for a subtle approach rather than a straight-on NIMBY (Not In My Backyard) campaign. He didn't want the opposition campaign to be viewed simply as a group of wealthy landowners who wanted to prevent a theme park from disturbing their fox hunting. As the meeting ended, Backer agreed to come up with a slogan.

A few days later, Backer presented his "Disney, Take a Second Look" slogan to the group. Backer's angle was to convince Disney that it should reassess the idea of building a theme park amid the beauty of the Piedmont. While the campaign addressed Disney directly, it would remind anyone who saw it of the Piedmont's unspoiled and now-threatened natural beauty. Within a few days, the slogan was running in radio ads and incorporated on a letterhead. The logo accompanying the slogan showed a balloon, with a barn and farmhouse inside, drifting away in the breeze.

This initial meeting was followed by dozens of others in the coming weeks and months. One week after the gathering at the Whitehouse home, over 500 people attended a meeting at the Grace Episcopal Church in The Plains, Virginia, about seven miles west of the Disney site. News of the meeting had been spread by word of mouth and posters placed throughout the region. Citizens from Prince William and the neighboring Fauquier and Loudoun Counties attended. The meeting's attendants represented a wide range of economic backgrounds, but they were united in their preference for the rural life they enjoyed.

Megan Gallagher, Whitehouse's co-chairman of the Piedmont Environmental Council, led the meeting, reminding the group of other local protest movements that had stopped big projects. Other speeches rounded out the audience's concerns: The park's estimated 9 million annual visitors would spark low-density ancillary development like that around Anaheim and Orlando. The pristine countryside would be overcome by cheap hotels, restaurants, and strip malls. Already problematic traffic congestion would be exacerbated. The park would create low-wage jobs and not provide the tax base that the Disney plan promised. During the meeting, the Piedmont Environmental Council, which had already committed $100,000 of its $700,000 annual budget to the project, emerged as the leading opposition group.

A few days after the meeting at Grace Episcopal Church, another meeting organized by the Prince Charitable Trusts of Chicago, another land preservation group, was held at a local restaurant. This meeting brought together several regional and national environmental groups concerned about the Disney's America project. Eventually, the Prince Charitable Trusts would give over $400,000 to 14 different anti-Disney groups that conducted studies, gave press conferences, and attacked Disney from every possible environmental angle. These groups included the PEC, the Chesapeake Bay Foundation, the Sierra Club Legal Defense Fund, the Southern Environmental Law Center, the Environmental Defense Fund, Clean Water Action, the Audubon Naturalist Society, the American Farmland Trust, Citizen Action, and the National Civic League. The largest grant went to the National Growth Management League, which mounted a local advertising campaign under the name "Citizens Against Gridlock." The campaign depicted I-66, already one of Northern Virginia's busiest and congested highways, as "Disney's parking lot."

In early December, the PEC held a news conference in a Washington hotel to increase the reach of its "Second Look" campaign. It retained a prominent Washington law firm as well as a public relations firm. The group began recruiting and organizing dozens of volunteers, from petition canvassers to bluegrass bands. It sent out a fundraising letter seeking $500,000 in contributions. It also commissioned experts to assess the park's impact on the environment, urban sprawl, traffic, employment, and property taxes.

DISNEY'S CAMPAIGN

Soon after the public announcement, Disney undertook concerted efforts to win over state and local government, as well as constituencies within proximity of the proposed site. Virginia's new governor, George Allen, immediately promoted the Disney project. He believed Disney's worldwide reputation would make Virginia an international tourist destination, bringing millions of travelers to the state. In numerous press releases, Allen endorsed Disney's belief that the project would create 19,000 jobs and bring millions of new tax dollars to state and municipal coffers.

By early January, Disney asked the state to bear some of the costs of the new park. Disney requested $137 million in state highway improvements and $21 million to train workers, move equipment from Orlando, pay for advertising, and put up highway signs directing tourists to the park. These funds would have to be guaranteed by the end of the current state legislative session to allow Disney to move ahead with development in early 1995. Now focusing on Virginia's state capital, Disney retained a well-connected Richmond law firm to handle its lobbying efforts. It also hired a Richmond event-planning firm to organize two large receptions. Lobbying expenses alone reached almost $450,000, including $32,000 for receptions and $230 for the Mickey Mouse ties given to state legislators.

Allen supported Disney's request and argued the highway improvements Disney planned would ease traffic problems that already existed in Northern Virginia, in addition to accommodating the extra traffic generated by the park. The state's support of the project, he said, would send a message that Virginia was "open for business." A team of Allen's top administrators also worked on getting the Disney project through the Virginia legislature.

Disney officials met with African-American legislators and promised to ensure that minori-

ties got a good shot at contracts and jobs. They invited a dozen officials from area museums and historic sites, including Monticello and Colonial Williamsburg, to a meeting in Orlando to discuss their plans for portraying history in the Northern Virginia park. In Richmond, Disney lobbyists portrayed opponents as wealthy landowners who simply did not want Disney in their backyards.

Disney sought and received strong support from the Prince William business community, especially realtors, contractors, hotels, restaurants, and utility companies. The Disney staff also poured tremendous effort into harnessing the support of local citizens, spending hours preaching the message of neighborliness to local groups. Groups formed to support the park, including the Welcome Disney Committee, Friends of the Mouse, Youth for Disney, and Patriots for Disney. Members of these groups attended state legislative hearings, gave testimony, and handed out bumper stickers and buttons. Disney sent newsletters to 100,000 local households and retained a second Washington public relations firm to handle grassroots support. Among other things, the firm set up a phone bank surveying people's opinions on the project. If a respondent was in favor of the project, the call was transferred to his/her state legislator's office in Richmond. The plan backfired when it clogged phone lines and angered several lawmakers.

Disney also entered negotiations with the National Park Service at the Manassas park, which was three miles away. The company agreed to limit the height of its structures to 140 feet so they would not be visible from the park and to develop a special transit bus system that would transport 20 percent of Disney guests and 10 percent of employees. The company promised to promote historic preservation and the Manassas National Battlefield Park within Disney's America, and immediately donated money to an allied nonprofit group. While these gestures placated some, the Park Service was still concerned about the traffic, congestion, and building heights of ancillary development that would be out of Disney's immediate control.[17]

THE PEC'S CAMPAIGN

The PEC mounted a strong effort in Richmond as well, including hiring two full-time lobbyists.[18] Its campaign was based on the premise that the park was a bad business deal for Virginia. The PEC claimed that the park would generate fewer jobs than Disney and Governor Allen had promised—6,300 rather than 19,000—and that the jobs would not pay well. They accused Allen of exaggerating the tax benefits. They emphasized the traffic and air pollution that would be caused by the park. They also suggested 32 other sites in the Washington area that would be more suited to the project than the current site. Finally, they suggested that the state should not have to fund any of the park's development. The PEC spent over $2 million in its campaign against Disney, including lobbying and public relations.[19]

THE VOTE

On March 12, 1994, when the Virginia state legislature voted on a $163 million tax package for Disney, the results clearly favored Disney. This wasn't even a close call for the state government officials. Disney won 35 to 5 in the Virginia Senate and 73 to 25 in the House of Delegates. Things were looking up for the Disney's America project, although a new bumper sticker appeared in the Piedmont that said, "Gov. Allen Slipped Virginia a Mickey."

THE HISTORIANS AND JOURNALISTS TAKE OVER

Disney officials were elated after their victory in Richmond. It seemed likely that construction could begin in early 1995 after all. Meanwhile, Disney's opponents were not ready to give up the fight. Public debate on local issues such as traffic congestion and pollution had failed to keep Disney out of the Piedmont, and the anti-Disney crowd realized they needed to change the theme of their campaign. They needed a grander, more significant argument—something that would gain national attention.

The kernel of that argument had appeared in December of 1993, in an editorial written to the *Washington Post* by Richard Moe, president of the National Trust for Historic Preservation and former chief of staff for Vice President Walter Mondale. Since earlier that year, Moe had begun broadening his organization's focus from individual historic properties to larger historic sites, such as downtown districts, especially those that were threatened by urban sprawl.[20] In his article, Moe suggested that Disney's development would engulf "some of the most beautiful and historic countryside in America."[21] He predicted that the park would reduce attendance at authentic Northern Virginia historic landmarks, including the Manassas battlefield. Moe also questioned Disney's ability to seriously portray American history when the success of its other theme parks was based on simply showing visitors a good time.

Moe's article was followed by a similar piece published in mid-February 1994 by the *Los Angeles Times*, the newspaper serving Disney's southern California headquarters. This editorial was written by Pulitzer Prize–winning journalist Nick Kotz, whose Virginia farm happened to be located three miles from the Disney site. Like Moe, Kotz based his article on the premise that Disney's park would desecrate land that should be considered a national treasure. He suggested that Disney would cheapen and trivialize its historic value. After the article was published, Kotz met with Moe over breakfast at the Mayflower Hotel in Washington to discuss anti-Disney strategy. This meeting was one of many that

[17] Ibid.

[18] Ibid.

[19] Ibid.

[20] Ibid.

[21] Richard Moe, "Downside to Disney's America," *Washington Post*, December 21, 1993, p. A23.

would follow among a growing network of the nation's most elite journalists and historians who were becoming increasingly concerned over Disney's plans.

As the network grew, several prominent historians joined the fight against Disney and formed a group that became known as Protect Historic America. An early recruit was David McCullough, the author of several best-selling books, including a Pulitzer Prize–winning biography of Harry Truman. McCullough was very well-known, particularly of late for his narration of the highly acclaimed Ken Burns *Civil War* series on PBS. Another prominent member was James McPherson, a Princeton University professor and author of the Pulitzer Prize–winning *Battle Cry of Freedom*. Exhibit 9.2 provides a list of many prominent authors and historians who joined Protect Historic America in its early stages.

By May, Protect Historic America was prepared to launch a national campaign in partnership with Moe's National Trust for Historic Preservation. Using funds donated by Piedmont residents, the group placed a full-page ad in the May 2 edition of the *Washington Post*, asking Eisner to reconsider the Haymarket site. The ad included a tear-away response form at the bottom and generated over 5,000 responses. Nine days later, on May 11, the group held a news conference at the National Press Club that featured McCullough and Moe among others. The prominent journalists in the group virtually assured that the conference would receive national news coverage.

During the well-publicized news conference, the speakers argued that Disney threatened the Piedmont countryside, including historic towns and battlefields. The region's rich heritage made it valuable to all Americans. David McCullough stated, "We have so little left that's authentic and real. To replace what we have with plastic, contrived history is almost sacrilege."[22] James McPherson, in a written state-

ment presented to reporters, said, "A historical theme park in Northern Virginia, three miles from the Manassas National Battlefield, threatens to destroy the very historical landscape it purports to interpret."[23]

The press conference, along with personal correspondence from McCullough and McPherson, convinced over 200 historians and writers to endorse the fight against Disney. Several historians wrote articles in national publications, attacking the Disney project. C. Vann Woodward, the noted Southern historian, wrote an article for the *New Republic* in which he stated:

> What troubles us most is the desecration of a particular region . . . historians don't own history, but it isn't Disney's America either. Nor is it Virginia's. Every state . . . in the country sent sons to fight here for what they believed, right or wrong. They helped make it a national heritage, not a theme park.[24]

The historians and journalists attempted to limit their arguments to the importance of preserving the Piedmont land and its historic heritage. Concerned that they would be regarded as cultural elitists, they tried to avoid the argument that Disney should not attempt to portray history in a theme park. There were several notable deviations from this strategy, however. McCullough once referred to Disney's plans as "McHistory."[25] Shelby Foote, a Civil War historian, made it clear that he believed Disney would sentimentalize history as it had done to the animal kingdom.[26] Commentator George Will asked facetiously, "Is the idea to see your sister sold down the river, then get cotton candy?"[27] Around this

---

[22] Larry Van Dyne, "Hit the Road, Mick," *Washingtonian Magazine*, January 1995, p. 59.

[23] Paul Bradley, "Prominent Historians Join Disney Foes," *Richmond Times-Dispatch*, May 12, 1994, p. B1.

[24] C. Vann Woodward, "A Mickey Mouse Idea," *New Republic*, June 20, 1994, p. 16.

[25] Sarah Skolnik, "The Mouse Trapped: Horton Gives a Hoot; Professor James Oliver Horton Retained by Walt Disney Company as a Consultant," *Regardie's Magazine*, September 1994, p. 44.

[26] Bradley, "Prominent Historians Join Disney Foes," p. B1.

[27] Van Dyne, "Hit the Road, Mick," p. 122.

EXHIBIT 9.2   The Third Battle of Bull Run: The Disney's America Theme Park. Partial List of Historians and Authors in the Anti-Disney Campaign

James David Barber	Professor of political science, Duke University
Frances Berry	Professor of American social thought, history, and law, University of Pennsylvania
William R. Ferris	Director, Center for the Study of Southern Culture, and professor of anthropology, University of Mississippi
Barbara J. Fields	Professor of history, Columbia University
Shelby Foote	Author of four-volume *Civil War*, which was made into a popular PBS miniseries
George Forgie	Associate professor of history, University of Texas at Austin
John Hope Franklin	Former president, American Historical Association
Ernest B. Furgurson	Journalist and historian
Gary Gallagher	Chairman, History Department, Pennsylvania State University
John Rolfe Gardiner	Piedmont Virginian and author of novels set in the Piedmont region
Doris Kearns Goodwin	Professor of government, Harvard University
Ludwell H. Johnson III	Professor emeritus of history, College of William and Mary
Richard M. Ketchum	Editorial director, American Heritage Books
Nick Kotz	Journalist, author of four books on American history and politics
Glenn LaFantasie	Deputy historian and general editor of the *Foreign Relations of the United States* series, U.S. State Department
David Levering Lewis	Professor of history, Rutgers University
David McCullough	Author, Pulitzer Prize winner, *Truman*
James McPherson	Professor of history, Princeton University, and Pulitzer Prize winner, *Battle Cry of Freedom*
Holt Merchant	Professor of history, Washington and Lee University
Richard Moe	President, National Trust for Historic Preservation
W. Brown Morton III	Chairman, Department of Historic Preservation, Mary Washington College
Neil Irvin Painter	Professor of American history, Princeton University
Merrill D. Peterson	Professor emeritus and former chairman, History Department, University of Virginia
James L. Robertson Jr.	Professor of history, Virginia Polytechnic and State University
George F. Scheer	Author specializing in Colonial and Revolutionary War history
Arthur Schlesinger Jr.	Author of 16 books on American history
William Styron	Author, Pulitzer Prize winner, *The Confessions of Nat Turner*
Dorothy Twohig	Associate professor of history, University of Virginia
Tom Wicker	Former Washington bureau chief of the *New York Times*
Roger Wilkins	Former advisor to President Johnson and professor of history, George Mason University
C. Vann Woodward	Professor emeritus of American history, Yale University

Source: Paul Bradley, "Prominent Historians Join Disney Foes," *Richmond Times-Dispatch*, May 12, 1994, p. B1.

same time period, a lively online discussion took place on the H-Civwar listserve whose members included academics and historians who were Civil War buffs.[28]

[28] Archived by Avon Edward Foote, "Disney Documents Plus," last modified March 26, 2002, http://www.chotank.com/disvasav2.html (accessed on May 20, 2002).

DISNEY'S RESPONSE

Following the May 11 press conference, a Disney spokesperson reiterated the park's intended effect: "Disney's America will bring America's history to life, celebrate America's diversity, provide a road map to other attractions throughout the region, and encourage

Americans to go further into their history."[29] Governor Allen also defended Disney after the press conference, saying, "I majored in history. I love history, and I think it's one of the best selling points for tourism. As much as I respect Shelby Foote and enjoyed the *Civil War* series, we shouldn't set ourselves up as censors." He added, "Hopefully, it will get people interested and want to go see the real thing."[30]

At Disney the situation seemed reminiscent of a 1991 controversy over an exhibit on Abraham Lincoln, which was criticized for its cursory treatment of slavery. Disney responded by redesigning the exhibit with the help of Eric Foner, a history professor from Columbia University who had made the complaint. To avoid costs associated with designing and redesigning an entire park based on varying interpretations of history, Disney had already begun to seek advice as early as mid-December 1993.[31] The company turned again to Foner, as well as other historians. As Weis put it, "We all share a common interest to make sure that our treatment of history is sensitive, honest, and balanced."[32] Disney invited a group of historians to Orlando to help them envision what Disney had in mind for Disney's America. Though at first skeptical, some came away thinking that Disney's America might work.[33] James Oliver Horton, a professor of African-American history and American Studies at George Washington University, who also designed exhibits for the Smithsonian, took the view that Disney's technological expertise might indeed help audiences learn more about history.[34]

Even with this much foresight, the strength of Protect Historic America's objections caught Eisner off guard. In April, the U.S. Transportation Department had decided to assess the environmental impact of Disney's proposed development. In light of impending federal involvement and PHA's national campaign, Eisner decided to personally visit Washington in mid-June to meet with reporters and editors from the *Washington Post*, Interior Secretary Bruce Babbitt, U.S. House Speaker Thomas Foley, and 30 other legislators. Eisner defended the company's intentions and expressed his frustration openly to the press, saying:

> "I'm shocked because I thought we were doing good. I expected to be taken around on people's shoulders. . . If this was any other city in the country, the (Federal government) wouldn't even be interested. . . (I was unaware) so many wealthy people (lived west of Washington). . . Disney's America will offer an alternative approach to history that may have more effect on people than conventional history. . . It's private land that is in the middle of a historic area, but it's not in the middle of a battlefield. . . We have a right to do it. . . If people think we will back off, they are mistaken."[35]

Then Eisner threw in at least one other comment that came back to haunt him, "I sat through many history classes where I read some of their stuff, and I didn't learn anything."[36] A few days later, PHA responded with a full-page advertisement in the *New York Times*. The ad headlined "The Man Who Would Destroy American History" reiterated the quote and commented, "Unfortunately, he means it."[37] In an attempt to generate some positive publicity for Disney, Eisner's visit coincided with the Washington movie premier of *The Lion King*. The plan backfired when the event attracted over 100 protesters from the PEC and other organizations, including a couple dressed as lions carrying a sign reading "Michael Eisner, the Lyin' King."

[29] Bradley, "Prominent Historians Join Disney Foes," p. 1.
[30] Ibid.
[31] Eisner, *Work in Progress*, p. 326.
[32] Skolnik, "The Mouse Trapped," p. 44.
[33] Eisner, *Work in Progress*, pp. 329–31.
[34] Park Net, National Park Service, "More Battles."
[35] William F. Powers, "Eisner Says He Won't Back Down," *Washington Post*, June 14, 1994, p. A1.
[36] Ibid.
[37] Van Dyne, "Hit the Road, Mick," p. 123.

CONGRESSIONAL HEARING

Protect Historic America's leaders next met with several U.S. senators and congressional representatives. As a result, Arkansas Senator Dale Bumpers, chairman of the subcommittee with jurisdiction over national parks, agreed to hold a hearing on the issue, which was held on June 21. McCullough, McPherson, and Moe represented the historians' point of view, while Governor Allen and several Disney executives presented their side of the issue. The historians presented a legal brief prepared *pro bono* for the hearing by a Washington law firm, stating that the Interior Department had a responsibility to investigate the project, given its proximity to the Manassas battlefield and Shenandoah National Park. They added that Virginia's historic landmarks were threatened, and because the landmarks were national treasures, the federal government had a responsibility to protect them. Allen and the Disney officials countered, arguing that the park was a local land use issue that should be handled within the state of Virginia.

Most of the congressmen sympathized with Disney, believing that Congress and the federal government should stay out of the situation, and Bumpers said he would take no further action. While it had no legislative impact, the hearing spurred thousands of newspaper stories, cartoons, and editorials nationwide, greatly increasing national awareness of the issue. Protect Historic America's clipping service pulled over 10,000 items covering the hearing. At this point, national television and radio shows began covering the issue in depth and political cartoonists were having a field day.

THE DEBATE CONTINUES

Despite outraged or lampooning overtones in the press, a few columnists supported Disney in the debate. For example, columnist Charles Krauthammer wrote,

> Those who fear that a children's entertainment will destroy real history have little faith in his-

tory. Disney's America is an amusement for kids who bring their parents along for the ride. The issue of urban sprawl is serious. The suggestion of cultural desecration is not. As the kids would say, "Lighten up, guys."[38]

In another instance, William Safire of the *New York Times* called the opposition group "a little band of well-credentialed historians, litigating greens, liberal columnists, and self-protected landowners."[39]

Overwhelmingly, however, press opinion sided with the historians, and the criticism became increasingly vicious over time. George Will called Eisner a "Hollywood vulgarian" and suggested that he should learn, like the South's Robert E. Lee, when the time was right for surrender. Pat Buchanan suggested that Eisner should "take his billions and go back to Hollywood . . . where they are impressed by . . . swagger." *Washington Post* writer Jonathan Yardley wrote, "It's difficult to say what's more astonishing, the gall of the show biz creeps at Disney . . . or the millions of saps out there who can't wait to be fed this pabulum masquerading as history."[40]

Eisner remained steadfast as he continued in his attempt to build public support for the project. On July 12, *USA Today* printed Eisner's retort to the historians' arguments to build national support for the project. Eisner wrote, "When we began developing plans for a northern Virginia park to celebrate America's heritage, we expected to encounter hurdles. . . But we did not expect that our creative reputation and talent for educating while entertaining would be attacked with such invectiveness." He continued, "We see Disney's America as a place where people can celebrate America, her people, struggles, victories, courage, setbacks, diversity, heroism, dynamism, pluralism, inventiveness, playfulness, compassion, righteousness, tolerance. . .

---

[38] Charles Krauthammer, "Who's Afraid of Virginia's Mouse," *Time*, June 6, 1994, p. 76.

[39] Quoted in Van Dyne, "Hit the Road, Mick," p. 123.

[40] Ibid.

[O]ur goal is to instill visitors with a desire to see and learn more."[41]

Meanwhile, the U.S. Department of Transportation began its environmental impact study during the summer. The agency planned to bring other agencies into the study, including the Environmental Protection Agency, the Interior Department, and the Army Corps of Engineers. During the same period, several environmental lawsuits had been filed by an organization called Protect Prince William, and several were expected to follow from the Sierra Club Legal Defense Fund and the Southern Environmental Law Center. In response, Disney retained several environmental lawyers and lobbyists. Disney continued its local efforts in Prince William County, continuing to build relationships with its supporters there.

On September 12, Protect Historic America and the National Trust for Historic Preservation invited journalists and politicians to a program at Ford's Theater in Washington celebrating Virginia as the "Cradle of Democracy." Foote, Styron, and several other authors gave readings from their work, and each guest received a binder of anti-Disney news clippings.[42] Don Henley, co-founder of the rock group the Eagles, also read a brief passage and donated $100,000. Several years earlier, Henley had been involved in the fight to save nineteenth-century American essayist Henry David Thoreau's Walden Pond in Massachusetts. Then, just five days after the Ford's Theater event, the anti-Disney national mall demonstration and the pro-Disney parade in Haymarket took place concurrently.

THE DECISION

Eisner watched the beautiful California sunset and pondered the situation. Could he come up with an argument that would sway public opinion in Disney's favor? Would the public tire of the issue, or would the debate continually resurface? How many lawsuits would Disney have to become involved in, and what would be the cost of litigation? What would the historians do once the park opened? Would Disney continually be engaged in a costly process of redesigning exhibits that were objectionable to various factions of historians? Could the park's theme be changed or repackaged?

If Eisner ended the Disney's America project now, the company would upset countless Virginia politicians, including Governor Allen, who had fought on its behalf. The various groups of Piedmont residents who had supported Disney and were counting on the park to provide jobs and tax revenues would be upset as well. Giving up now would mean that Disney had lost a very public, hard-fought campaign. Eisner had said publicly that Disney would not give in, so ending now would risk going back on his word. But were these previous commitments worth the costs of keeping them in light of the vocal opposition and the risk to Disney's reputation?

Eisner considered the options. He had reached the point where he needed to make a decision regarding Disney's America so he could focus more closely on other business concerns.

[41] Michael D. Eisner, *USA Today*, July 12, 1994, p. 10A.

[42] See Protect Historic America, "Reaching the People: News Media Coverage of the Controversy over the Siting of 'Disney's America,'" Washington, D.C., May 11, 1995.

CHAPTER TEN

Crisis Communication

Unlike many of the other topics covered in this book, a crisis is something *everyone* can relate to. The death of a close relative, the theft of one's car, or even a broken heart—all can become crises in one's personal life. Organizations face crises as well. Exxon's *Valdez* and Enron's and WorldCom's accounting scandals all became crises for the companies and people involved.

Thirty years ago, such events would have received some national attention, but would more likely have been confined to the local and regional area where the events occurred. Today, because of changes in technology and the makeup of the media, any corporate crisis is covered in a matter of hours by the national and international media, and Webcast over the Internet—further hastened by an ever-growing population of online "bloggers" who document and critique companies' every move. Thus, a more sophisticated media environment, as well as a new emphasis on technology in business, have created the need for a more sophisticated *response* to crises.

This chapter first defines what constitutes a crisis. It turns next to a discussion of several prominent crises of the last quarter century. Once we define what crises are all about, the focus shifts to how organizations can prepare for such events. Finally, the chapter offers approaches for organizations to follow when crises do occur.

What Is a Crisis?

Imagine for a moment that you are sleeping in bed on a warm evening in southern California. Suddenly, you feel the bed shaking, the light fixtures swaying, and the house trembling. If you are from California, you know that you are in the middle of an earthquake; if you are from New England, you might think that the world is coming to an end. Or picture yourself on a friend's boat, out for a leisurely sail on a sunny afternoon. Two hours later you discover that you have been having such a good time that you didn't notice yourself moving farther and farther away from shore into open ocean. Storm clouds are gathering on the horizon, and the sun seems mysteriously to be setting a bit early.

All of us would agree that, in these situations, we as individuals would definitely be facing crises. If the earthquake turns out to be "the big one," or if your friend is a novice sailor and you are in fact drifting into a severe storm, these scenarios could turn life-threatening.

How do crises affect organizations? Organizations also face crises that occur naturally: A hurricane rips through a town, leveling the local waste management company's primary facility; the earthquake we imagined earlier turns the three biggest supermarkets in the area into piles of rubble; a tsunami devastates a coastal area, crippling the local tourism industry for months if not years in its aftermath; a ship is battered at sea by a storm and sinks with a load of cargo destined for a foreign port. While all of these incidents create havoc and most can't be predicted, they all can be planned for to some degree.

Natural disasters cannot be avoided, but there are many crises—those caused by human error, negligence, or, in some cases, malicious intent—that planning could have prevented in the first place. In fact, most of the crises described later in this chapter—such as those that beset Tylenol, Perrier, Pepsi, and several online retailers and banks—were *human-induced crises* rather than natural disasters. Such crises can be more devastating than natural disasters in terms of the costs they entail for companies in terms of both dollars and reputation.

All human-induced crises cannot be lumped together, however. One type includes cases in which the company is clearly at fault, for instance cases of negligence. One example of this was the June 2000 sinking of a Panamanian tanker, the *Treasure*, which spilled 400 tons of heavy bunker oil off the west coast of South Africa and threatened 40 percent of the world's African penguin population. Financial or accounting frauds constitute another example of man-made crisis—a type increasingly exposed under the scrutiny of the 2002 Sarbanes-Oxley Act. A McKinsey & Company report revealed that more than 65 major financial crises took place between 1995 and 2005—nearly one and a half times the number that took place during the 1990s.[1] In these cases, a falling stock price and rising legal tab are not the only aftereffects a company must weather; often the most serious impact is to the company's reputation and the subsequent loss of trust with key stakeholders.[2]

The second type of crisis includes cases in which the company becomes a victim, such as Barclays, Citibank, eBay, and other major corporations targeted by online information theft attempts, discussed later in this chapter. The company falls prey to circumstances in these situations, just as when natural disasters unexpectedly hit. A company's role as either perpetrator or victim in a crisis is the distinction upon which public perception often hinges. The general public's attitude toward the company is more likely to be negative for crises that could have been avoided, such as the oil spills of the *Treasure* or the *Exxon Valdez*, as opposed to one that the organization really had no control over, such as the destruction of countless hotels and resorts when the December 2004 tsunami struck Southeast Asia. In all situations, however, constituencies will look to the organization's *response* to the crisis before making a final judgment. Certainly, some human-induced crises, such as the Tylenol tragedy, end up actually increasing the overall credibility of the organization involved.

---

[1] Allan Schoenberg, "Do Crisis Plans Matter? A New Perspective on Leading during a Crisis," *Public Relations Quarterly* 50, no. 1 (April 1, 2005).

[2] Ibid.

Thus, to define *crisis* for organizations today is a bit more complicated than simply saying that it is an unpredictable, horrible event. For the purposes of this chapter, a crisis will be defined as follows:

> A crisis is a major catastrophe that may occur either naturally or as a result of human error, intervention or even malicious intent. It can include tangible devastation, such as the destruction of lives or assets, or intangible devastation, such as the loss of an organization's credibility or other reputational damage. The latter outcomes may be the result of management's response to tangible devastation or the result of human error.

Crisis Characteristics

While all crises are unique, they do share some common characteristics, according to Ray O'Rourke,[3] managing director for Global Corporate Affairs at investment bank Morgan Stanley. These include (1) *the element of surprise*—such as Philip Morris finding carcinogens in its filters or Pepsi learning of reports of a syringe found in a Diet Pepsi can; (2) *insufficient information*—the company doesn't have all the facts right away, but very quickly finds itself in a position of having to do a lot of explaining. The Perrier example later in this chapter is instructive here, as it took the company over a week to figure out what was going on after reports of benzene contamination surfaced; (3) *the quick pace of events*—things escalate very rapidly (even before Exxon's crisis center was up and running in Valdez, the state of Alaska and several environmental groups were mobilized); (4) *intense scrutiny*—executives are often unprepared for the media spotlight, which is instantaneous, as answers and results normally take time. Think of how much air time Martha Stewart received from 2003–2005.

What makes this difficult for executives is that the element of surprise leads to a loss of control. It's hard to think strategically when overwhelmed by unexpected outside events. In addition, the media frenzy that typically surrounds a crisis can prompt a siege mentality to ensue, causing management to adopt a short-term focus. Attention shifts from the business as a whole to the crisis alone, forcing all decision making into the shortest time frame. For example, in the early 1990s, public relations firm Burson-Marsteller was hired six days after the Perrier benzene scare began, and already they had to undo three different explanations from the company—none of which were true. Perrier's uncoordinated and off-the-cuff statements only increased the likelihood that the crisis would escalate. When panic sets in, this is typically what happens in organizations.

Part of the problem in dealing with crises is that organizations have tended not to understand or acknowledge how vulnerable they are until *after* a major crisis occurs. Lack of preparation can make crises even more severe and prolonged when they do happen. Let's take a closer look at some major crises from the past 25 years to bring our definition to life.

---

[3] Ray O'Rourke, presentation to Corporate Reputation Conference, New York University, January 1997. At the time of this presentation, O'Rourke was with public relations firm Burson-Marsteller.

Crises from the Past 25 Years

For baby boomers, the defining crisis of their time was the assassination of President John F. Kennedy. Virtually everyone who was alive at that time can remember what he or she was doing when the news was announced that President Kennedy had been shot. Generation Xers in the United States today probably feel the same way about the explosion of the space shuttle *Challenger* in January of 1986. Certainly people everywhere will remember the terror attacks of September 11, 2001, in the United States as a defining moment of the new millennium. These events have become etched in the public consciousness for a variety of reasons.

First, people tend to remember and be moved by negative news more than positive news. Americans in particular seem to have a preoccupation with such negative news. Network and cable news broadcasts underscore this point. Viewers rarely see "good" news stories because they just don't sell to an audience that has become accustomed to the more dramatic events that come out of the prime time fare on television.

Second, the human tragedy associated with a crisis strikes a psychological chord with most everyone. A cable car detaching over the French Alps in 1999, American Airlines flight 587 crashing after take-off in New York City killing 265 people on board in November 2001, the terrorist attacks striking the London Underground and bus system in July 2005—such events make us realize how vulnerable we all are and how quickly events can make innocent victims out of ordinary people.

Finally, crises associated with major corporations stick in the public's mind because many large organizations lack credibility in the first place. A public predisposed to distrust big oil companies could not be completely surprised by what happened to the *Exxon Valdez* or by Texaco's racial discrimination suit. Indeed, these events validated the public's suspicions, so they took as much pleasure in the turmoil these corporations faced as a result of their actions as they took sorrow in what the *Valdez* accident did to the environment and how Texaco treated minorities. In other cases, crises have such an impact on us because they take us by surprise. Consider energy behemoth Enron, ranked in 2000 among *Fortune*'s most admired companies and praised for its internal culture of collegiality and open communication.[4] A short time later, its collapse resulted in the largest bankruptcy in U.S. history as well as 11,000 employees losing their life savings—a total of $1 billion invested in the 401(k) plans attached to company stock.[5] As we look at other major crises, we will start to see more clearly why these events linger in the public psyche.

1982: Johnson & Johnson's Tylenol Recall

Johnson & Johnson's (J&J's) Tylenol recall in the early 1980s is held by many as "the gold standard" of product-recall crisis management. Though more than

---

[4] Peter Lilienthal, "The Myth of CEO Accountability," *The Conference Board—Across the Board,* March/April 2003.

[5] Martine Costello, "Company Stock Slams 401(k)s," CNN/Money, December 10, 2001.

20 years have passed since the crisis, the lessons to be learned from it are still relevant. Johnson & Johnson's handling of the crisis was characterized by a swift and coordinated response and a demonstration of concern for the public that only strengthened its reputation as "the caring company."

In late September and early October of 1982, seven people died after taking Tylenol capsules that had been laced with cyanide. At the time, Tylenol had close to 40 percent of the over-the-counter market for pain relievers. Within days of the first report of these poisonings, sales had dropped by close to 90 percent.

Certainly the irony of something that is supposed to relieve pain turning into a killer made this episode one of the most memorable in the history of corporate crises, but many experts on crisis communication, marketing, and psychology have conjectured that it was Johnson & Johnson's swift and caring response that was primarily responsible for turning this disaster into a triumph for the company. Despite losses exceeding $100 million, Tylenol came back from the crisis stronger than ever within a matter of years.

What did Johnson & Johnson do? First, it did not simply *react* to what was happening. Instead, it took the offensive and removed the potentially deadly product from shelves. (In the end, 31 million bottles of Tylenol were recalled.) Second, it leveraged the goodwill it had built up over the years with constituencies ranging from doctors to the media, and decided to try to save the brand rather than come out with a new identity for the product. Third, the company reacted in a caring and humane way, rather than simply looking at the incident from a purely legal or financial perspective. Thousands of J&J employees made over one million personal visits to hospitals, physicians, and pharmacists around the nation to restore faith in the Tylenol name.[6]

Why did the company go to these lengths? Despite its decentralized structure, Johnson & Johnson's management is bound together by a document known as the "Credo." The Credo is a 308-word companywide code of ethics that was created in 1935 to boost morale during the Depression, and is carved in stone at company headquarters in New Brunswick, New Jersey, today. It acknowledges: "We believe our first responsibility is to the doctors, nurses, and patients, to mothers and all others who use our products and services." Then-CEO James Burke made sure that the principles of the Credo guided the company's actions during the Tylenol crisis, helping J&J react to tragedy without losing focus on what was most important.

What is most amazing is not that J&J handled this crisis so formidably, but that the perception of the company was actually *strengthened* by what happened. As Burke—who was brought in early as the lead person handling the crisis—explained, "We had to put our money where our mouth was. We'd committed to putting the public first, and everybody in the company was looking to see if we'd live up to our pretensions."[7] J&J management did, and the public rewarded them for it. Within three months of the crisis, the company regained 95 percent of its

---

[6] Harold J. Leavitt, "Hot Groups," *Harvard Business Review,* July 1, 1995, p. 109.

[7] Brian O'Reilly, "Managing: J&J Is on a Roll," *Fortune,* December 26, 1994, p. 109.

previous market share.[8] More than two decades later, Johnson & Johnson ranks consistently on *BusinessWeek* and Interbrand's annual list of the 100 Top Global Brands, with a brand portfolio valued at $3.04 billion in 2005.[9]

1990: The Perrier Benzene Scare

Perrier Sparkling Water faced a contamination crisis of its own nearly 10 years after the Tylenol episode. While Perrier's contamination crisis did not lead to any deaths, or even reported illnesses, it still demanded resolution and an explanation from the public and the media. Perrier's actions during the 1990 benzene scare provide as many lessons in how *not* to handle a crisis as J&J's did of how to handle one effectively.

In February of 1990, Perrier issued the following press release:

> The Perrier Group of America, Inc. is voluntarily recalling all Perrier Sparkling Water (regular and flavored) in the United States. Testing by the Food and Drug Administration and the State of North Carolina showed the presence of the chemical benzene at levels above proposed federal standards in isolated samples of product produced between June 1989 and January 1990.[10]

This press release marked the beginning of the end of Perrier's reign over the sparkling water industry. In 1989 Perrier, one of the most distinguished names in bottled water, sold one billion bottles of sparkling water, riding high on the wave of 1980s health consciousness. Then, in January 1990, a technician in the Mecklenberg County Environmental Protection Department in Charlotte, North Carolina, discovered a minute amount of benzene, 12.3 to 19.9 parts per billion (less than what is contained in a non–freeze-dried cup of coffee), in the water.[11] After receiving confirmation from both the state and federal officials, Mecklenberg briefed Perrier Group of America about the contamination.

Two full days after the crisis broke, after recalling over 70 million bottles from North America (but before identifying the source of the contamination), Perrier America president Ronald Davis confidently announced that the problem was limited to North America. Officials had reported a cleaning fluid containing benzene had been mistakenly used on a production line machine.[12] The real cause of the contamination—defective filters at its spring[13]—was discovered less than three days later, and contrary to what Ronald Davis had previously announced, six months' worth of production would be affected, covering Perrier's entire global market.[14] The firm was forced to change its story.

---

[8] Ibid.

[9] "Special Report: The Best Global Brands," *BusinessWeek,* July 25, 2005.

[10] Perrier press release, The Perrier Group, February 10, 1990.

[11] "When the Bubble Burst," *Economist,* August 3, 1991, p. 67.

[12] Ibid.

[13] "Handling Corporate Crises; Total Recall," *Economist* 335 (June 3, 1995), p. 61.

[14] Ibid.

Without an official crisis plan of its own, Perrier relied on the media to communicate its story during the crisis, which proved to be a fatal decision. The press only served to expose the lack of internal communication and the lack of global coordination within the company. At a news conference in Paris, when Perrier-France announced that it was also issuing a recall due to the presence of benzene, the president of Perrier's international division, Frederik Zimmer, offered the explanation that "Perrier water naturally contains several gases, including benzene."[15] From the contradictory messages released to the press, it was clear that the U.S. operations were not communicating well—if at all—with their European counterparts. Moreover, yet another story emerged to explain the presence of benzene, and it contradicted the previous explanations: According to Perrier officials, "the benzene entered the water because of a dirty pipe filter at an underground spring at Vergeze in southern France."[16] All of this hurt the company's credibility.

The cost of the recall and eventual relaunch of the product—ushered in by a pricey advertising campaign—meant that customers found the new 750mL bottles selling at the same price as the old 1L bottles. Perrier's pre-crisis 1989 market share of 44.8 percent had plummeted to 5.1 percent by 2005.

The Perrier benzene crisis illustrates not only the consequences of having a *reactive* strategy to deal with crises, but also the problems of not having a coordinated and fact-based approach to crisis communication.

1993: Pepsi-Cola's Syringe Crisis

Another beverage company, Pepsi-Cola, faced a highly publicized contamination crisis of its own shortly after Perrier's benzene episode. Pepsi's handling of the syringe hoax of 1993 starkly contrasts with the Perrier example. In addition to showing concern for the public and demonstrating resoluteness in getting to the bottom of the problem, Pepsi also skillfully leveraged two other critical constituencies—the government and, most importantly, the media—to help it combat the bogus tampering claims and win back the public's trust.

In June 1993, a man in Washington State reported that, after drinking half a can of Diet Pepsi the night before, he had discovered a syringe in the can the following morning when he shook out the rest of the contents into the sink.[17] This was the beginning of a major crisis for Pepsi-Cola.

The CEO of Pepsi-Cola North America, Craig E. Weatherup, did not let the surprise of the crisis overwhelm him when he was contacted at home by FDA Commissioner David Kessler and informed of the situation. His first action was to engage Pepsi-Cola's four-person crisis management team—made up of "experienced crisis managers from public affairs, regulatory affairs, consumer relations, and operations"[18]—to swiftly deal with the unfolding situation, including opening lines of communication with FDA regulatory officials, the media, and consumers.

---

[15] "Poor Perrier, It's Gone to Water," *Sydney Morning Herald,* February 15, 1990, p. 34.

[16] Ibid.

[17] David Birkland, "Couple Say They Found Used Needle in Pepsi," *Seattle Times,* June 11, 1993, p. 18.

[18] Sandi Sonnenfeld, "Media Policy—What Media Policy?" *Harvard Business Review,* July 1, 1994, p. 18.

Internally, Pepsi prevented organizational chaos by updating employees with daily advisories to over 400 Pepsi facilities nationwide.[19] Unlike Johnson & Johnson's immediate recall of Tylenol from the shelves, by the next morning Weatherup had decided *not* to recall the product—despite a flood of new reports to the FDA of dangerous objects found in Pepsi cans.

When television networks contacted the company looking for a response or any formal statements, Weatherup realized that the crisis was rooted in the disturbing imagery of syringes in cans—and decided to supply the media with an equally "visual" response. Weatherup had his staff prepare video footage of the canning process at Pepsi that showed how it would be virtually impossible to insert a syringe into the cans. Additionally, Pepsi later distributed a grocery-store surveillance tape of a woman stealthily dropping a syringe into her Pepsi can. After the footage appeared as the lead story on three major networks, no new reports of syringes were made.[20]

Weatherup also made several television appearances throughout the day, on *The MacNeil/Lehrer News Hour* and *Larry King Live*. In his last appearance, FDA commissioner David Kessler accompanied him. Both men stressed the implausibility of the claims and the criminality of making false statements (five years in prison and up to $250,000 in fines).

Pepsi's highly visible work with the FDA in investigating the crisis boosted its credibility in the public eye. Additionally, without an investigative reporting team of its own, Pepsi found that the government agency was invaluable to the company during the crisis. The FDA established a center in 1989 to provide the agency with a team of forensic science experts who can respond immediately to all tampering incidents and provide expert advice and scientific evidence to FDA officials. It was an FDA investigation that provided the evidence used to convict a tamperer who had falsely claimed to find a mouse inside a Pepsi can when she opened it. Several days later, the FBI arrested four individuals for making false claims, and the contamination scare appeared even more like the hoax it turned out to be. In the end, 20 arrests were made and the crisis was resolved.

Pepsi-Cola did not stop there, however. To ensure that consumers knew that the tampering claims were false, Weatherup took out an ad to address the concerns of employees and customers. As he explained, "On Monday, Pepsi will run full-page advertisements in 200 newspapers around the country, including the *Washington Post*. The ad reads: 'Pepsi is pleased to announce . . . nothing. As America now knows, those stories about Diet Pepsi were a hoax. Plain and simple, not true.' It ends with an invitation: 'Drink All The Diet Pepsi You Want. Uh Huh.'"[21] (See Fig. 10.1.) Pepsi-Cola remains one of America's leading soft drinks with a 31.7 percent market share,[22] demonstrating that negative publicity and crisis situations can be overcome when the crisis is successfully handled.

[19] Ibid.

[20] Glenn Kessler and Theodore Spencer, "How the Media Put the Fizz into the Pepsi Scare Story," *Newsday,* June 20, 1993, p. 69.

[21] John Schwartz, "Pepsi Punches Back with PR Blitz; Crisis Team Worked Around the Clock," *Washington Post,* June 19, 1993, p. C1.

[22] Chad Terhune, "Market Shares Drop at Coca-Cola, PepsiCo," *The Wall Street Journal,* March 7, 2005, p. B10.

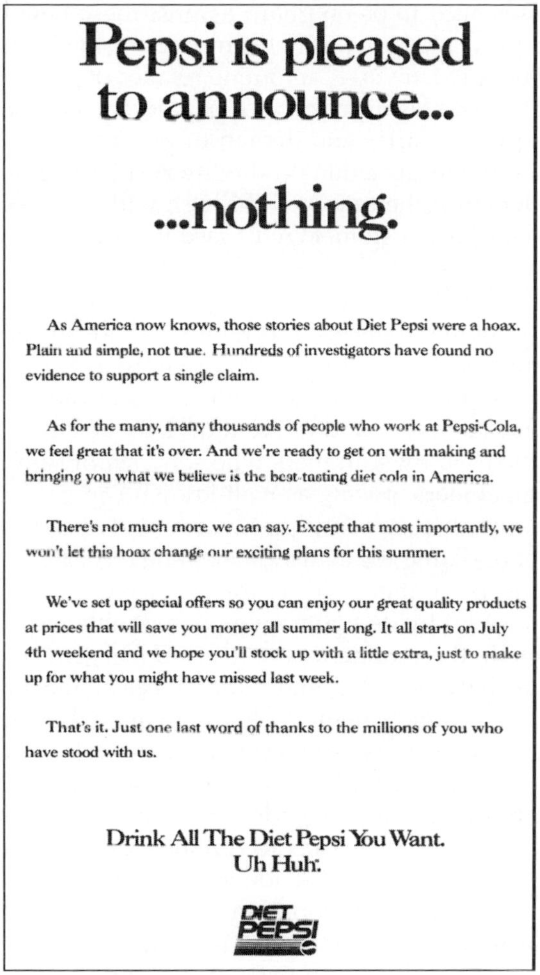

FIGURE 10.1
Diet Pepsi ad
run to
counteract
tampering
claims in 1993

Source: Permission
granted by Pepsi-
Cola Company.

Pepsi is pleased to announce...

...nothing.

As America now knows, those stories about Diet Pepsi were a hoax. Plain and simple, not true. Hundreds of investigators have found no evidence to support a single claim.

As for the many, many thousands of people who work at Pepsi-Cola, we feel great that it's over. And we're ready to get on with making and bringing you what we believe is the best-tasting diet cola in America.

There's not much more we can say. Except that most importantly, we won't let this hoax change our exciting plans for this summer.

We've set up special offers so you can enjoy our great quality products at prices that will save you money all summer long. It all starts on July 4th weekend and we hope you'll stock up with a little extra, just to make up for what you might have missed last week.

That's it. Just one last word of thanks to the millions of you who have stood with us.

**Drink All The Diet Pepsi You Want.
Uh Huh.**

The New Millennium: The Online Face of Crises—Data Theft and Beyond

With personal computers and the Internet now integral parts of the fabric of business, organizations face new challenges and the potential for crises that they have not dealt with before. The "I Love You" virus unleashed in 2000 cost businesses across a range of industries an estimated total of $10 billion in damages. Five years later, IBM released a report identifying the first viruses spreading beyond computers to attack and extract personal information from hand-held devices such as mobile phones and PDAs—the very tools upon which professionals, and certainly senior executives, rely to conduct daily business.[23] Companies of all kinds are also grappling with information security issues involving the theft or attempted theft of company and customer data.

[23] Rhymer Rigby, "Software Menaces Are Moving with the Times," *Financial Times,* July 22, 2005.

While all businesses need to be on guard against these new threats, Internet-based businesses in particular are on the front lines of the information security battle. In January 2000, CD Universe, an online retailer of music CDs, was black-mailed by an extortionist claiming to have copied the company's more than 300,000 customer credit card files and demanding compensation of $100,000 in return for not posting the information on the Internet.[24] When the company did not respond to his demands, he followed through with his threat and created a Web site where he placed the customer credit card files.

Hacking into Reputations

Today, the majority of online thieves are opting for more surreptitious tactics to steal confidential information. Viruses are now more commonly used to plant "Trojans" in personal or office computers—malicious software that steals sensitive information stored in a computer and relays it back to the criminal. "Phishing" is another popular tactic used by scammers who send spoof (but often legitimate-looking) e-mails to customers, posing as well-known companies and requesting personal information such as account passwords and social security numbers under the auspices of updating the company's online records.

The proliferation of such online security threats has resulted in crisis situations for myriad companies worldwide that now must redouble their efforts to protect against them to maintain the confidence and trust of their customers. The battle is not an easy one, especially as technological advances enable cyber-criminals to become more creative. George Samenuk, chairman and CEO of leading security software company McAfee, estimates that software piracy is costing the computer software industry more than $25 billion per year in lost revenues.[25] And according to the Federal Trade Commission (FTC), identity theft affects close to 5 percent of adults, costing businesses and consumers $53 billion annually.[26] Unfortunately, the threat is only increasing; in 2004, 246,000 identity theft incidents were reported to the FTC, almost triple the number reported in 2001.[27]

Why has the problem reached a crisis pitch for so many companies? Besides the reparations and damages businesses must cover for affected customers, doubts about online security have cast a shadow on many online retailer and banks' corporate reputations. And in the online arena, reputation may indeed be everything. A survey released in May 2005 by Gartner revealed that more than 42 percent of online consumers and 28 percent of people who bank online are "cutting back on their activity because of 'phishing' attacks and other assaults on sensitive data." Even more disturbing is the financial impact of this depleted confidence on online retailers and bankers—33 percent of those online consumers worried about fraud say they are buying less than they otherwise would if they weren't concerned;

---

[24] John Markoff, "Thief Reveals Credit Card Data When Web Extortion Plot Fails," *New York Times,* January 10, 2000, p. A1.

[25] Kevin Mills, "Software Piracy Costs Computer Industry over $25 Billion a Year," *Irish Examiner,* June 17, 2005.

[26] Christopher Conkey, "A Radical Tool to Fight ID Theft—U.S. Is Allowing Some Fraud Victims to Obtain New Social Security Numbers," *The Wall Street Journal,* July 6, 2005, p. D1.

[27] Ibid.

77 percent of worried online consumers report using online banking less frequently; and more than 4 percent have completely given up online banking.[28] Even
marketing can be negatively affected—with 80 percent of surveyed individuals
citing a reduced trust thanks to online security issues, people are playing it safe
and more than 85 percent delete "suspect mail" without opening it. More than
likely, businesses' legitimate marketing e-mails are lost to consumers as a result of
their personal defense mechanisms.[29]

What are companies doing to battle back? Some are responding more effectively than others. In May 2003, despite the heightened sensitivity of online consumers, Wachovia sent online banking customers an e-mail asking them to update
their user names and passwords by clicking on a link—a widely recognized
phishing tactic customers have been trained to ward against. While the request
was legitimate as Wachovia was migrating customers onto a new system, a quarter of their customers questioned the e-mail and flooded Wachovia's call centers
with calls.[30] More and more, businesses must understand and function within
today's context of increased customer suspicion and make concerted efforts to
quell those fears.

The most effective reactions have focused on clear, consistent communications
disseminated to customers prior to and in the immediate wake of an online attack.
Most importantly, communications should concentrate on consumer education.
Citibank, for example, highlights ways to ward off phishing on its Web site, including a "Spot a Spoof" chart that outlines ways to identify fraudulent e-mails.[31] The
company also has taken its preventative measures a step further: in May 2005,
Citigroup announced its collaboration with the National District Attorneys
Association (NDAA) to work with prosecutors nationwide to develop new strategies for the arrest and prosecution of identity thieves.[32] Companies also have
begun banding together and increasing intercorporate dialogues to communicate
best practices and experiences and better combat online security incidents. For
example, in 2003, the Anti-Phishing Working Group was founded in the United
States, comprising members from more than 400 companies.[33]

Internet service provider EarthLink has led the charge in increasing customer
awareness since it became a phishing target in early 2003. In fact, it makes its consumer education products—including a "ScamBlocker" toolbar—available to all
Internet users, not merely EarthLink subscribers, to promote a "better, safer online
experience" for all.[34] ScamBlocker displays a rating for each Web site visited, alerting a user before entering a page included on EarthLink's blacklist of fraudulent

[28] Riva Richmond, "Internet Scams, Breaches Drive Buyers off the Web, Survey Finds," *The Wall Street Journal*, June 23, 2005, p. B3.

[29] Ibid.

[30] Alice Dragoon, "Fighting Phish, Fakes and Frauds," *CIO*, September 1, 2004.

[31] Jeanette Borzo, "E-Commerce—Something's Phishy," *The Wall Street Journal*, November 15, 2004, p. R8.

[32] Citigroup press release, "Citigroup Teams with State and Local Prosecutors to Lock Up ID Thieves," May 5, 2005.

[33] Borzo, "E-Commerce."

[34] EarthLink Web site, http://www.earthlink.net/software/nmfree.

sites. For the greater good of the customer, EarthLink has gone so far as to share its blacklist with eBay to use in its own security toolbar.[35] Demonstrating genuine efforts to educate consumers and safeguard against threats is an important first step for a company to rebuild the trust many customers have lost in recent years, troubled by the potential threats of online transactions.

Online Opinions: Louder Than Ever

Data theft is only one type of threat companies need to guard against online. Another dimension of the new face of crises is how the Internet can be used to create anticorporate, antibrand "communities" where people can share information, opinions, and grievances about companies. One of the earliest examples of the influence of such sites is the crisis Dunkin' Donuts experienced in the summer of 1999 when a dissatisfied customer used the Internet to share his own bad experience at a Dunkin' Donuts store. When Dunkin' Donuts advertised coffee "your way," this customer was displeased to learn that they did not offer his choice of skim milk. Since the company did not have a corporate Web site where he could formally lodge a complaint, he created his own, writing: "Dunkin' Donuts sucks. Here's Why."[36]

While the site started out as a small section of this individual's personal Web page, it was not long before Yahoo! picked up the page in its consumer opinion section. Soon, it was generating 1,000 hits a day. Since Dunkin' Donuts had no official forum for customer suggestions or complaints, this fledgling site—out of the company's control—effectively became that forum. The complainant eventually purchased new Web space and the domain name www.dunkindonuts.org, moving the discussion to a place with a seemingly official name.[37]

It was a full two years after the site was launched that Dunkin' Donuts purchased it (after first writing a letter to the individual who created it, politely requesting that he close it, and then threatening him with a lawsuit) and built its own corporate Web site around it. Customers now have a wide variety of options for contacting specific franchise managers or company headquarters via e-mail or toll-free numbers to share feedback.

In the end, Dunkin' Donuts learned the value of offering its own Web-based forum for customer feedback and complaints, but it could have mitigated the crisis by acting sooner to take control of the situation. This example demonstrates the power of the Internet to make the voice of one individual louder than that of a major corporation, and also highlights how search engines are a cost-free means to further raise the visibility of anticorporate sites, however small and "home grown" they may be at first.

Since Dunkin' Donuts' online debacle, corporate "hate sites" have mushroomed; London-based mi2g estimates that, as of December 2004, there were more than 10,500 sites targeting major global brands. This is a huge leap from the 1,900

---

[35] Dragoon, "Fighting Phish, Fakes and Frauds."

[36] Joanna Weiss, "Dunkin' Donuts Complaint-Site Saga Shows Business Power of Internet," *Boston Globe,* August 25, 1999, Online Lexis-Nexis Academic, April 2002.

[37] Ibid.

hate sites online at the end of 2000, or the 550 posted at the end of 1997.[38] The sites are so abundant that *Forbes* magazine compiles a list of the 100 best anticorporate sites, "honoring the very best in online rage" by using a ranking system based on the following criteria: ease of use, frequency of updates, number of posts, hostility level, relevance, and entertainment value.[39] Among the top-rated are anti-Microsoft site www.MS-Eradication.org (modeled after the design of Microsoft's official corporate site), anti–American Express www.amexsux.com, or UPS-bashing www.UnitedPackageSmashers.com, featuring a photo gallery of damaged UPS-delivered packages along with the tagline: "turning parcels into pancakes . . . one package at a time."

In many ways, advocates and consumers alike now use technology to rally together and fuel or escalate a crisis—posing additional challenges for the corporation in question. Consider the thousands of text messages sent between mobile phone users in the Philippines to incite hundreds of thousands of protestors out into the streets, forcing out then-President Joseph Estrada in 2001.[40] In this way, the proliferation of online Weblogs ("blogs") has increased the visibility and reach of anticorporate sentiments. Twenty-three thousand new blog sites spring up on the Internet every day, enabling information to spread faster than wildfire—literally.[41] These electronic diaries often push a very specific agenda, one that can tarnish a company's reputation if read and shared by any of the estimated 70 million adults who go online daily.[42] Because postings tend to remain online for long periods of time—and are often not removed at all—blogs also can have a much longer-lasting impact than those transmitted through traditional vehicles such as print, recycled to the curb the next day.[43] And with services like the Wayback Machine and Google Cache offering an archive of Internet pages dating back up to nine years, online information may never disappear entirely.[44]

U.S. bicycle lock manufacturer Kryptonite experienced the influence of blogs first-hand, seeing sales plummet in 2004 after a blogger posted a video demonstrating how to pick one of its bicycle locks in under 30 seconds using a Bic pen.[45] Two million people read about the lock-picking tactic via blogs, resulting in Kryptonite spending $10 million on replacement locks.[46] The company settled a class-action lawsuit paying $3,000 for every stolen bike and issuing $10 coupons for any consumer who opted to keep the lock, on top of $690,000 in related legal

---

[38] Jack Kapica, "Anti-corporate Sites on Rise: Study," *Globe & Mail,* December 3, 2004.

[39] Charles Wolrich, "Special Report: Top Corporate Hate Web Sites," *Forbes,* March 8, 2005.

[40] William Foreman, "Text Messages Help Fuel Philippine Crisis," *Associated Press,* July 11, 2005.

[41] Adam Hill, "Reputation Management: Blogs Cast a Shadow," *PR Week Online,* July 1, 2005.

[42] "The Blogosphere: Separating the Hype from the Reality," *PR News* 61, no. 28 (July 20, 2005).

[43] Caspar van Vark, "Your Reputation Is Online," *Revolution,* March 4, 2004, p. 42.

[44] David Kesmodel, "Not Fade Away—Lawyers' Delight: Old Web Material Doesn't Disappear," *The Wall Street Journal,* July 27, 2005, p. A1.

[45] Christina K. Pikas, "Blog Searching for Competitive Intelligence, Brand Image, and Reputation Management," *Online,* July 1, 2005, p. 16.

[46] "Double-Edged Blog Power Puts Marketers on Guard," *Media,* July 1, 2005.

fees.[47] Though the same information had been published in 1992 in industry magazine *New Cyclist*, it took "the blogosphere" to give the information legs and escalate the situation to crisis level.

While many companies do not yet have an official approach to dealing with bloggers, a good place to start is identifying the most vocal and visible bloggers covering topics related to the industry and proactively supplying them with accurate corporate information.[48] In 2005, General Motors launched its first official corporate blog titled the GM "FastLane," written by GM vice president for global product development Bob Lutz.[49] "FastLane" has taken a bold approach, allowing consumers to post unfiltered feedback about GM, its products, or previous blog postings.[50] Many benefits have resulted, including free insights about products to share with the GM marketing team and, most importantly, a reputational boost for GM. Customers—particularly savvy Internet users who regularly research companies and products online—appreciate a company's solicitation for candid feedback. In times of crisis, this previously established credibility can be invaluable. The public will more likely give the company the benefit of the doubt, listen to the corporate response before casting judgment, or—at the very least—know where to turn to get the latest information if a crisis strikes. GM regularly uses its blog in noncrisis situations to manage its reputation and defend itself against "media articles that we considered unfair, unbalanced or uniformed," explains Lutz.[51] With the power of the blogosphere and Internet growing exponentially, companies have no choice but to join the fray and jump online to manage their reputations and deflect potential crises.

In the "new economy," these phenomena, coupled with widespread public concern over information security, now have the power to affect a company's bottom line substantially. Companies must recognize the increasing influence of the Internet on a growing number of its constituencies (see Chapters 6 and 7 for more on media and investor constituencies, respectively) and must keep this dimension in mind in planning for and handling crises.

These are just some of the other major crises that organizations have faced in the past 20 years:

- Credit-processing firm CardSystems is hacked into in June 2005, exposing 40 million credit card account numbers from Visa, MasterCard, American Express, and Discover Financial—constituting one of the biggest breaches of consumer data security in history.

- Boeing Co.'s board of directors forces out CEO Harry C. Stonecipher in 2005 over a consensual extramarital affair with an employee.

- Merck & Co. recalls pain medication Vioxx in September 2004 in response to a study revealing that the risk of heart attacks and strokes tripled in individuals taking the drug for periods of more than 18 months.

---

[47] Patti Waldmeir, "Blogs Are Shifting the Balance of Power," *Financial Times,* June 23, 2005, p. 11.

[48] van Vark, "Your Reputation Is Online."

[49] "The Blogosphere: Separating the Hype from the Reality."

[50] Ibid.

[51] Kyle Wingfield, "Blogging for Business," *The Wall Street Journal Europe,* July 20, 2005, p. A9.

- Accounting giant Arthur Andersen is convicted in 2002 for shredding tons of documents related to long-time client Enron Corp. While the Supreme Court overturned the ruling three years later in May 2005, Arthur Andersen's reputation was irreparably tarnished and its workforce plummeted from 85,000 to fewer than 200 after the fall.[52]

- Ford Motor Company recalls 6.5 million Firestone tires in August 2000 following a number of deaths and lawsuits surrounding Firestone tires on Ford Explorers.

- Coca-Cola issues a recall of its soft drinks in Belgium, France, the Netherlands, and Luxembourg in 1999 after more than 200 people report illnesses.

- TWA flight 800 explodes in July 1996, killing all 230 people on board the Paris-bound 747–100.

- Tainted meat served at a Jack in the Box restaurant kills two children in 1993.

- The FDA attacks Dow Corning's breast implants in 1992.

- The *Exxon Valdez* spills oil on the Alaskan coastline in 1989.

- Pan Am flight 103 explodes over Lockerbie, Scotland, in 1988.

- The Sandoz Chemical plant accident contaminates the Rhine River in 1987.

- Procter & Gamble's logo is linked to Satan in widespread rumors in 1986.

- A Hyatt Regency hotel walkway collapses in Kansas City in 1985.

How to Prepare for Crises

The first step in preparing for a crisis is understanding that any organization, no matter what industry or location it is in, can find itself involved in the kinds of crises discussed in the previous section. While these may be some of the most noteworthy ones from the last 25 years, those left out were likely just as devastating to the companies involved. Obviously, some industries—the chemical industry; pharmaceuticals; mining; forest products; energy-related industries such as oil and gas and electric utilities; and online retailers—are more crisis-prone than others, but today, every organization is at risk.

The terror attacks of September 11, 2001, proved to be an important test of many companies' crisis plans. For other companies, the attacks underlined the importance of having a plan in place. A survey of nearly 200 CEOs conducted by Burson-Marsteller and *PR Week* magazine in late 2001 revealed that a full 21 percent of CEOs surveyed "had no crisis plan and were caught unprepared" by the events of September 11. Fifty-three percent acknowledged that their plan was good but "not totally adequate for such events." In response to the question of whether they had readdressed their crisis communication plan since the September 11 disaster, 63 percent indicated that they intended to.[53] Despite those stated intentions, the

---

[52] Diya Gullapalli, "Andersen Decision Is Bittersweet for Ex-Workers," *The Wall Street Journal,* June 1, 2005, p. A6.

[53] Jonah Bloom, "CEOs: Leadership through Communication—The *PR Week* and Burson-Marsteller CEO Survey 2001 Finds U.S. Corporate Leaders Emulating the Strong, Open, Communicative Style of Rudy," *PR Week,* November 26, 2001, pp. 20–29.

numbers may be even more troubling several years on. A Harris Poll in 2004 revealed that only 22 percent of Fortune 1000 companies say they are completely prepared to face a natural or manmade disaster; 79 percent said that more than half of their employees are unaware of their companies' policies and procedures concerning disaster planning.[54]

Many companies located in the World Trade Center also had been tenants of the Twin Towers at the time of another terrorist attack. In 1993, an explosion blew out three of the underground floors of the World Trade Center, forcing the evacuation of more than 30,000 employees and thousands of visitors from the entire complex and a rescue operation lasting 12 hours.[55] After the 1993 bombing, many organizations developed or refined their evacuation plans from the Trade Center. When the second attack occurred in 2001, this preparation helped save many lives.

For example, the World Trade Center's largest tenant, Morgan Stanley Dean Witter, cited its own evacuation plan as critical to saving the lives of all but six of its 3,700 employees on September 11. A Morgan spokesman attributed the smooth evacuation to companywide familiarity with the plan: "Everybody knew about the contingency plan. We met constantly to talk about it."[56]

Communications managers must follow these examples and prepare company management for the worst by using anecdotal information about what has happened to unprepared organizations in earlier crises. There are so many to choose from that managers should not be hard pressed to find crisis examples in virtually every industry from experiences over the last 25 years. Once the groundwork is laid for management to accept the notion that a crisis is a possibility, real preparation should take the following form.

Assess the Risk for Your Organization

As mentioned earlier, some industries are more prone to crises than others. But how can organizations determine whether they are more or less likely to experience a crisis? First, publicly traded companies are at risk because of the nature of their relationship with a key constituency—shareholders. If a major catastrophe hits a company that trades on one of the stock exchanges, the likelihood of a sell-off in the stock is enormous. Such immediate financial consequences can threaten the organization's image as a stable ongoing operation in addition to the damage the crisis itself inflicts.

While privately held companies do not have to worry about shareholders, they do have to worry about the loss of goodwill—which can affect sales—when a crisis hits. Often the owners of privately held companies become involved in communication during a crisis to lend their own credibility to the organization. So all organizations—public, private, and not-for-profit—are at some risk if a crisis actually occurs. The next section examines how a company can plan for the worst no matter what.

[54] Mike Walsh, "Post-9/11, Does Your Company Know the Drill?" *PR News* 36, no. 60 (September 20, 2004).

[55] Carol Carey, "World Trade Center," *Access Control & Security Systems Integration,* July 1, 1997.

[56] Daren Fonda, "Girding against New Risks: Global Executives Are Working to Better Protect Their Employees and Businesses from Calamity," *Time,* October 8, 2001, p. B8.

Plan for Crises

First, the person in charge of corporate communication should call a *brainstorming session* that includes the most senior managers in the organization as well as representatives from the areas that are most likely to be affected by a crisis. For example, this would include the head of manufacturing in some cases because of the potential for industrial accidents in the manufacturing process. It also might include the chief information officer because of the danger to computer systems when accidents happen. In the case of the explosion at the first World Trade Center attack in 1993, most of the organizations were service organizations. After the loss of lives, the loss of critical information was one of the worst outcomes of the explosion.

During the brainstorming session, participants should work together to develop ideas about potential crises. They should be encouraged to be as creative as possible during this stage. The facilitator should allow participants to share their ideas, no matter how outrageous, with the group and should encourage all participants to be open-minded as they think about possible crisis scenarios.

Once an inventory of possible crises exists, the facilitator should help the group to determine which of the ideas developed have the most potential to actually occur. It might be useful, for example, to ask the group to assign probabilities to the potential crises so that they can focus on the more likely scenarios rather than wasting time working through solutions to problems that have a very low probability of occurring. But even at this stage, participants must not rule out the worst-case scenario. The risk for an oil spill the size of the *Exxon Valdez* occurring was very low according to outside projections. Thus, neither the oil company nor governmental agencies prepared for the worst possible accident.

Determine Effect on Constituencies

Once the probability of risk has been assigned to potential crises, organizations need to determine *which constituencies would be most affected by the crisis*. Crisis communication experts spend too little time thinking about this question. Why is it so important? Since some constituencies are more important than others, organizations need to look at risk in terms of its effect on the most important constituencies.

When the World Trade Center came under attack on September 11, 2001, American Express CEO Ken Chenault phoned the company's headquarters across the street from the World Trade Center and instructed building security to evacuate employees immediately. As the day wore on, he contacted all his senior executives to check on their well-being.[57] Until Chenault was able to relocate the company's 3,000 employees to a new building across the river, AmEx's in-house communications staff worked from their homes to reach out to customers and let them know the company was open for business.[58] Two concerns guided Chenault in his actions following this crisis—employee safety and customer service.[59]

---

[57] Bloom, "CEOs: Leadership through Communication."

[58] "Corporate America's Reaction," *PR Week,* September 24, 2001, p. 10.

[59] Bloom, "CEOs: Leadership through Communication."

Employees and customers, in this example, were the constituencies determined to be most affected by these events, and Chenault's actions reflected this.

Determining how to rank constituencies when a crisis actually happens is more difficult because so many other things are going on. But thinking about risk in terms of effect on constituencies in advance helps the organization further refine which potential crises it should spend the most time and money preparing for. During the Tylenol crisis, for example, Johnson & Johnson could rely on its Credo to help the company set clear priorities and deal with its constituencies. In the wake of several regulatory and legal scandals, Citigroup CEO Charles ("Chuck") Prince met with Johnson & Johnson when creating the three "Shared Responsibilities" that all Citigroup employees signed on to in March 2005—with the intent of setting behavioral standards that will prevent mishaps or offer a framework of values to guide responses to any that occur.

Set Communication Objectives for Potential Crises

Setting communication objectives for potential crises is different than figuring out how to deal with the crisis itself. Clearly, organizations must do both, but typically managers are more likely to focus on what kinds of things they will do during a crisis rather than what they will say and to whom. Communication takes on more importance than action when the crisis involves more intangible things such as the loss of reputation rather than the loss of lives.

Analyze Channel Choice

Once the ranking of constituencies is complete, the participants in a planning session should begin to think about what their communication objective will be for each constituency. Whether this objective will be achieved often depends on the effectiveness of the communication *channel* the company selects to convey the message.

Perhaps the mass distribution of a memo would be too impersonal for a message to employees in a time of crisis. The company might consider personal or group meetings or a "town hall" gathering instead. The choice of communication channel often can reflect how sensitive a company is to its constituencies' needs and emotions. What would be the most efficient and most sensitive way to communicate with consumers or their families during a crisis? Johnson & Johnson's caring and highly personalized reaction to the Tylenol crisis—involving a host of personal visits to hospitals and pharmacies nationwide—won the company significant goodwill. In a time of crisis, constituencies crave information, and are often more sensitive than usual to how information is conveyed to them. In the case of the Kryptonite lock-picking debacle, four days after the first blog was posted about the trick, Kryptonite issued a generic statement citing the locks as a "deterrent to theft" and noting that the new line of locks promised to be "tougher."[60] Hundreds of bloggers were unsatisfied with the empty answer and continued to write about the locks, prompting hundreds of thousands more to

[60] David Kirkpatrick, Daniel Roth, and Oliver Ryan, "Why There's No Escaping the Blog," *Fortune*, January 10, 2005, p. 44.

PEARSON AND MITROFF'S CRISIS MANAGEMENT STRATEGIC CHECKLIST

STRATEGIC ACTIONS

1. Integrate crisis management into strategic planning processes.
2. Integrate crisis management into statements of corporate excellence.
3. Include outsiders on the board and on crisis management teams.
4. Provide training and workshops in crisis management.
5. Expose organizational members to crisis simulations.
6. Create a diversity or portfolio of crisis management strategies.

TECHNICAL AND STRUCTURAL ACTIONS

1. Create a crisis management team.
2. Dedicate budget expenditures for crisis management.
3. Establish accountabilities for updating emergency policies/manuals.
4. Computerize inventories of crisis management resources (e.g., employee skills).
5. Designate an emergency command control room.
6. Assure technological redundancy in vital areas (e.g., computer systems).
7. Establish working relationship with outside experts in crisis management.

EVALUATION AND DIAGNOSTIC ACTIONS

1. Conduct legal and financial audit of threats and liabilities.
2. Modify insurance coverage to match crisis management contingencies.
3. Conduct environmental impact audits.
4. Prioritize activities necessary for daily operations.
5. Establish tracking system for early warning signals.
6. Establish tracking system to follow up past crises or near crises.

COMMUNICATION ACTIONS

1. Provide training for dealing with the media regarding crisis management.
2. Improve communication lines with local communities.
3. Improve communication with intervening stakeholders (e.g., police).

PSYCHOLOGICAL AND CULTURAL ACTIONS

1. Increase visibility of strong top management commitment to crisis management.
2. Improve relationships with activist groups.
3. Improve upward communication (including "whistle-blowers").
4. Improve downward communication regarding crisis management programs/accountabilities.
5. Provide training regarding human and emotional impacts of crises.
6. Provide psychological support services (e.g., stress/anxiety management).
7. Reinforce symbolic recall/corporate memory of past crises/dangers.

Source: Christine Pearson and Ian Mitroff, "From Crisis Prone to Crisis Prepared: A Framework for Crisis Management," *Academy of Management Executive* 7, no. 1 (1993), pp. 48–59.

read about them, online and in print via *New York Times* and Associated Press stories.[61] An estimated 1.8 million people read at least one blog posting about Kryptonite throughout the crisis, largely because Kryptonite failed to stage a swift, cohesive online response effort to battle the bloggers head on in their own forum.[62]

[61] Ibid.
[62] Ibid.

Assign a Different Team to Each Crisis

Another important part of planning for communicating in a crisis is determining in advance who will be on what team for each crisis. Different problems require different kinds of expertise, and planners should consider who is best suited to deal with one type of crisis versus another. For example, if the crisis is likely to have a financial focus, the chief financial officer may be the best person to lead a team dealing with such a problem. He or she also may be the best spokesperson when the problem develops. On the other hand, if the problem is more catastrophic, such as an airline crash, the CEO is probably the best person to put in charge of the team and to serve, at least initially, as head spokesperson for the crisis. In crises like this that result in loss of life, anyone other than the CEO will have less credibility with the general public and the media.

But managers should avoid putting senior-level executives in charge of communications for *all* crises. Sometimes the person closest to the crisis is the one people want to hear from. For example, the best spokesperson for a global company may be someone located in the country where the problem develops rather than a more senior manager from the head office due to considerations such as cultural issues, language differences, and local community concerns.

Assigning different teams to handle different crises helps the organization put the best people in charge of handling the crisis and communications. It also allows the organization to get a cross-section of employees involved. The more involved managers are in planning and participating on a team in a crisis, the better equipped the organization will be as a whole.

Plan for Centralization

Although organizations can employ either a centralized or decentralized approach to corporate communication for general purposes (as we discussed in Chapter 3), when it comes to crisis, the approach must be completely centralized.

Conflicting stories from Perrier's U.S. and European divisions created problems in the company's handling of the benzene contamination scare, further compounding that crisis. Decentralized organizations often find it more difficult to communicate efficiently between divisions, especially if they have not given interdivisional communication full consideration in a crisis-planning phase. Planning for centralization can help strip away layers of bureaucracy, keep lines of communication open throughout the organization, and dissipate conflict, all of which are especially critical in a crisis.

What to Include in a Formal Plan

Every communications consultant will suggest that you develop a detailed plan for use in a crisis. These are formal in the sense that they are typically printed up and passed around to the appropriate managers, who may have to sign a statement swearing that they have read and agree to the plan. This allows the organization to ensure that the plan has been acknowledged by the recipients, and permits questions and clarifications to be discussed *in a noncrisis environment*. The last thing you want to happen is for a plant manager's first read of the plan to be when a real crisis occurs.

Research on crisis planning shows that the following information is almost always included in a crisis plan.

A List of Whom to Notify in an Emergency

This list should contain the names and numbers of everyone on the crisis team as well as numbers to call externally such as the fire and police departments. The list should be kept updated as people leave the company or change responsibilities.

An Approach to Media Relations

Frank Corrado, the president of a firm that deals with crisis communications, suggests that the cardinal rule for communicating with all constituencies in a crisis should be "Tell It All, Tell It Fast!" [63] To a certain extent this is true, but one should be extremely careful about applying such a rule too quickly to the media. Perhaps a friendly amendment to Corrado's rule might be "Tell as much as you can, as soon as you can," so that you do not jeopardize the credibility of the organization. For example, Perrier's hasty communication with the media, in the absence of accurate information, was a crippling mistake.

If the organization has done a good job of building relations with the media when times are good, reporters will be more understanding when a crisis occurs. Having a reserve of goodwill with the media is what helped Johnson & Johnson during the Tylenol crisis. Generally, the person who has the best relationships with individual reporters is probably the right person to get involved with them during a crisis. By agreeing ahead of time that all crisis-related inquiries will go to a central location, organizations can avoid looking disorganized.

A Strategy for Notifying Employees

Employees should be seen as analogous to families in a personal crisis. Employees finding out from the media about something that affects the organization can be likened to a family member hearing about a personal problem from an outsider. An organization should take pains to ensure that a plan for employee notification is created with employee communication professionals in advance and is included in the overall crisis plan.

A Location to Serve as Crisis Headquarters

Although consultants and experts who have written about crises suggest that companies need to invest money in a special crisis center, all companies really need to do is identify ahead of time an area that can easily be converted to such an operation. A contingency location should be determined in the event of a natural disaster or terrorist attack affecting the safety or security of the chosen location. Gathering the appropriate technology (e.g., computers, fax machines, cell phones, hookups for media transmissions) as quickly as possible when a crisis hits is also important. This headquarters location should be shared ahead of time with all key internal and external constituencies. All information ideally should be centralized

---

[63] Frank Corrado, *Media for Managers* (New York: Prentice Hall, 1997), p. 101.

through this office. Other lines of communication should then flow through the headquarters for the duration of the crisis.

A Description of the Plan

Companies should have their crisis plans documented in writing. In addition to communication strategy, a crisis plan should address logistical details as well, for example, how and where the families of victims should be accommodated in the case of an airline crash.

Following the development of an overall plan, all managers should receive training about what to do if and when a crisis strikes. Several public relations firms and academic consultants now offer simulations that allow managers to test their crisis management skills in experiential exercises. Companies including MasterCard, Southwest Airlines, and General Motors use simulations to help their organizations work out the kinks before a real crisis hits.[64] Managers searching for the right training should be sure that the simulation or training session includes a heavy emphasis on communication in addition to management of the crisis itself.

Beyond managers, all employees should be versed in and trained regularly on the company's emergency procedures and plans. Involve all employees in continuity of business tests; while a genuine crisis cannot be simulated, test runs will help ensure familiarity with emergency plans throughout all levels of the organization. British Airways conducts a companywide crisis simulation exercise every 12 to 18 months. Guiding those trial runs is BA's crisis manual—200 pages outlining employee roles, responsibilities, and actions in the event of an emergency; third-party contact information; press release templates; as well as maps and key information on BA's fleet and partners.[65]

Communicating during the Crisis

All the planning that an organization can muster will only partially prepare it for an actual crisis. The true measure of success is how it deals with a problem when it occurs. If the plan is comprehensive enough, managers will at least start from a strong position. What follow are the most important steps to take when communicating during a crisis. Every crisis is different, which means that managers must adapt these suggestions to meet their needs, but crises have enough common elements for this prescription to be a starting point for all crisis management.

Step 1: Get Control of the Situation

The first step is for the appropriate manager to get control of the situation as soon as possible. This involves defining the real problem with the use of reliable information and then setting measurable communication objectives for handling it. Failing to take this seemingly obvious, but crucial, first step can be devastating to

---

[64] "Crises: In-House, in Hand," *PR Week*, January 21, 2002, p. 13.

[65] Mary Cowlett, "Crisis Training: Prepared for Anything?" *PR Week*, May 6, 2005, p. 25.

crisis management efforts, as seen in the Perrier case. Perrier lacked sufficient information to *define* its benzene problem in the first place—though its spokespeople tried to convince the public otherwise—which only compromised its attempts to mitigate the crisis.

When a crisis erupts, everyone in the organization should know who needs to be contacted, but in large organizations this is often unrealistic. Therefore, the corporate communication department can initially serve as a clearinghouse. The vice president for corporate communication at the head office should know the composition of crisis teams and can then turn the situation over to the appropriate manager.

Step 2: Gather as Much Information as Possible

Understanding the problem at hand is the right place for communicators to begin dealing with a crisis. This often involves managing information coming from many sources.

As information becomes available, someone should be assigned to mine that information: If it is an industrial accident, how serious is it? Were lives lost? Have families already been notified? If the incident involves an unfriendly takeover, what are the details of the offer? Was it absurdly low? Have any plans been made for the company to defend itself?

Many corporations have been criticized for reacting too slowly during a crisis because they were trying desperately to gather information about the incident. If it is going to take longer than a couple of hours to get the right information, a company spokesperson should communicate this to the media and other key constituencies right away to make it clear that the company is not stonewalling. No one will criticize an organization for trying to find out what is going on, but a company can face harsh treatment if its constituencies think that management is deliberately obstructing the flow of information.

Step 3: Set Up a Centralized Crisis Management Center

At the same time managers are getting in touch with the right people and gathering information, they also should be making arrangements for creating a crisis center as described earlier in this chapter. This location will serve as the platform for all communications during the crisis. Organizations also should provide a comfortable location for media to use during the crisis, including adequate computers or Internet hookups, phones, fax machines, and so on. All communications about the crisis should come from this one, centralized location.

Step 4: Communicate Early and Often

The organization's spokesperson needs to say whatever he or she can as soon as possible. Particularly if the crisis involves threat to lives and property, communicators should try to shield constituencies from panic by allaying some of the probable fears that people will have about the situation. Employees, the media, and other important constituencies should know that the crisis center will issue updates at regular intervals until further notice. Even if they retain public relations firms to assist them in handling a crisis, companies need to put good *inside* people on the front lines of crisis communication and should encourage managers to adopt a team approach with others involved.

Above all else, avoid silence and delayed responses. In 2000, Bridgestone/ Firestone's tire recall crisis proved just how detrimental tardy communication can be. Hundreds of accidents and deaths were linked to Firestone tread separations on Ford Explorers. While the majority of the 6.5 million tires were recalled,[66] Firestone's response focused more on pinning blame on Ford and dodging responsibility than communicating clearly and thoughtfully with affected consumers who were frantic for information. As a result of this highly publicized crisis, Firestone fell to the bottom of the list in *Fortune*'s 2001 survey of the most admired companies, assuming the last spot among rubber and plastics companies.[67] In contrast, consider CD Universe's swift response to the blackmailing incident in 2000. The company promptly sent e-mail notices directly to its customers alerting them to the situation, explaining how the company was responding to the security breach, and working with the credit card companies to help customers in the event that their stolen numbers were used. Larry Kamer, chairman of GCI Kamer Singer, notes that "nine and a half times out of 10 you have to communicate before the facts are in."[68] So communicate values, such as concern for public safety, and show a commitment to coming to the aid of people affected by the crisis, even if you do not have all the details yet.

Step 5: Understand the Media's Mission in a Crisis

Members of the media work in an extremely competitive environment, which explains why they all want to get the story first. They are also more accustomed to a crisis environment in their work. What they are looking for is a good story with victims, villains, and visuals.

The Pepsi syringe hoax had all of these sensational elements. As we have seen, CEO Craig Weatherup recognized the impact that visuals would have in reassuring the public that the tampering claims it was facing were simply impossible. The video footage of Pepsi canning procedures and the grocery-store surveillance tape, shown on television, and the full-page newspaper ad are all examples of Pepsi's using the media to help it beat a crisis (see Figure 10.1).

Step 6: Communicate Directly with Affected Constituents

Using the media to get information out is good, but it's more important to communicate with your employees, sales staff, organized leadership, site security, operators, and receptionists, as these will be the media's best sources of information in the crisis. External constituencies need to be contacted as well. These

---

[66] Caroline E. Mayer and Frank Swoboda, "A Corporate Collision; Ford-Firestone Feud Accelerated after Effort to Head It Off Failed," *Washington Post*, June 20, 2001, p. E1.

[67] "Who's Up, Who's Down," *Fortune*, February 19, 2001, p. 104.

[68] John Frank, "What Can We Learn from the Ford/Firestone Tire Recall? As John Frank Explains, Unlike the Tylenol Crisis, the Problem Is That They Just Can't Seem to Put a Lid on It," *PR Week*, October 9, 2000, p. 31.

include the other three key constituencies besides employees—customers, shareholders, and communities—as well as suppliers, emergency services, experts, and officials. All available technologies should be employed to communicate with them, including e-mail, voice mail, faxes, direct satellite broadcasts, and online services.

Before communicating, companies also should consider which constituencies are top priority. One of Firestone's major blunders during the 2000 tire recall scandal was targeting its first round of PR efforts at dealers instead of appealing directly to the consumers themselves—the constituency most directly affected by the crisis in the first place. Distributing reassuring ads to local dealers, Firestone hoped to leverage dealers' strong reputations to help build back its own. Instead, the company should have channeled its effort and resources into targeting consumers *directly* and personally to bolster their view of the company. With the recall nearly seven months old, it was not until February 2001 that Firestone began to speak to consumers directly by moving their safety efforts online. The company launched the Web site TireSafety.com.[69] By acting so late and misdirecting its initial PR efforts, Firestone gave the appearance of only paying attention to consumer safety when backed into a corner, not because it was part of the corporate philosophy.

Step 7: Remember That Business Must Continue

To the managers involved, the crisis will most certainly be uppermost in their minds for the duration, but to others, the business must go on despite the crisis. In addition to finding suitable replacements ahead of time for those who are on the crisis team, managers must try to anticipate the effects of the crisis on other parts of the business. For example, if an advertising campaign is under way, should it be stopped during the crisis? Have financial officers stopped trading on the company's stock? Will it be necessary for the organization to move to a temporary location during the crisis? These and other questions related to the ongoing business need to be thought through by managers on and off the crisis team as soon as possible.

Step 8: Make Plans to Avoid Another Crisis Immediately

Postcrisis, corporate communications executives should work with other managers to ensure the organization will be even better prepared the next time it is faced with a crisis. Companies that have experienced crises are more likely to believe that such occurrences will happen again, and also will recognize that preparation is key to handling crises successfully.

Johnson & Johnson's experience in 1982 helped the company to deal with another episode of Tylenol contamination four years later when a New Yorker died after taking cyanide-laced Tylenol capsules. There is no better time than the period immediately following a crisis to prepare for the next one because motivation is high to learn from mistakes made the first time.

---

[69] John Frank, "Ethics in PR," *PR Week,* February 11, 2001, p. 8.

Conclusion

Webster's Dictionary traces the word *crisis* back to the Greek word *krisis*—meaning a decision, from the verb *krinein*, to decide.[70] Today we know crises as pivotal times of instability where leadership and decision making can determine the ultimate outcome of the situation—for better or for worse. As we've seen, sometimes companies can emerge even more respected in the wake of a well-handled crisis.

In this chapter, we explored some real-life examples of how companies across a number of industries dealt with crises of their own and saw that planning and preparation are key to effective crisis management and communication. As British author Aldous Huxley put it, "The amelioration of the world cannot be achieved by sacrifices in moments of crisis; it depends on the efforts made and constantly repeated during the humdrum, uninspiring periods, which separate one crisis from another, and of which normal lives mainly consist."[71]

---

[70] *Merriam-Webster Online Dictionary,* http://www.merriam-webster.com. Retreived June 9, 2005.

[71] Aldous Huxley, *Grey Eminence: A Study in Religion and Politics* (London: Chatto & Windus, 1941), chapter 10.

Case 10-1

Coca-Cola India

On August 20, 2003, Sanjiv Gupta, president and CEO of Coca-Cola India, sat in his office contemplating the events of the last two weeks and debating his next move. Sales had dropped by 30–40 percent[1] in only two weeks on the heels of a 75 percent five-year growth trajectory and 25–30 percent[2] year-to-date growth. Many leading clubs, retailers, restaurants, and college campuses across India had stopped selling Coca-Cola.[3] Only six weeks into his new role as CEO, Gupta was embroiled in a crisis that threatened the momentum gained from a highly successful two-year marketing campaign that had given Coca-Cola market leadership over Pepsi.

On August 5th, The Center for Science and Environment (CSE), an activist group in India focused on environmental sustainability issues (specifically the effects of industrialization and economic growth), issued a press release stating: "12 major cold drink brands sold in and around Delhi contain a deadly cocktail of pesticide residues" (see Exhibit 10.1). According to tests conducted by the Pollution Monitoring Laboratory (PML) of the CSE from April to August, three samples of 12 PepsiCo and Coca-Cola brands from across the city were found to contain pesticide residues surpassing global standards by 30–36 times including lindane, DDT, malathion, and chlorpyrifos (see Exhibit 10.2). These four pesticides were known to

cause cancer, damage to the nervous and reproductive systems, birth defects, and severe disruption of the immune system.[4]

In reaction to this report, the Indian government banned Coke and Pepsi products in Parliament and state governments launched independent investigations, sending soft drink samples to labs for testing. The Coca-Cola Bottling Company (Coke) stock dipped by five dollars on the New York Stock Exchange from $55 to $50 in the six sessions following the August 5 disclosure, as did shares of Coca-Cola Enterprises (CCA).[5]

Pepsi and Coca-Cola called the CSE allegations "baseless" and questioned the method of testing, but the CSE claimed it had followed standard procedures documented by the U.S. Environmental Protection Agency including gas chromatography and mass spectrometry. Pepsi's own tests conducted at an independent laboratory showed no detectable pesticides and led Pepsi to file a petition with the high court questioning the credibility of the CSE's claims,[6] while Coke's Gupta commented: "The allegation is serious and it has the potential to tarnish the image of our brands in the country. If this continues, we will consider legal recourse."[7]

Despite Coke and Pepsi's early responses denying the validity of the CSE's claims and threatening legal action, a survey conducted in Delhi a few days after the CSE announcement

Source: This case was prepared in 2005 by Jennifer Kaye, under the supervision of Professor Paul A. Argenti. The author wishes to thank Nymph Kaul for her research assistance and Rai University for their financial support in the development of this case, which was written with the cooperation of Coca-Cola India.

[1] "Toxic Effect: Coke Sales Fall by a Sharp 30–40%," *Economic Times*, August 13, 2003, p. 1.

[2] "Controversy-Ridden Year for Soft Drinks," *Business Line* (New Delhi), December 30, 2003, p. 6.

[3] "Toxic Effect."

[4] Center for Science and Environment, press release, "Hard Truths about Soft Drinks." August 5, 2003.

[5] "No Standards for World-Wide Pesticide Residues in Soft-Drinks," *Business Line* (New Delhi), October 3, 2003, p. 9.

[6] "Coke & Pepsi in India: Pesticides in Carbonated Beverages," http://www.vedpuriswar.org/articles/Indiancases (retrieved December 7, 2004).

[7] "Tests Show Pesticides in Soft Drinks, Claims CSE," *Economic Times*, August 6, 2003, p. 1.

EXHIBIT 10.1 Center for Science and Environment Press Release: Hard Truths about Soft Drinks

Source: CSE press release, "Hard Truths about Soft Drinks," August 5, 2003.

New Delhi, August 5, 2003: After bottled water, it's aerated water that has plugged the purity test. In another exposé, Down To Earth has found that 12 major cold drink brands sold in and around Delhi contain a deadly cocktail of pesticide residues. The results are based on tests conducted by the Pollution Monitoring Laboratory (PML) of the Centre for Science and Environment (CSE). In February this year, CSE had blasted the bottled water industry's claims of being 'pure' when its laboratory had found pesticide residues in bottled water sold in Delhi and Mumbai.

This time, it analysed the contents of 12 cold drink brands sold in and around the capital. They were tested for organochlorine and organophosphorus pesticides and synthetic pyrethroids—all commonly used in India as insecticides.

The test results were as shocking as those of bottled water.

All samples contained residues of four extremely toxic pesticides and insecticides: lindane, DDT, malathion and chlorpyrifos. In all samples, levels of pesticide residues far exceeded the maximum residue limit for pesticides in water used as 'food', set down by the European Economic Commission (EEC). Each sample had enough poison to cause—in the long term—cancer, damage to the nervous and reproductive systems, birth defects and severe disruption of the immune system.

WHAT WE FOUND

- Market leaders Coca-Cola and Pepsi had almost similar concentrations of pesticide residues. Total pesticides in all PepsiCo brands on an average were 0.0180 mg/l (milligramme per litre), 36 times higher than the EEC limit for total pesticides (0.0005 mg/l). Total pesticides in all Coca-Cola brands on an average were 0.0150 mg/l, 30 times higher than the EEC limit.
- While contaminants in the 'Dil mange more' Pepsi were 37 times higher than the EEC limit, they exceeded the norms by 45 times in the 'Thanda matlab Coca-Cola' product.
- Mirinda Lemon topped the chart among all the tested brand samples, with a total pesticide concentration of 0.0352 mg/l.

The cold drinks sector in India is a much bigger money-spinner than the bottled water segment. In 2001, Indians consumed over 6,500 million bottles of cold drinks. Its growing popularity means that children and teenagers, who glug these bottles, are drinking a toxic potion.

PML also tested two soft drink brands sold in the US, to see if they contained pesticides. They didn't.

The question, therefore, is: how can apparently quality-conscious multinationals market products unfit for human consumption?

CSE found that the regulations for the powerful and massive soft drinks industry are much weaker, indeed non-existent, as compared to those for the bottled water industry. The norms that exist to regulate the quality of cold drinks are a maze of meaningless definitions. This "food" sector is virtually unregulated.

The Prevention of Food Adulteration (PFA) Act of 1954, or the Fruit Products Order (FPO) of 1955—both mandatory acts aimed at regulating the quality of contents in beverages such as cold drinks—do not even provide any scope for regulating pesticides in soft drinks. The FPO, under which the industry gets its license to operate, has standards for lead and arsenic that are 50 times higher than those allowed for the bottled water industry.

What's more, the sector is also exempted from the provisions of industrial licensing under the Industries (Development and Regulation) Act, 1951. It gets a one-time license to operate from the ministry of food processing industries; this license includes a no-objection certificate from the local government as well as the state pollution control board, and a water analysis report. There are no environmental impact assessments, or citing regulations. The industry's use of water, therefore, is not regulated.

EXHIBIT 10.2 Pesticide Content in 12 Leading Soft Drink Brands

Source: CSE Press Release, "Hard Truths about Soft Drinks," August 5, 2003.

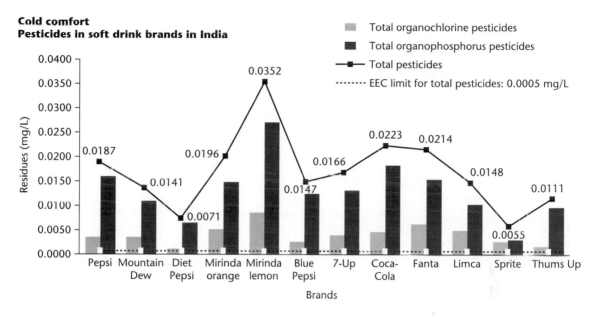

Cold comfort
Pesticides in soft drink brands in India

- ☐ Total organochlorine pesticides
- ■ Total organophosphorus pesticides
- ■— Total pesticides
- ········ EEC limit for total pesticides: 0.0005 mg/L

found that a majority of consumers believed the findings were correct and agreed with parliament's move to ban the sale of soft drinks.[8] The $1 billion Indian soft drink market[9] was at stake and Gupta had to act.

HISTORY OF COKE

THE EARLY DAYS

Coca-Cola was created in 1886 by John Pemberton, a pharmacist in Atlanta, Georgia, who sold the syrup mixed with fountain water as a potion for mental and physical disorders. The formula changed hands three more times before Asa D. Candler added carbonation and by 2003, Coca-Cola was the world's largest manufacturer, marketer, and distributor of non-alcoholic beverage concentrates and syrups, with more than 400 widely recognized beverage brands in its portfolio.

[8] "Coke & Pepsi in India: Pesticides in Carbonated Beverages."

[9] http://www.indiastat.com.

With the bubbles making the difference, Coca-Cola was registered as a trademark in 1887 and by 1895, was being sold in every state and territory in the United States. In 1899, it franchised its bottling operations in the United States, growing quickly to reach 370 franchisees by 1910.[10] Headquartered in Atlanta with divisions and local operations in over 200 countries worldwide, Coca-Cola generated more than 70 percent of its income outside the United States by 2003 (see Exhibit 10.3).

INTERNATIONAL EXPANSION

Coke's first international bottling plants opened in 1906 in Canada, Cuba, and Panama.[11] By the end of the 1920s, Coca-Cola was bottled in 27 countries throughout the

[10] Nymph Kaul, "Coca-Cola India," Rai University, 2004; Coca-Cola Company Web site, http://www2.coca-cola.com/heritage/; and Mark Pendergrast, *For God, Country and Coca-Cola* (New York: Charles Scribner's Sons, 1993).

[11] http://www2.coca-cola.com/ourcompany/aroundworld.html.

EXHIBIT 10.3 The Coca-Cola Company Income Statement

(in millions $ except per share data)	2002	2001	2000
Net operating revenues	19,564	17,545	17,354
Cost of goods sold	7,105	6,044	6,204
Gross profit	12,459	11,501	11,150
Selling, general, and administrative expenses	7,001	6,149	6,016
Other operating changes	0	0	1,443
Operating income	5,458	5,352	3,691
Interest income	209	325	345
Interest expense	199	289	447
Equity income (loss)	384	152	(289)
Other income (loss)—net	(353)	39	99
Gains on issuances of stock by equity investee	0	91	0
Income before income taxes and cumulative effect of accounting change	5,499	5,670	3,399
Income taxes	1,523	1,691	1,222
Net Income before cumulative effect of accounting change	3,976	3,979	2,177
Cumulative effect of accounting change for SFAS No. 142 net of income taxes:			
Company operations	(367)	0	0
Equity investments	(559)	0	0
Cumulative effect of accounting change for SFAS No. 133 net of income taxes	0	(10)	0
Net income	3,050	3,969	2,177
Basic net income per share before accounting change	1.60	1.60	0.88
Cumulative effect of accounting change	(0.37)	0	0
	1.23	1.60	0.88
Diluted net income per share before accounting change	1.60	1.60	0.88
Cumulative effect of accounting change	(0.37)	0	0
	1.23	1.60	0.88
Average shares outstanding	2,478	2,487	2,477
Effect of dilutive securities	5	0	10
Average shares outstanding assuming dilution	2,483	2,487	2,487

world and available in 51 more. In spite of this reach, volume was low, quality inconsistent, and effective advertising a challenge with language, culture, and government regulation all serving as barriers. Former CEO Robert Woodruff's insistence that Coca-Cola wouldn't "suffer the stigma of being an intrusive American product," and instead would use local bottles, caps, machinery, trucks, and personnel, contributed

to Coke's challenges as well with a lack of standard processes and training degrading quality.[12]

Coca-Cola continued working for over 80 years on Woodruff's goal: to make Coke available wherever and whenever consumers

[12] Pendergrast, *For God, Country and Coca-Cola*, p. 172.

EXHIBIT 10.4   Interbrand's Global Brand Scoreboard 2003

Source: "The Top 100 Brands: Interbrand's Global Brand Scorecard 2003," BusinessWeek, August 4, 2003.

Rank	Company	2003 Brand Value ($Billion)	2002 Brand Value ($Billion)	Percent Change	Country of Ownership
1	Coca-Cola	70.45	69.64	+1%	U.S.
2	Microsoft	65.17	54.09	+2	U.S.
3	IBM	51.77	51.19	+1	U.S.
4	GE	42.34	41.31	+2	U.S.
5	Intel	31.11	30.86	+1	U.S.
6	Nokia	29.44	29.97	−2	Finland
7	Disney	28.04	29.26	−4	U.S.
8	McDonald's	24.70	26.38	−6	U.S.
9	Marlboro	22.18	24.15	8	U.S.
10	Mercedes	21.37	21.01	+2	Germany

wanted it, "in arm's reach of desire."[13] The Second World War proved to be the stimulus Coca-Cola needed to build effective capabilities around the world and achieve dominant global market share. Woodruff's patriotic commitment "that every man in uniform gets a bottle of Coca-Cola for five cents, wherever he is and at whatever cost to our company"[14] was more than just great public relations. As a result of Coke's status as a military supplier, Coca-Cola was exempt from sugar rationing and also received government subsidies to build bottling plants around the world to serve WWII troops.[15]

TURN-OF-THE-CENTURY GROWTH IMPERATIVE

The 1990s brought a slowdown in sales growth for the carbonated soft drink (CSD) industry in the United States, achieving only 0.2 percent growth by 2000 (just under 10 billion cases) in contrast to the 5–7 percent annual growth experienced during the 1980s. While per capita consumption throughout the world was a fraction of the United States', major beverage companies clearly had to look elsewhere

for the growth their shareholders demanded. The looming opportunity for the twenty-first century was in the world's developing markets with their rapidly growing middle-class populations.

THE WORLD'S MOST POWERFUL BRAND

Interbrand's Global Brand Scorecard for 2003 ranked Coca-Cola the #1 Brand in the World and estimated its brand value at $70.45 billion (see Exhibit 10.4).[16] The ranking's methodology determined a brand's valuation on the basis of how much it was likely to earn in the future, distilling the percentage of revenues that could be credited to the brand, and assessing the brand's strength to determine the risk of future earnings forecasts. Considerations included market leadership, stability, and global reach, incorporating its ability to cross both geographical and cultural borders.[17]

From the beginning, Coke understood the importance of branding and the creation of a distinct personality.[18] Its catchy, well-liked

---

[13] Ibid.

[14] Ibid., p. 199.

[15] Ibid., pp. 200–201.

[16] "The Top 100 Brands: Interbrand's Global Brand Scorecard 2003," Interbrand Special Report, as seen in *BusinessWeek*, August 4, 2003.

[17] Ibid.

[18] Nicholas Kochan, ed., and Interbrand, *The World's Greatest Brands* (Washington, NY: New York University Press, 1997).

slogans[19] ("It's the real thing" (1942, 1969), "Things go better with Coke" (1963), "Coke is it" (1982), "Can't beat the Feeling" (1987), and a 1992 return to "Can't beat the real thing")[20] linked that personality to the core values of each generation and established Coke as the authentic, relevant, and trusted refreshment of choice across the decades and around the globe.

INDIAN HISTORY

India is home to one of the most ancient cultures in the world, dating back over 5,000 years. At the beginning of the twenty-first century, 26 different languages were spoken across India, 30 percent of the population knew English, and greater than 40 percent were illiterate. At this time, the nation was in the midst of great transition and the dichotomy between the old India and the new was stark. Remnants of the caste system existed alongside the world's top engineering schools and growing metropolises as the historically agricultural economy shifted into the services sector. In the process, India had created the world's largest middle class.

A British colony since 1769 when the East India Company gained control of all European trade in the nation, India gained its independence in 1947 under Mahatma Ghandi and his principles of nonviolence and self-reliance. In the decades that followed, self-reliance was taken to the extreme as many Indians believed that economic independence was necessary to be truly independent. As a result, the economy was increasingly regulated and many sectors were restricted to the public sector. This movement reached its peak in 1977 when the Janta party government came to power and Coca-Cola was thrown out of the country. In 1991, the first generation of economic reforms was introduced and liberalization began.

COKE IN INDIA

Coca-Cola was the leading soft drink brand in India until 1977, when it left rather than reveal its formula to the government and reduce its equity stake as required under the Foreign Exchange Regulation Act (FERA), which governed the operations of foreign companies in India. After a 16-year absence, Coca-Cola returned to India in 1993, cementing its presence with a deal that gave Coca-Cola ownership of the nation's top soft-drink brands and bottling network. Coke's acquisition of local popular Indian brands including Thums Up (the most trusted brand in India[21]), Limca, Maaza, Citra, and Gold Spot provided not only physical manufacturing, bottling, and distribution assets but also strong consumer preference. This combination of local and global brands enabled Coca-Cola to exploit the benefits of global branding and global trends in tastes while also tapping into traditional domestic markets. Leading Indian brands joined the company's international family of brands, including Coca-Cola, diet Coke, Sprite, and Fanta, plus the Schweppes product range. In 2000, the company launched the Kinley water brand and in 2001, Shock energy drink and the powdered concentrate Sunfill hit the market.

From 1993 to 2003, Coca-Cola invested more than US$1 billion in India, making it one of the country's top international investors.[22] By 2003, Coca-Cola India had won the prestigious Woodruf Cup from among 22 divisions of the company based on three broad parameters of volume, profitability, and quality. Coca-Cola India achieved 39 percent volume growth in 2002 while the industry grew 23 percent nationally and the company reached break-even profitability in the region for the first time.[23] Encouraged by its 2002 performance, Coca-Cola India announced plans to double its capacity at

[19] Kevin Lane Keller, *Strategic Brand Management.* (Upper Saddle River, NJ: Prentice Hall, 1998), p. 153.

[20] http://www.portobello.com.au/portobello/reading/memorabilia_cocacola.htm.

[21] "Brands of Coca-Cola in India," Rai University, November 2004.

[22] http://www.coca-colaindia.com.

[23] Sanjiv Gupta biography, Rai University.

EXHIBIT 10.5   Routine Tests Carried out by Bottling Operations and External Laboratories

Source: The Coca-Cola Company, http://www.myenjoyzone.com.report, 1989.

	Process Parameter	No. of Tests
1	Water	71
2	Water treatment and auxiliary chemicals	68
3	CO_2	50
4	Sugar	13
5	Syrup	17
6	Packaging material	25
7	Container washing	17
8	Finished product	18
9	Market samples	15
10	External lab	147
	TOTAL	441

an investment of $125 million (Rs. 750 crore) between September 2002 and March 2003.[24]

Coca-Cola India produced its beverages with 7,000 local employees at its 27 wholly-owned bottling operations supplemented by 17 franchisee-owned bottling operations and a network of 29 contract-packers to manufacture a range of products for the company. The complete manufacturing process had a documented quality control and assurance program including over 400 tests performed throughout the process (see Exhibit 10.5).

The complexity of the consumer soft drink market demanded a distribution process to support 700,000 retail outlets serviced by a fleet that included 10-ton trucks, open-bay three wheelers, and trademarked tricycles and pushcarts that were used to navigate the narrow alleyways of the cities.[25] In addition to its own employees, Coke indirectly created employment for another 125,000 Indians through its procurement, supply, and distribution networks.

Sanjiv Gupta, president and CEO of Coca-Cola India, joined Coke in 1997 as Vice President, Marketing and was instrumental to the company's success in developing a brand relevant to the Indian consumer and in tapping India's vast rural market potential. Following his marketing responsibilities, Gupta served as head of operations for company-owned bottling operations and then as deputy president. Seen as the driving force behind recent successful forays into packaged drinking water, powdered drinks, and ready-to-serve tea and coffee, Gupta and his marketing prowess were critical to the continued growth of the company.[26]

THE INDIAN BEVERAGE MARKET[27]

India's one billion people, growing middle class, and low per capita consumption of soft drinks made it a highly contested prize in the global CSD market in the early twenty-first century. Ten percent of the country's population lived in urban areas or large cities and drank 10 bottles of soda per year while the vast remainder lived in rural areas, villages, and small towns where annual per capita consumption was less than four bottles. Coke and Pepsi dominated the market and together had a consolidated market share above 95 percent. While soft drinks were once considered products only for the affluent, by 2003, 91 percent of sales were made to the lower, middle and upper-middle classes. Soft drink sales in India grew 76 percent between 1998 and 2002, from 5,670 million bottles to over 10,000 million (see Exhibit 10.6) and were expected to grow at least 10 percent per year through 2012.[28] In spite of this growth, annual per capita consumption was only 6 bottles versus 17 in Pakistan, 73 in Thailand, 173 in the Philippines, and 800 in the United States.[29]

[24] "Coca-Cola India to Double Capacity," *Kolkata,* March 8, 2003.

[25] http://www.coca-colaindia.com.

[26] Gupta biography.

[27] http://www.indiastat.com.

[28] Ibid.

[29] Ibid.

EXHIBIT 10.6 Soft Drink Sales in India

Source: "Soft Drink Sales Up 10.4%," *PTI*, September 29, 2004.

Fiscal Year	Million Bottles Sold
1998–1999	5,670
1999–2000	6,230
2000–2001	6,450
2001–2002	6,600
2002–2003	10,000

With its large population and low consumption, the rural market represented a significant opportunity for penetration and a critical battleground for market dominance. In 2001, Coca-Cola recognized that to compete with traditional refreshments including lemon water, green coconut water, fruit juices, tea, and lassi, competitive pricing was essential. In response, Coke launched a smaller bottle priced at almost 50 percent of the traditional package.

MARKETING COLA IN INDIA

The post-liberalization period in India saw the comeback of cola, but Pepsi had already beaten Coca-Cola to the punch, creatively entering the market in the 1980s in advance of liberalization by way of a joint venture. As early as 1985, Pepsi tried to gain entry into India and finally succeeded with the Pepsi Foods Limited Project in 1988, as a JV of PepsiCo, Punjab government–owned Punjab Agro Industrial Corporation (PAIC), and Voltas India Limited. Pepsi was marketed and sold as Lehar Pepsi until 1991, when the use of foreign brands was allowed under the new economic policy, and Pepsi ultimately bought out its partners, becoming a fully owned subsidiary and ending the JV relationship in 1994.[30]

While the joint venture was only marginally successful in its own right, it allowed Pepsi to gain precious early experience with the Indian

market and also served as an introduction of the Pepsi brand to the Indian consumer such that it was well-poised to reap the benefits when liberalization came. Though Coke benefited from Pepsi creating demand and developing the market, Pepsi's head-start gave Coke a disadvantage in the mind of the consumer. Pepsi's appeal focused on youth and when Coke entered India in 1993 and approached the market selling an American way of life, it failed to resonate as expected.[31]

2001 MARKETING STRATEGY

Coca-Cola CEO Douglas Daft set the direction for the next generation of success for his global brand with a "Think local, act local" mantra. Recognizing that a single global strategy or single global campaign wouldn't work, locally relevant executions became an increasingly important element of supporting Coke's global brand strategy.

In 2001, after almost a decade of lagging rival Pepsi in the region, Coke India reexamined its approach in an attempt to gain leadership in the Indian market and capitalize on significant growth potential, particularly in rural markets. The foundation of the new strategy grounded brand positioning and marketing communications in consumer insights, acknowledging that urban versus rural India were two distinct markets on a variety of important dimensions. The soft drink category's role in people's lives, the degree of differentiation between consumer segments and their reasons for entering the category, and the degree to which brands in the category projected different perceptions to consumers were among the many important differences between how urban and rural consumers approached the market for refreshment.[32]

In rural markets, where both the soft drink category and individual brands were undeveloped, the task was to broaden the brand

[30] Kavaljit Singh, "Broken Commitments: The Case of Pepsi in India," *PIRG Update,* May 1997.

[31] Interview with Nymph Kaul, September 20, 2004.

[32] Coca-Cola India, "Marketing: Questioning Paradigms," internal marketing presentation.

positioning while in urban markets, with higher category and brand development, the task was to narrow the brand positioning, focusing on differentiation through offering unique and compelling value. This lens, informed by consumer insights, gave Coke direction on the trade-off between focus and breadth a brand needed in a given market and made clear that to succeed in either segment, unique marketing strategies were required in urban versus rural India.

BRAND LOCALIZATION STRATEGY: THE TWO INDIAS

India A: "Life ho to aisi"

"India A," the designation Coca-Cola gave to the market segment including metropolitan areas and large towns, represented 4 percent of the country's population.[33] This segment sought social bonding as a need and responded to aspirational messages, celebrating the benefits of their increasing social and economic freedoms. *"Life ho to aisi"* (life as it should be) was the successful and relevant tagline found in Coca-Cola's advertising to this audience.

India B: "Thanda Matlab Coca-Cola"

Coca-Cola India believed that the first brand to offer communication targeted to the smaller towns would own the rural market and went after that objective with a comprehensive strategy. "India B" included small towns and rural areas, comprising the other 96 percent of the nation's population. This segment's primary need was out-of-home thirst-quenching and the soft drink category was undifferentiated in the minds of rural consumers. Additionally, with an average Coke costing Rs. 10 and an average day's wages around Rs. 100, Coke was perceived as a luxury that few could afford.[34]

In an effort to make the price point of Coke within reach of this high-potential market, Coca-Cola launched the Accessibility Campaign, introducing a new 200mL bottle, smaller than the traditional 300mL bottle found in urban markets, and concurrently cutting the price in half, to Rs. 5. This pricing strategy closed the gap between Coke and basic refreshments like lemonade and tea, making soft drinks truly accessible for the first time. At the same time, Coke invested in distribution infrastructure to serve a disbursed population effectively and doubled the number of retail outlets in rural areas from 80,000 in 2001 to 160,000 in 2003, increasing market penetration from 13 to 25 percent.[35]

Coke's advertising and promotion strategy pulled the marketing plan together using local language and idiomatic expressions. "Thanda," meaning cool/cold, is also generic for cold beverages and gave "Thanda Matlab Coca-Cola" delicious multiple meanings. Literally translated to "Coke means refreshment," the phrase directly addressed both the primary need of this segment for cold refreshment while at the same time positioning Coke as a "Thanda," or generic cold beverage just like tea, lassi, or lemonade. As a result of the Thanda campaign, Coca-Cola won *Advertiser of the Year* and *Campaign of the Year* in 2003.

RURAL SUCCESS

Comprising 74 percent of the country's population, 41 percent of its middle class, and 58 percent of its disposable income, the rural market was an attractive target and it delivered results. Coke experienced 37 percent growth in 2003 in this segment versus the 24 percent growth seen in urban areas. Driven by the launch of the new Rs. 5 product, per capita consumption doubled between 2001 and 2003. This market accounted for 80 percent of India's new Coke drinkers, 30 percent of 2002 volume, and was expected to account for 50 percent of the company's sales in 2003.[36]

---

[33] Ibid.

[34] Kaul interview.

[35] Ibid.

[36] Ibid.

EXHIBIT 10.7 Coca-Cola Principles of Corporate Citizenship

Source: Coca-Cola Company Web site.

Our reputation is built on trust. Through good citizenship we will nurture our relationships and continue to build that trust. That is the essence of our promise—The Coca-Cola Company exists to benefit and refresh everyone it touches.

Wherever Coca-Cola does business, we strive to be trusted partners and good citizens. We are committed to managing our business around the world with a consistent set of values that represent the highest standards of integrity and excellence. We share these values with our bottlers, making our system stronger.

These core values are essential to our long-term business success and will be reflected in all of our relationships and actions—in the marketplace, the workplace, the environment and the community.

MARKETPLACE

We will adhere to the highest ethical standards, knowing that the quality of our products, the integrity of our brands and the dedication of our people build trust and strengthen relationships. We will serve the people who enjoy our brands through innovation, superb customer service, and respect for the unique customs and cultures in the communities where we do business.

WORKPLACE

We will treat each other with dignity, fairness and respect. We will foster an inclusive environment that encourages all employees to develop and perform to their fullest potential, consistent with a commitment to human rights in our workplace. The Coca-Cola workplace will be a place where everyone's ideas and contributions are valued, and where responsibility and accountability are encouraged and rewarded.

ENVIRONMENT

We will conduct our business in ways that protect and preserve the environment. We will integrate principles of environmental stewardship and sustainable development into our business decisions and processes.

COMMUNITY

We will contribute our time, expertise and resources to help develop sustainable communities in partnership with local leaders. We will seek to improve the quality of life through locally-relevant initiatives wherever we do business. Responsible corporate citizenship is at the heart of The Coca-Cola Promise. We believe that what is best for our employees, for the community and for the environment is also best for our business.

CORPORATE SOCIAL RESPONSIBILITY

As one of the largest and most global companies in the world, Coca-Cola took seriously its ability and responsibility to affect the communities in which it operated positively. The company's mission statement, called the Coca-Cola Promise, stated: "The Coca-Cola Company exists to benefit and refresh everyone who is touched by our business." The company had made efforts towards good citizenship in the areas of community, by improving the quality of life in the communities in which they operated, and the environment, by addressing water, climate change, and waste management initiatives. Their activities also included The Coca-Cola Africa Foundation created to combat the spread of HIV/AIDS through partnership with governments, UNAIDS, and other NGOs, and The Coca-Cola Foundation, focused on higher education as a vehicle to build strong communities and enhance individual opportunity (see Exhibit 10.7).[37]

Coca-Cola's footprint in India was significant as well. The company employed 7,000 citizens and believed that for every direct job, 30–40 more were created in the supply chain.[38] Like its parent, Coke India's corporate social responsibility (CSR) initiatives were both community-

[37] http://www.coca-colaindia.com.

[38] Ibid.

and environment-focused. Priorities included education, where primary education projects had been set up to benefit children in slums and villages; water conservation, where the company supported community-based rainwater harvesting projects to restore water levels and promote conservation education; and health, where Coke India partnered with NGOs and governments to provide medical access to poor people through regular health camps. In addition to outreach efforts, the company committed itself to environmental responsibility through its own business operations in India, including[39]

- Environmental due diligence before acquiring land or starting projects.
- Environmental impact assessment before commencing operations.
- Ground water and environmental surveys before selecting sites.
- Compliance with all regulatory environmental requirements.
- Ban on purchasing CFC-containing refrigeration equipment.
- Wastewater treatment facilities with trained personnel at all company-owned bottling operations.
- Energy conservation programs.
- 50 percent water savings in the last seven years of operations.

PREVIOUS COKE CRISES

Despite Coke's reputation as a socially responsible corporate citizen, the company has faced its share of controversy worldwide surrounding both its products and its policies in the years preceding the Indian pesticide crisis.

INGRAM ET AL. V. THE COCA-COLA COMPANY—1999[40]

In the spring of 1999, four current and former Coca-Cola employees, led by information analyst Linda Ingram, filed bias charges against Coca-Cola in Atlanta federal court. The lawsuit charged the company with racial discrimination and stated: "This discrimination represents a company-wide pattern and practice, rather than a series of isolated incidents. Although Coca-Cola has carefully crafted African-American consumers of its product by public announcements, strategic alliances and specific marketing strategies, it has failed to place the same importance on its African-American employees."[41]

In the decades leading up to the suit, both internal and external warnings surrounding Coke's diversity practices were issued. In 1981, the Reverend Jesse Jackson, director of the Rainbow/PUSH coalition, instigated a boycott against Coca-Cola, challenging the company to improve its business relationship significantly with the African-American community.[42]

The Ware report, written by Senior Vice President Carl Ware, an African-American executive at the company, cited a lack of diversity at the decision-making level, a basic lack of workplace diversity, a "ghettoization" among blacks who worked for Cola-Cola, and an overt lack of respect for cultural differences as well as an implicit assumption that African-American employees lacked the intelligence to meet the challenges of the highest executive levels.[43]

Cyrus Mehri, one of the most visible and successful plaintiff advocates in the United States, represented the group and was skilled at leveraging the power of the media, creating a true crisis for the Coca-Cola Company and exerting

---

[39] Ibid.

[40] Nicola K. Graves and Randall L. Waller, "The Corporate Web Site as an Image Restoration Tool: The Case of Coca-Cola," *Proceedings of the 2004 Association for Business Communication 69th Annual Convention,* Cambridge, MA, October 25–29, 2004.

[41] H. Unger, "Coca-Cola Accused of a 'Companywide Pattern,'" *Atlanta Journal-Constitution,* April 24, 1999, p. H1.

[42] C. L. Hays, *The Real Thing: Truth and Power at the Coca-Cola Company* (New York: Random House, 2004).

[43] Ibid.

tremendous pressure for settlement. In 2000, the lawsuit was settled for $192.5 million after the company had sent mixed messages and damaging statements regarding the merit of the suit for over a year. Analysts identified the bias suit as a prime reason for the $100 billion decrease in Coca-Cola's stock price between 1998 and 2000.[44]

BELGIUM—1999[45]

On June 8, 1999, 33 Belgian school children became ill after drinking Coke bottled at a local facility in Antwerp. A few days later, more Belgians complained of similar symptoms after drinking cans of Coke that had been bottled at a plant in Dunkirk, France, and 80 people in northern France were allegedly stricken by intestinal problems and nausea, bringing the total afflicted to over 250.

In the days following the first outbreak, 17 million cases of Coke from five European countries were recalled and destroyed. It was the largest product recall in Coke's history and Belgian and French authorities banned the sale of Coca-Cola products for 10 days. Germany placed a temporary import ban on Coca-Cola produced in Belgium and the Netherlands, and Luxembourg banned all Coca-Cola products. Health ministers in Italy, Spain, and Switzerland warned people about consuming Coke products.

Coca-Cola sources explained that the contamination was due to defective carbon dioxide used at the Antwerp plant and that a wood preservative used on shipping pallets had concentrated the outside of cans at the Dunkirk plant. The European Commission, however, believed production faults and contaminated pipes were more likely to be the cause of the problem.

Though CEO Ivester was in Paris when the news broke, he flew home to Atlanta and kept silent, waiting over a week to issue his first public statement on the crisis, citing that "Coke would do whatever necessary to ensure the safety of its products." A Netherlands-based toxicologist Coke had hired issued a report on June 29 exempting the company from blame for the CO_2 impurity in Antwerp and the fungicide at Dunkirk. Though the product ban was lifted, Coke had a tremendous amount of work to do to win back consumer confidence.

An aggressive PR campaign included vouchers and coupons for free product delivered to each of Belgium's 4.4 million homes; sponsored dances, beach parties, and summer fairs for teenagers; and significant television advertising reinforcing "Today, more than ever, we thank you for your loyalty."

KINLEY BOTTLED WATER-2003

On February 4, 2003, the Center for Science and Environment (CSE) in India released a report based on tests conducted by the Pollution Monitoring Laboratory (PML) titled "Pure Water or Pure Peril?" Analysis of 17 packaged drinking water brands sold across the country revealed evidence of pesticide residues including lindane, DDT, malathion, and chlorpyrifos. The CSE used European norms for maximum permissible limits for pesticides in packaged water "because the standards set for pesticide residues by the Bureau of Indian Standards (BIS) are vague and undefined."[46] Coca-Cola's Kinley water brand had concentration levels 15 times higher than stipulated limits, top-seller Biserli had 79 times, and Aquaplus topped the list at 109 times.[47] In the wake of this statement, Coca-Cola remained largely silent and the buzz went away.

CORPORATE COMMUNICATION AT COCA-COLA

Corporate communication was a critical function at the Coca-Cola Company given the number of constituencies both internal and external to the company. In addition, the complexity and global reach of the company's operations could not be

[44] K. MacArthur and R. Linnett, "Coke Crisis: Equity Erodes as Brand Troubles Mount," *Advertising Age*, April 24, 2000, p. 3.

[45] "Coke & Pepsi in India: Pesticides in Carbonated Beverages," p. 8

[46] "Pure Water or Pure Peril," CSE press release, February 2003.

[47] Ibid.

centrally managed and instead demanded a matrixed team organization.

The senior communications position at the company, senior vice president, Worldwide Public Affairs & Communication, sat on the company's executive committee and reported to the chairman and CEO at the time of the crisis in India. Director-level corporate communication functions included: media relations, nutrition communications, financial communications, and marketing communications, but the geographic diversity of the company's businesses required regionally based communication leaders in addition to the corporate resources in place. As a result, five regional communication directors serviced North America, Latin America, Asia, Europe, and Africa with their own teams of communications professionals (see Exhibit 10.8).

NGO ACTIVISM[48]

NGOs (nongovernmental organizations) evolved to influence governments but by the early twenty-first century many realized that targeting

[48] Paul A. Argenti, "Collaborating with Activists: How Starbucks Works with NGOs," *California Management Review* 47, no. 1 (Fall 2004).

corporations and key corporate constituents such as investors and customers could be an even more powerful way to effect change. Along with their ability to focus, gain attention, and act quickly was the high level of credibility NGOs had cultivated with many constituencies. This credibility stemmed in part from their emotional, rather than fact-based, appeals and the impassioned nature of their arguments.

The most common tactic of NGOs was to develop campaigns against business through which they garnered support from consumers and the media. These campaigns, such as Greenpeace's attack on Shell Oil following the company's decision to dump the Brent Spar oil rig in the ocean in the 1990s, typically focused on a single issue; targeted companies with successful and well-known brands such as McDonald's and Nike; and were augmented by market trends such as the homogenization created by chains like Wal-Mart and Starbucks. NGOs realized that anticorporate campaigns could be far more powerful than antigovernment campaigns. Global Exchange's attack on Nike for sweatshop labor conditions in the 1990s, for example, was one of the most highly

EXHIBIT 10.8 Corporate Communication at Coca-Cola

Source: Case writer derived from Coca-Cola Company Web site.

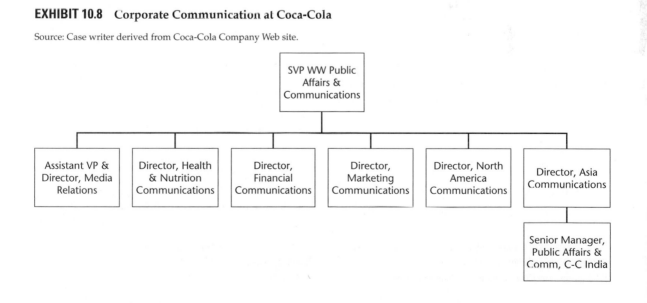

publicized and also one of the most successful antibusiness campaigns by an NGO.

CENTER FOR SCIENCE AND ENVIRONMENT

The CSE, an NGO, was established in India in 1980 by a group of engineers, scientists, journalists, and environmentalists to "catalyze the growth of public awareness on vital issues in science, technology, environment, and development."[49] Led by Sumita Narain, a former schoolmate of Coke India CEO Gupta, the CSE's efforts included communication for awareness, research and advocacy, education and training, documentation, and pollution monitoring.

Spurred by the February 2003 report on bottled water and questions like "if what we found in bottled water was correct, then what about soft drinks?" the CSE's August 2003 report claimed that soft drinks were extremely dangerous to Indian citizens based on tests conducted at the Pollution Monitoring Laboratory (PML). All samples contained residues of lindane, DDT, malathion, and chlorpyrifos, toxic pesticides and insecticides known to cause serious long-term health issues. Total pesticides in all Coca-Cola brands averaged 0.0150 mg/L, 30 times higher than the European Economic Commission (EEC) limit. PML also tested samples of Coke and Pepsi products sold in the United States to see if they contained pesticides and they did not.

The CSE report called on the government to put in place legally enforceable water standards and chastised the multinationals for taking advantage of the situation at the expense of consumer health and well-being.

INDIAN REGULATORY ENVIRONMENT[50]

The main law governing food safety in India was the 1954 Prevention of Food Alteration Act (PFA), which contained a rule regulating pesticides in foods but did not include beverages. The Food Processing Order (1955) required that the main ingredient used in soft drinks be "potable water," but the Bureau of Indian Standards (BIS) had no prescribed standards for pesticides in water. One BIS directive stated that pesticides must be absent and set a limit of 0.001 part per million, but the Health Secretary admitted, "There are lapses in PFA regarding carbonated drinks."[51]

Indian law enforcement was minimal with virtually no conviction under PFA. In the absence of national standards, NGOs such as the CSE turned to the United States and the European Union for "international norms." The appropriateness and feasibility of these standards for developing nations, however, remained a question for many. Under EU food laws, for example, milk, fruit, and basic staples such as rice and wheat would need to be imported into India to satisfy safety standards.

THE INITIAL RESPONSE

The day after the CSE's announcement, Coke and Pepsi came together in a rare show of solidarity at a joint press conference. The companies attacked the credibility of the CSE and their lab results, citing regular testing at independent laboratories proving the safety of their products. They promised to provide these data to the public, threatened legal action against the CSE while seeking a gag order, and contacted the U.S. Embassy in India for assistance. Coca-Cola India's CEO Sanjiv Gupta published the following statement for the Indian public:[52]

> You may have seen recently in the media some allegations about the quality standards of our products in India. We take these allegations extremely seriously. I want to reassure you that our products in India are safe and are tested regularly to ensure that they meet the same rigorous standards we maintain across the world.

[49] http://www.cseindia.org.

[50] "Coke & Pepsi in India: Pesticides in Carbonated Beverages," p. 3.

[51] Supriya Bezbaruat and Malini Goyal, "The Gulp War," *India Today,* August 25, 2003, pp. 50–53.

[52] http://www.coca-colaindia.com.

Maintaining quality standards is the most important element of our business and we cannot stand by while misleading and unaccredited data is used to discredit trusted and world-class brands. Recent allegations have caused unnecessary panic among consumers in India and, if unchecked, would impair our business in India and impact the livelihoods of our thousands of employees across the country.

This site is about the truth behind the headlines. It provides some context and facts on these issues and we hope it helps you understand exactly why you can trust our beverage brands and continue to enjoy them as millions of Indians do each day.

Sanjiv Gupta, Division President, Coca-Cola India

In the following days, the Delhi High Court asked the government to convene an expert committee to test and report on the safety of soft drinks within three weeks and to revise existing standards to include pesticide norms. Coca-Cola and Pepsi launched independent campaigns to reassure the public, taking out full-page newspaper advertisements and directing consumers to their corporate Web sites to review test results and safety protocol in greater detail (see Exhibit 10.9). In spite of these actions, the public seemed to believe the CSE's claims and the crisis was far from over for the beverage giants. With sales continuing to experience a precipitous drop, one Delhi medical student's sentiments appeared to be widespread: "For a person drinking at least one bottle a day, the report came as a rude shock. I haven't picked up a bottle today and most definitely will not consume soft drinks in the future. The reports of pesticides and other pollutants have made soft drinks a strict no-no and we will now stick to juices and plain drinking water."[53]

[53] "Shocked Delhites Stay Away from Soft Drinks," *The Hindu* (New Delhi), August 7, 2003, p. 1.

GUPTA'S DILEMMA

As he contemplated the crisis at hand, Sanjiv Gupta questioned what action, if any, was necessary. Coke India was well within the country's legal guidelines and the crisis had not been widely reported outside of India. Gupta knew that the Indian public had a short attention span and had reason to think that it wouldn't be long before the CSE's report faded, just as the Kinley water issue had earlier in the year.

On the other hand, he wondered if the situation might offer the company an opportunity to display higher standards of social responsibility at a time when it needed to differentiate itself from the competition. Multinationals had slipped in numerous situations of late and were blamed for not adhering to the same standards in developing countries as in industrialized nations. The additive effect of this negative press meant that the potential damage to Coke's reputation was even greater. Finally, an ineffective resolution would be a devastating blow to the momentum Coke had gained after three long years of work on the marketing front.

CASE QUESTIONS

1. What are the key problems that Gupta should focus on in the short term and in the long term?
2. How would you evaluate the crisis?
3. How well-prepared was Coke India to deal with the CSE's allegations?
4. What is your recommendation for Coke's communication strategy? Who are the key constituents?
5. Could Coke India have avoided this crisis?
6. What should Gupta do now?

EXHIBIT 10.9   Myths and Facts from Coca-Cola India Web Site

Source: Coca-Cola Company Web site.

Since August 5, 2003 the quality and safety of Coca-Cola and PepsiCo products in India have been called into question by a local NGO, the Centre for Science and Environment (CSE). The basis of the allegations are [sic] tests conducted on products of Coca-Cola and PepsiCo by CSE's internal unaccredited laboratory, the Pollution Monitoring Laboratory.

In India, as in the rest of the world, our plants use a multiple barrier system to remove potential contaminants and unwanted natural substances including iron, sulfur, heavy metals as well as pesticides. Our products in India are safe and are tested regularly to ensure that they meet the same rigorous standards we maintain across the world.

The result of these allegations has been consumer confusion, significant impact on the sale of a safe and high-quality product, and the erosion of international investor confidence in the Indian business sector. This situation calls for the development of national sampling and testing protocols for soft drinks, an end to sensationalizing unsubstantiated allegations, and co-operation by all parties concerned in the interests of both Indian consumers and companies with significant investments in the Indian economy.

The facts versus the fiction False statements made in recent weeks have led to false perceptions by Indian consumers:

Myth   Coca-Cola products in India contain pesticide residues that are above EU norms.

Fact   Throughout all of our operations in India, stringent quality monitoring takes place covering both the source water we use as well as our finished product. We test for traces of pesticide in groundwater to the level of parts per billion. This is equivalent to one drop in a billion drops. For comparison's sake, this would also be equivalent to measuring one second in 32 years, or less than one person in the entire population in India. These tests require specialized equipment at accredited labs to have accurate results. Even at these stringent miniscule levels we are well within the internationally accepted safety norms.

Myth   Coca-Cola products sold in India are "toxic" and unfit for human consumption.

Fact   There is no contamination or toxicity in our beverage brands. Our high-quality beverages are—and have always been—safe and refreshing. In over 200 countries across the globe, more than a billion times every day, consumers choose our brands for refreshment because Coca-Cola is a symbol of quality.

Myth   Coca-Cola has dual standards in the production of its products, one high standard for western countries, another for India.

Fact   The soft drinks manufactured in India conform to the same high standards of quality as in the USA and Europe. Through our globally accepted and validated manufacturing processes and Quality Management systems, we ensure that our state-of-the-art manufacturing facilities are equipped to provide the consumer the highest quality beverage each time. We stringently test our soft drinks in India at independent, accredited and world-class laboratories both locally and internationally.

Myth   In India the soft drinks industry is virtually unregulated.

Fact   There are no standards for soft drinks in the US, the EU, or India. In India, water used for beverage manufacture must conform to drinking water standards. The water used by Coca-Cola conforms to both BIS and EU standards for drinking water and our production protocols ensure this through a focus on process control and testing of the water used in our manufacturing process and the final product quality.

Myth   Coca-Cola has put out results for Kinley water only and not for their soft drinks.

Fact   The results of product tests conducted by TNO Nutrition and Food Research Laboratory in the Netherlands is [sic] conclusive and is [sic] available on The Science Behind Our Quality web page.

Myth   International companies like Coca-Cola are "colonizing" India.

Fact   The Coca-Cola business in India is a local business. Our beverages in India are produced locally, we employ thousands of Indian citizens, our product range and marketing reflect Indian tastes and lifestyles, and we are deeply involved in the life of the local communities in which we operate. The Coca-Cola business system directly employs approximately 10,000 local people in India. In addition, independent studies have documented that, by providing opportunities for local enterprises, the Coca-Cola business also generates a significant employment "multiplier effect." In India, we indirectly create employment for more than 125,000 people in related industries through our vast procurement, supply and distribution system.

Myth   Farmers in India are using Coca-Cola and other soft drinks as pesticides by spraying them on their crops.

Fact   Soft drinks do not act in a similar way to pesticides when applied to the ground or crops. There is no scientific basis for this and the use of soft drinks for this purpose would be totally ineffective. In India, as in the rest of the world, our products are world class and safe and the treated water used to make our beverages there meets the highest international standards.

CASE BIBLIOGRAPHY

Argenti, Paul A. "Collaborating with Activists: How Starbucks Works with NGOs." *California Management Review* 47, no. 1 (Fall 2004).

Bhatia, Gauri. "Multinational Corporations: Pro or Con?" *Outlook India,* October 29, 2003.

Centre for Science and Environment (CSE). "Analysis of Pesticide Residues in Soft Drinks," August 5, 2003.

Coca-Cola India. "Marketing: Questioning Paradigms," internal company presentation.

"Coca-Cola, Philips Win Marketing Awards." http://www.financialexpress.com, October 7, 2004.

"Coke, Pepsi Challenge India Pesticide Claim." http://www.ajc.com/business/content/business/coke/0803/06pesticide.html.

"Coke, Pepsi India Deny Pesticides in Soft Drinks." http://www.forbes.com/home_europe/newswire/2003/08/05/rtr1049160. html.

Dawar, Niraj, and Nancy Dai. "Cola Wars in China: The Future Is Here." HBS Case, August 21, 2003.

Dey, Saikat. Interview on Indian History and Economic Liberalization. January 10, 2005.

Graves, Nicola K., and Randall L. Waller. "The Corporate Web Site as an Image Restoration Tool: The Case of Coca-Cola." *Proceedings of the 2004 Association for Business Communication 69th Annual Convention,* Cambridge, MA, October 25–29, 2000.

http://www.coca-cola.com/flashIndex1.html.

http://www2.coca-cola.com/presscenter/viewpoints_india_situation.html.

http://www.coca-colaindia.com/.

http://www.indiaresource.org/.

http://www.killercoke.org.

http://www.myenjoyzone.com/press1/truth.htm.

Kaul, Nymph. Interview of Sanjiv Gupta, president and CEO of Coca-Cola India, June 2004.

Kaul, Nymph. Rai University, multiple interviews.

Kaul, Nymph. Rai University, "Coca-Cola India." 2004.

Keller, Kevin Lane. *Strategic Brand Management.* Upper Saddle River, NJ: Prentice Hall, 1998.

Kochan, Nicholas, ed., and Interbrand. *The World's Greatest Brands.* Washington, NY: New York University Press, 1997.

Pendergrast, Mark. *For God, Country and Coca-Cola.* New York: Charles Scribner's Sons, 1993.

"People's Forum Against Coca-Cola." Brochure.

Sanghvi, Rish. Interviews on Cola in India before liberalization and marketing/advertising of Coke and Pepsi in India, November 2004.

Society for Environmental Communications. "Colonisation's Dirty Dozen: Deadly Pesticides Found in 12 Leading Brands of Soft Drinks," August 15, 2003.

"Soft Drink Sales Up 10.4%." *PTI,* September 29, 2004.

Srivastava, Amit. "Coke with a New Twist: Toxic Cola." India Resource Center, February 15, 2004.

"Things Aren't Going Better with Coke." *BusinessWeek Online,* June 28, 1999.

"The Top 100 Brands: Interbrand's Global Brand Scorecard 2003." Interbrand Special Report, as seen in *BusinessWeek,* August 4, 2003.

Yoffie, David B., and Richard Seet. "Internationalizing the Cola Wars: The Battle for China and Asian Markets." HBS Case, May 31, 1995.

Yoffie, David B., and Yusi Wang. "Cola Wars Continue: Coke versus Pepsi in the Twenty-First Century." HBS Case, January 11, 2002.

BIBLIOGRAPHY

Aaker, David A. *Building Strong Brands.* New York: Free Press, 1996.

Adams, Walter, and James W. Brock. *The Bigness Complex: Industry, Labor, and Government in the American Economy.* New York: Pantheon Books, 1986.

Ailes, Roger, and Jon Kraushar. *You Are the Message.* Garden City: Currency Doubleday, 1995.

Angell, Marcia, M. D. *Science on Trial: The Clash of Medical Evidence and the Law in the Breast Implant Case.* New York: W.W. Norton, 1996.

Argenti, Paul A., and Janis Forman. *The Power of Corporate Communication: Crafting the Voice and Image of Your Business.* New York: McGraw-Hill, 2002.

Argenti, Paul A., and Janis Forman. "The Employee Care Revolution" in *Leader to Leader,* Summer 2004.

Argenti, Paul A. "Collaborating with Activists: How Starbucks Works with NGOs to Enhance its Emphasis on Social Responsibility," in *California Management Review,* Fall 2004.

Argenti, Paul A. "Keeping to the Fairway" case commentary in *Harvard Business Review,* April 2003.

Argenti, Paul A. "Crisis Communication: Lessons from 9/11" in *Harvard Business Review,* December 2002.

Argenti, Paul A., Robert Howell, and Karen Beck. "The Strategic Communication Imperative," in *Sloan Management Review,* Spring 2005.

Aristotle. *The Art of Rhetoric.* Cambridge, MA: Harvard University Press, 1975.

Barton, Laurence. *Crisis in Organizations II.* Cincinnati, OH: South-Western, 2000.

Brown, Michael. *Laying Waste: The Poisoning of America by Toxic Chemicals.* New York: Pocket Books, 1981.

Byrne, John A. *Informed Consent.* New York: McGraw-Hill, 1996.

Chajet, Clive, and Tom Shachtman. *Image by Design: From Corporate Vision to Business Reality.* 2nd ed. New York: McGraw-Hill, 1997.

Collins, James C., and Jerry I. Porras. *Built to Last: Successful Habits of Visionary Companies.* New York: Harper Business, 1994, 1997.

Corrado, Frank M. *Media for Managers.* Englewood Cliffs, NJ: Prentice Hall, 1997.

Cutlip, Scott M. *Public Relations History: From the 17th to the 20th Century.* Hillsdale, NJ: Lawrence Erlbaum, 1995.

D'Aveni, Richard A. *Hypercompetition: Managing the Dynamics of Strategic Maneuvering.* New York: Free Press, 1994.

DeBower, Herbert F. *Modern Business,* vol. 7, *Advertising Principles.* New York: Alexander Hamilton Institute, 1917.

Dozier, David M., Larissa A. Grunig, and James E. Grunig. *Manager's Guide to Excellence in Public Relations and Communication Management.* Mahwah, NJ: Lawrence Erlbaum, 1995.

Edsell, Thomas. *The New Politics of Inequality.* New York: Norton, 1984.

Eichenwald, Kurt. *Conspiracy of Fools*. New York: Broadway Books, 2005.

Eisner, Michael D. *Work in Progress*. New York: Random House, 1998.

Fombrun, Charles J. *Reputation: Realizing Value from the Corporate Image*. Boston: Harvard Business School Press, 1996.

Ford, Daniel F. *Three Mile Island: Thirty Minutes to Meltdown*. New York: Penguin, 1981.

Forty, Adrian. *Objects of Desire: Design and Society from Wedgewood to IBM*. New York: Pantheon, 1986.

Fritschler, Lee. *Smoking and Politics: Policymaking and the Federal Bureaucracy*. 3rd ed. Englewood Cliffs, NJ: Prentice Hall, 1983.

Garbett, Thomas F. *Corporate Advertising*. New York: McGraw-Hill, 1981.

———. *How to Build a Corporation's Identity and Project Its Image*. Lexington, MA: Lexington Books, 1988.

Garten, Jeffrey. *The Mind of the CEO*. New York: Basic Books, 2001.

Gibbs, Lois Marie. *Love Canal: The Story Continues*. New York: New Society, 1988.

Goodman, Michael B., ed. *Corporate Communication: Theory and Practice*. Albany: State University of New York Press, 1994.

Gottschalk, Jack, ed. *Crisis Response: Inside Stories on Managing Image under Siege*. Detroit, MI: Gale Research, 1993.

Handler, Edward, and John R. Mulkern. *Business in Politics*. Lexington, MA: Lexington Books, 1982.

Hattersley, Michael E., and Linda McJannet. *Management Communication: Principles and Practice*. New York: McGraw-Hill, 1997.

Heath, Jim F. *John F. Kennedy and the Business Community*. Chicago: University of Chicago Press, 1969.

Hoffman, Paul. *The Dealmakers*. Garden City: Doubleday, 1984.

Hughes, Jonathan R. T. *The Governmental Habit: Economic Controls from Colonial Times to the Present*. New York: Basic Books, 1977.

Huxley, Aldous. *Grey Eminence: A Study in Religion and Politics*. London: Chatto & Windus, 1941.

Klein, Naomi. *No Logo: Taking Aim at the Brand Bullies*. New York: Picador USA, 1999.

Levine, Adeline Gordon. *Love Canal: Science, Politics, and People*. Lexington, MA: Lexington Books, 1982.

Levitan, Sar A., and Martha R. Cooper. *Business Lobbies: The Public Good and the Bottom Line*. Baltimore, MD: Johns Hopkins University Press, 1984.

Lorenz, Christopher. *The Design Dimension: Product Strategy and the Challenge of Global Marketing*. New York: Blackwell, 1986.

Low, Jonathan, and Pam Cohen Kalafut. *Invisible Advantage: How Intangibles Are Driving Business Performance*. Cambridge, MA: Perseus Books, 2002.

McLean, Bethany, and Peter Elkind. *The Smartest Guys in the Room*. New York: The Penguin Group, 2004.

McLuhan, Marshall, and Bruce R. Powers. *The Global Village: Transformations in World Life and Media in the 21st Century*. New York: Oxford University Press, 1989.

McQuaid, Kim. *Big Business and Presidential Power*. New York: Morrow, 1982.

Munter, Mary. *Guide to Managerial Communication,* 7th ed. Upper Saddle River, NJ: Prentice Hall, 2006.

Olins, Wally. *Corporate Identity: Making Business Strategy Visible through Design.* London: Thames and Hudson, 1989.

Peters, Thomas J., and Robert H. Waterman Jr. *In Search of Excellence: Lessons from America's Best-Run Companies.* New York: Harper & Row, 1982.

Poster, Mark. *The Second Media Age.* Cambridge: Polity Press, 1995.

Postman, Neil. *Amusing Ourselves to Death: Public Discourse in the Age of Show Business.* New York: Penguin, 1985.

Riley, Charles A., II. *Small Business, Big Politics: What Entrepreneurs Need to Know to Use Their Political Power.* Princeton, NJ: Peterson's/Pacesetter, 1995.

Schenkler, Irv, and Tony Herrling. *Guide to Media Relations.* Upper Saddle River, NJ: Pearson/Prentice Hall, 2004.

Schultz, Majken, Mary Jo Hatch, and Mogens Holten Larsen, eds. *The Expressive Organization.* Oxford: Oxford University Press, 2000.

Slywotzky, Adrian. *Value Migration: How to Think Several Moves Ahead of the Competition.* Boston: Harvard Business School Press, 1996.

ten Berge, Dieudonnee. *The First 24 Hours.* Cambridge, MA: Basil Blackwell, 1990.

van Riel, Cees B. M. *Principles of Corporate Communication.* London: Prentice Hall, 1995.

Vogel, David. *Fluctuating Fortunes: The Political Power of Business in America.* New York: Basic Books, 1989.

Wallis, Allen W. *An Over Governed Society.* New York: Free Press, 1976.

Weidenbaum, Murray L. *Business, Government, and the Public.* Englewood Cliffs, NJ: Prentice Hall, 1990.

Welch, Jack, and John A. Byrne. *Jack: Straight from the Gut.* New York: Warner Business, 2001.

White, Jon, and Laura Mazur. *Strategic Communications Management: Making Public Relations Work.* New York: Addison-Wesley, 1995.

Wilson, Graham. *Interest Groups in the United States.* New York: Oxford University Press, 1981.

Index